NANGA PARBAT
PILGRIMAGE
The Lonely Challenge

HERMANN BUHL

NANGA PARBAT PILGRIMAGE
The Lonely Challenge

translated by Hugh Merrick

BÂTON WICKS · LONDON
THE MOUNTAINEERS · SEATTLE

Hermann Buhl's autobiography was first published in Germany in 1954 as *Achttausend drüben und drunter* (Nymphenburger, Munich). The first english language edition was *Nanga Parbat Pilgrimage* (Hodder and Stoughton, London, 1956) and that was published in the United States as *The Lonely Challenge* (Dutton, New York, 1956). Paperback editions were issued in London in 1981 and 1989 (Hodder) and 1982 (Penguin). © Copyright in English translation by Hodder and Stoughton.

Nanga Parbat Pilgrimage - The Lonely Challenge is published under license simultaneously in Great Britain and America in 1998 by Bâton Wicks Publications, London and The Mountaineers, Seattle.

All trade enquiries in Great Britain, Europe and the Commonwealth (except Canada) to Bâton Wicks Publications, c/o Cordee, 3a De Montfort Street, Leicester LE1 7HD

All trade enquiries in U.S.A. and Canada to The Mountaineers • Books, 1001 SW Klickitat Way, Suite 201, Seattle, WA 98134

British Library Cataloguing in Publication Data
ISBN 1-898573-27-1 (tradepaperback edition) ISBN 1-898573-33-6 (limited U.K. hardback edition). Catalogue records of these books are available in the British Library

United States Library of Congress Catalog Data
ISBN 0-89886-610-3 A catalog record of this book is available at the Library of Congress

Printed and bound in Great Britain by MPG Books Ltd., Bodmin.

PHOTOGRAPHIC ACKNOWLEDGEMENTS: Front cover, Peter Aschenbrenner (Deutsche Himalaja Stiftung)*; upper cover portrait, Sepp Barr, Weimar; lower cover portrait, Kurt Diemberger*; 1, Richard Müller; 3, A. Pfannenschwarz; 4, J. J. Schatz; 6. G. Ghedina; 7. John Hartley*; 8. Diadem archive*; 9. Leo Dickinson*; 10, John Galloway*; 11. John Cleare*; 12. Swiss National Tourist Office*; 15. Ivan Fiala/Michal Orolin*; 16, Diadem archive*; 17 and 18 Deutscher Institut für Auslandforschung; 19. Tim Greening (Karakoram Experience)*; other photos taken by the author. (Note: * indicates photos added in this new edition)

CONTENTS

IN THE MOUNTAINS OF NORTH TIROL

THE DOLOMITE FAIRYLAND

WINTER TRAINING

IN THE ICE OF THE WESTERN ALPS

DREAMS COME TRUE

PREPARATION FOR A GREAT OBJECTIVE

NANGA PARBAT

PHOTOGRAPHS

MAPS

TRANSLATOR'S NOTE TO
HERMANN BUHL'S BOOK

WHEN on July 4th 1953 Hermann Buhl returned to camp at 23,000 feet from a successful solitary attempt on Nanga Parbat's 26,620 foot summit, he set the seal on what must almost certainly remain the outstanding achievement by a single human being in the long and yet unfinished history of mountaineering. Whatever circumstances may have combined to drive him to a performance so wildly contrary to all known rules and standards of prudent climbing practice, however undesirable the pattern may be for imitation by other more normally-conducted expeditions, the cold facts are that he had achieved something so far beyond the accepted limits of human possibility that, without the incontrovertible photographic and other evidence he brought back with him, one might at the time have been excused for doubting the authenticity of this manifestly true story. The astonishing facts are that, singularly ill-provided with food and drink, without the aid of oxygen, and absolutely alone, he climbed the last 4,000 feet of a Himalayan giant which had over the years already claimed 31 lives, undertaking at times technically difficult rock-climbing over completely unknown ground at an altitude normally precluding any such physical effort, and finally reaching his objective late in the evening of a day involving 17 hours of continuous effort. There he methodically took a number of faultless photographs, changed a film in the process and even built a miniature cairn, before committing his exhausted mind and body to a descent he knew to be technically even more difficult than the ascent had proved. Darkness caught him high up on the peak, forcing him to risk the most incredible bivouac in climbing history— at 26,000 feet, a height at which, according to the rules, a night in the open meant certain death from exposure; but miraculously the weather was exceptionally still and warm by Himalayan standards and somehow Buhl lived through it. At dawn he renewed his lonely fight to escape from the mountain's clutches and battle his way back to shelter, sustenance and human companionship, still 3,000 feet below. Exhausted and suffering from wild hallucinations, he tottered, reeled and fell, on frost-bitten feet, back to life and safety. For reasons still unexplained, nobody came up to meet him and when at endless last he staggered into camp and his waiting team-mates incredulously set about restoring his injured body and his failing brain, he had been engaged on his solitary, forlorn struggle against the elements, disaster and collapse for *forty-one hours*. The remarkable photograph taken of this good-looking young climber of twenty-nine directly after his return shows the face of an old, old man, haggard, drawn and deeply-scored by the ravages of that unparalleled ordeal. If ever a thousand to one chance came home, this was it.

Only a short but unique section at the end of this book deals with that final triumph on Nanga Parbat. The rest is Hermann Buhl's climbing history from his days as a weakling among school-mates and a poor man's son, when an irresistible inner urge first drove him to become a frail and youthful climber, making straight from the start for difficult rock in his beloved homeland hills. Later, he was to qualify as a trained mountain guide, his physique fortified by seasons of heavy portering; and finally, by sheer persistence and restless endeavour on the severest of severe rock-climbs in his own Limestone Alps, in the Dolomites he adores, and, eventually, amid the rock, snow and ice of the great western Alpine peaks, he ploughed a lonely, individual furrow to reach a private pinnacle among climbers of the day, possessed by then not only of fantastic skill but of superhuman energy and endurance.

In Buhl's story one rock epic is piled upon another, snow and ice hazards are plastered on top and finally, still driven by the γνῶθι σεαυτόν admonition of a daemon unsatisfied that he had yet discovered the ultimate limits of his capabilities, he is to be found climbing alone, if possible in the fiercest winter conditions, frequently by night, and often in half the time, the great "impossibles" previously only mastered by a few combined ropes of legendary climbing-aces. From the earliest days a Voice as clear as any heard by Joan of Domrémy had warned him that one day he would be called upon to face some mountain experience transcending all previous limits in difficulty, danger and magnitude.

Buhl had long decided to be ready when the call came; the whole of his climbing life was, in fact, dedicated to that end. Why he was ready and able to meet it when it sounded, as it did on that ill-assorted and strangely-conducted expedition to Nanga Parbat—and there, reading between the lines, one senses a master not only of mountaineering, but of moderation—will be clear to the reader who has followed this incomparable story of mountaineering skill, courage and hazardous achievement to its tremendous climax.

HUGH MERRICK

PUBLISHER'S NOTE FOR THE 1998 EDITION

Nanga Parbat Pilgrimage was first published in Britain in 1956 and later in America as *The Lonely Challenge*. This was at a time when the great Himalayan first ascents were taking place and spawning a succession of worthy but repetitive expedition books. Buhl's book, with its evocative mixture of alpinism, eastern alpine rock-climbing, and with a great Himalayan ascent thrown in almost as a bonus, struck an immediate chord with the ambitious young climbers of the day. Appearing at the same time as Guido Magnone's *The West Face* and Gaston Rébuffat's *Starlight and Storm* it marked the change in climbing attitudes that had been taking place. The old guard had been preoccupied with classic alpinism whereas the writings of Magnone, Buhl and Rébuffat recorded the emerging brave new world of technical climbing. The new focus was for repeating the great alpine North Walls and the hard rock climbs on the awesome precipices of the Dolomites and the granite faces of the Dru and the Grand Capucin. Magnone's writings on the Dru and Buhl's and Rébuffat's Eigerwand accounts laid down an irresistible agenda for the ambitious climbers of the day. Perhaps they were subconsciously preparing themselves for the obvious challenges of the Greater Ranges that were already beckoning as the first ascent phase drew to an end – all the 8000-metre peaks, with the exception of Shisha Pangma, having been climbed by 1960.

With the passage of time Buhl's solo completion of the Rakhiot Route on Nanga Parbat, sensational when it was done, is now confirmed as one of the greatest mountaineering feats of all time. Since then, this notorious first ascent route, that took so many lives during the various attempts in the 1930s, has been largely shunned in favour of more direct, steeper, but less serious lines on the Diamir and Rupal flanks. The Rakhiot Route waited eighteen years to be repeated when the Slovaks Ivan Fiala and Michal Orolin reached the summit. Their photograph of the upper reaches of the mountain above the Bazhin Gap (see plate 16) shows technical mixed ground of considerable difficulty. It speaks volumes for Buhl's inner confidence and doggedness that he pressed on when he saw this. "Before me lay a sharp rock ridge with a slabby face scored by countless gullies . . . I soon found myself facing a vertical rock face, to climb which seemed to me a sheer impossibility."

Michal Orolin, writing in the *Himalayan Journal* in 1971 described sustained technical difficulties on ice and rock above the Bazhin Gap including a 60ft, grade IV chimney and several awkward steps. From a camp on the Diamir Gap (7,600m) they reached the summit at 2 p.m. and regained the camp at 6 p.m. after a gruelling day. Their account underscores the speed and sustained technical difficulty of Buhl's ascent.

Three years later on Broad Peak, as the evening shadows lengthened, Buhl, hampered by his Nanga Parbat injuries, made painfully slow progress on the final section of the climb. With only a short period of daylight remaining his companion Kurt Diemberger, with Buhl's encouragement, pressed on alone to catch up Wintersteller and Schmuck to complete the ascent. As Diemberger returned from the summit he was amazed to meet Buhl still ascending. "Hermann kept coming up, slowly, step by step, his face drawn, his eyes set straight ahead. It was close on half past six. Surely it would be madness to go on to the summit now?" Diemberger, spellbound by Buhl's determination, accompanied him back to the summit – "ahead of us gleamed a radiance, enfolding every wish life could conjure, enfolding life itself. Now was the moment of ineffable truth . . . this was utter fulfillment . . . There we stood, speechless, and shook hands in silence. We looked down at the snow underfoot, and to our amazement it seemed to be aglow. Then the light went out."*

Soon after this second momentous 'first' of an 8000-metre peak Buhl was dead. During a sudden squall on Chogolisa a cornice collapsed, he fell and was never seen again. But despite the passage of years, and with so many fine climbs since completed in the Himalaya, his inspirational presence is still with us. Those great ascents of Nanga Parbat and Broad Peak resonate down through the decades. Here was an almost superhuman climber, not so much for his display of physical and technical prowess, but more for his drive and deep inner serenity – he was a true mountain apostle. He, of all climbers, deserves a statue in the hall of fame. Like de Saussure and Balmat in Chamonix, Buhl should join Maria Therese in the main street of Innsbruck, a gaunt figure on a high pedestal pointing yearningly towards his beloved Tyrolean Limestone ranges – aloft and heroic – a timeless symbol of the spirit of adventurous alpinism.

K.W. 1998

---

* *Summits and Secrets* (Allen and Unwin, 1971) and now collected in *The Kurt Diemberger Omnibus* (Bâton Wicks, 1998).

IN THE MOUNTAINS OF
NORTH TIROL

"THEY'LL NEVER
MAKE A CLIMBER OF ME"

I WAS born in Innsbruck; the Hills looked down into my cradle and I must have inherited my love for them, for my father loved to wander among the mountains. My mother was from the Grödnertal, in the very heart of the Dolomites, but I lost her when I was only four; she was spoken of as a fine, sensitive woman whose intelligence reached out beyond the cramped confines of everyday existence to those things on which it is impossible to set a material value. Her picture and my sense of loss have been with me all my life.

My desire to become a climber, the unquenchable fire that burned within me for the world of peaks, faces and ridges, were hardly sensible things. I was so delicate, so weak a child that I could not even go to school till a year later than usual. But I still dreamed of the mountains. On school outings I used to stop at waterfalls and such romantic places. It was as though the Hills had a special language for me, to which I had to listen. When teachers or the other boys scolded or laughed at me, I held my tongue. If they couldn't hear the voices I heard, how could they be expected to understand me?

On my tenth birthday my father asked me whether I would prefer to celebrate it by the train journey to distant Bregenz on the Lake of Constance, or a stroll up the local knob, the Glungezer. I didn't have to think long. The Glungezer was, after all, over 8,500 feet high. And so we walked all the way up on to the mountain-top which looks down on Innsbruck. From there, across the valley of the Inn, I could see the whole of the Northern Range, a welter of teeth and towers, of exciting rock formations and long, fierce ridges. One would have to be big and strong to go climbing there, from peak to peak—from tower to tower. . . .

Not many years later Innsbruck's Northern Range had become the regular field of my activities. I was up there almost every Sunday. But that wasn't so simple, either, for we had been very strictly brought up. Sunday had to be given its right reverence and recognition by attendance at Mass; so there was no question of going mountaineering without having been to Service first. Luckily for us who lived at Innsbruck, where the needs of the mountaineer have long been reconciled with the claims and dignity of the Church, there were special early celebrations, services held on the borders of night and day; but if you wanted to go to church and still be up in the mountains in time, you had to be up before four in the morning.

People who pitied me because I looked so frail, or thought of me as a poor specimen of a boy, were wrong. I was not too weak for the mountains. I walked and played about, I climbed and ran—up hill, down dale. Going up-hill seemed so easy to me. And wherever bare crag grew upwards out of rubble or snow I stuffed my boots into my small "Schnerfer" rucksack and climbed up the rock in my woollen socks. I had no money for proper climbing shoes; though that did not in the least depress me. In fact nothing depressed me, so long as I could be up there among the crags. By evening I was back in the Inn Valley again, and maybe I stopped in one of the streets of my home-town and thought, as I looked up at the Northern Range: "So you have been up there? On one or another of those spikes?" I was small and delicate and I expect that in the eyes of the worthy people coming back from their Sunday walk I presented a slightly comical spectacle. All the same, my childish pride in my achievement gave me a great sense of superiority over them. At home my enthusiasm was for the most part soon quenched. All they saw was the factual manifestation—my torn socks. I tried every kind of excuse and explanation; in the end I always stood there, my cheeks nicely reddened. Yes, I would look after my socks better in future. Till next Sunday, in fact!

A man grows with his highest aims, even when as narrowly confined as I was. The time came when I wanted to do something really worth-while with my chum Ernstl from school—a proper climb, with a rope and all the outward show laid on. In the windows of the sports shops there were maddeningly lovely ropes. Those were for people who could afford them, not for small boys with big ideas in their noddles. But a rope there had to be. That was why my stepmother's washing-line found its way from our balcony into my rucksack.

When we got outside the City Gates it changed places again. We took turns in wearing it round a very puffed-out chest—a most exalting thing to do. It did not occur to us that we were the least bit ridiculous; we simply saw ourselves as daring heroes of the mountains, like in the climbing books or in such songs as—

"With a rope around my breast . . ."

Our objective was the Brandjoch, whose 9,000 feet would be a height-record for me. Even then, as a thirteen-year-old stormer of peaks, whose importance must have been clear to everyone the moment they saw the washing-line round his shoulders, I could not bear the idea that there were other tourists ahead of us. We ran up the path, overtaking them, feeling like really confident "Tigers" of the rocks—though we and real rock-climbing were leagues apart. And all because of a length of washing-line. . . .

We reached the base of "Frau Hitt"—a fine-looking rock-outline into which, according to the legend, the noble and exclusive lady had been transformed. Even in the stony form into which God had condemned her, she had lost none of her unapproachability. Steep rock; smooth and holdless. Some of our youthful confidence began to ebb.

Others were by now reaching the foot of the pinnacle. Proper tough people with brown, sun-scorched, fine-drawn faces—the way climbers ought to look. Our approach earned us a few questioning, slightly scornful looks; but we did not let them point out our lack of safety precautions. While the others were tying on to a real climbing rope, we were undoing our ridiculous cord with all the composure we could assume.

And how they could climb! They tackled the stony old lady by firm hand- and foot-holds, gaining height without noticeable effort. Then it was our turn, and our anxiety was soon forgotten. There really were holds and stances; one really could make headway. Up we went, and not too badly at that. When we joined the others on the narrow summit platform, the scornful looks had vanished.

We looked down the North Face, with its definite overhang—a rock-wall leaping 130 feet sheer. If we could only climb a thing like that, we should be full-blooded, real climbers. Would we ever reach that standard?

For the moment the main thing was the descent of the precipice; we should have to rope down it. An *Abseil* which sounded rather alarming! We tried to forget that we had never done one on a proper mountain, watching exactly how the others did it. Then it was our turn to slide down into space. At first it gave one an odd feeling in the pit of the stomach, but with a growing sense of safety, it began to be rather fun.

We were very proud when we joined the climbing party afterwards. One of them, whose handsome face was shadowed by a broad-brimmed hat, made a special impression on me. There was a badge on his hat: an *edelweiss*, a rope and an ice-axe struck obliquely through it. One would have to belong to a body, to a club, like him, some day. I was immensely impressed, being only a child, by these young men. I said very little, but listened all the more breathlessly. There were the names of mountains, faces, climbs—the Hohe Warte, the Grubreissen, Kumpfkar, Schüsselkar. . . . Each name opened up an exciting, savage world of its own—a world I must attain. But would we ever even get as far as that? I must see to it that we did!

The Grubreissen Towers . . . they became my dream objective for a whole year. Those crags behind the Hafelkar—in my dreams they embodied all the joys of climbing, nay all earthly joys. For was there anything lovelier on earth than climbing? I was just fourteen. Although I was still unusually thin and "soft", I felt thoroughly seasoned the next time I stood on the Hafelkar. Of course I had come up from Innsbruck on foot. Who could afford the funicular and luxury of that kind?

I stood there looking across at the grey rock pinnacles to the north in the Karwendel ranges. Far away I could distinguish a few little dots there, moving about. Climbers! Perhaps they might take me along, if I. . . .

I hurried down the short slope, crossed the gully to a snow *couloir* opposite and climbed up it to the saddle at its top. There they were, my rock pinnacles, the Grubreissen Towers. On the right, the harder one, the South Tower, sometimes called the Melzer Tower. That was the North Tower, at the back. I knew it all from hearsay, even the approach routes. I had seen pictures and read accounts, too. Was it worth tackling the easier one? No, it had got to be the difficult one, the Melzer Tower.

I went straight at it, just as I was, in heavy ski-ing boots and a waterproof cape—in my highly unsuitable attire. I went up quite a long way like that. Then I couldn't go any further. There I was stuck like some comical bat against the rock. But bats can fly; upwards, if they want to. The only way I could fly was downwards. . . . It was a nasty moment.

Then I heard voices, and remembered the climbers whom I had seen earlier as little points in the distance. They had spotted that I had got into serious difficulties and were offering the silly young idiot a rescue-party. I would have been only too glad of the help, but I obviously couldn't accept it. How could I start my career as a climber in the rôle of a rescue-party's prize? So with due pride and outward show of confidence (though inside I was feeling pretty desperate) I refused their kind offers.

As I couldn't get up any further, I had to get down. That didn't seem possible either. But I must make it possible, in spite of the smooth-soled ski-boots. I kept on casting glances downwards and seeing the way I would have to take if my strength gave out. There would be no return to life if I took that way. So I *mustn't* fall!—I didn't; and eventually reached firm ground safely enough.

The others had been watching me and now rewarded me for my self-control.

"Like to join us on the North Tower?"

I could hardly believe my ears. I was proud and happy beyond words.

I was being asked to go along with experts; it was they who were inviting me to tie myself on to their rope.

"Where are your 'slippers', laddie?"

Of course I hadn't any—only my wonderful new ski-boots, whose
smooth, leather soles—totally unsuitable for difficult climbing—I
proudly displayed. They laughed, but took me along all the same. I
revelled in my good fortune. Sometimes my expensive boots didn't
offer enough purchase and I had to rely on some assistance from the
rope. But what did that matter? One can let men like these help one.
I have since learned their names. Every mountaineer knows them:
Aschenbrenner, Mariner, Douschan—all of them "famous".

As we were coming down the gully my leaders showed me the tower's
sundering South Ridge. "That is pretty severe," they told me. "Nothing
for you yet awhile—in a year or two, maybe."

Apparently my time-consciousness had gone a little astray. I did not
wait a year or two. Exactly a week later my school-friend Ernstl Vitavsky
and I were standing at the foot of the South Ridge, under the vertical
approach wall. We were choking down our usual breakfast of bread and
cream cheese, and watching a party climbing the ridge above our
heads. At the same moment the party discovered us and shouted down,
asking us to bring the rope they had left lying at the start, up to the
saddle.

True enough, there was a rope lying there, a lovely, real climbing
rope; and they wanted us to walk it up the snow gully to the saddle for
them. But that rope was an irresistible temptation; for with that rope
we could climb the South Ridge, too, and hand it to them at the top.
It would make no earthly difference to them; but for us this would be
the great adventure itself, for which we were longing.

The other party was out of sight overhead by now. We unlooped the
rope. Knots? We hadn't a clue about them—an ordinary "granny"
would have to do. So we roped up—we were a real "rope" at last. The
line felt just like an artery through which new strength and courage
were flowing for both of us.

There was a "carabiner" lying there, too—one of those funny clip-
rings used for passing the rope through the eyes of pitons hammered
into cracks in the rock. I had seen the experts using them. This time
we left our boots behind. We hadn't any "slippers" as yet, so socks it
had to be.

Ernstl started to lead up. I stood below, "safeguarding" him, letting
the rope run quietly through my hands, quite sure I could hold him
whatever might happen. Our practice work had not been in vain. My
friend went ahead very quickly. Presently he hung the "carabiner"

on a piton, just like a grown-up; a grown-up and a big one at that, would have been able to manage the long stride that followed rather more easily. But Ernstl was just the same size as myself, a small boy hardly out of his baby-shoes. I watched him bending and stretching; then he was across quite nicely and soon on a firm stance. "Come along up!" he called, most professionally.

This was the great moment for me. I was climbing in a real independent party, on the rope. My first steps were a bit tentative; but I soon found complete confidence. Roped like that, climbing is a jolly, harmless exercise. Fall off? Who could fall off? I gained height swiftly. I met a few pitons Ernstl hadn't noticed. I put my fingers in their rings to test them; they afforded splendid holds. On and up again, over a smooth slab and an airy ledge: then I was at the broad and delicate stride.

To my right was the split-ring on the piton, with the safeguarding rope running through it. Ernstl kept it nicely taut while my hand was exploring for a grip behind an edge, then my body swung across and I was standing in a chimney. Joy upon joy! "We are the lords of creation . . . !"

Ernstl was sitting comfortably on a ledge, slowly taking in the rope. We were both laughing, and completely happy after our first successful pitch of independent climbing. Then I went into the lead. We would take turns at it, as experts of equal skill always do. What could happen to us, anyway?

We heard voices above us. Were we lads really overtaking the party ahead of us? We were indeed, and at the foot of the "Auckenthaler Crack" we came up to them. Our reception was not exactly friendly, and we had to listen to a proper "pi-jaw". We had expected that, and just took no notice of it; it certainly didn't damp our enthusiasm. But on the final wall they revealed themselves as prudent Elder Brethren, determined to look after us youngsters properly. They lowered a safety-rope to us, so that we could enjoy the last difficult pitch under full protection. Then we were sitting on the warm summit of the South Tower and formally delivering the rope, as requested. We all laughed and shook hands. The others called us "clueless greenhorns".

Although it sounds more like a disguised compliment than a reprimand, its true force was to be brought to my consciousness in the grimmest fashion in a very short time. A few weeks later, during a mad attempt to climb the Auckenthaler Crack solo, my chum Ernstl fell and was killed. And so I lost my first partner on a climbing rope.

None the less, during that summer of 1939 I continued to visit the Grubreissen Towers frequently. Gradually I began to learn a little about rope-management, rock technique, the assessment of difficulties and the rest of it. Every free hour I had was devoted to training.

In the meantime I had been accepted into the Innsbruck Youth Section of the Alpine Club. We were thirty or forty young people, all mad about mountains, who went out into the Hills in a gay rabble every Sunday. Our bounds were fairly close-drawn, for we only had enough money for tours which could be accomplished from Innsbruck on foot or on a bicycle. We saved all through the week, scratching the halfpence together so as to have the necessary funds for Sunday.

We kept on improving our technique and soon began to believe that we were approaching the mastery of our craft. But the mountains see to it that trees don't grow into the sky and that young climbers get kept on the rails—even when they own proper climbing "slippers" with Manchon soles and no longer have to pay for torn socks with reddened cheeks when they get home.

One day Karl Glätzle—known simply as "Glatzen" ("Baldy") in our circle of friends—and I roped up, to do a climb in the Karwendel. It was broken rock and Karl was leading up it. I didn't think the rock looked very sound when he came to a block barring the way up; so I took up a position from which I could protect him, on a narrow rib of rock below. I had already learned how to safeguard my climbing partner properly, and as he climbed I watched his every movement. He reached the block next to which there was a rusty old piton sticking out, bent somewhat downwards. Karl clipped the rope to it with a carabiner—but would the piton hold? He reached up to the edge of a small platform, then pulled upwards and gave a short heave. . . .

There was a sudden crack. A shadow flitted across the wall. I clamped down on the rope with all my might, pressing myself hard against the rock. The next moment must be decisive. When the rope with my falling friend at its end went taut I was bound to take a terrific jerk. Would the old piton hold? Very little hope of that. Odd, how long split seconds can seem to last. . . .

There came the jerk! The miracle had happened—the piton had held. But it had catapulted me in a wide arc from my stance and I went swinging across the wall. I had but a single thought—that I must hold, hold, hold the rope somehow. Obediently, my fingers obeyed my behest: they held firmly on to the rope. . . .

At that very instant, before the pendulum motion of my body had even ceased, the block—weighing several hundredweight—came crashing down on the precise spot where I had been standing and splintered into a thousand pieces. There would not have been much left of me if the rope had not pulled me from my stance.

Now we were both hanging from the same rusty piton. The rope ran over a clip hanging in a piton-ring just like over a fixed roller. By a simple physical law my companion, who weighed nearly three stone more than me, had pulled me right up. And still the piton held. Obviously, that couldn't last very long. Karl must get on to the rock again somehow, very quickly. So I paid out rope very gingerly to him—fortunately he was quite unhurt—till he was able to get a firm stance under his feet again. It wasn't till it was all over that we realised what incredible luck we had had—the kind of luck a climber must have, but on which he has no right to count. It is a good thing for a young climber to go through nasty, serious experiences, provided he survives them. The mountains have their own way of dealing with over-confidence.

A new field of adventure was thrown open to us, thanks to a training-tour by the Youth Section—the great range of the Wilde Kaiser, which had till now been a dream and a distant desire. At last it was to become reality. In my mind's eye I could already see the sheer slabs slanting to heaven. I cannot describe the ecstasy of anticipation; my fertile imagination conjured up for me pictures which the real thing could never succeed in matching.

The express took us to Wörgl and on to Kitzbühel. Many solemn passengers were furious about the wild gang with whom they had to travel. After all, we were only fledglings. We had to be serious and sensible, responsible and prepared to behave like experienced men when we were on our mountains—on the train we behaved as our youth, and the bubbling excitement about pleasures to come, dictated. It is too late after all these years to apologise to the fellow-voyagers whom we shocked so badly that day; in any case they would probably never have understood that a funny hat can give rise to mirth unbounded. And if it were possible for me to be once again as young, as enthusiastic, as cloudlessly happy as I was then, I should no doubt behave in exactly the same way again. And so would all the rest—those who are still alive, those whom the War, a prison camp or the Hills themselves have not since taken.

The famous Gaudeamus and Grutten Huts—of which we knew from hearsay that they had housed generations of climbers in the Wilde Kaiser Range—were full to overflowing when we arrived; so some of us went on up the way to the Ellmauer Tor, to experience our first *bivouac*— a word which had always unleashed a flood of romantic imaginings in my mind. Now, sleeping out among the hills, we were to taste its real meaning for the first time. We stumbled up the narrow track by the light of torches, through pitch-black night, invaded by the spectral light of the flickering flames. Dark gulfs went plunging down under us: a torch went flaming down into them and we watched it until it was dowsed, far, very far below.

We reached the Ellmauer Tor at midnight and lay down behind a rock, where we tried to sleep, covering ourselves with every available piece of clothing. We had soon had more than our fill of romance. We were but inexperienced boys, with chattering teeth and a great longing for the warmth of the Hut, or even of a hay-rick—a long, long way from being real mountaineers.

Then, with the worst of the cold, the dawn was there. The towers and spires were illuminated. Hardship and the discomforts of the night were soon forgotten. A few steps took me to the top of the gate-like gap in the back-bone of the hills. It was a gateway to a world of wonders. . . . There at my feet lay the famous "Steinerne Rinne", a narrow gorge, bounded by walls that towered to the sky, sensationally steep and smooth; a landscape fashioned by primaeval forces. There they stood, the Guardians of the Gorge—the Predigstuhl on the right, the Fleischbankspitze on the left. Yes, and over there was the notorious Fleischbank East Wall, which opened up the cult of the difficult climbs in the Kaisergebirge; the Wall which Hans Dülfer and his partner Werner Schaarschmidt were the first to conquer, before the First World War, twenty-eight years ago.

Though the Wall at the time created an Alpine sensation, it was no longer reckoned as one of the more difficult Kaiser climbs; but it was still the Fleischbank East Wall, and one needed to have shed one's baby-shoes as a climber a good long time before venturing on it. Dare I? My intelligence answered "No!" but my desire was screaming a pitiful irresistible "Yes!" I knew that some of the older, more experienced members of our Youth Section were going to be allowed to follow in Dülfer's footsteps that day. Hannes Schmidhuber, our team-leader, had not judged me, the youngest and physically weakest, as fit for it yet. So I was certainly not going to be taken along officially.

Well, then, it had to be unofficial. I crept to the bottom of the climb and hid behind a boulder, waiting for the rope which had permission to do the Dülfer route. There they were, coming—a small party, descending the short slope in climbing-shoes, with Luis Vigl and Hugo Magerle among them; I could hear the rattle of the "ironmongery", pitons, carabiners, hammers. And there, bringing up the rear, was Hannes Schmidhuber. He had spotted me at once in my hide-out. There was no need to explain anything; he knew exactly what I was there for. The expression on his face was not encouraging.

"No, my lad," it said. "You can't smuggle yourself on to the East Wall—not while I'm in charge. You are too young, too green. . . ."

I could have howled aloud for rage and mortification as the strong hand of Hannes fell upon my shoulder and forced me back with him to the Ellmauer Tor. The others had already started off on the East Wall. I could only watch, admire and envy them. Perhaps I cursed Hannes then; for he did other things to me, that day. Not only did he warn me off the difficult Wall, but he parcelled me out to a newly-joined member—yes, as second on the rope, too—to do the ordinary route, the so-called "Herr-Weg" on the Fleischbank. So I, who thought I was pretty good, was to potter, under someone else's protection, up a climb which really didn't need a rope at all.

To-day the incident looks quite different to me. To-day I only think of Hannes with kindness and gratitude. I learned so much from that splendid climber and responsible leader, who gave his life on an expedition to rescue others. He knew well enough that if I had been allowed to let my enthusiasm run straight on, blindly, towards destruction, he could never have tamed my overmastering passion. Diagnosing my case perfectly, he wanted to teach me what was wanting—self-control. But it is hard to master an obsession which fights to burst all bounds and barriers. . . .

Then came another Whitsuntide in the Wilde Kaiser. The weather was perfect and the activity on the walls of the Steinerne Rinne tremendous. From every route, wall, *arête*, gully, crack and chimney you could hear the exchange of climbers' talk, the voices, shouts and yodelling accomplishments of those at work on the rocks. From opposite, the climbers looked like tiny flies on sky-raking walls.

We had just finished a nice climb, the North *arête* of the Predigstuhl. Fredl Schatz, on leave from Service, had insisted on leading; Helmut Weber was middle-man, while I was last on the rope. We were traversing from the North Summit to the Main Summit of the mountain by way of the Central Summit. Fredl reached a difficult bit, at which he had several tries, while Helmut protected him as he went up, came back, went at it again. I was also anxiously watching, but without a thought in my head about a fall of any kind.

Just at the moment the whole Steinerne Rinne was filled with a menacing roar, as if all the peaks were collapsing into it. The noise echoed a hundred-fold in the crannies of every wall and rose to a deafening inferno of sound. It was just an airman carrying out the hair-brained stunt of flying slap through the middle of the "Steinerne Rinne" —well below my stance. A mad type, that pilot—I could look down into his cockpit. Then, like a ghost, the 'plane was swept from my sight.

I looked at the place where my companion had been clinging to the Wall; he was not there. But there was a shadow flitting like a flash downwards across the rock-face. Fredl had come off and was falling. . . . Like lightning I grabbed the rope and wedged myself behind a bollard. Hold it, hold it! . . . The jerk was fairly gentle, for there were two of us to take it. Fredl stopped and swung, spinning on the rope, seventy feet below us. We let him gently down further, till he could find a stance. Then I climbed down to him.

"Is it bad, Fredl?"

"No," came the plucky answer. "Only bruises on my legs and thighs; but I can't climb any more."

Six hundred feet below us lay the safety of the Rinne. Between us and the haven of that level ground was a dark repulsive gash, with water running down over its rocks. The Botzong Chimney is normally a quick, airily-amusing way down, when you can rope down it pitch by pitch, step by step, without any worries or any dead-weight. But how would it go, with our injured comrade?

Time was pressing. We only had a hundred-foot rope with which to ensure the rescue of our friend and our own safety during it. We were determined not to shout for help, though there were quite a lot of people standing at the bottom, little dots, now quite motionless, staring up towards us. We were not going to shout for help, and it wasn't likely to arrive of its own accord.

Helmut and I had no experience of rescue work with such primitive resources. But somehow we must get off the Wall and down the Chimney with the injured Fredl, and without anybody's assistance. We let him down on the rope; all he had to do was to keep himself away from the rock with his hands, we did all the rest. Then we climbed down, safeguarding ourselves with the same rope, as best we could; yard by yard as we got further down into the cold, watery gash. Not only water, but ice as well; for no ray of the sun ever reaches this part of the Wall. Soon it was so cold that we were frozen stiff all over, for we were wet through to start with. We couldn't have shouted then, if we had wanted to, we were all so hoarse. And we began to wonder miserably why none of the crowd which had in the meantime collected at the foot of the chimney was coming up to help us. Couldn't they see what trouble we were in? Were they trying us out? Or weren't they taking the whole thing seriously?

There was little time for solving such riddles. We had to get down, and down and down, so as to escape once and for all from our grim, numbing prison. Neither Helmut nor I were "Strong Men". Getting our companion down used up our last reserves of strength. Our hands were wet, stiff and without feeling, from the cold: but we still had to manage a rope with them, a rope which had gone rigid as wire. Our muscles rebelled when we had to drive in some big *Abseil* pitons with the heavy hammer. It took us two hours to reach the edge of the débris slopes at the bottom of the Botzong Chimney, and we were on the verge of exhaustion. The people gathered at the bottom of the Chimney, who included some well-known climbers, took Fredl over.

We had an odd reception. They held us responsible for Fredl's fall. I protested, and tried to clear up their mistake. They told me to shut up. They were a crowd of big, tough men using harsh words to a slight, half-grown youth, hoarse with exhaustion, as they tried to shatter that dream-world of his, born of a raging passion for the Hills and of his youthful self-confidence.

"Why don't you stay at home? You don't belong in the mountains. You'll never make a climber."

I was too tired, too cold, too hurt to offer any serious defence. But I did wonder how such a misunderstanding could arise, and where any fault of mine might lie. Ought we perhaps not to have allowed Fredl, who was out of climbing practice because of his military service, to take the lead? But he was the oldest, the most grown-up, the most experienced. Perhaps I ought not to have allowed the 'plane to take my mind off the safeguarding job, although it was the middle man's responsibility, not mine. Everyone on the rope is, after all, responsible for everyone else on it; if you are aiming at the highest things, the standard you set yourself must be the highest, your demands on yourself must know no limits at all.

I had surely made mistakes, though at the time I felt the reproaches to be as unjust as they were hurtful. But courage was soon re-born out of my dejection. Even if I was a half-grown boy, whose frail build made an impression diametrically opposed to that of the popular conception of a hero, I still felt myself superior to the others in one respect—the sheer consuming strength of my burning passion for the Peaks.

"Me not belong in the Mountains?" Why, I couldn't go on living without them! My thoughts, my dreams, my whole life were nothing but the Mountains! And I swore a secret oath as I stumbled down the Steinerne Rinne in the wake of the others:

"I'll be a climber just the same!" I promised, all unheard.

I think I have kept my promise.

A LESSON FROM DEATH

My companions have never really been able to get undiluted pleasure from being with me. They never could have; I admit it freely. Even when there was a storm outside, or a blizzard, or when the monotony of heavy rain blanketed a disconsolate world, it was still fine for me. There was no stifling the urge within me. I always wanted to be off. When my comrades, safe in the knowledge that the rain was drumming on the roof, burrowed more deeply into the blankets or the hay, I was always up and about, bothering them to start in spite of everything . . . until someone hurled a boot at my head. True, they forgot their anger the moment the weather cleared and we were at work on the rock-faces up there. We were glad of life and of the Hills. Sometimes they even thanked me for having disturbed their early-morning sleep.

During those years my chief discovery was that it is very difficult for a boy whom Nature has not equipped with outsize biceps, to stand up against a group of older lads, most of them as strong as horses. I found it difficult, too, to take the jibes of these strong young men. It has been said that a sense of humour means laughing in spite of everything. I tried hard to laugh "in spite of everything", but sometimes could only manage a wry grin. Let me confess: I didn't find it amusing to be thrown unexpectedly into the Lake of Seefeld, wearing tricouni-nailed boots and all my clothes, and then having to make my dripping way home. My risible muscles were not exercised by finding myself, on a day of filthy weather, pushed plumb into a deep pool of rain-water, because one of the stronger ones happened to want some momentary activity for his muscles. I would also much rather have found in my bottle the tea I had made the evening before than the water made by my companions. I am probably wanting in the objectivity required to appreciate such jokes, which the others found screamingly funny. Perhaps I haven't the right feeling either for that kind of hardening process. I didn't want to be either an all-in wrestler or a mercenary. The toughness a climber needs is of quite a different brand.

But, apart from such occasional inconveniences, our comradeship was a close and happy bond. And I look back on this early youth with pleasure, even if the mountains always seemed to me to speak a more intelligible language than the people among them.

In the summer of 1940, my old friends of the Youth Section, particularly Herbert Eberharter and Ferry Theyermann, had invited me to join them on some climbing in the Wetterstein Range. I remember the invitation with special pleasure, even now.

Our base was a hay-shed near the Kühtaierhof in the Leutasch. As our evening exercise we made the neighbouring larch-woods unsafe. The object was to get as far as possible up the slender, branchless trunks in tricounied climbing boots. Herbert finished his winning climb by a crash-landing on his back, which put an end to the competition.

We were on the way early next morning. We strolled over the Wang-alm, that little piece of fairyland at the foot of the Wetterstein Walls, to the place where you start off on the South Wall of the Scharnitz-spitze. Herbert and Ferry wanted to do the "direct", which they said was not my pigeon as yet. I did not dispute the fact, and gladly joined Seppl Fuchs in an attempt on the so-called Kadner route.

Below us a solitary figure was making his way up the débris tongues somewhat diffidently. The man kept on stopping, looking up, and then going on a few more steps.

Odd to see a man on his own, up here. We wondered what he wanted. He certainly seemed to have some special plan. Watching him carefully, we noticed that he seemed to be battling with himself all the time.

However, we had no spare time for watching solitary wanderers; so we started off. It was a splendid climb. The rock was like that of the Kaisergebirge, hard as iron, every hold a sound one, a real joy to climb. After an over-hang we came to a chimney, which grew narrower and narrower, forcing us out to its extreme edge to left and right. The wall went down into the thin air, smooth, wrinkleless rock.

We had come up about 700 feet; then there was another narrowing, an enclosed chimney, almost a crack. I snaked my way upwards, panting a bit, and soon Seppl was standing next to me.

At that moment a mop of hair appeared below us in the chimney. Could it be another party? But we immediately recognised the solitary climber, who had approached the foot of the climb in such hesitating fashion. He was alone—quite a creditable performance. His hands were torn and bleeding a little. We asked him how he did that.

All he said was: "Getting on to the climb."

We offered him the protection of our rope. He thanked us, but refused. The hardest part was over, he said. . . . He climbed past us and went up more quickly than we, being alone. Soon he was out of sight.

We worked over to the left, where there was another pretty smooth slab. I made my way up the holdless wall by the friction of my slippers and found a good stance. Then it was Sepp's turn to do this awkward bit.

We were startled by a clattering sound. Falling stones? We ducked close into the rock, waiting for the hail of stones which never came.

Instead, a dark, heavy object—rather long, like a sack full of something—sailed past through thin air. I recognised it suddenly as a human body—that of the lone climber! A cold chill ran down my spine. It was flying straight at Sepp, clinging to the wall below me. Bound to knock him off, I thought, and gripped the rope more tightly than ever. But the lifeless body missed my friend by a couple of feet and went hurtling out into the void.

Endless seconds went ticking by till we heard the last thump down there at the bottom. . . . A shattering silence followed.

Over there, on the Scharnitzjoch, the sheep were bleating—it sounded for all the world like a ghastly dirge. I was shivering from head to foot. I kept on hoping it had been some kind of a ghostly manifestation; but Sepp pointed to the blood splashes all around us. A human life had been snuffed out; the life of the man with whom we had been chatting only a few minutes before. It goes as quickly as that, then?

We reproached ourselves bitterly for not having insisted on his joining our rope. A lot of good that was, now. Anyway, what climber worth the name would let himself be forced like that?

Our own confidence was almost shattered. How could we go on? But we *had* to get off this ghastly Wall, and as quickly as we could. . . . If we went down, we might still be able to help. Perhaps he was still alive? But those were idle hopes; the bottom lay down there 700 feet below. . . .

So up we went again; Sepp following me with faltering steps. I too had to take a firm hold on myself. My partner could not get a grip on the smooth slab, and slipped. I held him, as best I could, without a protecting piton, on the rope, my back jammed against the wall. The rope cut my hands painfully, forcing me down and down on to my stance, almost dragging me from my perch. I shouted to Sepp: "Get hold of something, or I shall be coming off after you. I can't hold you much longer!" (Sepp weighed three stone more than I did.) Beads of sweat stood out on my forehead; I dared no longer look down the Wall. But Sepp had taken hold of himself and managed to get a firm stance again; he moved slowly forward, and presently came up to me safely. It took our last reserves of will-power to climb, with the utmost caution, the rest of the way to the summit.

We shook hands, without a word. None of the joy and laughter this time, born of the thrill which a successful climb of great difficulty usually brings. Downwards we hurried, roping down from the Wang-scharte. When we got back to the start we found others attending to the dead man. They laid a larch-wreath on his body. Then we followed him down on his last journey.

For days and weeks after this fearful experience I was so shaken that I could not bear the sight of my mountaineering equipment. For a time I thought I should have to give up my climbing career, which had hardly even begun. I kept on seeing the body of a warm-blooded, living man, hurtling down through the empty air. I dreamed about it at night. What I had learned was that climbing can be a dangerous business and that it can lead to a sudden end.

END OF AN ALPINE APPRENTICESHIP

THE year 1942 threw open to me the realm of Grade VI. I felt good enough to enter this world of "Extreme Severity". I started my series of Severe and Super-Severe climbs with a Winter ascent in the Schüsselkarspitze's South Wall, the Spindler route on the Wetterstein. That began a new climbing era for me. During it, Waldemar Gruber, mustering like myself seventeen summers, was my trusted partner.

On a lovely sunny Sunday at the beginning of March, we stood under the Schüsselkar rocks at the start of the Spindler route. The yellow-black rock lifted in splendid contrast above the level snow at its foot. The solemn silence of this corner of the Hills was not even disturbed by the bleating of sheep. The Spring sunshine had already warmed the rocks nicely. On the light traversing rope we slid down the slabs and over bulging out-crops, using every corrugation in the rock to push off with the tips of our rubbers. Moving over to the left, we met a small overhang, the "Heave up!" I found a firm stance, to which Waldi would come up and join me. We took off the traverse-rope, but found a knot at the end of it. We gave it a tremendous jerk. No use, the knot was jammed too tight in the ring. And as we had to get on, we just left the rope hanging there, intending to pick it up on the way back.

The Spindler slabs, and the series of cracks above them were a joy that day. How easy climbing seemed this season! Where last Summer I had had to exert myself, I could now go up without any application of strength, just like that.

We soon reached the exit cracks, just as the sun disappeared behind a ridge, and it grew suddenly very chilly. While knocking out a piton, Waldemar lost his hammer, which disappeared into the bottom of a chimney. It would have taken too long to climb down and fetch it. We climbed on, determined to manage without it. At the final niche my companion again suffered the same misfortune; a second hammer went flying down. Now, we had to have one hammer. So this time it meant going down the chimney which had, in the meantime, become an icy shaft. Armed with a hammer, but very late indeed, we finally climbed out at the top.

By the time we were at the bottom of the Wall again, the sun was already vanishing in the West. We climbed the cracks again to the traverse where the rope had remained wedged in the ring. We yanked it down and were soon able to bid the foot of the Wall good-bye. Swiftly we got into our boots and put on our skis. Unfortunately the beautiful buttery snow had been transformed into horrible crust; so instead of the lovely descent we had been looking forward to so keenly, we had a fearful plunging and poking about. The only way to change direction was to stop and do a full-turn swing of each leg. We ploughed through the sticky white mass in primitive fashion, often losing sight of each other, only to pass again on the next turn below. The forest down into the Puitental is uncommonly dense. In our difficulties, we frequently embraced a tree-trunk or used a branch as an emergency grip. As dusk fell, we unstrapped our skis, preferring to stamp our way down. One of my "boards" had, of course, to go sliding away down the hill. I found it after a tedious search. We arrived back at the Leutasch very late.

* * *

At Whitsun we were back in the Wilde Kaiser.

The Gaudeamus Hut was full to overflowing. Mobs, scrums, milling around noisily. You have to expect that at Whitsun in the Kaiser. But the climbs are a sufficient compensation. The urge to get going drove us away from the Hut early indeed. Our enforced bivouac had ensured that getting up would be no hardship. We had already tried our hand on the East Wall of the Fleischbank and the South *Arête* of the Christa Tower the day before. Now we felt in right form for the Fleischbank South-East. At last, too, we felt we need no longer mess about so tentatively and unconfidently with the "ironmongery". Now we could let it rattle while we ignored it and relied with greater confidence on our own climbing skill. Our Alpine Apprenticeship was over.

Leaping neatly from boulder to boulder, we came to the foot of the rock-face and over a little ring of crags, to the start of our climb. Waldemar and I roped up together; Herbert Eberharter and Manfred Bachmann made up a second rope. We were not the only ones with our eyes on the Fleischbank climbs. There was a whole Club on the way: they would probably need to reserve places in the queue for dishing out tickets. The time when a "Climber's Lift" would sling one in a few minutes from the Hut to the start of the difficult climbs didn't look very far off!

The first red light of day was glowing on the Predigstuhl teeth; the night-frost was still nesting on the walls. We were met by the sun's first beams, comforting and warming. It would probably be quite hot by mid-day; so I left my pullover behind. We went through all the usual preparations for the climb. The torn soles of my rubbers were already allowing a few inquisitive toes to peer out. They would have to last

for to-day, anyway. To-day my calves would have to go bare, because
I was stuffing my stockings into my pack, to spare them unnecessary
damage. But what did it matter? My legs were hardened. My Anorak
hood—a bit soggy by now—would also have to do for this summer.
My trousers, on the other hand, were beyond repair; they didn't even
perform their most elementary duties. For instance, they let the hammer
slip time and again through the sieve of a back pocket, so that its own
iron head dug uncomfortably into my seat. I should have preferred to
do without the useless garment altogether: but even in the mountains
you can't go about the place "stark"!

Starting up the foot of a difficult climb always produces a funny
feeling; when, after getting on to the rock, you look down and have to
admit to yourself that this isn't just a "stroll". All the same, just to
prove our good form, we decided to climb everything under our own
steam, without the protection of intervening pitons. But when we were
agreeably surprised to find how soon we reached a firm stance, we
pretended to be disappointed and asked our partners whether the rope
had really run out so soon.

The older generation likes to accuse us youngsters of lacking all
respect for the mountains nowadays. So far as my own experience goes,
there has been no change in the respect paid to the mountains; it is
only the attitude towards actual climbing and to the technical difficulties
encountered which has changed. I do not believe that to-day's young
climber, standing at the foot of such a climb, experiences any different
feelings from those who climbed it before him: that strange mixture of
an upward surge, excitement, the pleasures of anticipation, reverence
for Nature and its Creator and—let it be freely admitted—a good
sampling of fear. We know the Hills and their dangers; why then should
we have lost our respect for them? For every time we do another climb
we renew our struggle with Nature, who can be a kind friend but also
a pitiless enemy. And that, too, is the explanation of the elation by
which we are moved when, after a successful struggle with Nature, the
enemy, we stand joyously conscious of victory, exhausted though we
may be, on the summit, with the defeated giant beneath our feet. Then
we are at friendly unity with Nature and with every lovely thing on
earth—but knowing full well that it is not the great Nature of the
mighty peaks which we have conquered, but ourselves. And perhaps
it is just we "Extremists" among all mountaineers who can best recognise men's tiny insignificance in the surrounding Universe.

But to get back to our South-East Fleischbank climb, that Whitsun.
It had been done for the first time in 1925 by those great cragsmen
Roland V. Rossi and Fritz Wiessner, the Dresden climber, since natur-

alised in America. Their achievement caused the greatest sensation in the Wilde Kaiser since Dülfer's day. On the upper part of this huge Wall of flashing Kaiser rock, it is possible to "wriggle off" along a narrow band to the left into the notch between the Fleischbank and the Christa Tower.

We never gave it a thought. Quite a crowd had gathered at the Ellmauer Tor in the meantime. The Alpine spectators were sitting down there, as if on a grand stand, excitedly watching the thrilling gamble between us climbers and the pull of gravity. Great parties were moving along the floor of the Steinerne Rinne.

Behind us, another party was getting ready. We had no wish to hang about and were soon on our way. Draped with the doubled-rope which exerts a fair downward drag, we started by testing and trying everything with extreme care. One always has to get used to one's material all over again; and one has to find the right spiritual and mental approach at the same time. The first rope's length therefore went a little hesitantly, but soon the rope was running more freely through the hands of our friends. The fighting spirit and the sheer joy of climbing were soon in evidence again. Presently I was laying back foot after foot of Wall below me with absolute freedom. There was a ladder of pitons above me and I climbed to the top. Almost too far, but then I noticed a rusty hook in a smooth slab down to the left. So that was the start of the notorious traverse . . . I edged myself over to the left, supported by the traversing rope, along the polished, almost holdless face of the rock, in a "Dülfer Chair"—one of the rope-tricks I had already learned. Another spring-clip—very comforting to the nerves—and I had reached the start of the cracks rising beyond the sundering wall-sector. I was hanging from a piton, supported by the rock; I could only see down into the bottom of the cracks by leaning the upper part of my body way out from the face. We rigged up a rope bannister, and the others came sliding up to me, one by one, on the improvised lift.

The weather was lovely. We could see the far-off Gross Venediger shining across between the ridges of the Karlspitze and the Bauernpredigstuhl. Rope's length by rope's length we mastered the Wall, till we were perched under a great bulge, the Rossi Overhang, one of the keys to this magnificent climb.

Then suddenly a keen wind got up. In a trice a coal-black cloud crept over the summit of the Fleischbank; a cold damp mist settled on the Walls and was driven on the wind along the Steinerne Rinne below. The cheerful sound of voices and chatter from all the ridges and faces around died suddenly away. It began to rain; soon it was pouring as if the Heavens had opened. We didn't want to turn back, so kept on climbing. We still aimed at climbing the Wall to its very top. Soon we were all at the grass terrace which cuts across the whole Wall and offers the last chance of traversing to the Fleischbank Saddle and, from it, quickly down to the bottom. The party behind us decided to make good use of the opportunity and so left the Wall. We thought it over for a moment: here we were in the Wilde Kaiser, more than half-way up our climb—the precious "South-East". We weren't likely to get another chance in the near future . . . there were the fares to think of. Up, then, and on! We traversed to the right and found the exit-crack. It had gradually begun to hail; it didn't bother us much as we wriggled on up the overhanging crack, for we were wet through already. The Walls were running with water like a gutter. It was noticeably colder and the first snowflakes were beginning to float down—typical Whitsun weather in the Mountains.

I was soon regretting my pullover. My hands and feet were bitterly cold now. My calves were blue; what a godsend stockings would have been, but we must get on with it. Perhaps it would have been better to use the Terrace and get off the Face, after all; but now the chance had gone for good! For two more rope's lengths the climbing was difficult, then the slope eased off a little. It was now snowing in earnest. We caught occasional glimpses, when the mists parted, across to the Walls of the Predigstuhl, all sugared white. Lucky not to be over on that side, where the West wind was lashing the snow straight into the mountain's faces!

We had no idea how late it might be. Time had lost all meaning for us—a watch was a luxury we could not afford. As for our good understanding with the sun, nothing doing to-day! An icy wind clawed hold of us, blowing the snow vertically up over the summit. Hurriedly we entered our names in the Summit Register; then down as quickly as possible by the "Herr-Weg". The rock, so warm under the sun only an hour or two ago, had put on its winter robes again. We slid down snow grooves, hiding mirror-smooth, tricky rock under their white covering.

Suddenly two figures loomed up. A man and his wife; he wearing shorts, his better-half a training suit, both pitifully frozen. Soaked to the skin, they looked at their last gasp. They told us they had come up in fine weather over the North Ridge of the Fleischbank, intending to traverse the summit. There in the saddle the storm had caught them, and the mist had closed in on them. With precipices falling away on every side, they had not dared to move on; so there had been nothing for it but to wait. Waiting—in such weather, such clothes and such a condition—meant waiting till this lowered temperature brought unconsciousness with it, in fact it meant waiting for certain death.

Without further ado we took them on to our rope, and continued downwards, though rather more slowly, with them in the middle. We were ourselves almost freezing. But two hours later we were safely at the bottom, on *terra firma* again. There we could stick our hands—which had lost all feeling—into our trouser pockets again, for warmth and comfort; gloves, of course, are things only brought along in Winter-time! The couple shook hands with us and left us, on their safe way to the Stripsen Joch Hut close by.

We were not the only ones that day to hug the stove in the Hut, wrapped in warm blankets, drying our wringing-wet clothes at it. Late in the evening a thoroughly frozen party arrived, still roped together. The wet body-knots had refused to yield to feeble, stiffened fingers; now they set to on them with a piece of iron.

None of which prevented our standing on the Ellmauer Tor again in lovely weather next morning. The grooves and crevices on the mountain flanks still harboured traces of yesterday's snow, now melting visibly under the warm spring sunshine. The Kaiser Walls shone across at us, sunlit, wet with rain, apparently oblivious of what had happened among them during the last twenty-four hours. They looked their friendliest; but it was heartless Nature's most cynical smile. For fantastic as the changes in the weather had been, they could not hide last night's drama. On all sides sounded shouts for assistance; rescue parties were on the way. The parties reached four climbers too late to wake them from their eternal sleep; cold and exhaustion had killed them. Even the West Gully of the Central Predigstuhl Summit could offer us no real cheer in such circumstances. It was with a feeling of deep depression that we left the Kaiser Range and the galaxy of climbs above the Steinerne Rinne.

GRADE VI—IN THE LIMESTONE CLIFFS

OURS was a modest home. My father was a small craftsman in State employ, whose restricted salary was just enough to provide the bare necessities of life. We usually had dry bread for breakfast, and I had to buy my lunch out of my own pocket money, which I earned as an apprentice in a Forwarding Agent's business. So, in order to save enough for my Sunday outings, I developed a real diviner's sense for the cheapest feeding-places. My normal commissariat consisted of bread and cream-cheese, because I couldn't afford anything else; but I was quite happy.

The eternal shortage of funds of course affected my choice of tours, too. I could rarely manage expensive railway journeys. What a boon a bicycle would have been! Still, thanks be to God, there are mountains just at Innsbruck's front door, so to speak. And what mountains! Take the Limestone Group, the Kalkkögel, for instance—a veritable treasure-trove. We practically made a base of the Adolf Pichler Hut. By the plural, I mean our bunch of friends from the Innsbruck Youth Section. Almost every week-end we met there on our gay—sometimes rowdily-gay—round; maybe it was the Hut-keeper's daughter that had such a special attraction for us.

A few easy practice climbs soon got me accustomed to the brittle rock of the Kalkkögel, with its splinter-like texture; in a very short time I felt perfectly at home on it. The climbing was not on iron-hard holds like in the Kaiser, but more like in the Karwendel—a cat-like stealthy ripple over the stone, with extreme care at every step. No pulling or propping, no violent "heave-ho!", but a cautious feeling of the way upwards, often made more difficult by vertical stratification. In no circumstances might one try to put one's weight "outwards" on the holds, as one can in the Wetterstein, for instance. To friction, keeping well away from the rock, would be quite the wrong technique here. Here the basic requirement is to hug the rock and only apply a pressure-technique on the holds. This range is a splendid school which has produced a host of first-class climbers: Hias Auckenthaler, Hias Rebitsch, Kuno Rainer—to mention only a few outstanding names.

Waldemar and I, teamed up once again, were sitting among the huge boulders at the foot of the great débris shoots, our necks craned upwards, as so often before. We had just done the North-West Face of the Riepenwand; but it was still only the middle of the day and we felt like tackling something else. We took a short walk along the bottom of the Riepenwand's yellowy-black walls, pottering from the start of one climb to another, assessing the comparative difficulty of each.

Just then I had a sudden thought. How would it be if we climbed up a bit to where the Wall swings away so steeply from its basic foundations? Not very far up, we should reach the place where our famous predecessors had found their way on to the West Face—that great climb had only been done twice.

We were at the extreme right-hand end of the West Face, standing at the outer edge of a broad terrace, a few yards from the Wall itself, with water sprinkling down on us. Two hundred feet above us, the Wall disappeared from view and only the outer edge of an enormous roof separated us from the sky. Up there on the left must be the start of the climb.

I sounded Waldi. "It doesn't look so frightfully difficult—I can't believe it's an impossible wall to climb. What d'you think?"

"One can but try," he answered.

Away went our boots into the pack, on went our rubbers in their place, and I climbed up without another word to the start of operations. It all looked so ridiculously easy. But the rock had completely taken me in and the Wall bared its ugly teeth from the first. I got stuck on the first three feet of it. The rock was sheer, overhanging slightly and demanding the last ounce of finger-strength—the whole weight of one's body came on to the very tips of one's fingers. I had to go back several times. Waldemar refused utterly to believe that one couldn't make any headway, so he had a go, but also had to give it up very soon. As a precaution, I banged a piton into the rotten rock, but it didn't sound very encouraging. Turn by turn, we tried again, several times—without any success—each time we had soon had quite enough of it.

"The rock just curls one's fingers up," said Waldemar. At last we saw what a waste of time it all was, and decided to pack up, for there was no sense in staying. Anyway, we could only have made a partial attempt on the climb; it was much too late now to complete it.

It was only when I was knocking the piton out that I realised how much more reliable an aid it promised to be than we had thought at the beginning. So I decided on just one more attempt. This time I could take a bit of a risk, for the piton would certainly break my fall. I climbed cautiously out over it. Very slowly, inch by inch, relying on its holding, I tried out every hand- and foot-hold within reach from it, insofar as the strength of my fingers could cope with the requirements. Every inch took me further from the piton. I tried to drive a second one into a wrinkle, but the rock was solid and offered not a single weakness. I was just wasting my strength; so I tried the thing without any protection. My fingers were already threatening to give out, but I had to get on somehow; there was no question of going back any more. Waldemar was about sixty feet below me, but there were still quite thirty feet to go, up to the Band. Till I reached it I should not find a place where I could stand normally, and get my strength back.

For about an hour I clung to tiny nicks and wrinkles. It was thanks entirely to the strength and endurance of well-trained fingers that I did not come off. Every yard had been a crucial struggle, and now I could hardly hang on any longer, except that I had to, and there was no choice left me. . . . I should fall a hundred feet sheer, and then out over the base of the mountain. I kept on telling myself that there wasn't a single piton on the rope, and that I simply must hold on somehow. I was no longer thinking of the Wall below me, but was beginning to look up towards the Band above, counting the very inches that lay between.

Then at last and at last, I got a touch on the very outside edge of the Band. I could hardly keep my fingers tensed any more, but just managed to swing the top part of my body up over the rim, and there I lay, gasping and exhausted, while I allowed my nerveless fingers to recover a little. I knew well enough that this time only a hair-line had separated me from a fall—a fall which would have meant an early end to my career as a climber and a human being. Waldemar must have known it, too, but he kept wonderfully quiet about it. Now it was his turn to discover what it feels like to master an "Upper Six", that is to say, to climb close to the limit of human capabilities.

It was only then that the hang of the rope, which nowhere touched the rock, revealed the true steepness of the pitch to my eyes. No wonder that this route had only been twice climbed in the course of ten years; even though it lies in a climbing ground where a dozen climbers operate every Sunday!

Waldi joined me. Sheer inquisitiveness lured us on. Above us, things looked definitely easier. While the first rope's length had been a sheer unjointed wall, in which you couldn't even fix a piton, now there was at least a crack ahead, with more of those comforting features looking down from above. The crack leaned heavily outwards. My body was soon hanging way outside my companion's, far out beyond the vertical. But once again there was a broad Band cutting across the sheer wall. At first we were very surprised to find a wide and friendly ledge, a veritable promenade like this, in so inhospitable, "impossible" a wall.

We decided we could get back if we wanted to, so we followed the Band to the right. We could move comfortably, standing upright.

"Almost a bicycle track," said Waldi. A small buttress interrupted the Band, then it continued across the Wall, though a little narrower. Overhead, the yellow walls went sweeping to the sky. I imagined the North Wall of the Grosse Zinne in the Dolomites to be like that. Nothing to stop the eye, which looks up, to the left and to right, always over the same picture—smooth yellow, unbroken up-thrusts of wall. I put my hand on the rock, but it slid off, for there was nothing to hold. So, on towards the right.

The Band narrowed continually, and now I could no longer go up-right; so I lay down flat on my stomach and crawled on, wriggling like a snake. The Band became a ledge, with the Wall overhanging it; 200 feet below was the outer edge of the mountain's base, where we had stood some hours ago. Directly beneath me, the wall turned straight inwards. I seemed to be poised on the outer edge of a monstrous bulge. My right hand and foot supported my body and kept it from slipping off the ledge, which was now about as broad as my hand. A hundred feet back along the Band stood Waldemar, "protecting" me. He knew as well as I did that this protection was merely "moral" and pure eye-wash. If I fell, he was bound to come too.

In places like that, there is nothing to help one except one's companionship on the rope, one's life-and-death interdependence, the great feeling of responsibility, the knowledge that the other fellow's life is in your hands, too.

The harder it got, the more slowly I moved. Waldi could only judge what difficulties I was encountering by the way the rope ran out through his hands, evenly or in jerks. I had clean forgotten that we had ever thought of turning back. Now it was too late, anyway: no retreat from where we were now. This exiguous crawling-shelf was a real mouse-trap; once in it you hadn't a hope of getting out again. The ledge kept on getting narrower. Somehow I had to get out of this crawling position. The overhanging rock kept forcing my body down. I tried to move feet foremost, so as to get out of this horizontal state back into a normal climbing position. Still the ledge narrowed, until it became an inch-wide wrinkle and then simply a hand-traverse. That traverse demanded everything it takes. Climbing on and down a little, I found a precarious stance; but just sufficient support to allow me to knock in a protecting piton. I hooked on with much relief.

It was now a question of getting through, of climbing the whole Wall, whatever it might still produce. The next bit looked considerably easier; but appearances don't count for much in such places, it is actualities that matter. And they were pretty grim. . . .

The overhang bulged far outwards. Waldemar tiptoed past me and started off on it. I marvelled at the way he tackled the rough, sharp stone bare-footed. With his naked soles he straddled the rock, crooking his toes into the wrinkles, and the last I saw of him was his heels, as tough as shoe-leather, disappearing over the bulge.

Then on again.

Hard work took us upwards in smooth chimneys, over wet, slippery rock. Whenever time allowed, we looked far down to the green bottom of the valley, in whose peace and calm we sought both the necessary relief for our nerves and the stimulus for the next struggle. We looked out far and wide over to the westward, where the sun was dipping behind the Kühtaier Hills. It must have been about eight in the evening —five hours since we began the climb. Surely we must be somewhere near the end? Above us the crack grew deeper, and the angle of the rock seemed to ease off up there. Could that be the end of the Wall? We took a short breather on a band.

"We've got it in the bag!" I told Waldemar, and was thrilled to think that we had brought off this terrific climb, only the third ascent ever of the Riepen West Wall, one of the hardest climbs in the Tirol.

Waldemar wanted to lead the next bulge, though I wasn't too keen to let him. Still I couldn't complain of my day's share. . . .

He had to come back and try again. Again he failed. A little impatiently I said: "Surely, it can't be as hard as all that!"—"All right, you try it," he answered.

But I stuck, too, about six feet up. The rock was pushing me furiously outwards, there was hardly any hold for my feet, the holds being scanty and far too low down. I tried it with a *Steigbaum*, but even that failed. The rock was obdurate and would not take a piton. I had to come back and let Waldi have the next go. The next time he came off he was furious. "This blasted Wall!" he fumed.

The sun had left the valley now.

"We've got to hurry!"

What's the use of all that, when you simply can't move forward? But there's no hope of going back, either. And we can't stay here. . . . Should we shout for help?—Not on your life! We racked our brains for some other possibility to the right or to the left; the rock was if anything more repulsive. The only way out lay straight on up! I simply refused to believe we were at the end of our resources, telling myself that, what others were able to do, we could do, too. Gradually I worked myself into a fury at our helplessness. "You're a coward!" I accused myself, then talked new courage into myself. I sent Waldemar to a moderately safe position. "I'm going to have one last go," I told him. "This time it's up or bust!"

I was soon clinging six feet up at the critical spot, but this time there was no more looking back. I was no longer interested in the Wall below us; whatever went on down there, it was up we had to go. I tried the tiny sloping hold to the right again, for it was our only hope of progress. This time my strength must hold out. I had to draw on the last of my reserves but, at last—at last, it went! Sweat was standing in beads on my forehead. It was a beast of a spot, but we had done it.

The rest of the climb was just easy rock. It was deep twilight when we traversed off the Wall, found a couloir and climbed down over the boulders in the dark. Waldemar's toes were bleeding and he could hardly walk. It was close on midnight when we stood once again at the foot of those thrusting overhangs, which we had regarded in the morning with such respect that it had not even occurred to us to try climbing them.

*　　*　　*

Pleasant as it is to return home on a Sunday evening after a success on a difficult climb, one's thoughts are inclined to switch to the next objective, which may perhaps yield a more important achievement. But let it never be said that we "Extremists" of the climbing world see nothing but mere overhangs, cracks, traverses, pitons and have no eye any more for the beauties of Nature; and that we never do a moderate climb any more. Far from it; we are not quite so poverty-stricken as all that.

The limit of what is climbable is reached comparatively soon. After all, an "Extremist" who could only find enjoyment in increased difficulty and danger would have to go in search of some other branch of sporting activity—maybe motor-racing or some such game, where he could go out after speed records. Of course there are people like that among our young climbers, but they are a very small minority. The true mountaineer, even the most extreme type, gets as much pleasure out of an easy climb or out of a good walk as he does when next he returns to the borderline of human capabilities.

I spent many more Sundays in the Kalkkögel, the so-called Dolomites of North Tirol. They were a hard school. We were always at the foot of some climb early in the morning, in the shadow below some North Wall. The rock was often still plastered with ice; but we could not wait, for the great difficulties up above drove us on to an early start to our climbing.

Once again the series of obstacles began with a loamy, sheer hand-traverse, typical of the rock here. Water poured down on us and we were soon soaked. It ran in at our sleeves and out at our trouser-legs. Waldemar had to undo the string with which he always used to tie up his long trousers below the knee, to leave the water a free exit and prevent its being dammed up. It is asking too much of fingers soggy with water to do this kind of climbing. Our heavy task for the day was the "Riepen Gully", the hardest climb in the Kalkkögel.

At mid-day we rested on a débris shoot. The Great Gully, the most difficult part, lay behind us. It had been a stiff job and a dangerous one, because of the brittle nature of the stone; but it had gone all right.

Behind us rose a great cleft. Moving on into it, we found ourselves in a deep shaft. Overhead an enormous roof swung outwards cutting off the whole chimney. How did one get out? I climbed upwards in the very bottom of the cleft. A little tower of rock required delicate circumnavigation and delicate handling of the rope, too, for it tottered ominously at the slightest touch, and Waldemar was standing exactly under it in the line of fire. I straddled up the top part of the chimney to its extreme upper edge. From it I gained a marvellously impressive view down into the abyss, my eyes sweeping the whole lower half of the Wall.

There I found a little hole, the only way by which to crawl out. Droppings of birds, feathers, old nests . . . then the screeching of jackdaws. "My dear good beasties, I don't mean you any harm. I only want to get out and up!" I pushed the upper part of my body through the chink; my feet kicked out over thin air for a moment and then I was through. I was in a fearful mess, just as though I had emerged from a sewer.

The Wall put up one more defence. A big overhang barred the next gully. Since there was no place for a piton, it had to be climbed without assistance; but I had sufficient skill for that. My hands searched outwards over the edge till I found a firm grip. Then I had to hold my whole weight on them for a short time, while my feet were feeling around for holds on the uttermost rim of the roof. Then I was able to take the weight off my hands, and we were through.

We had paid no attention to our hunger, but now it made itself felt beyond denial. We ate a piece of dry bread and some sugar, which seemed a princely feast to us. We didn't need anything else, for we were happy enough to be in the warm sun again. And in the evening I went back to Innsbruck on a borrowed bicycle.

THREE ROUTES ON THE SCHÜSSELKAR

I HAD by now a good many Severes and Super-Severes behind me, and still I felt like a beginner. Not just because I was only eighteen years old; it was as though I were under orders, working under some inner law, which commanded me to get better, tougher: "You are under the spell of the Hills, but you must make yourself worthy of them, too." I could not bear the idea of coming to grief somewhere among them through my own unfitness. I must learn to cope with whatever they might bring upon me. I must get better, better. . . .

My constant companions in the evenings were books, periodicals, accounts of climbs, pictures of mountains in foreign parts, stirring my imagination wildly. My thoughts went winging to those distant peaks; among them I enjoyed the most thrilling adventures. But there were awaiting me tremendous experiences on Mountains and Walls, close at home, too.

The South-East Wall of the Schüsselkarspitze, the great Face which Rudolf Peters was the first to climb long ago, but which has shed none of its grim, gigantic reputation in all the years between. I should soon be ready for that!

But I must be thoroughly fit for it. I used every moment of my spare time on training, though there wasn't much of it during the week. Sheer common sense and the wishes of my nearest and dearest urged me on to be a hundred-per-cent efficient distributor and salesman; but my heart wanted to be on the Schüsselkar Face. In order to comply with both dictates, I got up at five every morning and hurried to the Höttinger Outcrop, Innsbruck's climbing-nursery, and still got to work by the prescribed time. In the evenings, I went neither to the Pictures nor the Pub, nor walking out with young ladies, but straight back to the climbing-nursery.

I soon knew every hand- and foot-hold by heart. Things which seemed impossible at the outset in rubbers later became possible in boots with smooth leather soles. Indeed, the improvement was so rapid that I went up and down, up and down, time and again, like a lift. All this, of course, only a few feet above safe ground; but the important part was that my fingers were getting trained.

I had memorised the description of the "Südost" in every detail. There wasn't a sentence in which the word "roof" or "overhang" did not occur. We naturally kept our plans secret, but at last we judged the moment to have come. We spent the night in the Leutasch. It was still dark as we moved upwards under our heavy loads; climbing equipment weighs heavy and we had everything with us we might need. Nobody spoke, but we were all thinking long, long thoughts—an odd sensation, like the calm before the storm. Yes, and to-day would be a stormy day, or at least a red-letter day in our lives. We knew that anybody who has done the Schüsselkar Wall has won the respect and admiration of all climbers; he has taken the great stride from Apprentice to Master.

We were at the start by seven o'clock; above us on the Wall we heard voices. Someone shouted down: "What cheer, Hermann?" Immediately we recognised the voices. "Cheers, Manfred: cheers, Josl," we shouted up. "What are you two doing, there?" Down came the reply: "The same as you, of course."

"Oh, gathering grapes?"

"No, mushrooms!"

We laughed about it, but we were secretly a little narked that those two were ahead of us. We all belonged to the Youth Section, but the "Südost" was no place for a massed assault.

Waldemar, knowing my weakness for leading, let me take the first pitch without any argument. We hadn't been spoiled by any expectation of firmness from our rock, so to-day's stuff seemed to us, in very contrast to past material under our hands in the Kalkkögel, like a Christmas treat.

It is a strange thing, on a route like this up a rock face, how the impossible does become possible at the very last moment. Whenever you think you are at the very end of your powers, there is always a hidden hold or a wrinkle into which a piton can be forced, to bridge the difficulty. So the first rule of climbing is: "Look first—then climb!" The whole art is to recognize all the helpful features quickly. But what one man grasps at the first glance, another frequently misses. The one who sees correctly has the advantage. Finally, of course, the decisive factors are the personal degree of technical skill, a sense of balance, the extreme ability to use friction and even the slightest unevenness in the rock. But what good is the finest technique, if you don't take time to look, if you mess about and do your own bungling variation of every move, simply because you haven't the gift of assessing the relative difficulties?

I sometimes feel as if the Faces were specially built for climbers. Nature has formed them in a million years in such a way that they only seem to be there for crazy men in a crazy age to crawl about on them like flies, winning thereby a kingly delight. Especially this Schüsselkar South-East! It provides everything one can want—especially pleasing to me was the absence of a single chimney on the whole route. The overhangs and roofs are perhaps a bit exaggerated in the climber's guide, but climbers often like to think that a merely vertical pitch overhangs a bit. The route is so pre-ordained that it is quite unnecessary to follow the description, for there is no place where you can deviate from it. On either side of the series of crags great holdless slabs go winging up and down.

We followed close on the heels of the two ahead of us, with a certain amount of mutual interference. Manfred disappeared over a jutting edge, but Josl had to wait a bit and so we two were constrained to rest a moment. The climbing had so far been most pleasant, without a single difficulty. We had done much harder stuff in the Kalkkögel. This was sheer joy and we could do with hours of it.

I shifted impatiently from one foot to the other. This enforced idleness was sapping my small supply of patience. At last Josl was able to move on: then another overhang held him up for quite a time. He seemed to lose strength and nerve, tatting around for a hold; then the stone came away from the rock, the hold broke off, and Josl went flying out backwards, to be held at once on the rope by Manfred. But the broken hold still came flying down at me, a boulder as big as my head. I pressed myself as flat as I could against the wall, but the stone hit me smack on the forehead, tearing a clump of hair out of my head. I felt the blood running warm over my face and neck. I climbed down quickly to Waldemar and sat down next to him; then I began to feel like hell. Everything went round and round, but Waldemar had a close grip on me. After a quarter of an hour the vertigo eased off: I ate a little sugar and began to feel better. Meanwhile Waldemar had fitted me out with an emergency bandage, but I could hardly see out of my eyes; everything was gummed up with blood.

However, the old upward urge was back in me; so I climbed up again, trying to avoid the critical spot, circumventing it to the left, where the rock seemed easier. A steep ramp went straight up and ended in a smooth overhang step; there were a few old pitons sticking in the wall above it, so it must be possible to get up there. The awkward part on really steep faces is that you can only see a few feet up, then a projecting ledge or a bulging overhang cuts off the view of what follows; it is therefore really essential to study the route in detail from the bottom of the climb and fix the important places firmly in your mind, so as to know exactly where you are during the actual climb. As an example, from where we were lodged, we could not assess the continuation of the Wall because of the many outcrops.

I climbed on with the aid of the doubled rope, in a kind of "Paternoster Chair Lift" from piton to piton. That kind of climbing is known as "Fire Brigade Practice" in mountain jargon. I reached the last step that way: but there was the end of it. Above my head there was nothing but mirror-smooth, beetling rock. I tried every inch of the face within reach for the slightest corrugations, searching with my eyes and with my hands, time and again.

Waldemar wisecracked: "Just give it a miss and carry straight on."

"And you, of course, have left the 'Climb-Easy Compound' at home again," I jibed back.

The drag of the rope was pretty tight round my chest. Waldemar was hanging with his whole weight on the other end to take the strain off me.

"Perhaps we're on a wild-goose chase," I shouted down to my friend.

Auckenthaler was said to have gone wildly astray during his first attempts, I remembered now. I glanced down the slabs to the right . . . the way must surely be down there in that little depression in the otherwise unvaried downward sweep of the slabs. I let myself down and tried to traverse to the right. Every movement required the utmost caution—such traverses are only a question of touch. One has to make the most of friction, a delicate adjustment of balance against the drag of the rope, which acts as a counter-weight to lower the centre of gravity from the vertical to the horizontal. There is no other way of moving horizontally across absolutely holdless slabs except against this sideways pull of the rope. I was now thirty feet from the piton; the rope's drag threatened to pull me off the wall. My fingers clung with an iron grip to the slight unevenness; it was only thanks to them and the tips of my corrugated Manchon soles that I was maintaining contact with the wall at all. In between them hung my body-weight, ten stone or more of it. Only the correct position of that body permitted me to distribute the exact load to my arms and fingers. I had to maintain the maximum possible friction-grip on the rock by pressure on those soles. The further one's body leans away from the wall when climbing, the greater is the pressure and therefore the friction maintained against the rock, but the greater also the strain on the fingers. The establishment of the best counter-poise between friction and finger-strength is simply what is meant by "technique". A word easily spoken. . . .

I straightened my body and leaned out as far as I could to the right —almost at right-angles to the face now. My right hand was feeling quickly around a corner for a usable hold, and my fingers were crooking themselves again. . . .

"Give me a bit more rope," I called back.

My feet went searching for wrinkles, my body moved on after them. and there was another half-yard gained.

"Quite decent!" I called back to Waldemar, as I rested on my tiny stance. The firm foothold gave me new confidence and at last I could get my breath back.

We had circumvented the awkward place where Josl had come off. A crack and a continuing slab, which was dealt with by a "lay-back", brought us to a splendid platform. A real invitation to a mid-day snooze.

Manfred and Josl were waiting for us. Josl apologised for the accident, but I had already forgotten about it; and in any case climbers don't need to apologise to one another for things like that, which can happen to anybody. It was only then that we noticed that we had already reached the bivouac-place of the first ascent; we could hardly believe that the main difficulties were already below us. We had been waiting all the time for a "key problem". But there was only one more steep pitch, requiring our complete concentration, and then we were at the top of the Wall.

We were thus comparatively early on the summit of the Schüsselkar-spitze. There was a summit register under the cairn; we fetched it out and turned its leaves over. It was full of famous names—almost all the élite of the climbing world were in it—though some of them already had crosses against them. . . . "Whom they love, they take"—it is true of the Gods and it is true of the Hills. We felt very proud as we entered our names.

In the evening Manfred and Josl took me out to Seefeld to see a doctor, while Waldemar remained in the Leutasch; for we had something planned for the next day. The doctor found two tears in the casing of my skull; their scars remain a visible memento of the Südost to this day. He dealt with the situation with some clips, a tonsure and a head-bandage. By midnight I had rejoined my partner. We had a short sleep, then we set out again by the same path as yesterday.

This time our aim was the South Face "direct". It was only a few years since Kuno Rainer and Paul, Peter Aschenbrenner's brother, made the first ascent, and after several attempts had failed. The climb is notable for some huge roofs and overhangs. I already knew the "way" to the top of the buttress from having done the Herzog-Fiechtl route—the most difficult Wetterstein climb in the classical days. I will not waste any words on a description of that fine ascent, made by those two great climbers, Herzog and Fiechtl, both Hans Dülfer's equals; it has been described too often already, especially the notorious "Swinging Traverse" and the Slab Gully. I will confine myself to our new, infrequently trodden climb.

We branched off to the right before the "Eight Metre Wall". Waldemar climbed a steep gully which petered out under a big overhang. The stances were stuck to the Wall like swallows' nests; roof was piled on roof; the view down into the abyss grew ever more terrific. The rock fell away inwards from under our feet; we were hanging so far out that we could no longer see the bottom of the climb, but looked straight down on to the débris-cones which spread from the foot of the Wall. At the moment I was not sure whether I wouldn't prefer to be lying on the boulders down there sun-bathing; but when one is sitting down below, one longs to be up among those forbidding cliffs, fighting and venturing one's way up them. The eternal craving for the opposite extreme exerts its pull.

We both seemed to be having an off-day. Nobody is always in the same form. One's inner approach has a lot to do with it. Yesterday we had accorded the greatest possible respect to the "Südost", to be pleasantly surprised by the comparatively slight degree of its difficulties; to-day was just the opposite. After yesterday's climb we imagined we could manage anything in the world with the greatest of ease, so we underestimated all the difficulties. But we soon began to notice that this climb was "larning" us; not till we discovered the right approach were we able to master with complete confidence what confronted us.

There was one more diagonal crack, the crux of the whole climb. The rope disappeared beneath me, over a projection. If I hadn't known that my partner was tied to the other end of it, I should have believed that I had climbed up alone from the bottomless abyss into this chaos of steeply-piled masses of rock. The upward way ahead—steeper than ever—was a question-mark for us. Yet the description said one ought to get along quite well, through these huge outward-curving chunks of rock. Great rock-masses must have come away here since time immemorial, and it seemed strange to us that these gigantic blocks, bulking out huge above us into thin air, hadn't long ago obeyed the dictates of gravity. But Nature obeys different laws from those to which our human architects are subject.

I climbed a steep slab. The green-speckled stone was eaten away by water, whose deep runnels facilitated my progress. But that brought me close under those gigantic square blocks and I could not spy a single possibility of getting any further. In vain I searched the rock above me for rope-rings or pitons. This was a trap, built by Titans, in which to catch bothersome trespassers. Nobody could make headway here.

At that moment Waldemar shouted up that he had seen a rusty spike away up to the left, so that was probably the way. I climbed down to him and then up again leftwards between the great bulges, moving comfortably from step to step, without any serious difficulty. Then we took alternate leads again.

Waldemar was in the lead. Stones went whizzing close by me. A little worried by my yesterday's injury, I reminded my friend that my head wasn't in a fit state to stand another sample of that treatment. But Waldi was in any case being as careful as he could, and the mountain also decided to be kind.

Yet another entry in the register followed: "Schüsselkarspitz; South Wall Direct. 5th Ascent."

We hastened down, by the West Ridge. The sky was full of threatening thunder-clouds, pressing lower and lower upon us; mists began to gather round the flanks of our mountain. We roped-down from the Wangscharte, went loping down the lush meadows into the Leutasch at a run, and hurried on the way to Seefeld, to avoid getting caught in the impending downpour. But heaven opened its sluices far too soon; rain and hail poured down and in a very few minutes we were soaked through, as we moved on towards Seefeld, resignedly, through a perfect cloudburst. Let those who were safe under roofs or hay-ricks laugh at us; we couldn't care less. The very idea of the possibility of having been caught by this irresistible flood in the middle of those bulking slabs now sent a shiver down our spines. Valley rain isn't always very comfortable —but it isn't dangerous.

* * *

Then the Schüsselkar once again.

This time we spent our night in the rickyard. A fearful noise awoke me with a start. Rain and hail were drumming down on the roof of our abode, dimming all hope of a successful climb. The Schüsselkarspitze East Wall—our goal this time—seemed to be literally washed away under the descending deluge. We got up at five o'clock, and had a dubious look at the weather. The rain had stopped, but thick cloud was still veiling the flanks of our mountain and hanging low into the valley. How could we guess that it was fine up above?

Waldemar and I went together again. We had decided at least to go up to the foot of the Wall, come what may. Slowly the cloud wrack began to lift; as we arrived at the foot of the climb the sun even managed to struggle through.

Our early start was rewarded by a magnificent climb. The difficulties increased gradually on this, the most difficult of all the Schüsselkar routes. The titbit of the climb is a hidden chimney, high up. I loathe chimneys; but I had, of course, not been consulted. . . . We reached a belt of smooth wall-like overhangs. Where did one go from there? There was only a hole, a kind of cave; I went through it into the bowels of the mountain. Below me gaped a black, bottomless pit; above me it shot up as a dark shaft, with a feeble glimmer of light at its very top. We climbed up towards the faint illumination, the climbing made easier by a kind of stalactite formation, whose rock was uncommonly rough and it was necessary to exert care to avoid injury on it. It grew darker and darker; a torch would have been useful here. Feeling my way from one stalactite to another, I drew nearer to the pale ray of light. After more than 130 feet I finally reached the narrow fissure and wriggled through it into the light of day. We were up; at my feet the great Wall went plunging down into nothingness. . . .

Muffled rumblings heralded an approaching storm and robbed us of our longed-for and well-earned hour on top. Down we went by well-known ways.

We got through a long list of climbs that summer, climbs of all sorts; difficult struggles, light-hearted experiences, contemplative pleasures— but my longings were not yet satisfied. Evidently such is my nature. Many of my wishes were fulfilled; each time fulfilment gave birth to another wish. The successful outcome of each climb was at the same moment the upward urge for the next. And as I lay resting in the sun on the summit after some grim upward struggle, my thoughts were already far, far away, somewhere else. It was the kind of passion which knows no frontiers, no constant, attainable end.

THE DYING MOUNTAIN—
THE NORTH WALL OF THE
PRAXMARERKARSPITZE

KUNO RAINER, of whom I had heard so much, was on recuperative leave, brought home by a war wound. It had been pretty serious—a stomach wound—but now it had healed properly, and Kuno was making fresh plans. It was with great pleasure that I accepted his invitation to climb together; and we met the very next week-end. We were crossing the Lafatscher Joch in the Karwendel when a tremendous thunderstorm burst right overhead; not wishing to act as lightning-conductors we broke into a run but, before we could reach the shelter of the Club Hut close by, we were knocked off our feet by a lightning flash. We got up in a daze. The following thunder-clap was deafening indeed. Quick, quick . . . into the Hut, just over there!

The guide-book in the Hut described our proposed climb in detail. The growling of the thunder ebbed away gradually into the distance as we studied our route, but the thunder-showers had given way to a steady, drenching downpour; down it poured ceaselessly, so we had to wait. It was getting dark by the time the rain stopped; but we set out on our way just the same, for we still meant to get to the Lafatscher-Hochleger up there, so as to be at the start of our climb when we woke up in the morning.

It was a typical late autumn night. Presently it was pitch-dark, so that we could hardly see an inch in front of us, as we went on up.

"Black as a bag," said Kuno.

The woods grew thicker and thicker, almost like a jungle. We could no longer see the tiny track we were following, could only feel it through our slippers. Occasionally we could recognise, against the tops of the trees which alone enabled us to detect the sky, where the path went on. It was pouring again, now, on the pine-needle roof of the forest. The sky was pitch-black; not a star to be seen. The distant lightning-flashes provided momentary opportunities for a vague kind of direction-finding. But after each of them it was all the darker; we stood there, blinded, compelled to shut our eyes again, so as to get used to the darkness again. We stumbled into puddles and tripped over stones, slipping on wet wood underfoot. At last we got out into the open, but the track immediately became muddy and our feet sank into the morass. . . . We cursed and prayed. . . .

Beyond the meadow, we couldn't find the continuation of the path, as we stood at the edge of a tangle of dry, decaying wood. Upturned trees lay around on the mossy floor, barring our onward way. For better or worse, we turned back; but this time we failed to find the place where the path had issued from the forest. We searched the whole edge of the woods right round the meadow for it, but found not a sign of it.

At last we found our way into the forest just anywhere, through dense undergrowth. We couldn't even see the floor; we could only hope not suddenly to find a yawning abyss under our feet. We felt our way forward with hand and foot, reeling like drunkards, our feet slipping on the wet wood under them as if on polished ice. We hardly dared think of our climbing-rubbers; they were wringing wet. Each of us was taking his own line, where he thought he might best force a way through this jungle. That took us further and further apart, till we could just avoid losing each other by shouting to one another.

"This is nonsense!" I shouted across to Kuno. "We'll never get any further this way. Let's stop here!"

Kuno tried to light a fire so that we could at least dry our sopping clothes, but everything was wet through including, unfortunately, the matches; there was nothing to be done. So we just lay down on the wet ground and tried to snatch a little sleep; but the cold kept shaking us awake again. Desperation drove us on our way again, and we tried at once to gain height. Perhaps we could traverse above the tree-level, if we could get out above it, for the Hochleger must still be a long way over there. We took a look from a slight rise and saw something shining down below: perhaps it was the path? . . . We climbed down to it, and found nothing but a piece of rotten wood, phosphorescent and shining in the darkness. The rain stopped after midnight.

A few single stars began to twinkle through the heavy clouds, but it got no lighter for all that. At last all progress was brought to an end by the thick tangle of larch undergrowth. It cleared overhead and a bitter cold set in. Shivering, we waited for the morning. Ursa Minor, Ursa Major, the Milky Way—they have all been going their appointed ways since the Creation; they could teach us how minute and insignificant are we human beings, who take ourselves so seriously.

We moved on again in a grey dawn. Soon enough we found the little track we had sought so frantically in the darkness of night—but it took us another two hours to the Hochleger; and from there it was a long way over shoulders and combs before we reached the final hump of a ridge.

There we were at last, standing at the foot of the North Wall of the Praxmarerkarspitze, a huge, reddish-yellow wall, towering up before us.

It made a terribly repellent impression on me. Even from there you could see the brittle nature of its rock. Black watery streaks slash down and across it. A gigantic débris-cone splits the base of the Wall, reaching down and away to the tree-level, a witness to the terrific artillery-fire of stone.

This was Hias Auckenthaler's Empire. There are countless climbs bearing his name on these Karwendel Walls; a lasting memorial to that unforgettable climber. The Eastern Praxmarerkarspitze fell northwards, towards us, in a fearsomely steep face. Even the bottom part looked impossible, yet this was our to-day's objective. Hardened as we already were, we didn't care for the look of it at all. It was ten years or more since Auckenthaler and Schmidhuber fought their way up it together; since then the Wall had slept the safe slumber of a Sleeping Beauty.

Two figures were coming up towards us. It surely wasn't possible that, after a lapse of ten years, two ropes had chosen this particular climb for their attentions—on this particular day, of all days?

We went down a bit over loose rubble-chutes. Two steps forward and one back brought us forward with difficulty over the knobbly boulders. At this stage the two figures revealed themselves, to our great surprise, as our friends Josl Knoll and Manfred Bachmann. They had been cleverer than we, riding across on their bicycles from Scharnitz, and spending the night in the Hunting Lodge.

Even now, in September, there were still occasional relics of last winter at the foot of the wall—hard snow, frozen to an icy consistency, snow that refused to melt this year.

The mountain's base, a great buttress, gave us a taste of what was to come. Age-long stone-falls had planed the rock as smooth as glass; fine dust counselled caution and speed at the same time; the stones came cracking down on to the buttress incessantly. We got ready for the main business on a narrow, débris-covered ledge. The rock above us was overhanging; at all events falling stones could not affect us any more, for the line of fire now carried everything far out into the rift below. Enormous roofs spread their protection over this part of the wall.

Kuno allowed me to lead. I felt my way gingerly forward. It was vital to avoid any kind of jerky movement; this kind of rock has to be caressed, or it turns nasty. I could feel the hand- and foot-holds giving, and the movements of the rock, which held reasonably under pressure. Above all one must not dally, but must keep continually moving. Each hold had to be made use of for the shortest possible time, be it for hand or foot.

Kuno was looking up expectantly. "This is one solid rubbish-chute!" I told him, resignedly.

Every now and then a stone came out under my shoes and fell sound-lessly on to the projecting rocks at the foot, without touching anything on the way. A rusty old piton and a soggy rope were signals left by our predecessors. Perched on a rickety stance, I brought Kuno up to me, knocking in a second piton for safety's sake, in case the old one decided to part from the loose rock. It was a marvel that anything held here, that there were holds one could trust—even momentarily in passage.

A second, lesser buttress, separated from the Wall, allowed further progress up the otherwise unbroken rock-face. It, too, had to be handled with the utmost caution, for it vibrated noticeably, when one leaned against it. Water, cracking frosts, the passage of Time have destroyed the stone-masonry. The mountain was dying. When attacked, it defended itself, with deadly brittle stone, threatening to hurl one into the depths.

We reached a wide Band. As we were traversing along it to the right, we were startled by a fearsome clatteration. We clung close to the rock, thinking the whole mountain was coming down on us. Behind us a great dark dust-cloud rose to the heights; the buttress had broken away—our buttress! For a long, long time its broken stones went rattling down the face, clattering down the slopes below it into the cauldron at the bottom. A herd of chamois went darting away in fright. Then at last there was peace and silence again. . . .

Another thirty feet and the Upper Band would be ours. The weight of the rope dragging on me was almost unbearable. I climbed on, countering the pull desperately, taking the utmost care not to dislodge a single stone from the face, for every hand-hold, every foot-hold, was vital. Then the rope jammed and I could hardly pull it after me. That was the last straw. Then it came free, just as suddenly; and I was free again, too. A few feet more. Then—the Band.

It proved a dreadful disappointment. It was covered in rubble and very airy—no kind of a stance at all. I crawled up on all fours, slipped back again, tried to get some kind of a hold somewhere, but met nothing but loose stones. There was no more rope now—and at that very moment I found a precarious stance. I did not in the least envy the others, still standing at the foot of this pitch. Kuno and I waited in case the two coming up behind us might need assistance. But Manfred and Josl were in tip-top form: and they were too proud to want any help from us. Afterwards they told me that the narrow ledge broke off just an inch behind their feet after they had crossed it. You have to have the luck, or you get nowhere!

There was still half the Wall, which stands more than 2,000 feet in all; but all the excitements were over. We climbed on together to the summit ridge with our ropes coiled around us.

There our ways parted. Bachmann and Knoll went down the north side again, while we traversed along the ridge to the Kaskarspitze, intending to descend southwards to the Pfeis Hut. We tried a short-cut, but soon got entangled in a thick larch-forest and had to come up again. It was there that Kuno, who had noticed nothing at all till then, suddenly collapsed, complaining of frightful pains. His recently-healed stomach wound had opened again, as a result of the excessive exertion. It had really been much too soon for him to attempt such a climb; but his will-power was tremendous. After a short rest he was soon in good enough condition to proceed. Kuno is like that!

We reached the Pfeis Hut by evening and, although they tried hard to persuade us to stay the night, we had to go on. Kuno had to be at the hospital next morning without fail, so that the doctor would not notice anything wrong. So we started down the scree-slopes from the Arzler Saddle for Innsbruck. We were soon enveloped in the veils of night, while below us lay a sea of lights—Innsbruck itself. We knew every inch of the way—so the darkness, which was hardly any less than yesterday's —could not do us any harm. Even so, in the belt of larches above the Mühlauerklamm we only just avoided having to camp out in full view of the brightly-lit city. Somehow we just managed to detect the steep little track through the larches down to the ravine. To add to Kuno's troubles, he had cut his ankle on a stone and could hardly walk any more. It was long after midnight when we reached our home-town, swaying, tottering, and utterly exhausted.

HEAD-FIRST TO LIFE

IT was Whitsun, 1943. I had grown old and fit enough for Service. Field-grey had been fashionable for years, but I had not been old enough. Now I had arrived, though I hadn't yet reached the stage of listening to those deadly little singing birds, the bullets. At the moment my billet was in a particularly beautiful holiday resort in my own native Tirol, St. Johann in Tirol, at the foot of the Kaisergebirge—and at the State's expense, too. It was, at the time, the location of the Army Mountain Ambulance School of Training. . . .

What a mixture of stiff discipline and of mountaineering! I found it especially difficult—I, who had always visited my beloved Hills at my own sweet will and caprice—to mould myself to discipline's tight clamp. It was a contradiction in terms: climbers have to be self-reliant, headstrong blockheads or they would come to grief every time the mountains demand initiative or power of decision of them. In the Army you are only allowed to exhibit those fundamentals of the climber's self-imposed training and life's basic aim at times of danger, at the front when attacked by the enemy, and so on. In the early stages of instruction and drill, such characteristics are frowned on; they got me into trouble time and again. What an extraordinary paradox: A Climber-Soldier! I certainly hadn't yet discovered how to fuse the two careers, for at eighteen, I was still more the climber. All the more so, at St. Johann in Tirol, where the ridges, faces and teeth of the Wilde Kaiser are more or less on your doorstep.

It was June and I had one day's leave. Waldi and I were together again. Once again we went along the Steinerne Rinne, descending it a little further than usual. Over our heads the Walls stood sheer, leaving room for only a narrow strip of sky. If you lie down on a boulder there and look up to where the two opposing Walls almost touch, you get the feeling that they are both coming crashing down on you. On the right was the Predigstuhl, the West Wall of the central peak still in deep shadow—far too cold for us; so we turned to the sun-drenched Eastern Walls, where rose the precipices of the Fleischbank. The rays of the sun outlined the Plattenwülste even more sharply, till we could recognise that prominent black rift in its exact detail. It was Peter Aschenbrenner and Hans Lucke who found the way up it, many years ago now.

It is not often that a party approaches that part of the Wall; the

"Asche-Luck" hasn't the reputation of being an exactly pleasant climbing-ground. All the same, we wanted to sample it.

"Try a fall with Death," said Waldi, who likes to face hard facts. In his view one should never underestimate things.

We climbed the first few rope's lengths unassisted. We took no notice of a piton, full of confidence in our own grand form. The next traverse made us quite glad of the rope; but it was not until we reached a roomy pulpit that we got ourselves into full array for Grade VI "severe" stuff, with twenty-five carabiners, twenty pitons, two 130-ft ropes and some rope-slings as our outward accoutrement. An unquenchable upward urge and sheer joy of living were our inner driving force. And somewhere in between was strength, which would be a first essential here. It was the factor which had given me furiously to think on the very first few feet of the gully and had acted as a spur to rouse all my will-power. Extreme difficulties demand extreme bodily and mental concentration. Unassisted climbing was out of the question there; yet there wasn't a piton to be seen on the whole Wall. Could our predecessors have knocked them out on purpose, to rob others who might chance to come that way of the opportunity of using them? We don't know the answer to this day.

We drove piton after piton into the rock, with extreme effort. If I climbed a few feet unassisted, in between, I was so exhausted that I had to knock in another protecting spike immediately. Often I only succeeded at the last possible second. The shaft went ringing into a wrinkle; it had better grip, or——I soon felt my fingers growing soft as butter, giving way as if they had no bones in them. Quick, in with the carabiner, then pull on the rope—a few more bangs with the hammer: the piton simply had to hold! There I was, hanging from it. I let the hammer slip through my hands and depend from its cord, while I took a short, highly necessary rest, at least till my unfeeling fingers had recovered a little. I wasn't allowed much time for that, because the pull of the rope was making itself unpleasantly felt on my thorax, about which it had become so tightly drawn that immediate release was absolutely essential. "So it's up to you again, my dear little fingers!"

Another piton driven firmly into the rock, and a sharp upward pull on the rope. I was using every corrugation for my toes. I leaned away, trying to reach up as far as possible, and to place the next spike in another crack at the extreme end of my reach. I placed it perfectly and gave it a well-aimed bang . . . and still it went wrong. The iron shaft flew out and went clinking down into the gulf.

"One piton less, and a 'special' at that!" I accused the Fates.

Very carefully I fetched out another, and placed it with extreme care.
A lusty bang with the hammer, and the spike went singing into the rift
with the old comforting melody, and this time it held. In with the
carabiner—hurry now!—and now the rope. But in my haste I hung it
in upside down. Never mind!

I was glad to rest after such exertions, even if there wasn't an arm-
chair handy—only a loop of rope round my chest and a couple of tiny
projections under my feet. God knows the "Asche-Luck" of the
Fleischbank isn't exactly comfortable.

My legs went doing the "splits" on the outer edges of the crack, and
the climbing became an exercise in acrobatics. My fingers were bleeding,
though I hadn't noticed it till I saw the red blotches on the rock.

Another couple of feet gained! Now the carabiners were running out;
I had only two left. So I had to retrieve the ones below me each time,
which increased the labour and the danger. The sun was getting pretty
hot in the meantime. Voices sounded from the Walls all around, but I
hardly noticed them. . . . People in the ribbon of a path down there
were staring up inquisitively at us. Well might they shake their
heads at our choice of a Sunday pastime. Not that I cared—tastes
differ.

I wriggled into a crack, forcing my way up. Only a few feet above me,
I could see an inviting stance, where I could have a rest; but the rope
wouldn't let me move. I cursed and complained. . . . "Let's have some
rope!" . . . There I was, stuck, and couldn't move an inch forward.

Waldemar started agitating the rope; looking down between my legs
I could see him manoeuvring it. Still the damned cord ran all over the
place; I must have fixed it wrongly somewhere—my own fault. Using
the last reserves of strength I could still summon, I tugged at the rope
myself; taking it between my teeth, I climbed gingerly up the smooth
crack. The slightest slip would mean coming off altogether. At last I
reached the stance. Well, stance? Call it a little indentation in the overhang. Those 130 feet had taken me hours.

Then it was Waldemar's turn to come. Almost gloatingly I shouted
down: "Up you come!"

It was particularly difficult for him to follow, especially near the top
where I had retrieved all the carabiners. At the start it still went all
right, for he was able to pull himself up from piton to piton by the
necessary strength of arm, while I hauled the rope in at each movement;
but where the carabiners were missing, that method wouldn't do any
more. There was only one way; to resort to the technique of the Prusik
Knot. He hung the slings on one of the ropes, and I made them fast
with the so-called Prusik Knot, which has the peculiar virtue of tighten-

ing when any weight is thrown on it, so that it grips the rope, and loosening when the weight is withdrawn, so that you can move it along the rope.

Waldi put his feet into the two slings and went swinging out into space until he was vertically under me in them. Then we were in a position to start the manoeuvre and while he climbed very slowly upwards in the slings, I kept on pulling in the second rope to give him protection. At the end of it, we were both completely exhausted, he from the sheer effort of the climbing, I from continually taking the strain on the rope.

Changing stances was a fearfully chancy business, for there was only room for one man at a time, and then there was all that rope into the bargain. We had to ensure that it didn't get hopelessly "knitted", to avoid a "cat's cradle", to use the trade jargon.

I hung the ironmongery round me once again and started off up another chimney. It narrowed quickly, till its walls were almost touching. The rock pressed heavily downwards and I could only just wedge myself in between by main force. I could see neither up nor down and had to test every hold. I moved carefully forwards by snake-like motions, so as not to go sliding down that open maw again.

When we both stood on a splendid stance in the bottom of a broad chimney above, I said to Waldi: "I think we've done the worst of it." But he looked doubtful.

To reinforce my opinion, I told him: "There's not the slightest doubt it goes straight on up, as Nature dictates."

I was soon high up on the walls of the chimney. Disgusting country! I shall never learn to like these cold, damp, slimy chimneys; but I was gaining height rapidly, and we could almost see across to the North Summit of the Predigstuhl now. It couldn't be very far to the Ridge now—only another steep bit of rock-wall, overhanging slightly. Only. . . .

At a small breach, I spent some time in providing a good, reliable piton. At last I managed to get one in a few inches.

"It'll do in case of emergency," I thought, and brought my partner along up.

I said to Waldemar: "How'd you like to fall into that one?—I shouldn't!"—but continued on my way upward. The chimney widened again, till it was too wide to straddle. I climbed up its bottom, close to the wall, then traversed out to the right. About sixty feet above my friend's head, I stood on a little stance, panting a bit and examining the way ahead with a critical eye. No, the main difficulties were not finished, after all. . . .

I shouted down to Waldi, warning him to take the firmest possible stance: "It seems to get difficult again!"

Down in the chimney I could see a little pedestal. It looked reliable enough and, besides, here in the Kaiser, every hold is a sound hold. I straddled in, got my other foot on as well, and stood there quite comfortably on my little plinth, gently massaging my over-worked fingers.

All of a sudden there was nothing under my feet—the block had broken away and was sliding down from under me! I grasped what was happening, instinctively pushing away from the wall with lightning speed. What ensued took seconds to happen. During those seconds I looked out over the edge of life. . . .

Two hundred feet down the chimney, I found myself upright, clinging close to the wall, on a tiny shelf. The rope was taut above me— between me and what? That was where Waldemar must be. Everything was so quiet. I hardly dared call up to him. I could only hope the block hadn't hit him. . . .

"Waldi, where are you? Are you all right?"

Down came a voice, choking with joy and amazement: "Yes! Are *you* alive?"

It was only then that I realised I must have fallen two hundred feet. Two hundred feet, and I was still alive . . .!

Gradually memory began to supply the details—how the block broke away: how I was just able to push off from the rock. Then I was falling: no, rather Waldi seemed to be flying up to meet me . . . past me. Then I felt as if I were floating in thin air—no weight to me any more—rather a pleasant feeling. Finally a dull thump, not in anyway sharp or terrifying . . . only as if I had fallen on a sofa or something soft like that. But that wasn't the finish of it. . . . Down I went, from one wall to the other. Suddenly I remembered the piton, of which I had said to Waldi that I shouldn't like to fall down on to it. I felt every bump, but not the slightest pain. Ridiculously enough, I began to think of my new climbing-trousers. I hoped they wouldn't come to any harm from this tumble, they could so easily get torn on the rock! Then my thoughts began to work feverishly. My pocket-knife in my trouser pocket: I mustn't lose that, at all costs. The fall began to seem endlessly long to me. Surely I must be almost down in the ravine at the bottom—only a thousand feet down below, the Rinne! Why didn't the jerk come on the rope? Wildly confused thoughts occupied my mind, but all of them harmless to a degree. Logic, common sense were entirely absent. It never occurred to me that anything serious could happen to me, such as a bad injury; or, if I was to finish up in the ravine, a quick finish to everything. I could feel quite clearly how I was turning over and over—now I was going down head-first. And then at last, the long-awaited jerk. My body was yanked upright, and I was in a normal position again, feet downwards. But I was still falling, falling. . . . Then came a momentary fright: the rope must surely have broken!

Then another jerk . . . my trip had come to its surprising end. By some miracle I was standing quite suddenly on a minute ledge in the wall at the back of the chimney, with the rope as taut as taut above me. I dared not move a muscle, in case I should lose my balance.

At first I felt nothing at all. Only that there was something warm flowing down my forehead. I must have cut my head, for the rock was a little red. But as soon as I tried to grip the wall again, I was aware that my left hand was out of action. Probably I had damaged the bones a bit.

Then Waldemar began to give me assistance with the rope. I climbed up to him and he bandaged my head. Otherwise, except for my left hand, everything seemed in good order. We had to have a good laugh, then, about our incredible luck in such a serious mishap.

Waldemar began to tell me the story, as seen from his watch-tower . . . I had gone sliding down like an angel—an angel in a hurry, perhaps. Then, head-first, into the chimney, which swallowed me up. A horrid sight, that: unimaginably horrid! Then Waldi had waited for the jerk —the inevitable jerk, which must bring the end. The rope went taut as a fiddle-string, on the verge of breaking, but it held. Then came the moment he had been waiting for, with horror in his heart. The piton would obviously not hold; it didn't, and out it came. The tug of the rope yanked it away from the rock, but the full momentum of my headlong rush had been checked. And then on it went. . . . Then the rope went taut again; only this time there was no piton between me and him, nothing to act as a brake. It dragged him off and out of the bed of the chimney, to where there was a bigger level spot with blocks piled on it. Desperately he had tried to hold himself and me, but the rope kept on pulling him further out towards the broken edge, towards the abyss below it. . . .

A few more feet—eighteen inches more, now, and the moment would be there when the rope joining the two of us must drag him over the rim. He knew he was for it; the end was staring him in the face . . . at that very instant, at the extreme outer edge of the platform, the drag on the rope suddenly ceased. The rope went loose and Waldi came to rest, there on the uttermost edge. . . . He didn't dare to move or even to shout. Then suddenly, like a deliverance, my voice, from down below.

I do not know even to-day what Patron Saint stood by us then; but I do know that the whole thing hung on a hair. The more I thought about it afterwards, the more incredible became the whole incident. It wasn't a case of mere luck any more; some kindly Fate took a positive hand that day. Our time had simply not come. God in His Goodness did not want us written-off yet. I had not fallen to my death, but into life itself. . . . We promised to celebrate this miraculous second birthday regularly, on its recurrent date, in future.

But as yet it was too early for celebration; we had still to extricate ourselves from the Wall. Waldi still wanted to go on up; I felt it was useless to try. All the same he had a go, but soon agreed that there was no future in it. So down we went, back again, by the long staircase of chimneys. But the huge overhang below gave us plenty to think about. It simply had to go!

Soon I was beginning to feel the effects of my two-hundred-foot fall. I could feel bruises everywhere, and soon could hardly move my limbs. I lowered myself into the depths in a rope-chair, like a cripple. It was just all right while I was roping down, but when I was on my feet again and had to do a little climbing, it seemed as if I had my legs in splints.

We were now once again in the bottom of the chimney above the huge undercut rift. The sky had meanwhile turned menacingly dark.— "Please put it off till we are down in the Steinerne Rinne; just an hour's respite, please—don't let it come down now!" But St. Peter was stony-hearted and sent his wet benison in full heavenly measure. . . .

Our 130-foot ropes hung straight down, dangling well clear of the Wall. Was everything safely anchored? Were the ropes slung properly, so that we could fetch them down after us, when the time came? No question of a retreat, if anything went wrong.

Another look, to make sure, then I went roping down first, in a so-called "Dülfer Chair". That is, with the rope round my thigh, chest and shoulder, then hanging down loose behind my back.

I grudged every yard of the height we had fought so hard to gain as I went down on the rope, spinning like a teetotum, to the right, to the left, faster and faster. Now it was the Predigstuhl going past, now the overhanging rift was plumb opposite me again. The weight of the rope was unbearable, pulling me fiercely backwards. I could nowhere get a support for my feet on the rock, for the Wall was still some feet away. I felt I couldn't stand it much longer. Supporting one's whole weight with one hand was far too exhausting. So I let myself slide down the rope faster than usual.

That "Misfortunes seldom come singly" is as true in the mountains as anywhere else. So the seam of my Anorak hood had to choose that moment to tear and provide more trouble, for now the rope lay against my bare neck and its friction produced unbearable ·heat and horrible burns; but I was quite helpless and could do nothing about it.

At last I reached the top of the stance under the rift. I had very little rope left, so I tried to start a pendulum-like motion, backwards and forwards, and waited for the moment when my face was towards the Wall, to give a jerk; but I was still a little short.

I swung to the left again like an acrobat on his trapeze. Only here there was no net and I was higher up than the dome of the "Big Top".

Again—and I could just get a touch with my feet, while my body pressed heavily on them; at the same instant I had to let go of the rope, to avoid swinging back again, pendulum fashion. This time I managed it.

At last I was standing at the foot of the rift and could shout up to Waldemar to come on down.

"Take care that the rope doesn't stick or get twisted anywhere!"

Then he was wafting down like a spider on its own thread. Opposite me, he swung a bit, till I could get a hold on him and pull him over to my side.

But now came the real moment of tension. Could we yank the rope down? We had to have it for the next *abseil*: without it we could neither rope down nor climb up again. We had taken great care to note the end we had to pull. It was a little difficult, but it went—a little jerkily. We let go of the one end and it disappeared above us; but then, suddenly, it stuck. What was the matter now? It simply wouldn't budge—not an inch!

It *must* come down! We couldn't stay on the Wall, captives for ever. We used every available ounce of strength on the single end; still it didn't budge—obstinate with the cold and the damp. We swung it about, trying to loosen it, then gave a united "Heave ho!" That shifted it at last. Very slowly and carefully we began to take it in; faster and faster it ran through our hands, till the joyful moment when it came hurtling through the air like a giant snake. We took a deep breath. We were saved.

One more *abseil* took us down to the Steinerne Rinne. It was quiet down there, not a sound of human life by then. Cold, wet and forbidding, the Walls frowned down upon us. I looked up again at that Chimney! ... That was the first time I realised how high up we had been. My next thought was: "And where would we be now if the mountain hadn't been kind beyond words to us?"

My contusions were making themselves more painfully felt every moment. I stumbled on ahead, while Waldemar was straightening out and packing our equipment. At the Gaudeamus Hut they told us we had got hopelessly lost, had climbed far off the proper route. Then I understood for the first time why we never saw a single trace of human existence, after we passed the Rift, not so much as an ancient, rusty piton.

I had to stay in bed some weeks: and as my health came flowing back I lay and looked up at the towers and spires of the Kaisergebirge with an ever-increasing feeling of home-sickness.

AT THE EXTREME EDGE OF THE
ABYSS—MAUK WEST WALL

I DID not return to the Hills till autumn drove me up into them; though circumstances were not exactly helpful. Sunday passes weren't easy to come by. So I had to resort to the time-honoured device of a dummy stuffed with straw to register my presence in my barrack-room bed after "Retreat". Mostly the deception worked. My subsistence allowance passed into the keeping of my room-mates to keep them sweet. My own nourishment on these outings was still confined to a hunk of cheese, a little piece of butter and some stale ration-bread. My small change was just enough to buy a drink with; the modest pay of my lowly rank wouldn't run to more. But that in no way diminished my joy in Nature's beauty and my longing for freedom and independence. All I wanted was to get out of the daily round—and for one day a week not to hear the Sergeant-Major's strident voice.

One of my fellow-sufferers, Hans Reischl, from Salzburg, who could mostly be seen leaving barracks at mid-day on Saturdays, came to me one day and asked what I thought of an attempt on the Mauk West Wall.

"We shall get at loggerheads with that awkward chap Wastl Weiss, I'm afraid, if we try to take that one off his toes," was my reply.

Yes, that magnificent climber Wastl Weiss and I had much in common; so did he and the West Wall of the Maukspitze, that prominent eastern corner-buttress of the toothy, spiky Wilde Kaiser Range. What he and I had in common was mainly ideological: we had both decided to celebrate Whitsun with a headlong fall and had yet survived. Mine—already described—was in the "Asche-Luck"; his on the Mauk West Wall, that virgin, vertical wall. No, not vertical, for the Mauk Wall is not only vertical, it . . . well, we shall see presently, what it does.

So Wastl's relationship with the Mauk Wall was very close; not only spiritually but bodily, and robustly-painful-bodily at that. Since then he had given the Wall itself a miss. But he had never forgotten it; it ruled his every thought. And he was guarding it jealously, to see that nobody else came. . . .

Perhaps the prospects of success were too slender. But I do know that in the meantime Wastl, hearing of the intention of two Munich climbers to make good use of the work he had already put in, solemnly roped down from the top and cleared the Wall of each and every one of his pitons he could lay hands on.

Still, one might discuss the thing; so we decided to go up the follow-ing week-end to the Ackerl Hut in the Eastern Kaiser, where Wastl had set up his abode. In the evening Reischl and I sat on a wooded spur close to the Hut, using a fine pair of binoculars to have a good look at the utterly unbroken Wall. We made a particularly careful survey of the middle section, where the finest glasses in the world cannot discover the slightest sign of a crack. There was nothing to see but smooth wall. Just to make things more difficult, this part of the Wall is overhung by an enormous bulge, cutting clean across it. I shrugged my shoulders and said: "Not a ghost of a chance; but we can always try. . . ."

Wastl had recognised us and came up to join us. I spotted that he wasn't a nice customer to deal with where the Mauk West Wall was concerned.

"Don't you dare think of going up there!" he said, threateningly.

I knew him too well not to realise what it meant if he—normally such a decent chap—started issuing threats. It showed that the Wall meant absolutely everything to him and that he obviously still intended to do it.

"You do the Fleischbank Gully . . . that's where you ought to go!" he suggested, trying to turn us aside.

I replied: "Rebitsch tried that and came off; so there's no point in *our* having a go. But what do you say to our teaming-up?"

Wastl thought it over and then put forward the proviso that he should have the lead at the critical spot. We certainly had no objection to that. Agreed!

Wastl promptly set to work with the greatest enthusiasm on the preparations, getting the ropes and "ironmongery" into order—30 pitons, 30 carabiners to match and, most important of all, the special pitons, made to measure, which he had got ready long ago. He also packed in something undisclosed.

At about 7 a.m. we were at the start of our climb. We had two ropes between me and Wastl, one between him and Hans, and carried the fourth, a "reserve" rope for the traverses in the middle of the Wall. The last man had our rucksack with a little provender and some tea, a simple bivouac outfit for an emergency and the camera.

The Wall bared its teeth from the first step, starting with a difficult chimney. We were still cold and stiff, and not functioning properly as yet. I always have to warm up. We came to a fork in the crack and took the right-hand branch, which led on through a shaft opening gradually outwards. The inside was smooth rock, with a few chock-stones barring the way and forcing one out again and again on to its outer lip; but that didn't offer any holds either. The top half of one's body kept on threatening to slide downwards and outwards, as we tried desperately to jam ourselves in it with back and knee. A tiny rock-wrinkle at the left-hand outer edge of the chimney offered a momentary anchorage for one's weight. With great relief I thrust myself out of these restricting narrows to the very outside edge of the chimney. My body was already lying practically horizontal between its walls; but my feet still had to get up an inch or two more. A little help from one hand, and the soles of my rubbers had reached the little wrinkle. I straightened up and stood upright.

The gain had been six feet and the barrier of the chimney lay behind me. I was panting for breath. I could not imagine any increase in severity; there must be a limit somewhere. But Wastl with a sanctimonious expression—as if he were telling me something comforting—remarked that there was much worse to come.

Vertical cracks in series took us up and on. At about noon we reached the grassy, rather more level zone of the Wall, just below the main difficulty.

There we took a light snack and then a *Hä-jua-hä* yodel went floating down, just to show how calm and peaceful we were; but it was sheer self-deception. We could feel our inner unrest; our nerves were on edge. In order to relieve them we began to sing, to yodel and to shout—as so often happens when people are climbing in the Kaiser. Especially in the area of the Steinerne Rinne, where on Sundays the climbing has almost become an exhibition and where one hears all sorts of delectable tit-bits from the "V.I.P.'s" of the Rope Department.

A smooth crack goes serpent-fashion upwards, but only for a short way. I was standing under an enormous roof, cutting off all upward view. Here I let the others come up. The Ackerl Hut down there was minute, the people outside it hardly recognisable as little dots. To the right our Wall fell away from us in a sheer riot of slabs, as far as the eye could follow downwards. And as a perfect contrast, down at the bottom, the green meadows of the Vale of St. Johann and Kitzbühel.

I tried to drive a piton into a crevice at the highest point under the overhang, but it came out again at each stroke; so I wedged a second in with it. It didn't look very promising, but it would have to do for this traverse. Then Wastl handed me his special pitons, short four-sided shafts. I gave one more hopeful look back at the piton—then, on with the dance. . . .

I was prepared for the very worst. Thirty feet away over me, horizontally, was a tiny projection, hardly sufficient for the front half of my rubber soles. Between lay a bulging, vertical, utterly holdless wall, the like of which I had never tried to traverse. I pushed forward to the right, inch by inch, leaning against the drag of the rope which Wastl was paying out with extreme care and attention, watching my every movement. Whenever he began to fear that my body-lean would tip me over backwards he tightened the rope again. Eventually I got my hands on to the projection, but that wasn't enough. I must somehow get my feet there and stand on it. There wasn't a hold in sight. Then I went all the way back to the start of the traverse, so as to begin it again a little higher on the rock.

Frequently the two ropes were my only support. Suddenly they gave way. I fell off the Wall as if someone had swatted a fly, and went swinging back and forth thirty feet lower down, like the pendulum of a clock. But that put me in the right mood. It was just what was needed! Like a flash I was up again, and banged the slipped piton home once more into its cranny, and was back on the traverse, supported by both ropes. Just as a tight-rope walker cannot allow himself a false movement, so now I was forced to study every motion of my body: I dared hardly breathe, hardly dared move, as I could feel my body slowly trying to part company with the Wall again.

Only an inch or two to go. . . .

"Let it come, gently." I hardly dared raise my voice above a whisper; but Wastl was managing the rope as if he were part of me. I had reached the little platform.

I stood cautiously on my miniature pulpit. There was a little hole in the rock above my head: just the place for one of the special pitons, of course. I had also far-sightedly brought some plastic wood along. Picture-hanging technique, this. The piton gets wedged between the wood and you drive it in with everything you can give it; it doesn't go in very far, even so, but it will hold some weight for a short time. I gave it a couple more hefty bangs. I had to be careful not to lose my balance when I lifted my arm to hammer.

I snapped a carabiner in and hung a sling from it, to act as a rope ladder. I pressed up with my hand on the piton, while my other hand explored the rock above—not a hold anywhere. With envy in my heart I watched the jackdaws wheeling about the Face, coming to rest on tiny ledges. How they must be laughing at me, as they watched what hard work I was making of it! I spat at them. With a single beat of their wings they rose from the Wall and sailed out sublimely into the void.

My right foot was swinging backwards and forwards in the sling, and had begun to quiver—a condition we call "the sewing-machine" and denoting the start of muscular cramps. A little balancing stunt followed, feeling the way with my left foot, bringing it up on to the piton, which I was still using as a grip for my right hand. The open palm of my left hand went stroking the rock as if it must find a hold somewhere. Very slowly I uncoiled myself, pushing myself upwards, following through with my knee, and stood upright on the piton.

"Just a second longer," I besought the piece of iron, to which the whole of my weight was now committed, "then you can break away as much as you like!" Beyond, there were isolated holds, with a crack slanting upwards, till I was standing once again under the bulging, massive roof. But I was a whole rope's length further on; and now I was in a position to see my two friends safely up on the rope. To-day they were saved the toil and trouble of knocking the pitons out—Wastl found most of them in his hands as soon as he touched them; Hans got hold of the rest without much trouble.

I was puzzled as to how to proceed. It was impossible to continue over the roof; so we had to try to traverse again across the slabs from one step to the next, from one wrinkle to another. The further I pushed out to the right, the steeper grew the plunge of the Wall below me, the smoother the lift above. That uncanny smoothness—it was beginning to have a depressing effect; nowhere could the eye detect a single hold. Pitilessly, the Wall went sweeping down—down, hundreds of feet down. In vain did one seek for a stance to rest on; it was shattering! After two more crossing movements I found myself at the extreme end of this long, long traverse. Nowhere to go from here, except straight up overhead. I wriggled into a little niche and sat doubled-up on a little cushion of turf, with my feet swinging in thin air. They were aching from having stood for hours on exiguous foot-holds; my fingers were leaden; my eyes closed for sheer weariness, and I nodded off. My body leaned more and more forwards. . . .

Oh, the comforting warmth of the sun . . . but far less comforting the abyss which yawned before my eyes when I tore them open again. This mid-day snoozing was far too dangerous. I stood up again and waited till Wastl joined me. I could only congratulate him humbly; he had been even higher than this at Whitsun. And the worst was still to come. . . .

Wastl took my stance over, carefully knocking in another piton, and handed me his whole ironmongery outfit. I moved out on to the open Wall, heavily laden. A very narrow crack ran up it, with occasional interruptions. The particular difficulty now was to get over the missing bits. Although we were all used to difficulties, to-day's job went beyond anything we had ever met before. We examined the rock as if with a magnifying glass, trying to find the slightest possibility of going ahead. Now was the time to use the smallest pitons we had brought along; they only went half an inch or so into the rock, though, and I hardly dared put any weight on them. There was no question at all of snapping a foot-sling in and entrusting my whole weight to it.

All the same, it had to go; there was no other way out. I had started by giving the Wall below me frequent appraisals, to judge about where I should land if a piton broke; now such thoughts were automatically laid aside. As I gained height and the distance between me and my companions lengthened, the climbing demanded even greater concentration. There just wasn't any time for looking down, for thinking what would happen, if. . . . There was only one permissible thought: how to get on up without dithering, and as quickly as possible. For I couldn't dawdle about on those pitons; to load any of them for any length of time was a dangerous risk. I could just imagine the result if they came away one after another. It would be like undoing a zipp-fastener.

I had done about sixty feet, when the world really seemed to come to an end. I had only two pitons left. Only a few feet above me I could see a stance, and I called down to Wastl: "How do I go on now? Everything's petered out!"

I kept on looking up. Six stupid feet more and I should be there. I couldn't understand it: just six more feet—the vital six feet! I certainly couldn't go back. One or two of the pitons had already been pulled out of the wall by the movement of the rope and gone tinkling down it in their carabiners. "Damn it!" thought I, "Wastl has done this once before me. He has only two hands and two feet, like myself; but perhaps his fingers are stronger?"

Away with all inhibitions; no more looking down into the pit! My only interest now were the six feet immediately above me. Very slowly I managed to push myself upwards, but the rope was dragging very heavily on me: it was threaded through too many carabiners. There I found a wrinkle opening at the bottom into a little crack, offering the only place which might take a piton—my only hope of safety, perhaps? I used my very shortest shaft. The wrinkle sounded abominably hollow —it wouldn't hold much. Of course, the piton might go in a bit further, but then a piece of rock the size of my hand might come away, too, taking my last support with it. I could see plainly that I dared not put any downward weight on my piton. I took hold of it and pushed the eye upwards, so that it would jam in the crack; then I began to pull gently on it.

"Pull a bit more," I ordered. Then I straightened up. The piton was at knee level now, but I still had nothing for my hands.

"Let go a little." I stretched up as far as I could, and felt a hold. I clung harder than ever to my flake. For a moment I wondered was the hold big enough? Could I trust my whole weight to it?

I shouted down: "Let the rope go loose!" No more drag now. Up went my second hand, my fingers literally clawing on the rock. Then my whole weight was hanging on my finger-tips. My feet slid off the rock and went dangling over thin air; the piton which, a few moments before, had been supporting my whole weight, flew out and went rattling down the rope. There were only two choices left me: to let go meant a tremendous fall into the abyss, and both my friends would have to come along. So I must get up, somehow!

I gritted my teeth . . . quick now. The rope wouldn't follow; it was dragging at my back; my fingers were beginning to throw up the job. I heaved desperately upwards, assisted by my knees. At the very last gasp I was over the edge of the bulge. With utter relief my hoarse throat croaked: "Up you come!"

In order to ease the work for the others, I rigged up a fixed rope with buttons and slings in it, so that they could haul themselves up. Soon Wastl, using these aids, was standing by me, congratulating me on my success on the key-pitch of the climb. Only then did he admit that his fall had been *below* it and that no one had ever laid a hand on it till to-day.

I was absolutely all in and was glad to let Wastl take the lead over.

It was 10 p.m. when we stood on the summit, not a little proud to have beaten the Mauk West Wall, the hardest face-climb in the whole Kaisergebirge.

But our "first ever" was not fated to go entirely unpunished. Next day when I crept into barracks—and about mid-day at that—my absence had been noticed. My "Buddy" promised me three to five days' C.B., the moment I got in. "Well, the Wall was certainly worth that," I thought, and worried not a whit about the future.

Everybody soon knew exactly what we had done—it had at once become a topic for much discussion. In a Company consisting of climbers one might have thought a "first climb" would get a little recognition. Only a couple of my superiors remarked more in scorn than in praise: "Well, I suppose it was worth while!"

I was court-martialled for breaches of the Regulations and over-staying my leave. The sentence was: Transfer to the draft unit.

I listened to it with equanimity. I had to hear the bullets whistling some time or other, thought I. And very soon I was, in fact, hearing them.

STRAIGHT ON UP—THE
LALIDERER WALL

WAR, prison-camp, a two-year gap—nothing could repress my longing for the Hills. My attitude towards climbing had never varied and my mountain passion had only been inflamed by my compulsory absence. Thanks, however, to hard months spent at the Front, and behind barbed wire, my condition left much to be desired. I had to start all over again from the beginning. Into the bargain, all the normal conditions of mountaineering had become noticeably harder.

Now it was only the Hundred-per-cent Idealists who could be seen going up into the mountains. Their rucksacks were bigger than ever for, in an era of war-rationing, everything had to be carted along on one's back. Not having any marks, we could buy nothing on the spot. Even so, what they doled out to us in the way of food was precious little, and when the rucksacks were unpacked at the Huts the general stringency became painfully obvious. One climber would produce a gherkin, backed up by a piece of dry bread and sugarless tea, for a whole day's ration; another would be busy peeling potatoes—a very fine delicacy when salted. The favourite dish of all was *polenta*—"The Yellow Peril"—which was in evidence wherever one went, in every saucepan, in every rucksack, in its solid form to make up for lack of bread, in liquid as a substitute for soup. In every possible disguise, as a brew, as dumplings, as a paste to spread on bread, this cooked maize mass was being forced down everybody's gullet. Even on the climb itself, a portion of *polenta* went along in one's trouser pocket as a snack for the road.

It was not the kind of diet to produce strength and fitness.

I made my first cautious essays at climbing, but had reluctantly to admit that it wouldn't go at all properly. My strength was soon used up; I was utterly unfit, and my permanent starvation diet since being taken prisoner, had weakened me terribly. But it was no good letting oneself be got down by such things; slowly, very slowly indeed, I began to regain my normal form.

While our famous patterns of earlier years were busy getting ready ice-pitons, crampons and axes for attacks on the great Western Alps, my thoughts never strayed further than over the Northern Range into the Karwendel, where there were still so many unattempted face-climbs. The Western Alps seemed something altogether beyond my powers—

I was too weak, too slight, would certainly never have the necessary physical endurance for such big things. They were meant for quite a different type of person; at least, that was what I had been told over and over again, and I believed it. . . .

"Stick to your rock-walls, Hermann, that's your mark. The Western Alps will keep!"

The Karwendel were far from the madding crowd, unsullied by the noise and bustle of everyday life. They were a Paradise for the *connoisseurs*, for the lonely wanderer, and for the highly skilled climber, too. The mere climber-for-sport would find them disappointing and hurry away: which was also a good thing.

In the heart of these mountains, piled up like some prehistoric upheaval, there was a Wall which shot up to Heaven, incomparable in its sweep and splendour—the Laliderer North Wall.

It was in the summer of 1933 that Hias Auckenthaler—a master chimney-sweep from Innsbruck and an inspired craftsman—first stood at the foot of that Wall and surveyed its every inch. His aim was to climb it just where it was at its most forbidding, straight up under the Laliderer Summit; but his first attempt failed even on the lower half of the Wall, where unclimbable overhangs forced him down again. But that did not deter him; he climbed the lower part of the face at a point 300 feet to the left and, by a wide détour got into the great gully which goes up to the ridge just to the left of the direct line to the summit. He and his partner, Hannes Schmidhuber were successful in completing the climb after a hard fight lasting two days. "Auckenthaler's Route" is still one of the most exacting rock-climbs of the classical kind.

I remember well when in September 1943 Waldemar and I tackled that enormous summit gully as rain began to fall, how we counted the ropes' lengths up to nearly one hundred, and still there was no end in sight, no summit ridge to rescue us; also how just before dusk, in heavy mist, we jumped down at last into the rubble-shoot; how, glowing with joy, we ate our last apple in the winter quarters of the Falken Hut; how we did not let even a night march through the Karwendeltal daunt us, and next day in Seefeld proudly informed our comrades: "We've just done the Laliderer Wall!"

Three years after Auckenthaler, Rebitsch had had another attempt on the Wall. He planned to climb it straight up, as if a line had been drawn by a ruler. But after his first attempt had also failed, this gigantic precipice was given a long rest.

As the summer of 1946 was drawing on, talk of the "Direct" began to be heard in "Extreme" climbing circles. Hardly were the North Walls in fit condition when certain stalwarts were to be found at the

Falken Hut, among them Hias Rebitsch and Sepp Spiegel. They had all trained thoroughly and it looked as if someone must succeed this time. Hias, who knew the Wall, at least in part, believed the Gully could be directly reached by way of a slender crack; but the rock was too wet and he had to give that plan up. So he, too, tried his luck further to the left, and he succeeded in getting on to better stuff by way of a hazardous traverse. However, continuous heavy thunderstorms, almost daily, prevented Hias and Sepp from reaching the Gully and kept on driving them down to the bottom again. Several times they had to rope down hundreds of feet with a veritable torrent pouring down over them; three times they were compelled to go back because their hammers broke; as a last straw, Sepp contracted a poisoned arm, which put them out of action for quite a time.

Meanwhile Rebitsch climbed the upper part of the Wall with Kuno Rainer, straight to the summit from the Gully. Once again a storm broke on them, compelling them to traverse off the Face on to the North Ridge barely 300 feet below the top. In the pitch-darkness of the night they climbed down the "Spindlerweg" to the Falken Hut, which they did not reach till dawn. The connection between the upper and the lower halves of the Wall was thus established; it only remained to climb both parts in one attempt.

Sepp Spiegel was fit again by the autumn. At 5 a.m. one morning of settled weather he and Rebitsch were standing at the foot of the Wall, with every hope of success. They made rapid progress and, after four hours, they were just short of the Gully. But ill-luck pursued them once again. Sepp fell 60 feet clear on to the rope, a fall Hias was just able to check; but both suffered sufficient injuries to compel the unlucky pair to retire once again, putting "paid" to it for the time being.

Soon the hills and dales were clothed in white ermine and even I had to join the "wood-workers", as we called the pilgrims of the downhill snow-shoes. A new fairy landscape, an entirely new kingdom was opened up to me by this return to skis. But I was rarely to be found on the crowded slopes frequented by townsfolk, in the close proximity of funicular railways. I find a definite lack of proper traffic control in those places.

But the coming of spring, when ski-ing really begins to be a pleasure, found me back on airy, corniced ridges or on steep faces following the precept: "The steeper the wall, the less snow lies on it," Winter is always pretty short for me. May and June of 1947 were unusually dry months. Everybody, except us climbers who were happy, was complaining about a water shortage; never had I seen the North Walls so dry so early in the year.

I had my eye very much on the "Laliderer Direct", but Alpine etiquette demands that those who have begun to attack a new route must be allowed their chance of seeing the job through; but once again Rebitsch had to wait, for Sepp had an inflamed ankle. Half the Summer went by, in glorious conditions, which I had never seen equalled.

By the end of July, I thought I had given them enough time. I did not want to let the perfect weather—which is so essential on this kind of climb—go absolutely for nothing; so I agreed plans with a climbing partner of a few years back, Luis Vigl.

The following Friday we met in Schwaz, so as to approach the Falken Hut by the Stallental. Luis arrived on a heavy racing bicycle, quite worn out with the pace at which he had been pedalling, and found himself totally unable to adjust to a decent gait. Our top speed was about that of a tramp's and we had to put up with some searching looks. In order to avoid every ounce of excess weight, we were travelling light of foot in so-called "Rubble Sneakers", fitted with a stout sole against heavy work.

Luis had to call on a friend somewhere on the way. After a while he came back bringing a long stick of sausage; just the kind of friend one wanted in those days of stringency! We were of course tremendously cheered by this unexpected delicacy and felt that it was a definite omen for success on the following day.

On our left we could already see the peaks of the Rotwandlspitze. There, too, was the Lamsenhütten tower. "Nice climbing there," suggested my insatiable "Specialist" companion. We crossed the Lamsenjoch and stopped at a little Alp for a short rest. Soon we were being refreshed and our hunger was being stilled by glasses of fresh milk—no marks to pay!—and, better still, served by a charming girl. We would have liked to stay and keep the pretty Alpine dairymaid company, but we had a target for the day and it was still a long way to the Falken Hut. So it was "Cheerio!" and on our way again.

The path zigzagged steeply down to the Ahornboden—a wonderful little oasis, a jewel of the Hills. Tall acorns stud its lush green carpet, in vivid contrast to the dour grey slabs of the Grubenkar's North Wall.

Beyond, a track led us up to the "Hollow Saddle"—and there once again we were facing the magnificent Laliderer Wall. We had seen it over and over again, but every time one sees it anew one has to stop and stare at it, overcome by its magnificence. Surely this is one of Nature's masterpieces!

We heard voices above us, but couldn't see anybody. A man against a Wall like this is only a dwarf, a tiny point, diminutive, hardly to be seen. We went stumbling over the massive boulders, hardly looking where we were going, our eyes drawn up to the Wall overhead. It is miraculous with what magic power the naked rock, mere dead stone, can take a living man in thrall!

We reached the Hut—a very hive of activity, but we enjoyed a certain influence. The Hutkeeper always had a corner for genuine climbers and, while our sausages were sizzling in the frying-pan, we took a good look at the Wall, in the late evening light, through a telescope. Our survey of the series of cracks was, however, not exactly encouraging. They called us in to supper; this evening we still had something to laugh about, at any rate—our sausage supremacy. . . .

I kept on tossing and turning on my paillasse, unable to sleep; my thoughts were up there on the Wall. It was as clear as if I were really looking at it; I saw myself gaining height in smooth cracks. I found cast-iron holds everywhere, exactly where one would have wanted them. Just what the doctor ordered . . . only a few more rope's lengths and we're up. . . .

Someone was shaking me. "Up you get, Hermann. It's four o'clock!"

In a sulky and bemused kind of way I answered: "You might have left me to it. Only a few more ropes and I would have been on top. Then I needn't have got up at all and could have gone on sleeping!" But my dream was over and I suddenly realised that I had to face grim reality.

We crept silently down the steps, like thieves. Breakfast was ready. The Hutkeepers hadn't been to bed at all. A few hours ago a party had come in from the North Wall, after going astray on the Auckenthaler route.

We passed out into the mysterious silence of the night.

Nature herself seemed to be sleeping. Over in the Ravine a few stones were clocketing down, disturbing some chamois into startled flight; then there was peace again. We were enveloped in a huge black shadow, ghostly and menacing: the shadow of the Wall—our Wall.

Gradually the dawn came up behind the Karwendel foothills, bringing us the light we needed. The sun rose in a riot of colour; we watched the gorgeous spectacle from the rocks at the base of our climb.

Separate abrupt minor Faces connect the lower bands which sweep across the whole Wall; these yielded some pleasant climbing. A long traverse to the left led us to the start of the series of delicate cracks. The Falken Hut below had woken to a new day's life. Two Viennese shouted up:

"Hi, where are you off to?"

"To the top," we laughed back.

"Is that the 'Auckenthaler'?"

"No," we shouted down, "the 'Direct'."

They shook their heads and moved off.

Dark roofs lowered overhead—they would be coming to us later on. In the meantime, we were on marvellous rock: totally different from other Karwendel climbs. And to-day climbing was the greatest fun. "All because of my stick of sausages," explained Luis.

"Don't forget yesterday's milk," I reminded him, as I went on up.

Down, down, went the ravine below us. At every upward step the view broadened out over the Rofan and across the Valley of the Inn. Over yonder we could hear the voices of a party at work on the "Auckenthaler"; everything close about us was peaceful and earnest in character. At a fork in a crack we moved out towards the right, guided by the presence of pitons; this was the only rope's length on this part of the climb where the things were absolutely necessary. The route continued up a 140-foot overhanging crack, barred at the top by a big jutting roof.

"This is where Sepp must have come off," I suggested.

The whole 140 feet, the height of a church tower, had to be climbed without aids; twice only did a piton ensure a short breather. The rope went straight down, clear of the rock, but we were quite used to places like that; we had met plenty of similar places in the Kaiser and the Kalkkögel. I was glad, however, that Luis when he came up spoke of the last rope's length with great respect.

Soon we could see our predecessors' old traverse-rope overhead. Only one more short crack and we had the yellowing, bleached hemp in our hands, to our great delight.

With no great feeling of confidence in the old rope, we preferred to put in our own, hanging it in a piton-ring and lowering ourselves on to some small protuberances. Then we pushed forward across a smooth slab to the left—to the kind of traverse we really enjoy, a sheer delight. I reminded Luis of the complete contrast with the traverse on the Mauk West Wall. That was a very different story. . . .

We didn't count the rope's lengths. Everything had been going without any particular effort or strain—the kind of climbing that is a real joy.

Full of expectation we drew near to a *gendarme* which, we had been warned, constituted a very unsafe kind of barrier to progress. From the Hut it had been barely recognisable as a little yellow stripe; from close to, it revealed itself as a tall, bulky pillar completely separated from the Wall. But Nature had only equipped this independent Tower with the smallest of bases; it rested on a plinth about sixteen feet square. Above, it broadened continually and in addition leaned far outwards from the Face—truly an architectural masterpiece.

It was separated from the Wall proper by the narrowest of fissures. This crevice, a narrow chimney contracting in places to a mere crack, offered the only means of upward progress. Everything round about was terribly brittle; and everything which wasn't clinched and riveted to the Walls disappeared soundlessly down into the depths. I tidied up in order to spare my partner any risk of injury from unexpected stone falls, once I got going. Up above, the crack steepened considerably, till it built up into an overhang; but I carefully avoided the use of a piton. I was not prepared to trust the Tower to stand that kind of treatment; it was wobbling quite sufficiently under the weight of my own delicate movements.

I crawled deeper into the crack, to give myself a greater feeling of safety. My idea was: "Nothing much can happen with all that rock round me." But a rucksack was a horrid encumbrance, digging into one's back and catching on every roughness in the rock. I wondered what it would be like inside—the fruit, the biscuits, the bread—all mashed up in a lovely mess!

Sweating, I reached the top of the Pillar, and looked down to my right, into the huge central funnel, a most impressive downward glimpse. Far down the Face I could see the fine series of cracks, up which we had come hours ago. Below it the Wall curved under, out of sight; 1,300 feet below that lay the scree-shoots.

We were genuinely relieved to get away from that Tower standing on such weak legs. A short but fearfully exposed traverse led to the overhanging portion of the Gully. All the rock here was wonderfully polished by the regular down-rush of waters and the continual bombardment of stones; but to-day there was blessed peace from both menaces. To be caught in such a spot by a storm would be Hell itself.

About 10 a.m. we reached the foot of the great Gully and felt pleasantly sure we should find some water, for we were roasted to cinders by the heat. The bed of the Gully went up ahead in a series of steps like the bottom of a torrent; but even its smallest pools were dry as a bone. We climbed on with parched tongues, and it was still a long way to the entrance to the Auckenthaler Route. But—thanks be to God!—the sun gradually worked round behind the teeth that crowned the ridge above us, and we were in shade; then we allowed ourselves the short rest to which we were certainly entitled after our efforts. Ravenously we swallowed the indefinable mush which emerged from the climbing rusksack.

"D'you think we're over the worst?" I asked Luis. "It's only noon, so we ought to get to the top still to-day all right."

We now had to cross the Summit Gully to get a lodgment on the Face which goes straight up to the peak. "Look! The way goes up there, between those two big pillars!"

The rock became very brittle and we had to use the piton-hammer for the first time. We could see a couple of pitons up above, too.

"This must be a tough bit," I said. "Kuno never knocks a piton in, unless he's absolutely got to."

It certainly was tough, though the first part seemed easy enough. We were alerted by a horrid whistling sound, familiar enough to our ears, but going right through one's body—falling stones! We flattened ourselves against the rock as they went clattering by, leaving a cloud of dust, a sulphurous smell befouling the air, as the only legacy of our seconds of fear.

We hurried up the next pitch, exposed as it was to stone-falls, together, to collect ourselves, completely out of breath, at the foot of the big double *gendarme*. There was a slender crack splitting the 300-foot Wall above and I went straight at it. Up and up I went. . . . I could hear Luis grousing and upbraiding me because I was climbing it all without the aid of pitons.

"Hermann, you clot! For Pete's sake knock a hook in—you're crazy!" came up from below. I took no notice and went on climbing. He would soon be able to see for himself what splendid holds there were; indeed, when he followed me up, he was soon convinced that I had been right.

We could see up the Face now. To our disappointment, we found ourselves at the foot of yet another precipice of brilliant yellow rock—not a sign of the top yet. Would there never be any end to this Wall, on which we had been at work the whole day? And we hadn't been dawdling, either, God knows! Still, something over 3,000 feet takes time; *it just has to be climbed*!

We felt small and very lonely. After all, it was sheer lunacy to be fighting a Wall like this, which falls vertically for 3,000 feet; but we hadn't much time for that kind of thought. We only had one objective; the way to the top—out at last into the daylight at the top.

Impatiently, we climbed on, traversing back leftwards to the Gully. A final overhang brought us to a firm halt with its yellow, splintering rock.

We looked down 1,000 feet into the abyss of the Gully—slicing down into the Wall like the approach run to a giant's ski-jump. On the easily recognisable white, scored slabs of the Gully Traverse we could just make out two tiny dots—a party climbing. What an undertaking, to pit oneself against Nature just in the very place where she is at her most savage! The other climbers moved on like ridiculous little toys; and yet they were human beings—possessed by the same inner urge as ourselves. And if a layman asked them why they were doing it, they would give the answer Norman-Neruda gave half a century ago: "Because we like it!"

But how can there be any pleasure in it? Or in any activity in which Life often hangs on a mere thread? The non-climber will never understand it . . . but we who climb know what Life really means: for we have continually to battle in order to keep alive. Not till you have been to the edge of the abyss can you know how good life is and what a lovely place is the world.

At last the slope began to ease off. "Look up there, Luis—the top!" We unroped, moving on simultaneously, strolling along above the great precipices towards the North *Arête*. At last the tension under which we had so long been climbing relaxed—that tension which heightens all awareness and sharpens the senses, so that the body reacts instantaneously to every stimulus. And into the place vacated by tension, flooded a boundless joy.

We were at the summit. Eleven hours after the start of our effort we were shaking hands up there, light of heart and full of joy. It was the first time I had ever stood on this particular peak in sunlight. We looked down into the shadowy abyss and could hardly believe that we had come up out of it. Deep down there, like a matchbox, stood the Hut. How rich we were, we to whom Nature had given the ability to move about in so magnificent a setting; how thankful was I that I had been cradled in the heart of the Hills. I wondered what my mother, who died so young, would have said, could she have seen her weakling problem-child at this very moment. Over there to the south was the land of her birth—over there southwards where, beyond the white comb of the Zillertal snows, the unseen Dolomites must be standing ranged; over there, where my own home-sickness was even now winging, across the stupid material frontiers that hem a man in. . . .

We did not leave the summit till the sun was bending far down to the rim of the world. We were proud and glad to have come a journey not granted to every man to travel—perhaps the most tremendous journey to be found in the whole of the Northern Limestone Alps.

CHANGE OF OCCUPATION—
THE SKI-RACER

WINTER came in overnight. Everybody grabbed their skis and joined the ski-hordes, positive armies debouching on to the treeless slopes, the corridors in the forest above Innsbruck. It was complete mass psychology—and that winter I gave way to it, visiting the steep slopes on the Hafelkar up in the Northern Range much more often than usual. I soon learned that this is a place where people learn to ski and, secondly, that in these realms of ski-lifts one gets more down-hill running than in a whole long mountain tour.

Possessed of the idea that somewhere deep down in me there were the makings of a down-hill racer, I climbed up to the Pfriemersköpfel one week-end. This was no high mountain tour, nor a particularly long down-hill run, but it certainly was a proper race-track, with special training going on that day; for there was to be a down-hill race next day, and one or two "Fliers" were to take part in it.

I stood at the place where to-morrow's race would be starting and watched the Aces flit down the narrow forest-ride, to shoot out at the bottom as if from a gun. One jump over the "leap" and then they were out of sight. "Very daring," thought I, secretly annoyed at not being one of them. "Aren't you brave enough?" I asked myself. "You ought to try it once, you know! All you have to do is to put yourself in position —and then go to it." Once away, there would be no question of checking or turning aside; one would have to go through with it, like the others. I simply couldn't see why I, of all people, who don't mind precipices, hadn't the confidence to push off down that ridiculous little slope.

What could happen to me, after all? I could fall down, break a ski, at the worst damage a bone. "Come on, then, Hermann, pull yourself together—don't be such a softy!"

I pushed off. My "boards" went gliding away down, only inches from the trees. I got round the sharp bend. All this in spite of my decrepit old "Schwärtle" ski, lacking in tension and steel edges. I couldn't help thinking, at the smooth icy places, how much better proper racing skis would have been.

I got down the second slope, too. A lift into the air, over the so-called "leap"—I took it like a veteran—and then on down. Presently the slope eased; in next to no time the down-hill run was a thing of the past.

One of those who had been training hard asked me if I was competing next day.

"Me—competing in a downhill race?"

"Why not?"

Come to that, why not, after all?

I was up there again next day. They were handing out numbers, checking watches. Everyone was waxing up, testing the snow for its smooth, racing condition. They began to call the roll of the runners. Number One—Ernst Spiess—Number Two—Egon Schopf." . . . The race was for the Club Championship of the Innsbruck "Gymnasts"; one or two first-class runners were competing.

They called Number Seven, but no one answered.

I thought a moment, then asked if I could take Number Seven. Agreed! So as Number Seven I joined the starters.

It was with somewhat mixed feelings that I fastened the number on and fixed my ski-bindings. I hadn't noticed till then how well-equipped the others were. How ridiculous I must look with my old ash-boards on my feet! How I envied the others their marvellous equipment. When I realised the standard I had got mixed up with—all first-class Club runners—I would dearly have liked to withdraw. What a brick I had dropped in coming in at all; but now it was too late to back out!

The first man was off, now. I suddenly felt weak and feeble. The first six went off down the strip, "skating" to get up speed more quickly, and even helping themselves on with their sticks.

Then my number was being called—"Seven!"

"Fifty-six—fifty-seven—fifty-eight——" I looked down the steep drop in front of me almost as fearfully as if I were going to the gallows—"—fifty-nine——Go!"

A slap on my shoulder. I heard someone shout: "Good luck!" I had time to think: "All right for him to talk!"—then I was in the woodland ride. My fear fell away from me—this was it! I went flying down over the waves of the ground. My skis were too light and wouldn't bite, but somehow I just managed to keep upright. Another group of spectators—I whizzed between them. Somebody gave a sudden shout—was it meant for me? A branch hit me in the face; I almost went down then. My skis were tearing downhill under me. Suddenly, no floor—a chasm beneath my feet; not exactly like the Laliderer Wall, but quite sufficient for me. I hit the ground hard on one leg and visualised myself strewn about in several pieces . . . yet nothing seemed to have happened. I had got away with it again. This was like dancing on a tight-rope. . . .

The worst was over and I could draw breath for a moment. Of course I had under-estimated it—and there I was, in trouble, clean off the course; but I was up on my feet again in a trice. Now the thing was to make up the lost seconds. I hunched myself up as small as possible, so as to present as little resistance as possible to the air. There, at the bottom of a couple more slopes, lay the finish. I must pull myself together; it would be infuriating if it tripped me up now, in front of all these spectators. I shot down the final slope like a practised performer, sticks jammed under the arms, even waggling my hips. What a relief, to be through with it; a solo climb on severest rock would be better than another down-hill run like that!

The prize-giving was in the evening. I attended just as a matter of interest. When they called my name, it sounded like a bad joke; I had won the fifth prize—a silver ski and a tin of ski-wax.

*   *   *

Is it very surprising that I then saw a chance of testing myself in the Winter too? I trained assiduously on week-days, on Sundays I went racing. One week-end the Pert Fankhauser Memorial run was to be held at Telfs. On Saturday, as befits a real ski racer I was on the course, training, training, training. . . .

This time I even had two pairs of skis along—clear evidence of a real ski racer. I had a pair for down-hill racing and a pair for slalom. If there was any difference between the two, I was the only one who could detect it; but that isn't the point. I filed the edges, as part of the morning "toilet" and set out for the top of the down-hill run.

Of course I could no longer go up by the most comfortable way now, but had to climb straight up the course. I looked at every ripple in the surface as if with a direction-finder and tested the consistency of the snow. At places I stuck pine-twigs in to indicate the shortest possible line—a silly occupation, because you mostly fail to see them when you come shooting down in the race, but it was the proper thing to do.

At last I reached the upper rim of the forest. I realised for the first time how gorgeous the weather was and how lovely it would be to go wandering on towards the top of the mountains, with not a care in the world. But to-morrow was the great day—the race. . . .

I laced my down-hill boots on tightly; they grip one like a vice. I went over the course mentally once more, before pushing off. . . . There were two young lads in front of me, running like the very devil; but I couldn't afford to be left behind by such novices. So I put everything into it and gave it "the works"; in spite of which I didn't make any impression on them and could see them holding their distance in front of me, till they disappeared at a bend in the course. One mustn't underrate these "locals"—but catch them I must. There was a fearsome slope ahead of me. I leaped into it, hitting the snow again a long way down, but recovering my balance well. The two ahead were just flitting through a gap in a fence at the bottom, swinging to the left, out of sight. . . .

The pace was terrific. Certainly "forty", probably more; then fifty and sixty, the speed of an express train.

I came to a sharp bend. I pressed with all my might on the steel rims, but the slope was too icy and they didn't grip. Carried on by my skis I went flying through the air for ten or twenty yards.

Crack, bang . . . there I was on the floor amid a heap of wreckage. For three yards around me lay bits of wood, long stakes of it, as if a bomb had exploded. I had landed on a wood-pile; but luckily ski-first.

When I got up, I noticed that my skis felt remarkably light. Damnation! They were broken off, front and back, both of them, and only the bindings remained fixed to my feet. My best skis, too—I could have cried with rage!

The long walk down to Telfs in deep snow sensibly heightened my anger. A kind of deep defiant fury came over me when I saw the two lads standing grinning there by the roadside. I recognised them then as the two Gabl brothers, one of whom was later to win a world championship in America.

As soon as I reached Telfs, I grabbed my second pair of skis—the old, light ash-boards. Then I went straight back up the course. I cut out the top part; I knew it well enough by now. The part I had to practice now was the finishing stretch—the last steep slope down to the post. Quite a stretch that, full of obstacles.

Half-way down now—missing here a shed, there a clump of trees by a hair's-breadth, as I went tearing down. Just before the finish my skis decided to go different ways. A perfect dive landed me head first on an icy patch.

My skull can stand quite a bit, but it wasn't going to put up with that particular treatment; it buzzed so that I could neither see nor hear. I stood there in a complete daze. So much for racing to-morrow; indeed, I realised that this marked the definite end of my career as a ski-racer. It was a thought I could bear with equanimity.

Chastened, I returned to the solitudes among the high peaks. Far from the madding crowd, free from the irksome restrictions of the race-track, I cut my lonely furrow once again in unsullied snow, enjoying to the full the beauty of the Hills. If I had ever envied the others, the feeling did not last long.

AVALANCHES, PLASTER-CASTS AND
A HINT OF SPRING

SNOW is an odd thing. Its starry flakes are so gentle and so orderly—a miracle of loveliness and perfection. But Beauty is not always trustworthy; her character is mainly superficial, unstable. And so it is with the beauty of snow. You have to be pretty well acquainted with it, if you are to get away with it for long. Rock is much more reliable. It is either sound or sick, firm or friable; and it rarely tricks those who understand it. It is far less deceitful than that white pall which originally fell from Heaven upon the Earth beneath in little six-pointed, magical starlets.

Take avalanches, for instance. If you want to invade the mountain fastnesses in Winter you have to learn to know them and the laws that govern them. You have to gather experience—such experiences. . . .

One morning in winter Karl and Franz Glätzle and I left the Adolf Pichler Hut in the Kalkkögel together, with the Kleine Ochsenwand as our objective. The slopes crackled suspiciously under our skis. We climbed the *couloir* to the Alpenclub Saddle, well spaced out on the rope, and thus avoided any lengthy traversing. The top surface of the snow was packed hard, but we knew that therein lay the very danger. There was an unnatural tension on the slope; you could feel it weighing you down. Karl was breaking the trail, keeping as close as possible to the projecting rock-rib, so that he could use it as an island of refuge if the snow threatened danger. He was quite high up, almost at the bottom rocks of the Kleine Ochsenwand. We climbed on towards him with a feeling of relief—nothing could happen any more now.

"Avalanche!" His sharp sudden shout came down to us. At the same time we heard its penetrating rumble, and then—like a thundering waterfall or a tidal bore—the snow masses came rushing down on us. I did a quick jump-turn, just as the avalanche reached the broad slope on which we stood. There was a gentle report and like lightning a jagged line split its surface, as the slope disintegrated, tumbling into blocks. In a matter of split seconds I saw it all happening, even while I tried to get out of the danger zone by running sideways. Then I ran straight down the steep slope, a thing I would never normally do; but the avalanche was too quick for me. In spite of my own speed, I felt as if I were standing still. By now the whole slope was on the move. It was like being in water: there was nothing under my feet any more. It was just as if the ground were trying to swallow me up.

However, the improbable happened. I was just able to work myself clear of the wildly moving mass and, having reached the outer edge of the slope, was in a position to watch the rest of the avalanche's progress.

Only three yards from me there was a step, three feet high, the side-wall of the avalanche. Down below, the masses of snow moved out from the bottom of the slope, piling up into a dam, then came to rest. Suddenly all was still again, but I could see nothing of my companions. I moved quickly across to the other side of the avalanche, for the slope above me didn't look any too good. There I saw something moving. . . .

It was Karl. He had taken refuge behind an outcrop in the rocks. With the aid of his sticks he had just been able to jam himself between the snow and the rock, while the whole avalanche poured over his head.

But where was Franz? We ski'd down and searched the entire avalanche cone, which was more than a hundred yards wide. We soon saw the point of a ski, and quickly freed its owner. He was not deeply covered by the snow masses, but they were so solidly wedged that he had had to lie there, utterly unable to move, as if cemented in.

We gave up the projected tour, rather early in the day, but richer by one experience.

*   *   *

Yes, snow. . . .

Avalanches are not its only peril. It has even been known to dictate that I, in the shining springtime, with the rocks already warm and dry, enough to tempt one to the heights, stayed down in the valley or half-way up the slopes, strolling—or more correctly hobbling—about in the company of a pretty girl.

In February I had been for a last ski-run. Once again I was up on the Seegrube above Innsbruck and the good snow conditions lured me into a little too much "cocky" over-confidence. The run was in marvellous condition and, in order to make the most of my time, I used the Ski-Lift continually. No sooner was I at the top, than down again, Schuss—a one-man ski race, in effect. As a result, I pulled a tendon in my knee. Plaster-cast!

None the less, in the early spring I was back at the Höttinger Steinbruch trying out its practice climbs, even with a stiff, caged leg.

Two months later, just when the time had come for removing the plaster, I was running, as usual, up a staircase with long, bounding strides. I took three or four steps in one, slipped and came down—need I say?—on my bad foot. The plaster-cast broke in two—I must say to my great satisfaction. I took the broken wreck off and went straight to hospital to report the mishap. The doctor wanted to put another cast on straight away, but I implored him not to. I promised to take the greatest care during the next few weeks. I did: I took the greatest care to get into training as quickly as possible.

The call of the High Hills was irresistible. Innsbruck, after all, is ideally situated. All you have to do is to take the Funicular and, an hour from its top station, you are at the Hafelkar, 7,000 feet above the valley level. I was there soon enough, but it no longer satisfied me; the Kemacher Ridge, a favourite springtime climb, was so seductively close at hand. I didn't find walking very difficult, not even when breaking a trail in deep snow. So I went on, crossing several slopes covered with deep snow, wandering along the edge of huge cornices, ready to break away any moment. . . . Oh, I was back in my element!

I went on from the Kemacher—in such form, why not?—down the North Ridge, a very jolly climb. I had almost forgotten my bad leg.

What about the Rainer Pinnacle—a most attractive scramble, which must surely be ready by now? I went down a gully and came to the foot of the Pinnacle's West *Arête*. There was a small overhang there. Attractive scramble? No, a splendid bit of climbing. I went up on lovely warm rock. Up and again up . . . life was worth living! I was soon pulling myself over the edge of the roof and standing on the top of the slender pinnacle.

Short but often sheer pitches brought me back to the Kumpfkar Saddle. I was delighted both with the nice extension to my outing and with my splendid condition, so I followed the ridge on and over the Kumpfkarspitze to the Widdersberg. Here the ridge drops sharply, so I had to decide on a way down off it. I saw a most suitable snow gully, dug my heels in and went sliding down on the steep hard snow. I had forgotten all about bad legs and torn tendons. I felt as good as ever.

There was a sudden break in the snow, where the gully took a downward tilt, and a deep crack opened up in front of me. I was going too quickly to be able to put the brakes on, so I tried to clear it with a jump. I got over the gap with a broad leap of about fifteen feet. Then I felt a fearful pain, deep down in my knee.

My joint, which I had imagined quite fit again, had given way. Pain kept me lying in the snow for several minutes, and I only began very slowly to feel better. I hoped I hadn't torn a tendon again, but at the same time feared that I had. I tried to continue my downward way, but found it a very difficult business. Face inwards to the snow, I kept on kicking steps for both feet with my sound leg, for there was no strength at all in the other. The gully steepened and snow gave way to rock. In the end, I got down to the ravine at the bottom; but that wasn't the objective by a long way. I still had to cross the Kemacher Saddle back into the Seegrube and somehow or other to reach the Funicular Station. I gritted my teeth and forced myself on and up again; my knee was hurting terribly. It took me till sundown to reach the Saddle and then I went limping on down the steep slopes to the Funicular, only to find to my utter disappointment, that the last car had gone down.

I went stumbling on down towards the Valley. Gradually I got used to it. By the time I reached Innsbruck I hardly felt any ill-effects of the mishap any more. In fact I felt so well that I even visited the Club during the evening, to arrange a climb for the following Sunday. . . .

All in vain, of course, for next morning I couldn't get out of bed. The knee was hurting horribly again; so it was hospital, once more. On went the plaster-cast, hey presto! "Come back in two months," said the doctor, calmly. What could I do but obey?

Everything in the Inn Valley was already green. The meadows were starred with primroses and, a little further up, the crocuses were pushing up at the very rim of the last brownish shields of snow. Now only very few late skiers could be seen passing through the dry streets of the city: enthusiasts bent on seeking out the last of the winter snow. The boys were all barging about on football grounds. The still younger lads were to be seen at *Totzenhacken*—a round-game and one of Innsbruck's national sports—at which it is possible to pick up a penny or two. The deserted benches in the Hofgarten Park were glad to find regular visitors again. Lovers came to hold hands there. There was no denying it: Spring was here!

My plastered leg only permitted me very moderate excursions into the Lower Hills—but it wasn't a very harsh punishment. I had time to realise for once how lovely spring can be down in the Valley, too; how delightful it is to stroll about among Nature's signs of reawakening. The sound of many waters gurgling again was like a benison. Everything was waking up, budding and blossoming; only the last remnants of grubby avalanche snow up in the gullies remained as a reminder of the cold season. Even if I glanced up occasionally with a pang of regret at the shining snow-peaks, I had to admit that it was very pleasant to wander through the pleasing landscape of the Valley with a pretty girl by my side. And I realised that life has other pleasures in plenty to offer besides the joys of the Hills.

I was seen out with girls quite often, up in the Hills and down in the

Vale. But when my friends said: "We can see Hermann's finished, now that he's started with the girls!" I only smiled.

It is true that these charming creatures constitute a serious menace for many a mountaineer, often diverting him from his ideals and aims. But I understand myself well enough to know just how far the influence of the female sex was likely to get a hold on me. Just at that moment, when I happened to be a temporary invalid, I could think of no more pleasant way of spending the time than to go about in amiable association with a pretty girl.

That did not prevent the Mountains from remaining the Law of my life.

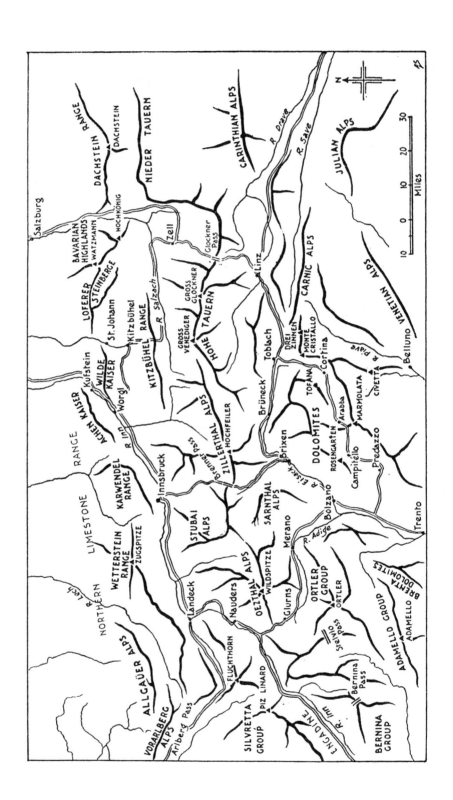

THE DOLOMITE FAIRYLAND

SMUGGLER'S JOURNEY INTO FAIRYLAND

THE Dolomites—an endless sea of mountains! Partly streaked with snow and ice, their sharp heads bit into the blue sky of the South, as if they were no part of this Earth of ours, but rather of the climber's dreamland Paradise. Proud and upstanding, like fairy castles, they soared above the green and pleasant vales—beyond counting, their spires, towers and needles crowning sheer ridges and walls. Exciting, wildly romantic; their yellow faces leaping perpendicular straight from the green leas or growing straight up from the grey tongues of rubble at their feet. And where else are the tarns, the rushing waters and the whispering woods so enchanting as here in God's Garden, the magic Dolomite country?

It was 1946. We were sitting in a comfortable inn near Sterzing, sampling our first Tirolese rendezvous. We had to laugh about our experiences of the past twenty-four hours.

A few days before, Herbert Eberharter had come to me and asked delightedly: "How would you like a trip to the Dolomites in South Tirol?"

"I'd like it all right. But how—we haven't a permit?"

"That's the easiest part," he replied.

It was all arranged on the spot. We were really going to the Dolomites!

Almost indescribable were the pleasures of anticipation. We were already dreaming of the things we would do—first the Drei Zinnen, then the Civetta. We would follow in the footsteps of Comici, Tissi, Solleder, Steger and Stösser—just as long as our supplies lasted.

The five of us left Innsbruck at noon one day. Fritz Bauer, lucky owner of a motor-cycle, ferried us by a shuttle service up to the Obernbergtal, near the Brenner Pass. Heavily laden, we went up a lateral valley in the darkness of the night. When I picked up my rucksack at home it had almost bored me into the ground. I estimated it at almost seventy pounds and couldn't imagine how I was going to reach the foot of the Dolomites under its crushing weight. There is, however, nothing one can't get used to, and the upward urge is always a good companion. We sent a harmless-looking advance guard on ahead. A few hundred yards behind followed Herbert, Reinhold Berger and I, carrying the valuable loads which were to earn us the necessary exchange. To put you at your ease at once, let it be said immediately that the loads weren't as valuable as all that. They consisted merely of small everyday articles of use. We certainly didn't feel like professional smugglers. All we wanted to do was to earn a few *lire*—enough to buy us a glass of wine and a bed at night-time.

We were working up the valley, alongside the stream, whose gurgling drowned almost every other sound. Suddenly we heard the agreed alarm signal, a little tune whistled by the advance guard. In one movement our packs were off our backs and trundling down the slope into the stream, while we proceeded, looking the picture of innocence. We could see vague outlines, a shape or two emerged; they gave us a very friendly "Good evening" and passed by. It was a false alarm; only some South Tirolese coming across from the other side of the frontier. We soon found our rucksacks lying down there in the burn, with the water swilling round them. We let them dry off a bit; even so a nice dollop of water splashed on our heads as we slung them on our backs again; not a very acceptable present—a free shower bath on a chilly night in the late autumn.

Up on the crest, where the real frontier lies, we met some more "smugglers". They were harmless lads from the South Tirol, coming across to look up relations in the north. We came to a board which read "Austria" on one side and "Italy" on the other; so we were already on South Tirolean ground. Very cautiously, avoiding every kind of noise, we crept down on the other side. We worked across to the road through thick forest and by dawn we were in Gossensass.

A hayrick gave us shelter till morning; then we started peddling our wares, which met with a lively demand. Much relieved, we continued on our journey next day, and now we could keep to the main road without any qualms. Presently a car gave us a lift. Its driver, from the South Tirol, knew his onions. He knew just where to put us down, in Sterzing, that charming little town, where he pulled up behind the ancient arched gateway. We jumped out, shouldered our packs and marched off to the Market Place. It happened to be market day so we were not likely to attract too much attention in the milling crowds. I was the rear-guard of our little party of five.

A man in uniform tapped me on the shoulder, remarking: "*Signore, venite qua!*" or some such words.

"Oh, Lord," thought I, "now they've got us!" However, I went calmly on,—pretending not to have understood. Meanwhile the Police officer had caught up with Reinhold, the next ahead in our column. He appeared to whisper the same words in *his* ear and then went on; by the time he had got to the head of our little column, we had reached the market-place. As previously agreed, we all scattered in different directions, throwing our rucksacks under the nearest stall, while the woman in charge looked at us in bewilderment—there was no time for explanations. We mingled with the groups of people and tried to get away without making ourselves conspicuous. I just had time to see the officer make a desperate grab at Herbert and hang on to him. Poor Herbert—at the head of the proceedings, he had no idea of what had been going on behind him. And now we were marked men!

By pure chance we all met again, Herbert excepted, at a small inn. The first thing we wanted was a refresher. Reinhold had already briefed a man to retrieve our rucksacks. Our peace was, however, short-lived. Another policeman came into the bar, had a look round, vanished again; but a few minutes later he reappeared and, making straight for us, demanded our personal papers.

Now we were for it!

We could see the Dolomites receding into the dim distance, and a dark cell in near-by Franzensfeste as our next lodging. Obviously they had summed us up as pretty bad hats; what else could such monstrous packs presage? They took us under guard to the Police Station. Herbert had already arrived there, and had been interrogated. The next thing was a personal search; they emptied our packs. Out came a mound of pitons, iron-work, ropes, climbing-boots and provisions, which piled up all round us. With every sign of disappointment, they ordered us to pack again. The only thing they commandeered was a knife which exceeded the measurements permitted by Italian regulations. Then they released us with a warning not to poke our noses into Sterzing again. We could hardly believe our luck and would have liked to hug the officers. . . .

For us the sun had come out again, smiling down on us.

And what a thrill next day when we stood at the foot of the Drei Zinnen! There they stood in all their splendour. We felt we were the luckiest people on earth; and yet we were only ludicrous dwarfs, minute beyond words, in face of those North Walls. They made us realise the size, the might of such giants.

It wasn't long before we were at the base of the enormous, oppressive sweep of the Grosse Zinne's North Wall. But as soon as we began to climb, we felt the firm holds of Dolomite rocks under our fingers. Up and up we went, till the ground below seemed almost flat. Had we not known that many climbers had come up this way before us, we might perhaps have lost our zest; indeed we might excusably have considered it impossible that there was a way up at all. From the psychological aspect alone, the climbing of this Wall is a tremendous effort and is always acknowledged as such. Its sheerness and exposed nature took some getting used to—our Walls in the North Tirol don't go shooting so furiously upwards. All the same, the Wall of the Zinne seemed friendlily enough disposed towards us; it was not till its upper part that we got into any difficulty, and had to disentangle a crazy mix-up of rope; but that was our fault, not the Zinne's. The rope had got completely out of control and we had to untie it for we could not just apply the Gordian solution to the knots.

In the evening we stood on the summit and entered our names in the thick book, full of hundreds of signatures. Darkness overtook us on the way down, a stone having chosen my head for its objective; so we got back to the Zinnen Hut very late. It was the end of the season, and things were very quiet. Mine host offered us a room with beds instead of the usual hard mattresses; he had noticed that we were just a group of youngsters and had taken pity on us. Before turning in we touched glasses to celebrate our day's success.

Next day found us on the ochreous rocks of the Kleine Zinne's Comici Ridge. It justified its nickname of the "Yellow Edge". I knew from the route-books that the climb went straight up, as if drawn with a ruler. So we went straight up a ruled line, overcoming one overhang after another.

Odd, I thought, that they rate this Ridge as easier than the North Face of the Grosse Zinne: I must be having an "off day"! I certainly made heavy weather of the climbing. Brittle rock and not a piton in sight: my head ached from yesterday evening's knock. I dared look neither up nor down, for everything seemed to be going gently round and round, probably as a result of that wretched stone. But I was not so bad that I couldn't judge the degree of difficulty—it was an "extreme super-severe".

"For goodness' sake, Hermann, use a piton!" Herbert called up to me from his niche 130 feet below. "Have a look round the right-hand Ridge."

"But I know it goes straight on up, this side of the Ridge," I answered, and moved out to the left on to a yellow facet of the Wall. The rope ran clear down to my partners—never a very encouraging sign for your "Number Two". It just couldn't be helped.

"There's no sense in starting the nail business now; it'd waste much too much time," I said. All the same, I was pretty near the limit of what one can do without adventitious aids.

I could see a party climbing the Grosse Zinne by the ordinary way. We were obviously pretty high up, but there was no end to the overhangs.

I was standing on a ledge about as thick as my finger, tatting the rock above me for the vestige of a hold. Suddenly my left foot gave way. I lost balance, but somehow managed to claw into the rock with my fingers. The ledge had broken away and, after long seconds, I heard the impact of stone on stone hundreds of feet down at the bottom. That persuaded me soon enough to bang a piton in with lightning speed.

There was another roof overhead. In it I caught sight of a few old pitons, the first we had seen since starting up; so we were definitely on the right route. The difficulty was to reach them, by way of a fearsomely difficult traverse, which took the last strength out of me. Jammed in a crack, I tried to knock in another hook, and at last wedged it firmly enough to rescue me from my unbearable situation.

Somebody shouted up from the bottom: "It's six o'clock—you'll have to hurry!"

We conferred. It was certainly too late to get to the top. We were left with no choice but to beat a retreat from this bitterly contested route, by roping-down from the overhanging edge.

It was only later that we were told our route constituted a completely new variation and that we had opened up the true "direct" when forced to go back; but we had not reached the top so, under mountaineering rules, it couldn't count as a first ascent. We also learned that we had already dealt with the worst of the difficulties.

We joined the two 120-foot ropes and drew them through the piton-ring, which didn't look very reliable, but it was the only way. It was only half its length into the rock and the weight of the two ropes was enough to make it vibrate in the most dubious way.

"Look after it a bit," I asked Herbert, and started to lower myself down as if I were on a silk thread. I had to avoid the slightest jerk or swinging movement. The thing held fast.

Time and again we floated down 120 feet of thin air, till at last we reached the foot of the wall. We looked up at it a little sorrowfully, as if we had lost something irreplaceable.

It was a Dolomite sunset. A fierce blaze lit every peak and ridge, till the rock-walls glowed like living coals—the peaks were unearthly torches licking the sky with their fires—a scene of indescribable beauty.

We emptied our glasses to the sound of old songs of our homeland and of the mountains. As the sun sank in the west, it drew a broad purple scarf across the horizon. The brilliance faded gradually, and dusk climbed up out of the valleys, till a heavenly peace enfolded all the hills. One after another the tiny lamps were lighted in the arch of the heavens. And we began to dream of yet another day. . . .

But even the loveliest of care-free days in our mountain life must draw to an end. It was time to go back by the way we had come.

We boarded the train at Franzensfeste and all collected in the last carriage during the journey. Up in front they had already started to examine passports. At the door of each compartment sat one of us in a state of nervous tension. We must be almost at Gossensass! The brakes screeched—we were running into the station.

At an agreed signal we threw open the doors and flung out our packs. Then we ourselves followed, while the train was still moving, and went scrambling down the embankment. There we grabbed our rucksacks, and away we went. We were out of the station precincts before the train had even pulled up.

It was a particularly dark night. We failed to find the little track by which we had come over the frontier on our outward journey. We were feeling fairly cocky—and walked bravely along the high-road feeling perfectly safe. We were talking quite freely, for the frontier block-houses must surely be behind us now.

"Halt, who goes there!" sounded a voice from the woods, taking us completely by surprise. We heard a rifle being cocked. There was no sense in running for it, standing as we were in the open, on the road; they must be able to see us quite plainly and there was no doubt they would fire.

Two Carabinieri loomed up, armed to the teeth. They didn't seem very happy—after all, they were two and there were five of us.

They seemed to be thinking: "A nice fat haul!" They looked at our packs almost affectionately, and marched us off to a barrack-room. By the light of a candle they rootled through the contents of our rucksacks. Once again—a mass of ropes, irons, food and dirty linen. What a disappointment for them! All the same—or perhaps because of it—they decided to take us down to Franzensfeste where, as they explained, they could lock us up.

We summoned up all our powers of persuasion. We pleaded that we weren't criminals; we hadn't done anyone the slightest harm. And the Italians understanding us vagabonds of the Hills, sympathetically told us to run away. Then, grateful beyond words, we demonstrated how we could run, when told to.

But we still had to get through the Austrian frontier-guard. We conjured every shadow into a policeman on patrol. We felt like desperate smugglers, wanted by everyone on the border.—"Look, there's another shadow!"

"Only a tree stump," whispered Herbert. After a long time we were back at the notice-board: "Italy-Austria." A few more steps landed us safely on the soil of our own homeland; nobody could want anything of us any longer; we had every right to be on the move here.

We got back to our native city with empty pockets, but rich in the thrills and labours of our adventure, and rich, too—for we had been tempered in body and spirit—in new-won experience.

ONCE IN A LIFETIME—
GOLDKAPPEL SOUTH WALL

EVEN in Innsbruck, that lovely city on the banks of the green Inn, life can be very hard. The crowds of visitors who admire the Northern Range from the Maria Teresia Strasse would of course not realise it, for it was golden holidaytime for them; but I had occupational worries.

When I returned from captivity at the end of the war, I found every job filled by older men with more experience. I had only my interrupted training as a salesman—but had never actually been one. I had gone straight from my course into the army, and served for three long years—three lost years, as I was now to discover.

There was a bed for me in my parents' house, but I had to provide for my own upkeep. So I seized the first chance that came along and became an assistant in a wholesale grocery concern. In the ruling circumstances that was a bit of luck, for we employees always got a picking at that time of strict rationing. But my second plaster-cast put a prompt end to my fortune—I was left without a livelihood by that light-hearted sacrifice of my fitness to earn a living.

Oh, those Mountains . . . if only someone tried to understand the power they exerted and with what relentless strength they drew me to them!

I was told: "With you, your career is a secondary consideration." My career? If my inner urge had anything to do with careers, I knew well enough what I wanted to be—the career of a Guide was my aim and object. That demanded time and money; meanwhile I had got to live somehow. So I got another temporary job—this time in the workroom of a Sports shop. Fitting ski-bindings and steel edges wasn't very difficult for me, even if my colleagues on the Sales side considered themselves a shade above me. I levelled that out on Saturdays by getting up into the Hills while they were still serving behind the counter.

On one of those Saturdays off, in the autumn of 1947, I was near a lonely mountain and its even more lonely Face—the South Wall of the Goldkappel in the Tribulaun Group. It was Hias Rebitsch, one of the greatest climbers of recent days, who had first climbed it; and he had described it as his most difficult climb. It wasn't therefore surprising that it had never been repeated. It was one of those climbs, however, about the difficulty of which there were differing views; and I, for one, didn't believe it was one to stretch a man to the uttermost. My companion was Ferry Theyermann, one of my "buddies" of the old Junior Section days. He had just come back from a prison-camp and was in pretty poor shape; but, somewhat light-heartedly, I thought he would do all right as second on a rope.

We made an early morning start. The rock was so broken that we made very slow progress, and it was mid-day before we reached the great rock-belt which forms the crux of the climb. A ramp leads up through the overhanging rock, which here swells outwards like the cupola of a Church, and provides the only way through. From a stance which seemed based on air I was watching Ferry come up. After a while it became almost impossible to take in the rope. A hoarse shout of "Hold it!" was the first confirmation that Ferry had come off.

He was dangling over the abyss, a few feet away from the Face, spinning like a top out in the void, first to the right, then to the left. There was nothing I could do but hang on, holding him. At the same time, I advised Ferry, who was being almost suffocated by the constricting rope, to use Prusik slings—the only way of escape from this diabolical situation.

But Ferry had no slings with him. Some of them were hanging on the Wall, and I had the rest; so the sling from which his hammer was suspended had to be brought into emergency use. I could not see Ferry, and my movements were dictated by what he shouted up to me. I could only pull in the one rope: the other had jammed. This was a very "dicey" manoeuvre, tedious beyond words and terribly exhausting. Ferry counted out the metres to the next piton—still ten to go . . . nine . . . eight . . . seven. . . . It took a whole hour to count those thirty feet.

I had learned my lesson. Nothing like that was going to happen again. I took the immediate precaution of providing my friend with some slings.

This was a "point of no return"—the only way was on, up, to the top. The next rope's length was even more difficult and dangerous; the rope almost dragged me off and cramped my every movement. I was just able to master the last few feet of the bulge, then there wasn't even a bare inch of rope left. It ran out over too many edges, through too many split-rings, though I had been careful to hang them only on occasional pitons. I could find no stance from which to protect my Number Two; it was difficult enough for me to stand upright. There wasn't even a wrinkle which would take a piton. I simply couldn't let Ferry come up like that—if he came off, we were both finished.

What was I to do? In the end I got a piton halfway into a minute crevice. It was the only chance. Then I called down to him: "Right. Move up now. But none of your coming off in this place!"

Very slowly he came up—I saw a hand feeling its way over the edge of the bulge. Ferry was standing in a sling. Suddenly the piton from which he was suspended came away. The whole of his weight now came on the doubtful bit of iron I had just driven into the cranny. I did my best to reinforce its holding power by applying my own strength; but that couldn't last long.

I think I uttered a short prayer: "Dear Lord, let this hook, on which two lives depend, hold fast!" Then I heard the stifled voice of my friend: "Let me down, I'm suffocating."

I couldn't let him down. He would never have got on to the rock again; he would simply have hung in thin air. It was a matter of seconds now, and there was nothing I could do to help, except to hang on to the rope and prevent his sliding down further. I shouted: "Fasten a Prusik sling on the rope!" With his last failing strength he managed to do it. He stepped into the sling, the rope relaxed around his chest and the murderous pressure eased. But he was still hanging over the void, jammed under the overhang and rotating gently. By a terrific effort of will-power he forced his body, emaciated as it was by his long captivity, upwards—slowly, inch by inch, but always upwards. I gave a last hefty tug and there he was, on his feet, above the projection. And, wonder of wonders, the piton had held! The rest of the way to the top was easy; we climbed down the West Ridge in the darkness of the night.

So we had achieved the second ascent of the Goldkappel's South Wall. But I shouldn't like to repeat it. No, never again.

THE NORTH-EAST WALL OF
THE FURCHETTA

I was in the Dolomites again, not secretly this time under cover of the night mists, but officially, with a passport, all in proper order. We had joined a rather larger party, motoring through the Grödnertal and then going up to the Regensburg Hut in the Geisler Group by a somewhat romantic night march. The Langkofel shone in overpowering beauty bathed in the moonlight, whose silver was tempered by passing clouds. It was midnight when we reached the hut.

At four o'clock we took a look at the weather. Dark rain-clouds were scudding across the sky. I lay down again—a rainy Sunday has the great advantage that one can for once have a peaceful lie-in. . . . At about seven there was a sudden stir in the hut; the rain had stopped and it had turned fine. We got up, determined not to waste what was left of the day.

"Perhaps there'd be time for the Furchetta North Wall," I suggested to my companions, who were all rather younger lads.

"We could at least go to the bottom of the climb and have a look," said Hans Gogl.

Time was now the essence. The Hutkeeper described the best way to the foot of the Wall, while our "Transport Officer" made us promise to be back early, because the car was leaving at 5 p.m. We left the hut and followed the prescribed route. At least that was what we thought, but it seemed to be taking us further and further from our peak. . . .

"Where is the Furchetta and where are we?" was the great question.

We had to cross a lofty saddle to reach the North Walls of the Geisler Group. There was not a sign of our Wall. We raced down débris slopes, crossed several ridges and crests, only to meet with one disappointment after another: no Furchetta to be seen. Surely a Wall, 2,500 feet high, couldn't have been sunk without trace?

It was not till after a long ascent and the traverse of a lateral ridge that we suddenly saw the whole expanse of the Northern Walls before us. Right at the back was our Furchetta. Among the loose and uneven boulders I came a purler and turned my already somewhat damaged ankle, which began to swell painfully; but I wanted to go on in spite of it. We had to go down again to the edge of the woods, then up again to regain the same level on the other side; then came endless scree-shoots along the foot of the North Walls. After all this wearisome traversing we reached the base of the Furchetta North Wall climb, towards noon.

"Aren't we too late?" asked Hans. We thought it over. There were 2,500 feet of rock towering above us. The route-book spoke of ten to twelve hours' climbing. And we were supposed to be down at the car in the Grödnertal by five o'clock; so there obviously wasn't any time. But there was the Wall, and we wanted to climb it.

The Furchetta North Wall is the highest, and probably the hardest in the Grödner Dolomites. Famous Alpine names are woven into its history. The first to cast envious eyes on it was the young Grödner apprentice guide Louis Trenker, who wanted to find a route straight up the Face. With this end in view, he teamed up with Hans Dülfer, the best rock-technician of pre-war days. In 1913 the pair got more than half-way up, to the narrow ledge or step still known as the "Dülfer Ledge". At that point the way seemed hopelessly barred, and they turned back. It was not till 1925 that this terrific Wall was mastered by Emil Solleder, the famous Munich climber, and Fritz Wiessner, the man of the Sandstone Peaks, who had been Roland Rossi's partner on the Fleischbank South-East climb. They reached the Dülfer Ledge, agreed that there really was no continuation up straight, looked round the corner to the left at the North-East Wall and came to the same conclusion as Dülfer twelve years before—absolutely no hope there. So they explored out to the right, that is, to the West. And there Solleder and Wiessner found an exciting, dangerous and exposed route up to the Summit Ridge; one of the most difficult Dolomite climbs of those days.

A few years later Hias Auckenthaler, one of the best rock-climbers of all times, turned his attention to the Wall. He also looked at the North-East Wall, out to the left; but he did not find it impossible. He found a route and climbed it, straight up to the Summit; his route had only been repeated three times since. We wanted to do it again, this very day. . . .

We started up, moving simultaneously, frequently forced to look for the way, because the route-description was inaccurate; all the same, we were standing on the Dülfer Ledge in two hours. Then the Wall shot up with terrifying steepness; huge roofs of reddish-yellow rock, with water pouring over them, jutted out over us—a most uninviting prospect. In an attempt to follow the route-instructions precisely, we traversed out two hundred feet to the left.

We got into a gully and climbed on up it, but I soon began to have my doubts; the way ahead looked too problematical. An immense dripping roof loomed overhead like a gigantic question mark—the sort that is only welcome as a protection against heavy rain. Under my feet the rocks fell away, undercut, into a gloomy abyss. The chasm was full of ice, and the stones thundered ceaselessly down in it; beyond it, jutted a steep, sharp edge—a scene of awe-inspiring magnificence, but of no great appeal to us at the moment.

There was no hope of traversing out in either direction; so the only thing was to go back—down the same gully again. Beyond it, we explored a little in the direction we had come from and found a yellow, gently-angled gully, which offered a way up from the rubble terrace, till presently I bumped on a couple of old rusty pitons. So this, at last, was the right way. The gully narrowed and closed; looking round its left-hand rim, I saw a chimney going on up.

It was a black fissure splitting the rock, terribly smooth, moss-coated; a runnel of water found its way down through it into the depths. It was obvious that the Wall had been climbed very rarely. We searched around for holds under the cushions of moss. A contraction in the chimney increased the difficulties even more—it became a real grind. We continued up it for several more rope's lengths, with overhangs providing plenty of variety; then, after a short traverse to the left, we were at the bottom of the Summit Gully.

Heavens, what a sight! I turned to Hans in my disappointment and said: "I thought we were through. Why, it only begins here!"

There was a glint of ice up there, and another rivulet came splashing down to the bottom of the rift, which started off with an overhang, with a few isolated protuberances of rock projecting through the ice. I tried them cautiously with the toes of my climbing shoes, for they offered the only means of support. Then I did a careful ice-waltz upwards, till I was standing under a jutting chimney, jammed full of ice. I was genuinely worried. How could I get up it, only in climbing rubbers, without "Ice-technique equipment"?

It looked a hopeless proposition.

I straddled as best I could up such ice-free rock as I could find at the extreme outer rim of the chimney, until the chimney widened so much that I was forced to climb out on to the left wall of the Gully. The wet rock was so cold that my fingers were numb and utterly without sensation; no ray of sunlight ever penetrated this spot—it was still last winter's ice.

I was forced by projections to move out on to the other wall, but it was too far away, and my legs could not reach it—the sort of place where you need extensible legs like a camera tripod. I had to let myself fall on to the opposite wall. My hands were then gripping rock again, but my body was bridging the chasm. Hans was standing directly under me, his teeth chattering, frozen with the cold, showing little understanding for my acrobatical exercises. Very carefully I drew my legs after me and at last reached easier rock, at which point the angle eased.

A few minutes later, I was standing on the ridge, directly below the Summit.

It was five o'clock—exactly the time we were supposed to be leaving Gröden. We stretched ourselves luxuriously on the warm Summit-slabs. It was a joy to be in the sun after the icy cold in the shadow of the North Wall below. I pointed over to the south-east.

"Do you see that enormous Wall—over there, beyond the Marmolata—the Civetta North-West Face?" I asked.

Lit by the lengthening rays of the setting sun, the Civetta stood drenched in rose-red radiance, its massive pillars erect to the sky like the pipes of a giant organ; pre-eminent among all the Dolomite Walls, with the names of those outstanding men—Solleder and Comici—carved for ever in its great rocky face.

But we could not stay long to enjoy that glorious summit view, for we could not keep our friends down at the car waiting over-long. How lovely life would be—how timeless, how free from care, how utterly at unity with Nature—if one didn't always have to work to some frustrating time-table. . . .

A day of tremendous experiences was drawing to its end; another climb banished to our yesterdays—but a day that would remain alive for ever in our memories.

Later, my way was to lead me over and over again southwards across the Brenner, to my home-from-home in the Dolomites; for good companions I had my bicycle, my sleeping bag and a cooker.

A CLIMB ON PROBATION

On a sultry August afternoon in 1949 I was labouring up the many hair-pins of the Brenner Road under a heavy pack. I reached the top of the Pass in a lather of sweat; the formalities were quickly disposed of. The stamp-entries in my passport, which I had possessed for a long time, had gradually increased in number. Then I went flying down the upper Eisack Valley, through Gossensass, Sterzing and Brixen, and soon found myself on the undulating road to Bozen. I was pedalling for all I was worth, urged on by my longing to be back on bright, sun-warmed Dolomite rock.

Erich Abram and Otto Eisenstecken were waiting for me in Bozen with their motor-cycle. I "changed horses" and, three-up on the motor-bike, we reached the Karer Pass late in the evening. We put up for the night in a convenient hayrick.

By the time the sun was up, we were at the foot of a high, repulsive Wall.

"That is the Rotwand," said Erich proudly, as if he owned it.

A most appropriate name, too; the Wall was red, which usually also means brittle. As in the case of all really difficult Walls, Nature had clearly indicated the "way up". A long series of overhanging cracks, gullies and chimneys cut through the lower part of its 1,300-foot height, a little to the left of the line of the summit, with a huge roof barring the middle sector. From its ugly bulge the route continued a little towards the right and on to the summit over grey, steep and apparently unbroken slabs. The first climb had been made two years earlier by the pair who were my companions of the day, after Italian climbers had launched assault after assault on it over the years; but my two friends had plucked the prize. The climb, one of the hardest in the Dolomites, had required eighteen hours of actual climbing time. And we were going to scramble up it in a day! They let me lead, and I wondered whether they were putting me to the test. If they were, I was quite agreeable.

I tied myself to the two 150-foot ropes and climbed up into the first overhanging gully. Up I went, as far out in it as spread-eagled legs would allow, thus overcoming the bulging protuberances in the bottom of the gully. The rock of the Rotwand is rotten, and has nothing in common with good, holding Dolomite. But on I went, up and up; and only the protecting rope, running out between my feet, reminded me of the presence of my friends at the foot of the climb. Then they shouted up: "No more rope!"

I was to hear that cry often before we stood as a threesome under the great roof in the middle of the Wall. Even in those first 500 feet the Wall overhung the base of the climb by nearly thirty feet. But at this point the bulge made it a point of honour, apparently, to out-vie its pals lower down several times over. A narrow crack ran up it, and a piton showed itself high up in it—the first I had met to-day.

Very slowly I drew nearer, and eventually reached it. I snapped a split-ring into it and passed the rope through it.

"Pull gently!" I called down, then went straddling almost horizontal out under the overhang. It was almost impossible to find a foot-hold anywhere. There was more than enough air beneath me. But I managed to gain height without knocking in any more pitons, defeating one over-hang after another. I felt exactly like a fly on a ceiling. All the same, the holds were mostly excellent, even if the first glance at the thing was terrifying—reality is never half as bad as imagination. There is nothing more wonderful than exposed climbing of this kind without the aid of pitons.

I reached a narrow rock-ledge, the place where they bivouacked on the first climb; this time it was only the middle of the morning. I drove in two ring-pitons with powerful hammer-blows, so that my companions could come up to me. I could see by their faces that they were quite satisfied with the way I had carried out the task they had laid upon me; but they were not so pleased with my climbing the overhang without any safeguards whatsoever—they thought it altogether too risky. I, on the other hand, had found it exhilarating and perfectly safe.

Our difficulties, however, were by no means at an end. There was a new gully running up ahead, moss-covered, by way of a change. "We ought soon to be coming to the tree-line," I surmised ironically.

Where moss is, there is water; sure enough, everything combined to make things as unpleasant as possible again. It was a tough piece of work. I had to get rid of each moss-cushion in turn, in order to get finger-holds; but the surface on which the moss had rested was invariably slippery. After about 120 feet, the rock at last became less obnoxious, offering firms holds and finally presenting a much easier angle. I fairly rushed up it, as if climbing solo. There were only one or two places where a piton or a wooden wedge served as a reminder that there were still difficulties to be dealt with.

We were on the Summit by three o'clock. Thrilled by our "second ascent"—and in such good time, too—I lay down on the summit plat-form, overcome by a pleasant lethargy, the reactions from the exertions and the nervous tension of the last few hours. In an ecstasy of fulfilment I lay there enjoying our success and the loveliness of this beautiful world. As so often before, my eyes wandered over the encircling summits, ever finding new things to linger on. Finally they came to rest on a mountain structure of outstanding magnificence—the Marmolata; we were looking at her South Wall. Sheer from her crest the notorious Buttress plunged to abysmal depths in sharp interplay of sunshine and shadow. I had heard and read hair-raising accounts of it; one would have to sample it oneself, to know just how true they were. Yes, I should have to have a go at it one day—that Southern Buttress of the Marmolata.

ICE-GLAZED ROCK, WATERFALLS
AND STONES

JUST a week later I was back again; this time my friend Manfred Bachmann was with me. It was eleven at night when we got to the Contrinhaus, that refuge for climbers who approach the Marmolata from the south or the west. We were used to sleeping on hay, but search as we might we couldn't find a rick anywhere; our solitary 1,000-*lire* note certainly didn't warrant invading the Hut. We searched all the outhouses for hay or straw; finally we discovered a perfectly good room with two mattresses and blankets in a shed close by. "Why, it might have been reserved for us," I told Manfred. We installed ourselves noiselessly, cooked a *risotto* quickly and fell wearily on our beds.

It was still dark when somebody knocked at our door and a voice cried: "*Sveglio!*"

"*Si,*" answered Manfred in perfect Italian, while I rolled over and asked him, still fuddled with sleep, whether he had given instructions to call us.

Soon there was quite a stir outside our room and just as we were ready to flit, we had visitors. Two young ladies came in and made the situation perfectly clear: "*Bagare*", commanded the two young charmers —but the 500 *lire* they demanded was far too much. Unable to reach agreement, we left our passports, promising to resume negotiations when we got back from our climb.

We reached the Ombretta Pass well behind schedule, going up past deserted war-barracks and decrepit dug-outs. It was nine o'clock by the time we set foot on the Marmolata's sky-raking South Buttress. We made good progress in spite of rapidly increasing difficulties. There were parties climbing on the South Face, but we were keeping pace with them, in spite of the enormously greater severity of our route. Everything was going like a clock. *Abseil*-rings and rope-slings which we encountered told of many a withdrawal from the Marmolata's South Buttress.

There was a sudden whistling and whirring. We looked up, expecting stones. But it wasn't: instead, in a thousand glittering fragments, a shower of ice splinters came pouring down the Face and whizzed over our heads. Falling ice—on a South Wall, in August! It didn't bode well; all the same, by noon we were at the Second Terrace, half-way up the Face.

To the right was the entrance to the Main Summit Gully, starting straight off with a considerable overhang. A stream of water as thick as my arm was pouring down over it, and though I explored every possibility from close to, there was nothing for it but to take a voluntary shower-bath if I wanted to master that overhang.

"Haul on the main-rope; now on the thin line; now let the main-rope out," I ordered. By the time I was up, my body-heat was some degrees cooler and the percentage of humidity in my clothes had risen sharply.

An exceedingly smooth crack came next. The pitons I had to knock in for protection simply wouldn't go into the resistant rock; perhaps, an inch or two, but no more. It was only after thirty feet that I found a hold for my left hand, sufficient for the tips of my two middle fingers; almost immediately afterwards, I had to bring my friend up, from a most precarious stance, then we had to traverse back to the left into the gully. At various points I had to climb through water again; it was only rarely that I could work out of the bottom of the rift to use drier rock.

There was no end to the desperate struggle. I hung on dubious hooks, supported myself on minute holds until my finger-nails actually bent; and still there were always fresh surprises ahead.

We were now asking ourselves what had become of the huge chock-stone, which we knew formed a great roof to the gully. We ought to have reached it by now. Or had Time blessed it by sending it down to its long rest at the bottom? That could only make our climb easier, any-way. . . .

For the umpteenth time I climbed out over a bulge, and there, at last, I saw the chock-stone, still fully 300 feet above my head.

But what an approach to it! The bottom of the gully was a solid silver band; every crack and cranny was solid with ice—hard, unyielding water-ice. The angle of the rock eased for a moment, then built up again rapidly. The sun had long ago deserted the gully, which was as cold as a cold-storage chamber; stones were pattering down the gully.

For better or for worse, I had to get back into the wet, trying to get up a damp overhang, followed by a polished crack. I tried to dispose of that dangerous bit as quickly as possible, fighting the tricky ice, which now allied itself to the running water. I couldn't beat it down, for Man-fred was standing directly beneath me, unprotected. I worked my way up—as so often before—as far outside as possible, using the few pro-jections of rock; an exceptionally dangerous performance. The last few feet consisted of wobbly blocks and loamy soil. Without the slightest protection, the whole 130 feet of rope ran clear down to my worried partner. The very slightest slip here could only mean our both coming off. I simply dared not think of such a contingency. The only possible attitude was an iron determination not to slip!

I watched Manfred up with chattering teeth; then we both had a look at the monstrosity above us. There were only two alternatives: We could try to find a hole behind the enormous chock-stone and wriggle through it; or, even more difficult, to climb over it on the outer side. There was a dank, weathered rope's end hanging down under it—what a saga it would have to sing, if it only could, of bitter struggles for very life! There were also a few rusty pitons, with a bannister of old soggy rope strung between them, and a few hooks that had worked out dangling from it.

I finally managed to get into the extreme top corner under the roof, where I wedged my hips between excrescences and blocks, while my feet dangled out over thin air. In that comfortable position I began to enlarge a hole about the size of my foot, by digging with both hands, sending everything loose flying down below me; it was comforting to know, this time, that my Number Two was safe under the shelter of the roof. But all my efforts did not result in much progress; there wasn't room for my head, let alone the rest of me, to get through that hole, so I thought I would at least try to thread a rope through it. Before I could do that, however, I had to untie one of the ropes, uncomfortably placed as I was; that was a conjuring trick in itself. At last one end was free; I fastened a stone to it and threw it through the aperture; but, because the block didn't fall away sheer on the other side, the stone kept on catching. Meanwhile, an icy jet of water kept pouring over my head, to add to the other joys, finding its way down my body and spraying out again at my feet. After an hour's vain labour I was so numbed by the cold of the ice-water that my hands ceased to function; as I couldn't bend my frozen fingers any more, I had to retreat to the stance below.

It looked as if the Wall was going to defeat us—near as we were to the goal. Wilting in every limb, wringing wet from head to foot, I stood there next to my partner. "Let me have a go," he said. "I'm narrower. I might wriggle through."

"If it doesn't go at once," I advised, "come straight down and try the outside of the overhang"—for we dared not use up all our reserves here. There were plenty of difficulties still to be dealt with.

Manfred put aside everything that might impede him, down to a matchbox. Soon he disappeared into the hole and I could only see his legs struggling and hear his breath rasping. Then I heard a gurgling sound; he was in danger of being suffocated by the weight of the water pouring into his clothes from above and out again at the bottom of his trouser-legs. He couldn't get through the obstinate hole either. But he

did succeed in passing the end of the rope through it, so that it hung
down, when he lowered it, on the outer side of the block; about eighteen
or twenty feet clear of the inside of the gully, way out over the abyss.

An extremely daring traverse enabled Manfred to get hold of the
loose rope, and with its aid at last to surmount the chock. I was very
relieved to watch my friend disappear from sight overhead, and soon it
was my turn again. The rock was so slippery that my shoes could no
longer get a proper hold. Of course, the rope running up to Manfred
had to choose that precise moment to jam, so that the protective tension
ceased; it was hanging loose in a great loop and it took all the energy
I could find to free the thing. I was just able to maintain myself long
enough for Manfred to pull it in quickly, then my fingers gave out. I
swung out under the roof, but was able to make a swift grab at the rope
and climb up to Manfred with his support. That single overhang had
taken us two precious hours. Time was becoming precious.

We shuddered as we looked up, in bitter disappointment—still not
a sign of the Summit.

Nothing but the same grey, oppressive chasm, hemmed in by smooth
walls, with black, water-sodden bulges overhead and the same ice-
armour filling its inner recesses. There was only a narrow strip of sky
to be seen between those beetling walls; the chock-stone was snow-
covered; above that there was steep ice. The piton-hammer would have
to take on the role of an ice-axe. Never had I met so much ice on any
Face in the Dolomites.

We climbed up along the edge of the ice-shield and reached the lower
edge of an overhang. Could we see this thing through, debilitated as we
were by cold and wet? Would we be fit to cope with the difficulties yet
to come? Suppose we hadn't enough strength left to escape from the
Wall? Retreat was out of the question—down all those pitches, over ice,
through torrents, on stiffened ropes; numbed by cold and, worst of all,
that roof! Were we going to get out of this at all?

It had just got to go—we couldn't give in. If you admit defeat, the
battle is already lost. I talked my spirits up, telling myself we had got
to get up it, and before the onset of night, at that!

After a highly-polished gully I found an enormous icicle barring the
way. I couldn't knock it off, because Manfred was below me. So willy-
nilly, I had to use it as a grip.

"Don't lose your head now!" I admonished myself. "No panicking
here. A fall here would be the end of everything."

I used up all the rope and managed to fix a piton; then I brought
Manfred up, perched on an exiguous stance. It was dusk by the time he
joined me there. We simply had to do the next difficult rope's length

before night folded her wings about us. So I pushed on almost before Manfred was established on the stance. I was driven far out by a narrow crack, only to meet more of that accursed ice—a six-inch sheet covering the rock everywhere. Thirty feet overhead there was yet another overhang with water pouring off it. After that, we hoped, the Wall would ease off a bit.

"It's all right," I encouraged Manfred, "I'm used to climbing in the dark."

"There's just thirty foot of rope left," he called back stoically.

Not a piton, not a protection anywhere—a ghastly sensation. Suddenly it was pitch-dark, without my having noticed its coming. I wanted to fix a piton, but couldn't find a crack in the dark. That was the end.

What I had feared most, but hadn't even dared to mention, had happened. We would have to spend the night in this bedevilled gully.

I climbed carefully down to Manfred. We would have to go down all those hard-won pitches, all the way back to the chock-stone—for there was no room to bivouac on that minute stance. We fastened the 120-foot rope to a piton, while the second rope was used to assure my partner, who was soon disappearing into the black darkness of the gulfs below me. A horrible cracking noise made him stop in his descent and ask: "What on earth's that?"

I called down: "Only the carabiner shifting a bit. You can go on down—don't worry."

Presently I heard his faint call from below:

"Right, I'm down. Come along."

The rope's friction on my soaked clothing was so strong that I let it run around one thigh only. As soon as I was plumb under the piton I heard the same horrible cracking sound; only this time it sounded much more frightening. I climbed up again and discovered that the hook had bent right downwards and was only held in the crevice by its very tip. No amount of hefty banging would persuade it to go any further in. So, as a safety measure, I had to climb down the 120 feet unprotected, with the rope wrapped around one arm as an emergency precaution. Thirty feet above Manfred my feet went from under me on some ice, and I went flying clear of the Wall; in the same instant I managed to drape myself round the rope and force myself in again alongside my bewildered companion. Sometimes one's luck is truly astonishing. . . .

We didn't want to go right down to the chock, because of the danger from stones. Manfred had already prepared a tiny place under an overhang, six feet from the edge of nothingness, where we could spend the night with icy water dripping continually upon us. It was so small that two people could just get a lodging on it somehow.

"Will those pitons hold?" I asked Manfred, giving him a shake.

"I hope so," came the reply, "but I'm not promising anything."

We slid under our Zdarsky Sack, put our feet in the rucksack and crouched down on that little pulpit. Had we let our feet hang over the edge we would have slid slowly off our sloping perch: so we had to keep them tucked in, to exert a continual pressure against the rock under us. After half an hour of that our legs were hopelessly cramped. The rock pushed mercilessly at our backs; worse still was the pressure of a few sharp stones through the seats of our trousers. Our wet clothes were uncomfortable beyond words and we were shivering with cold. We lit a candle-end, but kept on blowing it out through sheer carelessness, till finally our supply of matches was used up—our torch had already gone out of commission, owing to the wet. So we sat there in the inky darkness. Our only food was some small chunks of bread and a fragment of bacon, with a few small lumps of sugar, softened by water, which we found in the bottom of the rucksack. In the end our weariness got the better of us.

The icy cold soon shook us awake again. There seemed no ending to the night. The water dripped down on our bivouac with a monotonous . . . tack . . . tack . . . tack. . . .

And all the time there was that ghastly, clammy cold on our bodies. The inside of our tent-sack was soaked with condensation. To add to everything, the wind got up and rapidly gained in force. At short intervals missiles went whizzing past us. Their sound enabled us to judge whether they boded danger or not. The big lumps were heralded by a loud whizzing; then we pressed close to the rock. By contrast, if we heard a high whistle, it meant small fragments, and we knew we need not alter our position, even if a few of them hit the sheltering "tent" over our heads. The situation became even more worrying when a thunderstorm began to threaten and lightning flickered through the darkness of the night sky. Inevitably we remembered Leo Maduschka's tragic death on the Face of the Civetta. There would be no escape from a sudden spate in this gully; and it had been in such a spate that the young poet-climber had been drowned.

Suddenly the stones stopped falling; only occasional disturbances of the peace came rattling down; the wind fell, the storm had blown over. We had been spared once again and could begin to breathe anew.

Memories awoke. I reviewed the many lovely but hard nights spent out on mountains. We had always come out on top; so why should this Wall get us down! My old confidence came surging back. To while away the time we went over our predecessors' experiences on this Wall.

Stösser had been the first to attack it; he reached the great overhang, only to be driven back by impossible ice-conditions. After Micheluzzi and Perathoner had succeeded where he failed, he became the second to climb it. Two ropes, Steger and Kasparek, Vinatzer and Peters later repeated the route. The most recent attempt had been a few years ago when two Bozen men attempted the climb. One of them died of exhaustion at the great overhang; the survivor tried to climb on to the top alone, but fell to his death from the beetling cracks above our heads. Grim indeed, the history of the Marmolata's South Buttress.

We could judge the passage of time by the increasing cold. Our situation was now almost unbearable; our limbs ached painfully, our legs were crippled. We could only breathe with difficulty: all the air under our Batiste shell was used up.

At long last the blackness of night gave way to the pale grey of dawn. I wanted to get up and move about; but the cutting cold drove me back immediately.

A damp mist engulfed the gully and we were doubtful about the weather.

It wasn't till ten o'clock, when a glimmer of light shot through the fog and the sun's rays lit upon the outer extremities of the chasm, that life began to trickle back into us. We climbed down on to the chock, and let the sun warm us; we got out of our wet clothes, wrung them out and spread them to dry. It took a long time for the sun to waken warmth again in our bodies. The ropes were stiff as poles; it was not till we had given them a long overhaul that we dared to trust ourselves to them again.

At eleven, by which time the sun had warmed the rock a little, we started up the repulsive pitches again; but this time we knew them in detail. Using the icicle as a grip again we were soon at the questionable piton.

The effects of our vigil were all too noticeable. Where yesterday I had not used a single piton on the way up to our point of return, I now needed them to protect me. We used "safety-first" tactics: "Better one too many—than one too few."

An icy chimney brought me to an immense overhang; till then I had adroitly avoided water, now I could not escape a shower-bath. I clipped in one more sustaining carabiner, gave the order to haul in, and found myself fully exposed to the douche. In went another clip; I was hauled up and tried to bang in another piton. The water ran in at my sleeves and out at my trousers. I shouted, in desperation, as if there were someone there to hear it: "Oh, turn off the tap!" At last the hook, the ring and the rope were all in place and I could give the relieving words: "Haul up!" With a sudden clatter the old piton, on which I had just been hanging, went rattling down the rope to Manfred. Not that I cared any more. I was up the projection and in a very smooth crack, by then; but there was more of this disgusting ice there, too.

The rope ran out before I could find a stance. Pitons and holds were a rare phenomenon. This had got to go, somehow! We pushed past each other, flat against the Wall, which seemed to have no end at all. We were ravenously hungry—a good sign that we were alive—but things were almost blacking-out round me. A crazy tangle of barbed wire—the relic of the World War Number One—shook me out of my bemused state. Oh, joy, the Summit must be close at hand!

At about two o'clock we stood on the top of the 11,000-foot Marmolata, and my hardest fight yet was over, with the "directest" climb of the Dolomite Queen lying safe behind us. Our endeavours had been too exhausting, our nerves were still too taut, to let us taste the real pleasures of success yet. We warmed ourselves in the little shelter-hut on the Summit; and the last mangled and pulped crumbs of bread went down to satisfy our fierce craving for food.

THE ROYAL WALL OF THE CIVETTA.

I HAVE roamed the Dolomites from end to end, climbing their many peaks. My milestones have been the Furchetta—Rosengarten—Marmolata—Civetta—Pala and Brenta.

We had just come from the Pala Group and were still under the spell of its unique climbs. The "Scarf *Arête*" of the Cima della Madonna particularly—that heavenly ladder made by God for the climber. We had made a new route up the West Wall of the Cima Canale, a crack straight as a plumb-line defended by numerous overhangs and penthouses, greatly to my liking. Our hearts beat high with the delights of such climbing gems.

From Agordo we went on to Cencenighe and Alleghe. A charming lake lay in the bowl of the valley, with the houses clustering close at its shore and little southern alleyways running through the town. Above its roofs the gigantic Wall of the Civetta towered in all its pride, her massive pillars standing out prodigiously from the colossal mountain-face. The afternoon sun was throwing its slanting light on to the Wall, picking out every detail in sharp relief. We stopped to rest on the far side of Alleghe's lake; its water was clear as crystal. We could not resist the invitation to bathe in those cool waters—but they were damnably cold as well as clear. The meadows were already gay with autumn crocuses and the larch woods were a riot of lovely colour. Autumn was well on its way.

Hermann Herweg and I took a little track up the mountain-side through all this colourful glory until the rust of the meadows was fighting sheer rock for the right to survive. Beyond a saddle, the Pelmo lifted its broad head like some great castle of the Gods, built of lovely reddish stone.

We were the only guests at the Coldai Hut, when we got there. And the Keeper was all the better disposed towards us for that. At four next morning we left the friendly shelter, and it was the Warden who showed us the way to the foot of our climb. It was a rare and touching example of such thoughtfulness.

We had to cross tedious rubble slopes, with the Face looming black and demoniac above us. Gradually the peaks around us took on recognisable shape; a gentle light touched their crests. The last star was paling as we stood at the foot of the Solleder route into the Civetta's North-West Wall. It was in 1925 that Emil Solleder with his partner

Lettenbauer climbed that gigantic Face for the first time, a first-class Alpine undertaking in those days. The climb has not lost any of its prestige in the years between.

We were soon ready. A loamy ramp and a narrow crack brought us leftwards to the start of a long series of cracks and chimneys. I used a few pitons for my protection. Soon the rock got better, with the bulges seeing to it that I didn't indulge in over-confidence. We reached the débris-cauldron and I climbed out of it by another 100-foot crack to the left. The rock began to overhang steeply and increased in difficulty. Now where to? I looked around a corner; yes, it might go up that way. I traversed out across an exposed wall and soon reached the continuation of the cracks.

Here we had a little interlude—my partner had lost his Anorak while following me up. He had left it lying in the débris-cauldron. There was no point in being cross about the *contretemps*; I just had to go back and fetch the thing. I roped down 100 feet, my posterior getting very hot in the process, picked the Anorak up in the cauldron and then had all the fun of climbing the difficult pitch all over again.

We followed the line of cracks till beetling overhangs slowed us down. A damp, mossy ledge led us out to the right on the Wall. Then a succession of cracks, with good holds in them, brought us to a rubble terrace in the middle of the Face, where we decided to take a short rest.

The valley had fallen far away below us. The deep blue eye of Alleghe's lake shone up at us, Alleghe's little houses huddling close under the mountain. The white threads of roads cut through the valleys and wound over passes. Over to the north loomed the broad, stately Tofana with its vast buttresses; to the south, the valley broadened out. The sharp rock wedge of Monte Agner lorded it over the Val di San Lucano, lifting its 4,000-foot North Ridge in a single sweep from green meadows to its summit. In the background the hills died away into gentler outlines.

Lovely as was the prospect, we could not linger. We must push on, upwards, to our own sunlit summit. We climbed on by marvellous pitches, often moving together and so gaining height rapidly: the rubble terrace was soon far below us. Soon we reached the Summit Gully, which was mercifully dry to-day, thus sparing us some notorious showerbaths. The Summit already looked quite close, though there was still steep rock lifting above us, and we met a final overhanging pitch.

So we reached the Civetta's Summit Ridge. The contrast between the shadow of the grim North Wall and the brilliant sunshine flooding everything up there was tremendous, as we moved on to the Summit itself. Below us lay 3,500 feet of Wall, up which we had worked our way hold by hold and step by step. It seemed impossible that we had reached our goal so quickly, for it was only just after mid-day. In blissful enjoyment of the warming rays of the sun, we allowed ourselves to be lulled into the joy of a dreamless sleep.

My love of the mountains led me many a time to my mother's native land—my second Homeland of the Hills. Many were the hours of delight I found there, many the new joys of living I won for myself by toil and endeavour. For whenever, at their latter end, I sat on a summit with a world of ridges and peaks at my feet, I believed myself the happiest man in the world. Only he who knows that feeling can understand why we are always drawn upwards again on to those sunlit heights, into the "stainless imminence" of mountain air. My greatest wish is this: to be granted, for long years to come, the chance of seeking out, again and again, that lovely world, far from the hurly-burly of everyday life.

WINTER TRAINING

IN THE HELL OF A BLIZZARD—
SCHÜSSELKAR WALL

WINTER climbing had always been my particular passion. Over the years easy peaks had given way to difficult ridges and finally the limestone walls close to my home had become my winter province. The mountains in winter opened up for me a new world, in which skis were merely a means to an end. Where the tracks of the ski-runner ended, I found a realm of my own, full of new possibilities. Like the early climbers, on Shanks's pony, I broke a trail through virgin snow—a trail that did not halt however steep the slope before me.

I used my winter climbing as the best training I could get for the great climbs I planned to make later on, in the Western Alps. I did not want to be in any way inferior to my older friends who, while I was still enjoying myself among my local limestone walls, packed their equipment and got to grips with the icy giant peaks of Switzerland. I also wanted to avoid the stigma of being labelled a mere rock-climber who would soon be found wanting amid the ice-slopes of the Western Alps.

One idea crystallised. It was to do a winter climb on which I should really know that it was winter, on which the sweat froze on my forehead and rime caked my hair—a real fight against snow and ice, not mere springtime acrobatics up dry rock in the gentle sunshine of May. The more the idea took shape, the sooner I wanted to put it into practice; but the winter of 1948 seemed most unsuitable for such a venture, for the Föhn lay perpetually on the Mountains and continual violent variations of temperature, accompanied by sudden snowstorms, produced the most unfavourable conditions.

The first period of stable weather at the beginning of January went begging, to my great annoyance, because I happened to be suffering from a maxillary infection. But when I had only half recovered, my skis had taken me, by sunset one evening, to the top of the Birgitz-Köpfl above Innsbruck, and I saw the Walls of the Wetterstein on the other side of the Inn Valley glowing in the sunset, I decided to put my plan into practice. There was a full moon and the weather promised to hold.

I asked my old friend Luis Vigl to join me, but he couldn't get away from his work: so he sent me his brother Hugo as a replacement. Owing to his studies Hugo hadn't done much for some time, but he felt up to the proposal and was most enthusiastic about it. "Anyway, it'll stay in the family," Luis remarked as we parted.

We travelled to Seefeld on the evening of 26th of January and went up into the Leutasch. At five o'clock next morning we were already on our way through the darkness, up through the deep snow of the larch-forests, towards the Scharnitz Joch. The moon was hardly able to penetrate the veil of clouds that filled the sky; but we pressed on, heavily weighted under our rucksacks. We could still turn back if we must. By eight o'clock our tiring ascent had brought us through floury snow to the foot of the precipices under the Wangscharte. An icy wind was driving the clouds, which Hugo identified as a typical Föhn forma-tion; but I went on my experience of the last few weeks, during which the Föhn had always lasted for several days. So that, while the wind continued to whistle about our ears we had nothing to worry about; certainly no fresh snowfalls. We therefore decided to embark on our climb.

We left our skis and climbed down over a thirty-foot cornice. The wind blew a fine smother of snow into our clothes and even in mid-morning we were chilly enough. We ploughed on through slushy snow till at last we reached the foot of the Schüsselkarspitze. We intended to climb the "Direct", which Kuno Rainer and Paul Aschenbrenner had been the first to climb—but that had been in summer.

We were thoroughly wet by the time we reached the foot of the climb, and then moved on over steep snow to the start of the real diffi-culties. The first pitch was completely buried under a white mass. After that the Wall looked almost summery, though I knew it was a totally misleading impression. Up above the overhang, on the less abrupt places, which we could not see from there because of foreshortening, the snow would be clinging.

Still unsuspecting, we started up the rock, choosing the left-hand crack which, though harder than the normal one to the right of the buttress, is shorter. Its steep overhanging angle soon got us warmed up, though the cold and the wet were still most uncomfortable. Little avalanches and a few stones kept on coming down; these, however, boded us no ill, on account of the steepness of the Wall, and we regarded them merely as an *obbligato*.

It was not till we reached the terraces that winter really showed a hand. Great balconies of snow hung directly over the very line of the route; they stuck out above us far from the Wall, like swallows' nests. Surmounting these obstacles was an extremely dangerous job; for you can never judge how much weight such balconies will stand. A jutting snow-scoop ran up to the *gendarme* below the "Eight Metre Wall", obviously a very simple matter in the ordinary way. But now the wind had whipped the Face till a thick layer of snow had stuck to the Wall, and an ice-axe was called into play. Another icy, snowed-up wrinkle followed, with water pattering down as well. I had to bring up my companion's rucksack on the rope, for it was too much of an impediment for him when climbing on such overhanging stuff.

I was startled by an uncanny rushing sound. A shadow flitted across the Wall. One of the snow balconies weighing several hundredweights had sheared away above me and gone whistling by, only a hair's breadth from us.

"That was a lucky break," said Hugo. And I thought: "That might easily have wiped us out!"

We reached the hardest pitch, the notorious "Diagonal Crack", in the late afternoon. Water was pouring down here, too, but we couldn't get any wetter. The worst half of the Wall was still ahead of us. It was plain that we were not going to get through in daylight.

Gradually the sun dipped behind the Mieminger Hills. We had reached the niche below the huge roofs of the "Direct"; there we met a strong southerly wind, which immensely increased the difficulties of the climb, and the water lying on the rock had turned to a thin glaze of ice. We were being steadily numbed by the all-pervading cold; our clothes, soaked with melting snow, hardened to armour-plating. There was great danger of frostbite in the event of a bivouac.

The hundred feet above the niche were a gradually steepening snow-slope; but the snow had frozen into hard ice and was extremely difficult to grip with our climbing-boots, which were also frozen stiff. After the snow came sheer ice stretching right up to the overhangs. The transition from ice to rock and *vice versa* is always very trying and every step had to be thought out. Even here, under those enormous overhangs, where one might have thought the snow could not possibly lie, there were cornice-like banks, driven by the ferocity of the prevailing wind.

I was sixty feet away from my partner on a precarious stance, trying to bang a piton in, because the continuation looked too chancy without some protection; but all my efforts were in vain. Still, I couldn't bring Hugo up safely without some form of attachment to the rock. In the heat of the battle I had failed to notice the gradual fall of night; suddenly I realised that we had been caught by the darkness, just as I managed to get the piton into the crack, and was at last in a position to let Hugo come up and join me.

To bivouac in such a place would have been lunacy. So I promptly started climbing the icy groove overhead. Luckily, climbing in the dark was a strong point of mine. Dark overhangs loomed above me, looking more ominous than ever in the gloom; above them stretched a starless, stormy night sky. The wind grew stronger and stronger, threatening to sweep us off the Wall, fierce gusts flapped against the glazed rock; the ropes bellied out from the Wall in a great bend, frozen stiff and hardly manageable. In these exceptionally difficult conditions we dared not use more than from forty to sixty feet of rope.

Not till I had sent the ice fragments tinkling down under my hammer blows could I prospect with my finger-nails for some kind of a wrinkle. It seemed an age every time before I got a piton in; yet there wasn't really much point even when I had got it firmly fixed. We knew perfectly well that to come off here meant the end for both of us, though we didn't tell one another so; the mutual bonds of mountain-comradeship saw to that. A doubt expressed, an admission of our desperation could easily precipitate disaster; we had to convince each other somehow that we could cope with the crisis even if we thought we could not.

There was no feeling in our fingers, our toes had gone dead. We had to force our limbs back to life before each new pitch. Gloves, reposing in our trouser pockets, would have been useless here. What a good job my hands were so tough; I had been out and about without gloves the whole winter—and now it was paying off. I had also improved on that by carrying a ball of snow in my hand on most occasions, even after my fingers had gone green and blue with cold—evidently a repaying exercise.

Still no end to the Wall; still yawning black emptiness below us. I shouted into Hugo's ear:

"Lucky I remember the climb so well!"

The moon, on which we had relied, let us down utterly. We struggled up foot by foot, two minute dots on a huge, black slab on which we could see no further, but which resolutely refused to ease off. And as we went up, the Wall was plastered more and more with snow- and ice-armour. Snow slopes intervened: no skiable slopes those, but curtains of snow, almost vertical, framed by icy rock.

The most dangerous pitches of all came next. Every sinew in one's body, indeed one's whole mind and being, was stretched to the uttermost. Then, suddenly, the broad band of snow beneath the summit was there and we could breathe again, even if we still had to push on.

An amazingly steep snow-shield went straight up from here to the ridge, demanding extreme care and delicacy. It consisted of about ten feet of powdery snow, resting on a slab whose inclination was sixty degrees; not that one could see it, but I knew the supporting ground from my summer climb.

Beneath us, the face disappeared into the bottomless dark, as we set foot with somewhat mixed feelings on the snow-shield; but it went unexpectedly well. At last I could get out of my stiff slippers and into heavy climbing-boots; my numbed feet began to recapture some feeling.

At ten p.m., on January 27th, 1948, we stood on the storm-swept summit of the Schüsselkarspitze and, speechless, held out numbed hands to each other. It had taken us thirteen hours of bitter struggle not only with the Wall, but with the elements. The thought that we had to get down again robbed the triumph of all its joy; for in such conditions the ordinary way down the West Ridge would in itself be a difficult climb. But first we stilled our hunger, sitting on a partly-sheltered slab; our bread and our butter, both frozen solid, were the first morsels we had tasted since we left the Leutasch in the early dawn. A very odd "summit-hour"—at the dead of night, on a crag beset by the fury of the Föhn.

The fierce wind soon had us on the move again. We had hoped to be at the bottom once more by midnight, but the ridge soon began its pranks. On the north side it fell away in fearfully steep snow-slopes into the Oberraintal; to the south it was hung with three-foot cornices— jutting perilously over the unseen abyss. It would be fatal to step out on to such a cornice, yet there was no way of circumventing them on the northern side; places where you wouldn't need your hands in summer had been conjured into insurmountable obstacles. We had to sacrifice our few remaining pitons, in order to make progress at all.

We reached the Spindlerturm, only to be caught in a dilemma. Hugo wanted to rope down the North Face; I, unwilling to desert the ridge, wanted to go over the Tower itself. I had my own reasons for that, even if we should be exposed to the full violence of the storm. But when I looked at the Spindler Tower, it was a mass of ice and snow, its rock finely glazed. In a storm like this. . . . No, Hugo was right, there wasn't any future in it. So back to the North Face again.

To start with, there were some snow-gullies plunging downwards, but they got steeper and steeper, to break away in the end into perpendicular cliffs. To go on down that way was nothing short of suicide!

I shouted up to Hugo: "It's the Spindlerturm, after all. No way down here!" Then I climbed back to join him. Up there, the gale was howling its loudest organ notes. It fastened upon me with such force that all my desperate attempts to climb the Tower failed miserably. We were on the verge of despair. Where could we go now? We were trapped.

Then I tried to traverse the slabs of the North Wall, unprotected, to see if I could by-pass the base of the Tower and get back on to the ridge beyond it. The sheer rocks were covered with an inch of ice-glaze, and I had to use all the ice-technique at my command. I worked my way across, inch by inch, the ice-hammer in one hand, my axe in the other. Sparks flew from the rock as the axe bit into the thin cake of ice overlaying it.

My nailed boots "scratted" on hard surface below it, but I didn't know whether it was rock or ice I was on, and it was far too dark to see. Luckily, I couldn't see the gulf either, though we knew from our summer climbs, that it swept down hundreds of feet to the bottom of the peak. All the same, we were aware how dangerously poised we were.

It was even harder for Hugo in his climbing-slippers. I supported him on the rope as he knee'd and elbowed his way infinitely slowly across, finally to hang helplessly at the rope's end and swing across like a pendulum towards me. But we were back on the ridge at last, thank God!

Then suddenly we noticed something was missing. The wind had dropped, most strangely. . . . I looked at my watch; it said four a.m. Lord, where had all that time gone to?

An extraordinarily dark belt of cloud was sinking down, down, down into the Valley of the Inn. Spectral scarves of mist were wreathing about the Wetterstein's ridges. Sure as Fate, the weather was going to break and catch us up here, still a long way from the bottom of the mountain.

Half an hour later, the first flakes of snow fluttered down from the coal-black sky. The whirling flakes built up into a thick smother, which soon became a heavy blizzard. At first we paid little attention, finding it rather pleasant to feel that steady, gentle fall of soundless flakes, after the searing cold of the whistling Föhn-wind. But our quiet dream did not last long; it was all too soon a question of getting out of a raging inferno, if we were not to fall victims to its violence. Stumbling with sheer weariness, we fought to escape the venom of the elements. In no time, eighteen inches of fresh snow had fallen on the rocks, entirely altering their appearance. The merciless storm hurled whole loads of fresh snow at us, driving it into our faces. In vain did we search for the *abseil*-piton, so prominent here in summer; everything was covered in snow. In the end we wrapped the rope around a bollard and roped down, sitting in a coil of it. *Abseil*-ing may be great fun in good weather and with dry ropes; then, with the rope and our clothes frozen stiff, it was just hell, especially as we could see nothing at all through the whirling pother of flakes. After swinging backwards and forwards for a long time, I managed to find a stance just big enough for us both; but by the time Hugo reached me, the ropes had frozen so hard at the bollard above, that we couldn't get them off it.

We obviously couldn't go up again, and with great reluctance we decided to sacrifice those two 120-foot ropes; this left us only the belaying-rope, whose knots had frozen so hard we had to cut them, so we only had seventy-five feet of rope in all.

Thirty feet further down I was again looking vainly for a stance, having run out all the available rope. In the darkness I identified a projection, a rock platform, offering the only possibility. I took an outside chance and let myself down till I only held the very end of the rope in my hands, then swung across till I got a foot on to the rock. Somehow it provided sufficient purchase for me to get a lodging.

I used my last piton behind a block, which immediately broke away, to go clattering down into the depths—followed by that last piton of mine, clinking along in pursuit.

I hadn't time to warn Hugo, who was already on the way down on the rope. There we both were, utterly unprotected, hanging on the end of the rope, without the vaguest idea how to get down the last part of the Wall. If only we could see something! It might be safe to risk a jump down on to the snow below; but it might equally be twenty or 200 feet, for all we knew. In our plight we could not possibly dispense with the rope, which was our only means of assurance. We clung to it like children to their mother's skirts.

I had no sensation in my feet since leaving the summit; right up to my knees they felt like lifeless blocks of wood. The same went for Hugo, who was much worse off in his "slippers", the soles of which were by now coming off, to complicate matters. We feared the worst, for our soaked and benumbed legs were getting colder and colder every moment that we were kept immobile in our awkward position.

I searched every inch of the Wall, straining my eyes, for the possibility of another *abseil* which it must somewhere hold. Wherever I peered, I saw nothing but a holdless, snowy, icy Wall, bound into one smooth white surface as far as my eyes could see. The snow clung to the crags in a wind-driven plaster, hiding every projection, every cavity.

Was this the end, then? I turned questioningly towards Hugo and saw, to my horror, that, a yard away from me, he was hanging with his face to the smooth Wall, desperately seeking a hold. He was clutching the frozen rope with his last remnants of strength, having slid off the stance; it could only be a question of seconds, now. But I couldn't lose

---

A bastion of rock and ice, probably unrivalled in all the Alps; the buttresses of the Grandes Jorasses soaring skywards.

The impressive rock teeth of the Chamonix Aiguilles attract every true climber like a magnet. The idea of traversing them from end to end at a single attempt intrigued us. It had never been done. . . .

the partner who had shared every phase of this struggle! Somehow or other I clawed on to the ice-plastered bollard and leaned far out from it, grabbing at his rucksack: what is more, I got a hold on it and managed to pull him neatly back on to our ledge. No sooner were his feet firmly based again than his frozen gloves parted with the rope. Just in time! I looked at my friend's pale, ice-crusted face. Such moments are no times for "Thank you's", but one never forgets them as long as one lives.

It was now by common consent absolutely essential to get away from the place. In such situations one tries the impossible. Hugo stayed on the tiny knob of a platform, while I let myself down the smooth Wall, hanging only by my hands. Meanwhile he pulled the rope down and belayed it round the knob, which released me from my critical situation and enabled me to continue down on the rope. It just reached the Wangscharte Saddle.

Below the Saddle there is another steep Wall. We had to rope down more pitches, executing several daring manoeuvres as we swung across the mirror-like face, before we found another satisfactory stance. Hugo did another perilous slip on his completely disintegrated shoes and went flying past me; but I managed to hold him at the last moment, just above a precipice. Day had meanwhile dawned.

We got clear of the Wall at eight o'clock; utterly exhausted, we dragged ourselves valleywards. During a momentary lightening in the dark cloud-pack we cast a last glance back at the repellant, slabby walls of the Schüsselkarspitze, new-powdered with snow. We had been their prisoner for more than thirty hours. We knew what our fate would have been if we had let ourselves be forced into bivouacking. There was no need to put it into words.

TWENTY-FIVE SUMMITS IN
THIRTY-THREE HOURS

I WENT back again and again to the wintry Hills; they drew me irresistibly. The very breaking of a trail gave me the greatest joy; moving over the untrodden slopes, I revelled in the feeling that I was penetrating into untouched, virgin land.

Even as a boy I had, in my youthful enthusiasm, pottered up and down the ridges of Innsbruck's North Range in winter. There it was that I made my first sad acquaintance with the tricks snow can play. I remember how one day I was coming down the East Ridge of the Brandjoch alone and—with the difficulties of the ascent well behind me—paying little heed to the details of the descent. I meant to "skate" down over the hard-packed snow on my boots and to put the brake on when I reached a projecting crag; but I had failed to notice that the snow lay on an undersurface of ice. I gathered too much speed and sailed clean over the crag out on to the North Face below it, into a gully. I tried to get out of it and to arrest my swift progress. Meanwhile the heavy snow on the northern slopes had detached itself in an avalanche which moved with me, and bore me onwards. I devoted the whole of my strength—a commodity which was in short supply in those youthful days—to resisting the flood, without the slightest effect. I worked my way over the side, but the sliding mass caught hold of me again and dragged me along with it. Then I saw a precipice ahead. I braked desperately with my heels to stop my momentum, but at the next rocky projection I was sent diving into the seething mass; and this time I was hurtling valleywards head first. The precipice came nearer and nearer —another fifty yards and I had had it! The fear of death lent me superhuman strength; I paddled, swam and fought like a drowning man; somehow I managed to reach the edge of the sliding horror. Then the avalanche spewed me out.

I stood at the rim of the gully watching the hissing mass disappear below. Only its dull thunder sounded up to me. Cautiously I regained the ridge and only realised then how dangerous my little slide of a few hundred yards had been.

It is a good thing to harvest such experiences early on, provided of course one gets away with them undamaged. It is never too soon to learn the recognition and observance of the Mountain Laws. I owe it to such early experiences that I later dared to attempt

*1. As a small boy I used to look longingly up at the Northern Ranges from the
streets of Innsbruck, my home town ... it was up there that I wanted to be.*

2. The Wilde Kaiser [Kaisergebirge] – a landscape of primeval shapes. The huge wall of the Predigstuhl is seen from the Fleischbank, lifting steeply above the deep defile of the Steinerne Rinne.

3. I visited the Schüsselkarspitze in the Wetterstein Range again and again.
Everything a climber can ask for is to be found on its South Face.

4. At the heart of the wild and primitive Karwendal Range savage wall,
magnificent beyond compare goes reaching to the sky – the Lalider North Face.

5. *Firm Dolomit*
rock, rich in good
holds. Up I go; no
need for pitons he
There is nothing
than this kind of
unprotected climb
with the abyss ev
deepening below.

6. *At last t*
comes to
an im
mountain ma
Marmolata, (
of the Dolo
with her
southern wall
us. High time
to have a go
notorious bu

7. *The south Ridge of the Aiguille Noir has a height differential of 3,600 feet. The granite was marvellously firm and the ascent was a veritable joy . . . it was like a mighty staircase*

8. *We had chosen a great climb; the North Face of the Aiguille Blanche (left), menaced by its hanging glacier, a route done only once before.*

9. Our 1950 season closed with a finale worthy of a great year –
the North Face of the Western Zinne [Cima Ovest], which ranks
as one of the hardest climbs in the Dolomites.

10. The impressive rock teeth of the Chamonix Aiguilles attract every true climber like a magnet. The idea of traversing them from end to end at a single attempt intrigued us. It had never been done . . .

severe and even super-severe climbs in winter conditions and in the dark.

My inner urge to become a Guide was taking more concrete forms. I was firmly resolved not to resume my destined career as a shop assistant; nor could I permanently remain an extra hand. But the qualification for taking the Guides' examination is a good report after a two years' apprenticeship as a Porter. So I got myself a job that winter at the Glungezer Hut above Innsbruck. A porter's life is a hard one, but it has its silver lining. To be alone all day long in Nature's surroundings was my compensation for the actual heavy labour of porterage. You have to be a bit of a philosopher, though, to be satisfied with the modest pay for such hard work. No matter what the weather or the condition of the snow, I had to cover the weary way with fifty to seventy pounds on my back, often twice in a single day. And of course it was my business to break the trail.

The guests knew, of course, that the porter from the Glungezer Hut would be coming, so they waited happily till I had made a track—and, in view of the weight on my bent back, a nice deep one.

I came and went in burning heat, in Siberian cold and in hurricane-strength Föhn storms; night or day, rain or snow. I must have done that journey more than a hundred times.

In doing so I had become trained to a hair and exceptionally tough, an advantage that has remained with me to this very day. It was in fact the main reason why so exacting a job appealed to me at all.

An old, old idea of mine, which I had almost forgotten, resurrected itself. Years ago I had stood one day on the Katzenkopf near Scharnitz at the start of the Gleirschkette, with its twenty-five summits and more. It was a good thing that nothing came of a plan to attempt that *tour de force* then, for we were not yet ready for such an undertaking. But now I felt qualified for it; all I needed was a suitable partner.

Josl Knoll did not need any special form of invitation, particularly where winter problems were concerned; a telephone call could always fetch him out on any scrape. It was mid-February and the Mountains were clad in their loveliest winter raiment, heavily mantled in snow.

That day I had to tread the path once more from the Patscherkofl to the Glungezer and, of course, with an unusually heavy load, so as to work off the morrow's stint as well. I got back to Innsbruck very late in the afternoon, to find Josl ready for the trip. We took the Hungerburg Funicular, changed to the North Chain cable and an hour later we were on the Seegrube; but it was too late to catch a connection to the Hafelkar. So foot-slogging was the only way.

I pointed out across the Inn Valley and said to Josl: "Just two hours ago I was still over there!"

We went up by slopes which hordes of ski-addicts had ironed into smooth icy snow; they provided us with a pleasant ascent without any painful breaking-through. We were of course skiless, in view of our programme. We reached the Hafelkar at 7 p.m., the real pushing-off point for our "stroll". We gazed across the Gleirschtal to the end of the great Ridge, from whose spine lift twenty-five summits, each of them a climb in itself, with deep drops in between. It would offer a heavy enough programme for a day's climbing in summer, but I had no experience of it, even in summer conditions.

We had a friendly ally in the full moon, which enabled us to prolong the dwindling day. The snow on the south slopes was beautifully hard, where the night frost had solidified it; on the north side it was powdery and treacherous. It was a glorious walk and we made swift progress along the Ridge, with its pleasant ups-and-downs, high above the twinkling lights of Innsbruck.

"Perfect farming country," said Josl, who likes his little joke to hide more serious thoughts.

The descent from the Maundlspitze needed care. A steep rock-ridge led down to the Arzler Saddle and beyond it we hurried up to the Rumerspitze, which we reached at ten o'clock. Beyond it the Ridge presented continual rises and falls between the 6,600 foot and 9,000 foot levels.

From the Thaurerjoch to the Plattenspitze was a little more difficult. We left the row of little rock-towers on the right by climbing down a steep snow-slope. A tedious traverse brought us to the Stempeljoch across an unavoidable north slope, where we sank chest deep in the bottomless, floury snow.

It was the ghostly midnight hour, but there was nothing ghostly about the valley sleeping peacefully below us. The Stempeljoch Face lay ahead of us; that lovely slope on which we had so often enjoyed our down-hill ski-runs. We traversed the ski-slope and reached virgin ground again. Marvellous cornices hung like garlands between the summits; mushrooms of snow leaned against the east faces. A few stiff rock-pitches afforded the desired change and gave the necessary seasoning to the whole expedition. A broad stride took us across a notch in the ridge, where the walls fell away steeply on either side. We by-passed *gendarmes* wherever it was easiest, to right or left of the ridge. On and on we went, breaking a trail, climbing over or ploughing through the spotless snow. We were amazed at the speed of our own progress.

"If we're not careful we'll get to Scharnitz much too early," I told Josl jokingly. Well might we laugh; we didn't know then what was brewing for us.

The moon's round lamp moved steadily westwards. Far beyond the Tüxer foothills the dawn was already coming up. Once again we lived through the birth of a new day from our high perch. By sunrise we were sitting on the Kaskarspitze, enjoying the comfort of the first warm rays.

But how changed was the landscape by winter's touch! The summer-world of dead, grey rubble-cones and bare slopes had given way to smooth, dangerously steep snow-slopes. White streaks relieved the darkness of the rock-faces, outlining countless ribs and runnels. Along the crest of every ridge ran a lovely white seam of glorious corniced snow. On the north side steep, holdless precipices fell to the Hinterautal, far below; on them lay deep, bottomless drifts of powder-snow, piled by the wind. Where we found it possible, we avoided them.

The zigzag of our trail extended further and further along the ridge, ploughing deeper and deeper into the rapidly softening snow. Presently the sun's warmth changed the hard night-crust to a slobbery broth. The easy going gave way to a laborious plunging forward, sinking in at every step.

We climbed down steep gullies and traversed across exposed ledges above steep cliffs. The continued deterioration of the snow conditions forced us to keep as close as possible to the ridge; but there our way was often barred by dangerous double cornices arching out on both sides of the crest. In such places our only support was the ice-axe, and progress became slow indeed. We began to be racked by a furious thirst.

By mid-day the sun was beating down pitilessly; in the broad Kar-wendel troughs the air pulsated as in a distorting mirror. We had only added one summit to our tally since daylight came. The way seemed to stretch endlessly before us and the white top of the Katzenkopf, the last summit in the chain, the goal of our long promenade, still lay terribly far away, with all sorts of prominent upthrusts between us and it, all of which had to be crossed. Of course there were plenty of places where we could climb down off the ridge if we wanted to; but a retreat of that kind was neither to our liking nor very advisable, for the descents to the valleys were intersected by huge, craggy gullies. There was also a great risk of avalanches, unless we waited for the sun to leave the slopes.

We pressed on. We had long since given up laughing at the continual up-and-down of the ridge. Tower after tower, slope after slope, it loomed before us; and presently we were again at the rim of a deep indentation. We agreed it was about time the ridge decided to finish; but the Jägertürme with their savage clefts held us up for quite a time. The ground thereabouts was pretty mixed, with rock, snow and ice all combined; you could never tell what was hidden under those soft unstable masses. Cornices broke away, thundering down into the bowl beneath, and then we could see the brownish mass of an avalanche ebbing away.

We traversed the Jägerkarspitze, but evening was by then drawing on. Josl, normally indefatigable, was beginning to lag behind, and was following me at about a hundred yards distance. I had purposely opened up the gap, in order to spur him on to greater efforts, for we still had a long, fairly dangerous way to go.

A narrow, sheer-sided ridge, fortified with numerous turrets now lay ahead of us, without visible end—an outsize castle wall, stretching from top to top, from gap to gap. We were very tired by now, mechanically putting one foot down in front of the other, our eyes fixed on the next few yards ahead. Our eye for the beauties of the scene was sadly dimmed. Josl's leg, which he had damaged on a ski-run some time before, was hurting him. But we had to go on.

We reached the Katzenkopf at last, as the sun's red orb went down over the horizon. Then we climbed and slid the straightest possible way down the slopes, so as to get down to the valley while it was still daylight. We almost broke our necks on snowed-up larch slopes, where our feet caught in hidden roots; dreadfully slowly, we forced a laborious way down, till suddenly we found ourselves at the edge of a cliff above one of the typical ravines which bar access to the valley along the whole range.

Meanwhile darkness had fallen, so we decided to wait for the full moon.

There we sat in the tangle of larches, and very soon sleep had overcome us, for we were absolutely worn out; but the cold soon woke us up again. There was no sign of a moon until we finally made out its faint shape, almost unrecognisable in the cloud-veiled sky.

"It's an odd thing," I remarked to Josl, "but every time I go out by a full moon, the weather breaks, as if fated."

There was no point in waiting for the moon any longer; the question had become one of getting down as quickly as possible. Neither of us knew the way, and it was mainly by feel and by intuition that we moved carefully downwards—expecting at any moment to step out into space. There was no way to be found through the larches, so we tried below them, along the edge of a rock-precipice. So as to have some kind of support we felt our way from one drooping branch to the next, but nowhere could we find a way down, and though we had a rope along, we had neither pitons nor a hammer.

I tried to find a line down through a gully, belaying the rope round a boulder to protect me; all I found was a frozen waterfall. Back I came again. I tried another place—without any more success.

It looked as if we could get down using the ice-axe and crampons, but we didn't know how deep the cliff was. If we had to pull the rope down, we might never get back, and that was a risk we dared not court in these highly dangerous ravines.

I said: "It's no use, Josl, we've got to go back to where we came from—up to the ridge again, and then down over its next hump."

He agreed and offered to keep watch first, while I rested my weary bones among the larches. Truth to tell, I could no longer keep my eyes open; sleep was forcing the lids together irresistibly.

I heard my partner's voice. I was quite fuddled and wanted to be left alone to sleep. "Have I slept yet?" I asked him.

So now we had to go back, up the whole long way we had come down. On the way we even had to climb a few pitches, in total darkness, before we traversed the lateral ridge and found a clear way down lying at our feet, at last. By that time it was midnight.

Down in the Gleirschtal we luckily found a beaten trail, probably made by hunters or wood-cutters. It was just wide enough to afford progress if you put one foot straight ahead of the other—much too narrow for us in our half-bemused condition. We kept on getting off the track on one side or the other, where we immediately sank into deep snow. I went on in a daze, as if drawn forward by an invisible hand: I had long ceased to be able to recognize a track and was doing everything sub-consciously. Suddenly a voice startled me, shouting: "Hermann, what are you doing?"

I realised I had left the track and had started to go off in an entirely different direction, straight towards a ravine leading down into the stream.

"I must have been dreaming," I explained to Josl.

"It certainly looks like it," he replied.

We arrived at Scharnitz at about 3 a.m., frozen and hungry. An icy night wind was whistling through its streets. We searched everywhere for a lighted window, but nobody was awake and we found ne'er a one. So we knocked at the door of the Police Station.

"Could you please put us up?" we asked the Sergeant. "An empty cell would do."

"Sorry, I can't just lock you up like that," replied the guardian of the peace, very correctly, and showed us the door. So once again we stood like Joseph and Mary in the dark roadway, and knew not where to lay our weary limbs.

At last we found a made-up train at the station, and tried out its coaches. They were all equally uncomfortable, with cardboard instead of windows—it was 1949—and bitterly cold everywhere, but we had to put up with it. We sat down in the corner of a compartment. Our puttees were so firmly frozen to our boots that we had to cut them off with a knife; every stitch of clothing was stiff and solid. We managed to wring out our socks and stockings, till a brown soup ran on to the floor. Our only dry possession was a pair of mittens which we used instead of socks, pulling them over our bare, worn-out feet. We meant to have something to eat, but fell asleep before we could get round to it.

The bustle and speech of people woke us from our slumbers. Where on earth were we?—In the carriage, of course; it was already packed full. By a freak of luck the train was going in the right direction—to Innsbruck. I don't know what the people must have thought of our odd looks—our feet stuffed into gloves, all our wet clothes spread about on the seats, everything higgledy-piggledy. We dressed quickly and pushed everything that was scattered around into our rucksacks, unsorted. Half an hour later we were rolling homewards.

Well before noon, I was treading the familiar path again from the Patscherkofl to the Glungezer, with a barrel of raspberry syrup on my back. I kept on looking out across the Inn Valley, to where my eyes rested on the glorious range in the Karwendel to the north, of which we had done the first end-to-end winter traverse, inside thirty-three hours. It had been a tremendous test of endurance. To have seen it through was a tremendous satisfaction. And how little a barrel of raspberry syrup can weigh when you are satisfied with yourself!

THE COLD *ARÊTE*

EVERY year there is a traditional high-level ski race in the Glungezer district, called the Kreuzspitz Relay. The course runs steeply downwards from the top of the 9,000-foot Kreuzspitz, lying far back in the range and then equally steeply up again to Boscheben. From there a fierce downhill run leads to Sistrans, a village on the slope of the Patscherkofel above Innsbruck. It finishes with a ten-mile "Langlauf" stretch which circles right round the Patscherkofel from Sistrans into the Vikartal.

The chief fun of this particular race is that the teams are divided into two classes—racing teams and touring teams—and there is a prize for each stage of the relay into the bargain—a tremendous incentive. In the racing section the starters are mostly absolutely first-class men, of Olympic Games standard; the "tourists" represent the ordinary sports- and gym-clubs. My climbing club was taking part, one year; it had entered a full relay team in the touring section and in spite of my having sworn never to race on skis again, I was very soon roped in. It was a matter of the club's prestige, so I couldn't refuse. Besides, the prize was a rope, a wonderful new climbing rope.

I waited my turn to take over at the Meissner-Haus in the Vikartal. I had to cross a three-mile stretch with a climb of 1,000 feet in it. Here were the leaders tearing down the slope. There was Luis Vigl touching me off; I tore away as if shot out of a pistol. I ran as if my life depended on it, faster than ever I did in the war, when menaced by whistling bullets or bursting bombs. It took me seventeen minutes to cover my relay-stage to Boscheben, where I collapsed, gasping for breath and with a terrible stitch. But in the evening they handed me my rope: the club had done the best time in the touring class. Ever since then, I get the job of "trail-breaker" when our club goes in for ski racing.

That winter I frequently broke out of a porter's wearisome grind into the great adventure of high peaks. I had noticed, from the windows of the Glungezer Hut a certain sharp, indented and very attractive *arête*, lifting its dark streak against the background white, over there among the Kalkkögel, over by the Stubai Peaks. It was my next objective.

Once again I had worked hard to earn it; I had man-handled ample supplies for several days up to the Hut, so had no compunction in going down in the evening to the valley, where I met Josl in time for the last train at the Stubai Station. We marched off, as on all our winter expeditions, while it was still night.

This time we laboured upwards through a steep and narrow gorge. Our skis began to refuse, slipping back at every step in spite of skins, till finally we grew tired of the idiotic proceedings and shouldered the recalcitrant boards, to continue on foot, even if it meant sinking in deeper. We had to use great caution in breaking a trail up those immense slopes. Several times we were brought to a halt by the dull, terrifying roar of avalanches; but we reached the foot of the rocks which led to our *arête*—the North-East *Arête* of the Ochsenwand— in safety.

We now had to abandon our skis because the ground had become far too steep. We plunged our laborious way forward through masses of snow, but luckily it was not far to the point where the *arête* really became sheer. Not even our exertions could cancel out the biting cold, which flayed our faces. Were we really proposing to climb in such a temperature? It didn't seem to make sense. The yellow rock towered steeply before us, the *arête* surging upwards like a narrow streak; in spite of the winter's plentiful snow, it was almost clear, and only the white streaks indicating steps in the rock showed higher up in its course. We shivered from head to toe as we waited for the early-morning sun; but it was not strong enough to help much and we had to support it with some physical jerks. Finally we resorted to a real boxing match.

At last we were off. We left our rucksacks and our boots behind with the ski-sticks; then we struggled up to the foot of the climb through loose, dry grit-like snow.

I had done the climb before in summer conditions and knew it wasn't at all easy. It was in fact a genuine "Grade VI", that is, at the extreme end of the Alpine scale. No less a climber than Hias Rebitsch had made the first ascent; it had not been climbed very many times since.

The sun treated us with disdain, disappearing at once behind the edge of the *arête*, and we were left in the ice-cold shadow. As a result our spirits sank to zero, with the cold. I started climbing half-heartedly and clumsily. I didn't seem to have any zest for it to-day, but you have to ladle out what you've brewed for yourself. My gloves, useless on such miniature holds, disappeared into my trouser pocket, but my fingers were soon numb and blue. I dared not think what it would be like on the really difficult pitches higher up. I tried the time-honoured dodge of massaging my hands with snow to restore the circulation; they began to sting as I felt the blood flowing through my veins again.

This feeling of ants running about in one isn't exactly comfortable: but my fingers were soon warm enough for me to start off again.

My bare hands grubbed around in the cold powder-snow as if I were digging for buried treasure, looking for hidden holds, clinging to unseen projections. That cooled my fingers off again; so the whole performance had to be repeated, the same painful process endured till they were warm again. It was sure to happen again quite often, only it would be worse up above, where the rock was steeper and the holds smaller.

Very soon I couldn't feel my fingers at all any more, and only my eyes told me when I was gripping a wrinkle or not. I kept on stuffing one hand or the other into a pocket or into my mouth. If I met a piton or had to knock one in, the steel stuck fast to my bare skin. The cloud of breath issuing from my mouth and nose formed a thick white layer of rime on my Anorak. The continual battle with the cold, on top of all the ordinary difficulties of climbing, was exhausting to a degree.

Moving as we were on the North Wall from thirty to sixty feet from the rim of the *arête*, we could see the rays of the sun warming the rock just over there—tantalising to the sixth degree! Still, this was our choice, nobody had compelled us; so we struggled on against the cold and gravity—with such success that by the afternoon we were past the worst of the difficulties.

The Wall eased back a little, but that made way for treacherous snow again. We took a short breather, nibbled some food rather joylessly and gazed across enviously at the sunlit slopes; straight down below us, hundreds of feet, we could see our tracks leading to the foot of the climb and our skis sticking up in the snow.

January days are short and we had to hurry on.

Sheer pitches gave way to corniced terraces; it was quite a fight to force a way through the overhanging masses of snow. It looked easier out to the right and I was soon festooned in a chimney leading that way. Dusk drew down upon us once again with astonishing swiftness; how the hours had raced by—if only bivouacs passed so quickly, waiting for the morning would not be the ordeal it is. It was so dark in the chimney that very soon I couldn't distinguish the inequalities in the rock at all; on those occasions you have to replace eyesight by an equally efficient sense of touch and work your way up like an animal, alert to every danger. A contraction in the chimney drove me right out on to the wall, just where an overlapping balcony of snow barred the way. I hoped it would hold, as I very cautiously pushed upwards till I succeeded in getting my whole weight on to it and paused a moment for breath. At that very instant the whole thing collapsed under my feet. Luckily I had a good hold and was balanced again in a second, well splayed out across

the bed of the chimney, with the rope drawn taut; and there I waited
for the inevitable jerk. Josl was standing sixty feet below me, directly
below; even if the solid mass of snow didn't kill him it couldn't help
wiping him off the wall, thought I. But the jerk never came. Good, tough
old Josl—he didn't come off. I heard him grousing and swearing, but
once again disaster had been avoided. With great presence of mind, he
had been able to cover his head with his rucksack in one lightning-
swift movement before the clutter of snow hit him a heavy blow.

It had meanwhile become pitch-dark, and the rock was promptly
covered with a thin veneer of ice. Every hand- and foot-hold had to be
carefully felt over: the best of them were already under the glaze and
we had to do the best we could with what was left.

There was a ledge above me; the last five feet up to it were fearfully
exhausting. It was like climbing up the snow-covered roof of a Gothic
church. Loose, powdery snow rippled down over the ledge, ran through
my hands and disappeared silently into the depths.

I heard swear-words coming up from Josl, who was not in the least
pleased at receiving these deliveries on his head. I said: "Send me up
a broom, then I'll sweep the whole lot down at one go!"

My arms disappeared up to the elbows in snow, as I searched for
grips. My feet clawed at the vertical wall, trying to get an outward-
turned grip on anything free of ice. At last, very carefully, I managed
to lever the upper part of my body over the ledge, with my feet feeling
their way after it. Then at last I had something firm to stand on, and
I could rescue Josl from his uncomfortable situation. Little by little I
eased the rope in; I could not see him until he appeared directly below
me, a dark shadow etched against the snow-streaked wall.

Steep, snow-lined gullies led on upwards, to a light-coloured platform
which stood out from the surrounding blackness. We could now find
a use for gloves again. We tore a way upwards like snow-ploughs, with
only an occasional pitch to bar the way. The *arête* gradually merged
into the ridge formation. The sky had meanwhile become overcast and
a strong wind met us on the actual ridge, which runs up with its
numerous *gendarmes* to the summit of the Gross Ochsenhorn. Wherever
possible we turned the towers, traversing their bases, letting the rope
run for our greater comfort now on their right now on their left hand
side.

We didn't bother to walk up the last steps to the summit, whose
white shield of snow we could just make out in the darkness. We went
straight down from a col, sliding down to the depths, sinking almost to
our necks in deep snow; then, traversing to the right on exposed ledges
in the steep walls to the gap between the Kleine and the Grosse Ochsen-

wand. Here the face was swept clean of snow by the wind. The débris, frozen firm and covered by a glassy sheet of ice, spelled heightened danger to us in our slippers. The rope ran taut above the dark abyss, with nowhere a belay to safeguard us. We needed no great imaginative powers to picture our joint flight through thin air if either of us so much as slipped. The wind had risen to gale force, whipping fiercely at the ropes, which bellied out almost horizontally. With the blood well-nigh frozen in our veins, we fought our way on downwards.

We reached the gap and moved on down a snow gully which punished us severely: then we had to traverse more steep slopes below the northern precipices of the Grosse Ochsenwand. We reached the foot of the North-East *Arête*, sweeping like a dark menace straight as a lath into the dark, stormy night sky.

Two hours later we rang the bell at the door of the Schlickeralm. Mine host, who opened it, bemused with sleep, was horrified at our appearance, and asked us where on earth we came from. No wonder he didn't like the look of us—we must have been a fearful sight, covered in snow, which clung to every fold of our clothing, like a pair of "Abominable Snowmen". We couldn't help laughing at ourselves when we realised what we looked like.

After a short sleep we ran down on our skis very early in the morning to the station at Fulpmes. Josl had to be punctually at his morning work, and I had also a job to attend to.

Up and up I went in the car of the Patscherkofl cable railway. None of my fellow passengers could possibly guess that the porter from the Glungezer Hut had spent the night over there—up in the terrible black precipice of the Kalkkögel, up on that knife edge, cutting sheer and menacing into the stormy sky. So much the better!

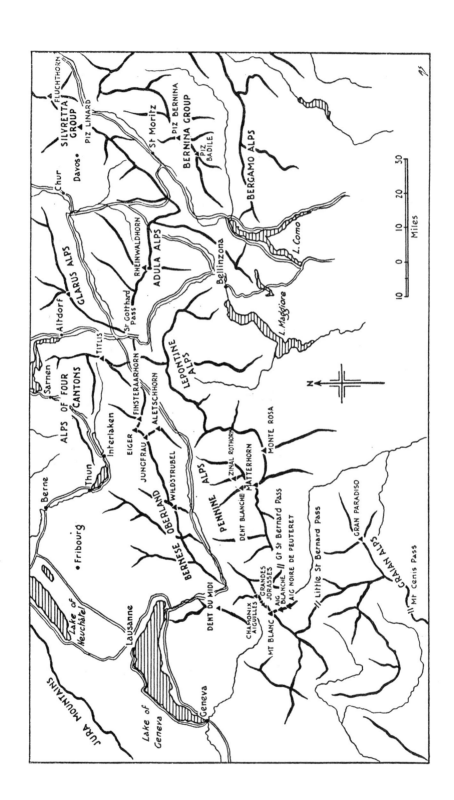

JURA MOUNTAINS

Lake of
Neuchâtel

• Fribourg

Berne

Thun

Interlaken

Sarnen

ALPS OF FOUR
CANTONS

Altdorf

GLARUS ALPS

Chur

Davos •

PIZ LINARD

SILVRETTA
GROUP

FLUCHTHORN

St Moritz

PIZ BERNINA

BERNINA GROUP

PIZ
BADILE

BERGAMO ALPS

L. Como

L. Maggiore

Bellinzona

LEPONTINE
ALPS

ADULA ALPS

RHEINWALDHORN

St Gotthard
Pass

TITLIS

FINSTERAARHORN

ALETSCHHORN

EIGER

JUNGFRAU

BERNESE OBERLAND

WILDSTRUBEL

ZINAL ROTHORN

MATTERHORN

MONTE ROSA

PENNINE ALPS

DENT BLANCHE

Gt St Bernard Pass

AIG NOIRE DE PEUTERET

Little St Bernard Pass

GRAN PARADISO

GRAIAN ALPS

Mt Cenis Pass

AIG
BLANCHE

MT BLANC

GRANDES
JORASSES

CHAMONIX
AIGUILLES

DENT DU MIDI

Lausanne

Lake of
Geneva

Geneva

N

0   10   20   50

Miles

10

IN THE ICE OF THE
WESTERN ALPS

THE WALL OF ICE AND GRIT

THE Western Alps—what stories I have heard of them! Tales of their 3,000-foot walls and their huge ice-slopes which allow of no return and no escape; of their hanging-glaciers lurking in wait, like over-ripe grapes, for some ridiculous dwarf of a man to stick out his neck below. They had told me stories of falling ice, of long hauls up to the Huts, of bivouacs and endless traverses under the crushing load of enormous rucksacks; of unimaginable ice-falls; of blizzards, fog and exhaustion— to say nothing of mountain-sickness. My lively imagination had no doubt exaggerated it all into something far worse than it really was; but I had long desired most passionately to get to grips with that reality. When would my dream come true, I wondered? It wasn't any longer a question of fitness, but simply of money. . . .

I had taken a special course in ice-work and learned from it how to go about expertly on crampons, how to use an axe and how to drive the long ice-pitons into the tough substance. I learned how to "winkle" holds and cut steps of the standard demanded by the conditions ruling in the Western Alps. I learned, too, why sometimes a piton driven into soft ice under the heat of the sun can be easily withdrawn by hand while on another occasion of great cold, or in deep shadow, the steel shaft, six to ten inches long, freezes in so firmly in the space of minutes that you have to hack away with your axe to the very tip of the piton before you can retrieve it from the ice.

In short, I could already claim to be experienced in ice-technique. I had realised that you have to use the same methods as on rock. Ice also boasts its cracks, chimneys, rope-work and traverses. But you had to take care to wear gloves even in the warmest weather, and to choose clothing essentially fitted for winter climbing. You can't take liberties with ice!

I had already been tested on ice on the North Wall of the Hochfeiler and the North-West of the Möseler, in the hot, dry summer of 1947. The ice at the time was polished as a mirror and hard as glass, so that the points of your crampons could hardly get a purchase on it. In spite of that, we dispensed everywhere with step-cutting. I soon had a nice object-lesson in the special dangers to be met. We were caught by a stone-fall; whole avalanches of them came hurtling down and hit the hard ice by which we were surrounded. Still, we safely disposed of the precipices of the Zillertal Alps and I had made myself at home on the steep ice of the Kaunergrat. When were we youngsters going to get our chance to prove ourselves in the Western Alps?

Then came the summer of 1948. . . . One day an invitation to visit Chamonix lay on the table; we could hardly believe it. It was like an outsize Christmas present and I thought I was the luckiest creature on earth. I imagined myself in the most extraordinary situations and began dreaming about it all at night. But I also knew that the moment had suddenly come for me to show—at long last—what I could do. "It's up to you now, Hermann," I thought.

That invitation from the *École Nationale*, the Chamonix Climbing School, ensured our getting passports and visas. The Austrian Alpine Club made us an allowance to help pay for our visit. When everything seemed settled, we met with a snag at the very last moment—the weather. It had snowed below the 10,000-foot level and now, in mid-summer, even the Wetterstein and Kaiser climbs had taken on the character of winter expeditions. It seemed absolutely useless to travel all the way to Mont Blanc in such conditions, though Luis Vigl and I naturally begged the question quite firmly: but the older and experienced members of the party, Erwin Schneider, the Himalayan expert, and Hias Rebitsch, the acknowledged master, had grounds for their doubts. They knew the Western Alps and their vagaries well enough. In weather like this we should just sit around in the valley. What sense was there in that?

But in the middle of July it was decided to travel all the same. We felt as if the whole of Innsbruck must know we were going; and some of our club-mates did, in fact, come to see us off. What a moment that was at the station!

We really were off to the Western Alps; it was an inexpressible thrill. Just to be travelling through my dreamland of Switzerland was enough —for years, when anybody breathed the name, I had immediately thought of the Matterhorn and those big slabs of chocolate.

We passed through Zürich and Berne; then on through the vineyards sloping down to the Lake of Geneva's lovely blue mirror, set in its wide basin. Sailing boats were moving on its calm waters. We came to Geneva, home of the Red Cross and the United Nations. We lugged our heavy packs from car to car, train to train—a typical West Alpine haulage operation.

We drove towards the Mountains through gorge-like valleys with creamy waterfalls dusting down from high above. This was France now. I could hardly believe we were approaching Mont Blanc itself. The very name was fascinating and represented for me the ultimate in High Mountain grandeur, with its peaks, the fierce shape of which is

nowhere rivalled in the Alps. I had browsed through the whole literature, pored over all the maps, till I knew every climb in the group, at
least theoretically. And now we novices were having our initiation into
this greatest and grandest of all Alpine groups. . . .

At Saint Germain our route curved to the left into the Valley of the
Arve. The air hereabouts ought by all the rules to have had a genuine
snow-scent. We pushed our noses out of the window only to get them
wet. It was raining—a thoroughly disappointing reception.

We man-handled our heavy luggage to Les Praz through the puddles,
to receive the friendliest of welcomes. Erwin, knowing the ropes, introduced us—"Monsieur Vigl—Monsieur Buhl!" Rebitsch needed no
introduction; he was already greeting our host with a *"Bon jour,*
Monsieur Franco!"

Our amiable host at once invited us to have a good chat. Luis and I,
the new boys, whose French extended to *"Oui"* and *"Non"*, didn't take
a great part in it; the other two talked all the more, to balance that.
I was mainly interested in the huge pictures on the wall—the Grandes
Jorasses, the Aiguille du Triolet, the Droites and other great peaks.
We were told that conditions were as bad as they could be, with fresh
snow newly fallen down to 10,000 feet and not a hope of any big climb
as a result. A party had come to grief on the Verte, because of the
wintry conditions. I was bitterly disappointed when I thought of the
Buttress of the Jorasses, which we had secretly decided to make our
main objective.

Next morning the sun was shining into our room. It was a glorious
day. The peaks were all powdered with fresh snow—and all the more
enchanting for that. The Dru, that slender, giant's tooth, shot up to
the sky like a white obelisk. There stood all the famous Chamonix
Needles—it was impossible to say which was the more wonderful, so
magnificently sharp was the challenge of that back-cloth of perilous,
fantastic towers. There were the Grands Charmoz, showing an enormous
black North Face, pitted and scarred by falling stones; the Plan, with
a hanging-glacier tumbling vertically from its summit comb down its
rock-wall; and the neighbouring Aiguille du Midi, a magnificent sweep
of ice. Above them all lifted the lofty, glittering snow-dome of Mont
Blanc itself, the Monarch of them all. Tremendous glacier-streams
poured from its very summit deep down into the valley, pushing right
down to the edge of the woods, their tongues licking the flowery
meadows on its slopes. I hadn't expected such a vision of glory—far
surpassing my most imaginative flights of fancy.

We left Chamonix at noon and took the cog-wheel railway up to
Montenvers, more than 6,000 feet above sea level. There we caught our

first glimpse of the Jorasses, arrayed like stately queens in their wintry robes, with the Mer de Glace curving from their feet down towards the valley. A short visit to that great river of ice gave me some comprehension of the immense scale of this overpowering scene and at the same time afforded a first good look at the field of our coming operations.

Next morning we got our first lesson in how short the nights have to be in the Western Alps. We were already groping round by candlelight at 2 a.m. Not long afterwards we were finding our way by electric torches outside. Not a mouse stirred at the Montenvers, where in the daytime whole hordes of people mill around.

We made our way along the lateral moraine of the Mer de Glace, over slabs, débris, and great boulders, then up steep slopes, in the first grey morning light, till a small glacier-crossing brought us to the foot of the North Face of the Grands Charmoz—our climb for the day. Every now and then a stone-fall echoed round the walls, a minatory voice, the speech of the mountains. Overhead ran the grey outlines of an immense smooth wall, shot through with white veins. The nearer we got to it, the more it leaned back.

It had looked very different yesterday from the Montenvers— terrifyingly steep and unapproachable. Then we had not been at all surprised that the route up that gigantic wall had only been repeated once, and otherwise shunned by climbers. A belt of ice half-way up turns it into a mixed rock-and-ice climb of the first order, indeed into one of the most dangerous in the Alps. Welzenbach and Merkl were the first to get up it in a desperate climb in 1931; Anderl Heckmair added the direct finish later on.

Erwin didn't come with us on this occasion, but the very presence of so experienced a climber—one of the most successful mountaineers of all time—was of incalculable value to us, for he knew the Mont Blanc Group as he knew the palm of his own hand. If he recommended a climb to us, we need have no qualms.

The wall started up without any preliminaries. Its lower part is only moderately steep and we climbed independently, not bothering to get the rope out of the rucksack; each took his own line up the rock. A waterfall flowing down from the snow-field debouched at the only place we could cross it.

Presently things got more difficult. The strata sloped outwards and the rock was highly polished by the action of water and falling stones. Every projection had a fine layer of rubble on it. We two youngsters thought it disgusting and were very disappointed with the climb, so far.

By noon almost half the face lay below us, and we had reached the lower rim of the ice-field. A few single stones came down, but they didn't menace us at all; they travelled down in the bed of a deep secondary gully. We stamped our way upwards in the soft snow of the moderately steep slope; but the angle stiffened gradually and the snow covering thinned out till we were moving on polished ice.

We traversed to the right across the steepening slope, with the snow-field looking almost flat below us; and above us black, almost vertical columns of ice, going right up to the Summit Gully.

We were on smooth, black water-ice. It was a most uncomfortable feeling to be anchored on that brittle substance by nothing but the front points of our crampons, not knowing at what moment that basis, covered by a gossamer-thin layer of hard rubble, would choose to break away suddenly. We dug our crampons in more firmly than ever, as if the idea was to cut right through the ice layer. Occasionally one of us slipped an inch or two and our hearts went into our mouths. Our calf muscles ached from overloading and excessive tension.

Only the very point of the ice axe scratched the surface. Its only use now was as a balancer to keep one upright; we no longer had any impression of being firmly in contact with the face, nor of making any progress at all—rather did we seem to be for ever standing in the same place. The only gauge of upward motion was the cry of: "No more rope!" from the next man on the rope below me, every hundred feet. It would be bliss to have something firm under one's hands again.

I took a line towards the rock bordering the ice gully, counting the yards as I moved forward. It was a great relief to be able to see it actually drawing nearer.

Luis, unlike me, seemed to feel pretty much at home in these conditions. I looked at his strong legs a little enviously: they were his particular pride and I couldn't help thinking how much more pleasant ice work must be on such massive supports.

We kept on changing the lead, to give each man fair shares. I purposely cheated mildly by moving forward a little too soon, before the rope tightened. With a few swift blows I cut a stance for my feet; my axe quivered and almost bounced off the tough ice, and ice splinters flew into my face. In went an ice-piton, with a couple of hard blows from the hammer, and I was glad to hear the carabiner click in, ensuring my position.

We were halted right on the traverse below the Summit Gully. Hias and I were at its extreme ends, Luis half-way across. Suddenly the air vibrated with a horrid whizzing sound—the noise of a stonefall, but even more unpleasant than usual; a moment later we could see a huge slab coming down. It came racing straight at us, up-ended like a mill-wheel, rolling and bouncing at a terrific pace, close to the surface of the

ice. Its roar grew more fearsome as it came. There we stood, absolutely
unprotected, on the open expanse of ice; something was bound to happen
this time! It was agonizing. . . . We let the rope go loose, so that if the
thing hit it, there would be enough slack to prevent our being hurled
from our steps. We crouched there, ready to jump aside, if possible,
at the last moment—but where was there to jump to?

Luis seemed to have been singled out as the victim, for the slab was
coming straight at him; it struck the ice just above him and, as he
flattened himself against the surface with a lightning movement, sailed
out clean over him. Its shadow flitted past; there was a dreadful rumbling
sound; but the rope still hung loose, as the block—weighing several
hundredweight—went out of sight below us and everything was still
once again.

We hurried out of the line of fire of this deadly artillery and kept
close to the right-hand margin of the ice. It was even tougher and
steeper there, spread over the rock in the thinnest of glazes. I was glad
to hand over the lead to Luis.

We only noticed then that the sky had filled with threatening clouds,
and the wind was rising. Gradually we realised that Hias's forecast was
coming true. Down there on the snow-field Luis and I had been sure
that it would take only a few hours to reach the top; but Hias had just
smiled and said: "We'll be lucky if we get off the face by evening."

The angle was just incredible. Our chests were touching the ice and
our knees kept on getting in the way. And it got still steeper, overhead.

Luis was going up with uncanny assurance. We had now reached the
point where we could take Welzenbach's route, away to the North-East
Ridge on the right. Its icy slabs, however, had no appeal for us and,
as conditions were equally bad everywhere, we decided we might just
as well follow Heckmair's "direct" to the summit. (It was hereabouts
that, seventeen years ago, Welzenbach and Merkl, on the first ascent,
had been caught for four days in a storm.)

"Sooner them than me," said Luis, when I told him about it, next
time we changed the lead. It was where rock began again and I didn't
mind taking over, for I prefer mixed work.

Narrow bands of ice and steep rock pitches alternated. I tried to
avoid the ice, for I had taken off my crampons and was levering myself
up from one rocky projection to the next. Ice plastered the vertical
stones and hung in the cracks, holding the disintegrating rock together.
Even Hias was moved to counsel great care on such an angle of inclination.

I caught sight of my boots while I was looking for a foothold, and felt
almost sorry for them. Their jaws gaped as if they were starving, their

soles hung down and my soaked, threadbare socks showed through the holes; but they had to see it through. I heard Hias mutter: "Thoroughly suitable rigout for the Western Alps!"

We began to move simultaneously at places, to speed things up. It was getting late and this was no place for a bivouac. We simply had to get to the top!

The rock now became terribly brittle. The only thing that kept the tottering masonry of this vertical rubble heap together was the frost that enveloped it. Solid pillars of rock stuck to the ice and huge growths of ice clung to the loose, crumbling rock. We had to manipulate the rope very carefully so as not to upset the balance of any of these swaying shapes. Before he could do anything about it, Hias loosened a block the size of a table, but managed to hold it balanced. Obviously that couldn't last long. Luis was standing directly below him, in the line it was bound to take when it fell. Hias couldn't move from where he was without letting the lethal boulder fall. Fortunately he had a sling with him and so managed—by a chance as happy as it was odd—to tie the stone to firm rock and then to move carefully forward. We knew from a loud crash when Luis had surmounted the obstacle and untied the sling; then we watched the boulder go bounding down its long flight into the cauldron below.

We came to snow again, a cheering sign that we must be getting somewhere near the finish; it got deeper and deeper. At our feet the wall fell 3,500 feet into the nothingness. Dusk was upon us as Hias led the last rope-lengths to the Summit Ridge. and in the last dying light we stood on the col just below the Summit of the Grands Charmoz. We were beyond speech—only glad that we were off that gigantic wall at long last.

To descend at such a late hour was out of the question, so we looked for a sheltered corner and, since there was some danger from lightning, we parked all our ironmongery some way off in a gully. The sky was ominously black; the mists were already enveloping us and, in order to escape from the imminent bad weather, we soon dived under Erwin's well-tried bivouac sack. Our clothes were soaked with water, snow and ice, but we felt nice and sheltered, and happy no longer to be imprisoned on the wall. The rain began to drum heavily on our roof.

"Worth a lot—a sack like this," said Hias, comfortably. But Luis complained of the wet, till we laughed at him. "You're inventing things!" we taunted him. Soon, however, Hias and I also noticed something wet running down our back, and we didn't take long to solve the mystery: the bivouac sack was absolutely porous, the proofing had gone altogether and it let water in everywhere.

"A nice sieve Erwin's sent along with us," we grumbled. "He'll have to pay for this," we agreed.

After midnight the rain turned to snow. Water continued to stream down our bodies and collected in our boots. How we longed to have Erwin with us; if only he were sitting next to us in his marvellous old Zdarsky sack!

Towards dawn it stopped snowing and became bitterly cold. Hias just sat there like a statue, with his hat well down over his face, quite expressionless. Luis and I were astonished by such peaceful relaxation and control; we were hardly able to sit still any more and kept on shifting about on our hard support. Finally we couldn't bear it any longer. We kept on sliding down the sloping platform till we finished up by dangling on the rope.

As the grey morning arrived, a terrific storm struck the Jorasses.

Clouds blotted out their entire North Wall for an hour, then cleared away to reveal a complete transformation—a winter landscape. Nothing to be done over there, this trip!

At last it was daylight. Stiff in every limb, we got up; at first we had to cling to the rock, for we couldn't stand up straight. We were giddy, almost as if we were drunk. As a result of the cold and the damp, we had cramp in every limb; it took a long spell of massage and muscle exercises to get us fit again.

Our equipment was frozen stiff; the ropes were like wires and refused to be stowed in the rucksack. There was fine grit off the wall in all our clothes and even in our food; grit on our fingers, grit in our teeth which grated as we ate. A careless movement toppled my rucksack over the edge, never to be seen again; or rather, to be seen once again far down the East Face, to disappear for ever from our view.

Stiffly and clumsily we climbed the Summit close at hand; it was not till we were well on the way down that our frozen joints began to come undone.

We stopped on a moraine above Montenvers and spread our things out to dry among the rugged boulders.

As we sat there Erwin came towards us.

"Well, how goes it?" he asked. "Surely you didn't get wet?"

Hias didn't bat an eyelid as he answered: "Look, Erwin, next time you needn't give us a sack one can't fold up because the air refuses to be squeezed out of it. They don't need to be as impenetrable as all that!"

THE NORTH WALL OF THE TRIOLET

WE were up at Montenvers quite often during the next days, but it was always misty or raining. We had long ago resigned ourselves to the filthy weather and didn't consider it normal if we got home dry from a climb.

We traversed the Grépon in a cloud-burst, followed by a blizzard. We went up by the West Face, climbing its polished cracks or roping down on frozen ropes, while a stiff wind blew fine needles of ice horizontally into our faces across its turrets and cols. On its steep rock *arêtes* the storm whistled about our ears and tugged our ropes out into space. At one point Luis went down a smooth crack in the rock and invited me to follow; it was only when we were both down that we discovered that there was no way on in that direction. There we were stuck in a smooth shaft, narrowing towards the top—a proper mousetrap.

"Now we're caught," I told Luis. "You might have had a decent look round before letting yourself down!"

I tried to push my way up the shaft again inch by inch, wriggling like a snake, performing extraordinary acrobatic contortions. Just when I thought I had got somewhere, I slipped back, every time. The chimney narrowed till you couldn't turn your head in it. By the time my fearful exertions ensured an escape through the aperture at the top, I was soaked with sweat and drenched by the weather.

On another occasion we climbed up towards the 3,000-foot high precipices of the East Face of the Grands Charmoz, looking in vain for my lost rucksack, while once again the sluices of Heaven were opened on our heels.

Things had quietened down at Montenvers. The endless stream of people, who are usually decanted there by the train, had dried up. Only a few optimists leaned on the balustrade of the terrace, staring out into the unvarying greyness. In vain did the Guides wait for newcomers with whom they might make arrangements for when the weather improved. The few people who hadn't gone home spent this rain-ruined time in Chamonix, where people live the strangest kind of life—the life of a great city—and every language in the world can be heard.

We sat with the "Aces" of the French climbing *élite* and listened to them, so far as our slight acquaintance with the language permitted, as they recalled many a great adventure. Luis was deep in an English conversation about the North Wall of the Eiger with Lachenal, who had recently made the third successful attempt with his countryman Lionel Terray. Lachenal was telling him about the difficulties and dangers, about a thunderstorm and about getting lost on that enormous wall. I kept on catching his "Terrible!" Luis was answering like an echo: "Beautiful! Really, very beautiful!"

The Clerk of the Weather was still against us. The mountains were wrapped in thick cloud and the rain never ceased to whip the windows of our shelter.

Then at last the sun we yearned for broke through, and revealed the Turrets and Needles of Mont Blanc shining in a glittering raiment of new snow! Lovely to look at, but not exactly desirable for the work in hand. Rock climbs were out of the question, so we had to think about a climb on ice. There was a picture on the wall of the *École Nationale*; it was of a magnificent ice face, the North Wall of the Triolet. We decided to tackle that. The mid-day train on the little Valley Railway took us to the foot of the wild, picturesque basin of the Glacier d'Argentière, whose retaining walls shot up more than 3,000 feet overhead. Half an hour on into the lateral cleft we came to the tongue of the glacier, which projects its ice masses far into the main valley, down to about 4,000 feet above sea level. We threaded our way up the endless hairpins of that Lognan path; the glacier plunging steeply down to our left was a wonderful sight, with blue-green ice glimmering through the darkness of the dense pine forest. It was very sultry and the weather looked unreliable. Just as we set foot on the upper level of the glacier, where we ought to have got our first glimpse of the chain of north walls, the veils of the clouds settled across their precipices. After walking for eight hours we reached the Argentière Hut and turned in almost at once, for we had to be up early in the morning.

It was another fine morning. The sky lay over the huge array of peaks like a starry cloak as, at about two o'clock, we moved across the almost level glacier towards the foot of our wall. Overhead the menacing barrier of the great northern ramparts of the Triolet, Courtes, Droites and the Aiguille Verte towered into the night sky. Everything was unnaturally quiet. Was this the calm before the storm? What, we wondered, would the next few hours hold for us?

By the first grey dawn light we were already at grips with our mountain. The sun shone fiery-red. Light scarves of mist swathed the sky and a much-too-warm wind was blowing down from the ridges. Was this all a pointer to one of Mont Blanc's typical sudden weather upsets, so dreaded by all climbers? We moved on up the ice wall. The clouds drooped on to the Peaks and in a trice we were swallowed up in a grey gloom. We held a long parley. Our urge to climb that wall was too strong for us to give it up altogether; but common sense won the day thus far. We decided to turn back, and reached the hut just as a snow-storm started; rightly, so it proved, for the bad weather raged without a break for the rest of the day.

Next morning at four we were back at the base of the Triolet Wall. This time there were six inches of snow on the glacier, but the Face itself glittered in bare ice. We must succeed this time!

We worked up to the first *bergschrund* over a huge avalanche cone which had appeared overnight, and crossed the chasm much more easily than on the previous day, for so much snow had slid down that it almost bridged it. We saved our energy by frequent changes of the lead; crossing, by means of slender bridges, two further *bergschrunds*, which cut across the precipice. Not till then did the wall really build up steeply; but hard streaks of frozen snow made for rapid progress, as we steered a course for a rock outcrop in the middle of the face, just below the mighty *séracs*—fantastic ice towers these!

Small wonder that we were out of breath, for we moved two to three hundred feet upwards without a break, at a considerable pace, so as to get away from below that threatening balcony of ice, which might easily collapse at any moment. Pretty exhausting work, that! The next lead was just right for Luis, our ice expert; we had to get across to a parallel rib, separated from us by a kind of hose-like ice runnel which carried away the melts from another belt of *séracs* above us. The ice here was as tough as steel, and cutting steps in it was a tiring job; but my friend got the better of a hundred feet of it, and I was glad to hear his summons to follow him up.

Narrow bands of hard snow took us up more quickly again. Luckily there were no falls of ice or rock; only a few baby avalanches of fresh snow trickled down on us like silver snakes and powdered us with white. As the angle steepened, the snow ribs grew narrower and less thick, till we were finally on bare ice. Up till now the inclination had been about sixty degrees, already fairly steep for an ice wall; but now things really began in earnest. The Face banked up, immense and steep above us. Every yard the ice grew steeper and more dangerous. We kept on changing the lead more frequently, for there were more and more steps to be cut. Our calf muscles ached to breaking point.

We were faced with two choices: on our left a narrow, terribly steep gutter ran upwards between the *séracs* and the rocks; we assessed its angle at seventy degrees at the steepest points. Lachenal and Contamin had gone that way before us. But on our right we could work straight up between the icefalls, and we decided it looked the better way. It only looked a bit questionable as far as the Ice Towers; after that it seemed to go on nicely, except for a few interruptions. Let's go up to it, then: "Well begun's half done!"

Luis started on the traverse, cutting steps at his furthest arm's reach, then balancing from one to the other on the two front points of his crampons. A few pitons in between gave him a surer footing, but the rope wasn't long enough for the whole traverse. Safely held by one piton he brought me along after him, first testing the steel shaft, frozen into its bedding, a second time for safety's sake. Even so, it was a pretty chancy protection, and we knew neither of us could countenance a slip here.

I climbed gingerly past Luis and took the lead again for the next rope's length. The sheerness of the wall pushed my body so far out that I could only keep my balance by using hand-holds. Every blow of the axe brought away whole slabs of ice, and my crampons only bit an inch or two into the brittle glassy surface. The exposure was appalling. True, we were not moving on overhangs like on a wall in the Dolomites, but this was in a way more discomforting. Only a few feet under us the ice curved over into a sheer drop, to reappear again far, far below.

The top surface now began to be soft and wet, and our axes kept on going through into hollows. A vertical sixty-foot ice chimney followed, but proved easily negotiable by straddling it and jamming one's axe as a support. We felt sure the angle must ease sensibly very soon now, and allow us to find a much needed resting-place; but still the face went on up above us at an average slant of sixty degrees.

At last we came out into sunshine. The cold had been a severe drawback all day, and we had lost all sensation in our toes. We were also feeling the altitude and were getting very tired. Above the belt of *séracs* we took a short rest and had our first nibble since breakfast. On either hand unbroken precipices of rock and ice fell steeply all the way to the Upper Argentière Glacier. Opposite stood the grim, dark face of Mont Dolent, where the frontiers of Switzerland, Italy and France meet.

There were about a thousand feet more to the Ridge. Here there were more snow-ribs to make the going easier. We were moving much more slowly now, but the glistening band which separated us from the Ridge narrowed rapidly.

At one o'clock we reached more level ground, though a sheer wall fell away on either side of it. Delicate clusters of cotton-wool hung from the mountain sides. Not knowing very much about the descent, we decided to forego the Triolet's Summit and content ourselves with the Petites Aiguilles de Triolet which, after all, stand very nearly 13,000 feet high. And, in any case, we had climbed that fearsome, gigantic face. Tatters of cloud were racing up and clinging softly to peak and ridge, enjoining us to go down. Fortunately they lifted for a moment to grant us a quick look down into the depths, otherwise we might easily have finished up on Italian territory. A little way down, we enjoyed a hard-earned rest on a little snow plateau; the afternoon sun began to suck the mists upwards, and soon they had all dissipated.

No words can describe the glory of the mountain scene before our eyes. It was an ample reward for our perilous approach. The Triolets are peaks of middle height and their central position assures an exceptional prospect into the heart of Mont Blanc's incomparable world of mountains. To the left lifted the shining dome of the Monarch himself, displaying the icy Brenva Face and the profile of the deeply indented Peuteret Ridge. Almost close enough to touch loomed the gigantic black rampart of the Jorasses, the most imposing mountain shape in the Group; below us, beyond the Mer de Glace, a row of teeth and spires, multiform and varied, the Chamonix Aiguilles, their dark granite rising in savage contrast from the white of glacier and snow-fields. It was certainly the finest summit-hour I had yet been privileged to enjoy.

We had to tear ourselves away. One last look down the abysmal depths of the face from which we had only emerged so short a time before, and it was time to take our leave.

We went down the steep, crevassed Triolet Glacier, wading rather than walking. The sun blazed down on us without mercy, transforming the snow to a slithery mass, till we were frequently ankle-deep in cold, melting ice water.

We hastened madly across the Mer de Glace so as to be in time to catch the mountain train down to Chamonix.

We only discovered from the admiring remarks of our French friends that this 3,000-foot wall of ice is counted as one of the most difficult in all the Alps, and that only four ropes had ever climbed it before us. We were very proud to hear it.

Unluckily, the end of our leave was at hand, all too short in the shocking weather conditions. The next day was overcast again; the snow-line had come right down into the valley. There was snow lining the permanent way as the train took us down towards the Lowlands. It was the beginning of August, but it felt like winter.

ONLY EIGHT HOURS—BUT PRODUCTIVE!

It was autumn in the Wilde Kaiser; another mountain summer was on its way out—always a sad moment. We had seen and accomplished much on faces higher and steeper than those overlooking the Steinerne Rinne. Of course they don't match up to the Dolomites or the Western Alps—but at the end of a season our Homeland Mountains of the north-west still stand as high as they did at the beginning. The look of the Wilde Kaiser alone was sufficient—so familiar and yet ever revealing new beauties, so savage and yet so friendly. Like pieces of stage scenery, the separate combs and ridges stand there in their well-known order: Lärcheck, Mitterkaiser, Predigstuhl, the buttress of the Fleischbank and, further on still, the Totenkirschl. And down below them the leafy woods in a blaze of autumn colour, with the pale grey limestone gleaming through. Home, sweet home!

All the same—I wasn't quite so much at home in the Kaiser as all that. At least not in the eyes of fervent local patriots from Kufstein, Kitzbühel and St. Johann. Coming from Innsbruck I was already half a "foreigner" and it is always a good thing for one's self-confidence if an immigrant of that kind bumps his head against one's own local mountains.

One afternoon, when Rudi Seiwald and I reached the Hut on the Stripsenjoch, the assembled body of Kaiser experts would leave us no peace. In the friendliest way they showed their concern about our arriving "out of condition". "He who rests, rusts, you know; you don't want to rust, Hermann, do you?—No? Then don't waste a moment but have a go at the 'Fiechtl-U' this very minute!"

A hand-hold had broken away on it; quite a small wrinkle but in a decisive place. Now that it was missing, there was quite a good chance of coming off; what rollicking fun for the elect of the Kaiser Circle to see someone fall off it—Hermann Buhl, for instance. Then my friend Rudi, though in a very different sense, joined the ranks of the prospective audience: "You'll do it easily," he said. "You just show them!"

O Vanity, Vanity! Of course I went off to the "Fiechtl-U"—not, obviously, with the idea of falling off, but of showing them how not to!

A word of explanation seems necessary. There are, in an otherwise unimportant vertical—or slightly overhanging—cliff near the base of the Totenkirchl, within shouting distance of the Stripsenjoch, two U-shaped cracks: these are the "Fiechtl-U" and the "Dülfer-U" respectively.

That famous Guide, Fiechtl, and Hans Dülfer, the most noted of Kaiser-climbers in the "classical" days before the War, had made the first ascents of those two short but extremely severe pitches. But, when a hold, which has sustained generations of climbers with its support, gradually grows brittle under the hand of man as it sweats with fear, and ceases to exist because it has broken away and fallen off—then such a pitch can become a devilish difficult proposition. Well, we should see. . . .

The Kufstein Section of Face-climbing Specialists, which knows every hold from the Predigstuhl to the Kleine Halt by heart, now took up their position on the Kaiserhof, armed with the kind of binoculars which would reveal every quiver of a finger, every twitch of an ear-lobe. For all I know, the non-paying spectators on that rock Grand Stand may also have had a stop-watch.

We were soon at the foot of the much-feared pitch. There it was, the U-shaped crack in the smooth slabs, only about 60 feet high, but quite a sufficient distance to fall. In the middle of it was a smooth overhanging bulge, the crux of the climb. True enough, a bit was missing: clearly there had once been something there approximating to a hold. My feet were lodged on sheer, smooth rock, and every time I tried to straighten up, in order to get a grip higher up, I had the uncomfortable feeling that they were starting to slip. This was a problem of balance, then! Very slowly I pushed myself upwards, flattening myself against the rock, till when next I straightened up I was able to get hold of something, very small but just enough to grip with my finger-tips. I pulled myself up, dealt with another exhausting projection above and that brought me to the top of the "Fiechtl-U".

We went back to the Stripsenjoch for the night, but in that hospitable refuge there was not a single mention during the evening of the "Fiechtl-U". Evidently they had made some kind of a miscalculation.

The next day was glorious, except that the rock was still a little cold and be-rimed. Rudi and I climbed the Weinberger route on the Predig-stuhl West. In those chilly conditions the overhang proved somewhat obstinate, but it gradually grew warmer and we began to enjoy ourselves. At noon we stood on the North Summit. Opposite us on the South-East Face of the Fleischbank I could see a rope of two, just at the first traverse. The sun-warmed rock over there looked thoroughly inviting. I thought: "What about doing the 'South-East' solo? Nobody ever has, but it ought to be possible."

I knew, of course, that Hias Rebitsch had climbed the top from the terrace alone, but not the whole Wall; and then I remembered that one attempt to do the whole climb had been made and had ended in a fatal fall. When I said to Rudi: "I've got a mind to try the 'Südost' solo," he answered: "Go on, you're kidding!" He didn't seem to think much of my plan, but added: "Well, you know best what you want to do, I suppose."

"I'd like to try it, anyway. I can always turn back," I told him. I called back: "See you on the Fleischbank Summit!" as I hurried down the Angermann Gully, the easiest way down the Predigstuhl and, crossing the hollow of the Steinerne Rinne, reached the foot of my climb in half an hour.

I could hear voices above me. It was the pair we had been watching from the Predigstuhl, and they were still stuck on the traverse. I took two slings, two carabiners and 100 feet of line with me. It was perfect bliss to be balancing upwards alone without the restriction of a rope or any ballast to weigh one down: that's what I call real climbing! I was determined to find out just what my own limits were; a solo climb like this was the only proper way to do it. Very few people understand that. The others are always full of gloomy prophecies—"One of these fine days you'll be lying at the bottom, you'll see!" But this was one of those things you can't do anything about. An irresistible urge lent me wings; an urge that ever ordered me to try something higher and harder, counselling me to try myself out to the uttermost.

I caught up with the second man on the rope at the traverse and asked his permission to climb past him. "Of course!" he agreed. Then I came to the leader's traversing rope and made my way over it.

I recognised a face popping out from behind an edge of rock. We knew each other from meeting at the Kaunergrat Hut. It was Heinz Labugger from Graz, a cheerful sort of chap but now, as I edged past him all by myself, he looked a bit nonplussed. He simply couldn't believe that there was no one else dangling on the end of my "tow-rope".

I tackled the Rossi Overhang. There were singularly few pitons on the "South-East" to-day; only two here, a pretty scanty ration, but I just had to do without them. First, I used the rope to give me a "leg-up"; I had to give myself a short pull up on it at two places, then I was up and on easier rock. Back went the carabiners into my trouser pocket. The wall grew airier and airier, a thing one notices more than usual when climbing solo, but that was really what I had come for—plenty of air round me and below me, and no one but myself to rely on. . . .

Somebody called over from the Elmauer Tor: "Look! There's some-one doing the 'South-East' alone!" But I wasn't there to collect admiring tributes or to provide a thrill for an audience. This wasn't a "Fiechtl-U" with its Grand-Stand seats. . . .

I reached the cave with the register in it, but I didn't stop, going straight on up the overhang above it. Suddenly I felt a strange feeling in my fingers. Now, I know perfectly well when my fingers are going on strike, and I certainly couldn't contemplate that when climbing solo. I wasn't prepared to take any risks, though that may seem odd in the context of a solo climb of the "South-East". Without more ado, I climbed down into the cave again and took a few minutes' rest. No wonder I was tired. Normally, you stop after every hundred feet of climbing, while you wait for the other man to come up, and that gives you time to recuperate for the next pitch; but to-day I had nobody to wait for.

It was not till I took my breather that I noticed what a marvellous spot this was. I seemed to have overlooked it before, on other occasions. Everywhere great precipices plunging down and away. I felt free and happy as a bird.

It does one good to be absolutely alone every now and then, with no one else to rely on. It is a fine and salutary experience; one finds new depths in one's own being, things one doesn't discover when there are other people along. I hadn't yet discovered the limits of my endurance or of my will-power, where mountains are concerned; but I intended to do so, even if others sometimes put my actions down to a kind of pathological search for notoriety. How superficial and facile are, often, the judgments of men!

I looked down over the grass-terrace to the Rossi-Overhang. I could see the blond mop of the boy from Graz popping up over the bulge. Those two were coming up like a good team, manipulating the ropes, protecting each other, in perfect co-operation. But climbing alone has its own real magic, too. My short breather had restored me completely. Happy again and perfectly at one with myself, I renewed my grapple with the overhang. Out to the right—up, and again up—and there I was at the end of the climb.

Rudi was already there, sitting on the flat top, to meet me with a cheerful grin.

"Now I feel better," I told him. "Now I'm happy. Nobody can take away the joy of having done that wall solo."

In climbing there should be no question of time-records or taking a stop-watch along, as I know well. But I couldn't help being pleased with to-day's success. Little more than an hour ago I had been over there on the Predigstuhl; now I was sitting on top of the Fleischbank; and between them lay a solo climb of the Südost. . . .

Up there, too, I met that most sympathetic of mountaineers, Walter Frauenberger, well past his days of hectic climbing. I had heard a lot about him and of his adventures with Schwarzgruber in the Himalaya and the Caucasus. Of course I could not guess that one day we were to be team-mates—and such team-mates, too—among Nanga Parbat's ice-mazes. . . .

Rudi and I loitered across to the South-East Ridge of the Totenkirchl, for full measure. It is a gloriously attractive climb and it seemed like precious relaxation after what I had been doing. With a sense of high well-being we lay down on the Totenkirchl's Summit platform, to an undisturbed rest, full of ease and contentment. Early in the afternoon we were sitting once more at a table decked with a white cloth, sipping a cooling lemonade. We had only been away from the Hut eight hours. Eight hours of supreme delight!

CHRISTMAS ON THE PRECIPICES

CHRISTMAS at the Gaudeamus Hut.

Nothing can be lovelier than Christmas at one of the Mountain Huts; to be at the heart of Nature and to commune with her on that Holy Night, after the last candle has been snuffed on the tree, up there in the lonely hills, far from the human herd! My imagination and my love for the Hills went farther than that; I would have found it wonderful to spend Christmas Night bivouacking on the face of a precipice, with the midnight bells sounding faintly up from the valley below. How I should have loved that! But this time I had to be content with hanging high between Heaven and Earth on the third night after Christmas, and without the sound of church bells.

That was still to come, though, as on Christmas Eve I climbed, heavily laden, up towards the Gaudeamus Hut, glancing from time to time at its lighted windows high above me. Up there, they had no idea that they were still to receive a guest. It was bitterly cold; the only sound breaking the stillness of the night, was the 'crunch' of the snow under my boots.

The only people at the Hut were the Keeper, Peter Hofer, and Steffi, his wife. I was a welcome intruder on their loneliness. Peter immediately pressed the guitar into one of my hands and a hot grog into the other. It turned into a typical, comfortable Hut-evening, helping one to forget that, down below, the whole world was quarrelling and fighting.

"Out you get; the sun's up!" I heard Peter call up to me. It was in fact ten o'clock in the morning and a faint light was coming in through the wooden shutters. Peter was too busy to come with me; he had visitors to look after during the day and all sorts of things to attend to in the Hut. So I went off alone towards the Ellmauer Tor. There had been so far very little snow that Winter, and the rock was sticking out everywhere. Just in case—after all, you never can tell—I had brought some slings and a carabiner or two along in my rucksack.

Nero, Peter's dog, had come along, very pleased to get a walk. He was still quite young and silly; all he wanted to do was to have a game. What he liked best was to tear along after you when you went skiing: he was obviously disappointed that I had left my skis behind. However, he plodded on cheerfully in my wake; when I sat down to rest, so did he. Neither of us was in any hurry.

We reached the Ellmauer Tor at mid-day. Nero barked furiously and without the slightest reason that I could see. The light covering of fresh snow on the walls of the Fleischbank glittered in the sunlight. Nero barked incessantly. Did he want to go on and, if so, where to? Aimlessly enough we pottered together towards the *arête* of the Christaturm.

Heavens, what a glorious day!

Suddenly I had the crazy thought: it would be fun to do the East Wall of the Fleischbank. I went over all its pitches in my mind and I remembered them quite well, though it was a long time since I had last climbed it. But solo, and in winter? Well, I could try it; conditions were not bad—very little snow as yet, only a powdering on the rock, and there oughtn't to be any ice about. It had been too cold and there hadn't yet been a proper thaw; besides, there wasn't a glimmer of ice to be seen in any of the chimneys. Off we go, then! "You'll have to find your way home alone, Nero. . . . See you later!"

I climbed up over the approach slabs, towards the spiral cracks, finding it necessary to dust away the loose snow from every hand- and foothold.

I had been there years before, with the same intention of climbing the East Wall in winter conditions, but there had been stupendous masses of snow clinging to the rocks then and, where in summertime it is a precipitous face, there had then been a thick blanket of snow. We had taken four hours for that traverse of 200-feet and been compelled by the fall of darkness to rope down, or we would have been too late to get back. Since then I had left the wall in peace—at any rate in winter conditions.

Nero definitely wanted to come up with me. He kept on trying to scrabble up the rock but, seeing that Nature had not equipped him with climbing-rubbers, kept on slipping back again. The further away I got, the more desperate became his attempts. He barked furiously at the wall and then began to howl heart-rendingly; but I could not help him.

The spiral cracks are pretty polished. I avoided every granule of snow with the utmost care. Little snakes of powder-snow were wriggling along the rock. I reached the first traverse, with a ready-made plan for tackling it. I joined my slings together and let myself across on them: they were just long enough for the first bit, then I had to climb the rest. It was not long before I was at the second traverse, while down below Nero was still complaining and whining forlornly, a tiny black spot continually jumping up at the rock and falling back again on to the snow.

The climb now stiffened. There was a slithery layer of snow on the grass terrace which affords such easy going in summer. Cautiously I tested its stability, treading warily on the snow surface. The terrace is only about a foot broad and there are no holds at all in the wall above it. Meanwhile the sun had disappeared behind the Predigstuhl and it suddenly got very cold. Nero had decided to give in and accept his fate. Slowly he disappeared through the Ellmauer Tor, surely thinking: "What fickle creatures men are!"

I was now all alone in the uncanny silence! There was ice in the upper gullies, and a glazed slab held me up for a while. I deliberated a long time whether I could risk setting a foot on it. I got good hand-holds on projections, pushed my body slowly forward, very smoothly so as to avoid a slip, taking my weight on the palms of my hands. Then I put the weight of my right foot very quickly on the icy treads, my hand reached out ahead and found an immediate fingerhold, my foot moved off its fearsomely slippery support, and the unpleasant spot was behind me.

There was one more steep pitch in the overhanging chimney; there was ice there, too, but it only filled the bed of the gully, and a little skill sufficed to avoid it. And so I climbed on, first to the ridge, then to the summit, up the steep gullies under their layer of soft loose snow, from six to ten inches thick.

I looked at my watch and was astonished to find I had only been two hours. The Christmas Spirit must have lent me wings; I had to laugh aloud at the thought of myself as a Christmas Angel.

I soon got down by the easy "Herrweg". As I came sliding out of the last gully, there was Nero, yelping with delight and wagging his tail. His greetings were so boisterously effusive that he knocked me over. Content to have found each other again, we ploughed through the snow together down to the Hut. A Merry Christmas!

Peter and I went to bed early that evening, with the alarm set for four o'clock. And what a morning—bitingly cold, with the trees all white in a shroud of hoar frost!

It was still dark as we forged our way up on ski over the frozen snow. Dawn found us near the Baumgarteneck; and there opposite us in all its might, soared the wall we had chosen for our day's work, the Mauk West Wall.

Peter seemed concerned. "Have you had enough rest?" he asked me.

"Yesterday's climb was just enough to get me into trim," I reassured him. "I'm not tired."

We got ready for the climb. I kept on staring up at the wall, remembering that day five years before, with Wastl Weiss and our other friend, when we got away with our great gamble. Several attempts to repeat our original route had been made since, but only one had succeeded. That was when my clubmates, Karl Gombotz and Hugo Vigl, climbed it and at the same time scotched the silly rumour that when we made the first ascent we intentionally broke off the critical hold at the keypoint, to prevent anybody from repeating the climb. What an idiotic accusation, anyway!

And now here we were, Peter and I, determined to try it in midwinter, at Christmastide—with what result had still to be put to the proof.

The series of chimneys were just as smooth as ever, the overhangs as forbidding, only this time there was ice to reckon with as well—chiefly at the most inconvenient places. We had to haul the heavy rucksack up after each rope's length, and the rounded bundle objected strongly to coming up through the narrow cracks. It was pretty hard work, but even so, we didn't get warm; we shivered from head to foot. Why had we just chosen a West Wall, which could not catch the sun till afternoon? That was our own fault; we could do nothing but clamber on, up and up. . . .

There I was, under the huge bulge again, staring up at it; but to-day the traverse had a more friendly look, for there was now a piton sticking out of the polished rock. I managed without great difficulty to reach the little plate-sized platform where our piton was still in place from our first ascent. Once again I performed the same balancing trick, using the piton as a hand-hold and a foothold simultaneously.

Soon after that we were standing huddled together at the start of the long traverse, right under the bulge which we had by-passed on our first ascent. Gombotz and Vigl, on the other hand, on their second ascent, had "nailed" themselves along it, as we say in climbing jargon. There were masses of pitons—and up there in the bulge itself a huge ring-piton. Full marks to whoever put it there!

I liked the look of this variation by my clubmates better than the route I had taken five years before. I was separated from the bulge by a thirty-foot slab; the rock was brittle and the shafts didn't seem to want to go into any crevices. Since there were no holds, I worked my way upwards in slings—I had to, little as I love the wobbly things in the ordinary way.

"Look out, the hook's coming away!" Peter warned me from below.

"Let it!" I said. "I've got to get on with things," and, at the same time, tried to take my weight off the piton in question by clawing on to a little knob. The hold broke off, the hook went flying and, before I knew where I was, I found myself hanging on the rope fifteen feet down.

No harm had been done, but my zest for the struggle had been mightily enhanced. I was soon on the rock again and went at it with a will—but this time very quietly. I squeezed in under the bulge like a burglar, and found a foothold; at last I reached the excellent ring-piton which had been so long the object of my desire and at last, too, I dared to shout down to Peter: "Haul away!"—and was I grateful for the support? I might have had to provide that blessed protection my-self—good for you, Gombotz and Vigl!

The rope weighed very heavily, almost dragging me off the wall. The familiar back-chat echoed among the rocks:

"Steady—you're pulling me clean off!"

"Don't be silly. I'm letting it go—look, it's as loose as can be. Why don't you pull it in?"

"But I'm telling you. I can't move on. I shall have to come back."

Then a tug on the rope as if there was a boulder tied to it, and some cursing and swearing. Then:

"Look out! I'm coming off!"

But somehow you do hang on, with your last ounce of strength; you brace yourself against the infernal tug of the rope, and at the very last second you find another hold somewhere else. Then you find a stance, clip a carabiner in like lightning, quite certain that you can't see it through for another moment. But it is astonishing what you *can* see through, and you do.

In the meantime the sun had said "good-bye" again and it was growing gradually dusk. I had only just noticed it and urged Peter to hurry; he trod on it nobly in response. This was no place at all for spending a night.

It was the old story again. Darkness upon us, and we hadn't found a place that would do; whenever I thought I had found the slightest promise of something to sit on, it turned out to be a phantom, and on we had to go. It was hours later, when the angle of the wall had begun to ease off, that we found a spot which could be used. We banged in pitons and, in the darkness, occasionally banged our thumbs instead of the pitons; then we tied everything for our overnight home firmly to the ironwork. We put on every stitch of clothing we had along, and crawled into the shell of our tent-sack, where we supped on bacon and tea.

Down in the valley electric flashes sprayed out from the overhead wires of the railway; we could see the trains quite clearly by them—sure evidence of how cold it was down in the lowlands, too.

We kept on sliding off our sloping perch and finishing up on the rope. If it tied us up too uncomfortably, we straightened ourselves out and climbed back again, but a few minutes later the rope would be taut again to the piton and the seat-slings tight about our thighs. At first we always got back to our position again; but presently we became apathetic and resigned to our fate; and all we did was to beat our hands together and rub our feet, to keep them from getting frostbitten.

Endless seemed the night hours. We talked about bygone days to make the time go by and said all the things we hadn't had time to during the day's climb. We sang, too, loud and clear, but not very beautifully. In between, we dozed off into a short nap, only to be awoken by cold and discomfort. While my partner slept, I counted up to a thousand or tried to identify the constellations, but soon gave that up, too; and for a long while nothing happened except that my teeth chattered and my body shuddered with cold.

Then I had a brainwave. There was a torch in our rucksack and we got it out and lit it. It served to pass a little time and even shed a little warmth around. Our immediate surroundings glowed, ghostly, in the garish light. It wasn't till then that we saw in what a precarious place we had camped for the night.

"I hope the Fire Brigade won't turn out when they see our blaze," I told Peter; then the increasing cold checked all desire to make jokes. We counted every stroke of the church clocks down in the valley. The worst moment was when we made a miscount and had to admit an hour later that they were striking the same time as before.

Slowly the grey dawn broadened. But the real test of our patience was still to come; in a great hurry we crawled out of the sack, had something to eat and got everything ready for continuing the climb. We gave ourselves a rapid massage and only realised when it was all over that it was all far too soon. It was still much too cold; the sun had still to come up. So we crawled miserably back under our shell. That last period of waiting was the slowest of all.

It was not far to the summit, but we were exhausted and weary. The last steep snow-slopes were agony. At ten o'clock we got off the wall, to our great relief. We had accomplished the first winter ascent of the Mauk West Wall.

That Christmas on sheer faces remains an unforgettable experience of tough, but not unbearable climbing. It was not lunacy, but a need to put myself to the proof, which the mountains were exacting from me. They are indeed implacable in their demands upon him who subjects himself to their Law. And I had to be obedient to that Law.

CLIMBING ON STEEPLES

HARDLY had I got down to Innsbruck when a very strange letter fluttered into my home. An undertaking called "Gearless Steeple Restorers" wanted a man who didn't suffer from giddiness. I wanted to save some money for a trip to the Western Alps in the Summer, so it arrived at a very convenient moment. My friend Rudl was in exactly the same situation, so he applied, too. Wonderful—a ready-made team for the job! So we switched our climbing skill from rocks to roofs for the time being.

We were taken to Aldrans, a village nearby, where our job was to go right up the sharp spire. We climbed through a trapdoor on to the outside of the steep roof. "Just like an ice wall," I remarked to Rudl, as I estimated the angle as from seventy to eighty degrees. I must admit that I didn't feel any too good as I stood on a wobbly ladder, fastened by a rope to the top of the tower. I took a tentative look down into the churchyard, where the wrought iron crosses on the graves stuck up like sharp spears—a downward glance that needed some getting used to.

Food was still a problem in those years, so our occupation was most acceptable; for we were catered for either by farmers or by the Padre, and in both cases there was ample provision for the Church Restorers. We were given five meals a day; and five times a day, with much pleasure, we climbed up and down our church-tower.

Of course there were drawbacks, too, to our unusual occupation. We had to keep a stricter watch on our lawless behaviour and restrain our normal mode of expressing ourselves: some of the remarks we occasionally let loose on rock-faces wouldn't have been appropriate here, and we had to show how well we had been brought up.

In the course of time we became more and more daring at our work. We had soon got used to this new form of climbing and balanced about on ledges and gutters without any safety device. At mid-day, when the sun was beating straight down on us we preferred to lie down for a snooze on the ball at the top of the steeple, where no one was likely to disturb us. We also learned to appreciate the skill of baroque church-painting, for it was our duty to restore everything on the outside of the tower.

Our rock-climbing technique proved a great help on the façades. We were soon doing the oddest traverses and pendulum manoeuvres, which often set on edge the nerves of the villagers below.

After closing-time we frequently had readings of the Book of the Law, with such additions as: "It's frightful: we daren't look up at you!"

Presently we gave up going down through the edifice of the church, but simply draped the rope around any old ornament and *abseiled* down the outside wall; we didn't even use our feet but simply let the rope run through our hands. We went sliding down like a lightning-flash out of a clear sky, and only checked our crazy flight by braking a few feet from the ground.

Those deeds of ours in a noble cause evidently amused the Padres. We often heard a whistle from below and then: "Rudl! Hermann! Come down quick!" "Orders is orders"—ours not to reason why. Down at the bottom were all the village worthies in a bunch, the Padre, the Schoolmaster, the Doctor and all, watching us come hurtling down like greased lightning.

But the most daring of all was our Boss, who thought nothing of risking his neck. Once, when the ladder was too short, he tried to go up to the very tip of the spire without one, and moreover without any protection whatever, just by using his hands on the wooden shingles.

There was a sudden flurry. Rudl and I rushed to the window in the tower just in time to see the Boss come bowling down the roof. We managed somehow to field him by the legs and pull him in through the window. That time even he consented to look a little pale; but he only thought it a good excuse for a drink, and washed his little scare away in no time in the neighbouring bar.

When Steeple Restoration gave out, I was offered the job of erecting a wireless-transmission mast, but I hadn't enough time left. Summer stood knocking at the door and, as I was in the happy condition of being sure that the touring-chest was sufficiently filled with shekels, I started getting ready instead for a second journey to the Western Alps.

TURNED DOWN BY THE JORASSES

I HAD recently met in the Wetterstein Hills a very young climber, but one who had already made a name for himself in climbing circles; in fact many were already saying that he was the best climber Germany had lately produced. This charming young man from Heidelberg was named Martin Schliessler. When Luis Vigl was unfortunately forced by business considerations to withdraw from our partnership, I suggested to Martin that he should come instead. He accepted with red-hot enthusiasm.

As a German citizen, Martin owned no passport, and since he didn't know the way across the Brenner, I had to go with him, counselling him first to keep his mouth firmly shut, whatever might befall. For I realised that everyone would know he was no Tirolese at the very first word he uttered. That was therefore Martin's only hope of getting across the Frontier.

We got out of the train at the station before the Brenner. A steady downpour suited our purpose admirably, and I prophesied cheerfully: "Nobody will be on guard in pig's weather like this." We kept on along the railway line; there was nothing in our rucksacks but food and clothes. . . . Just then a figure popped up right in front of us—the figure of a Frontier-guard.

"Good morning. How do we get to the Station?" I enquired innocently of the "Eye of the Law".

"Where do you come from?" he asked suspiciously.

"We come from the Habicht—we were caught up there by darkness and now we want to get back to Innsbruck. Perhaps you can tell us when the next train goes?" I reeled off in one piece, while Martin, heeding his instructions, uttered not a single sound.

"What's in your rucksack?" asked the Guardian of the Frontier.

I gave him a detailed list of the contents and at the same time showed him my passport.

"And what about him?" the officer enquired, pointing at my companion.

"Oh, he's with me," I said quickly, hoping against hope that the guard wouldn't ask for Martin's passport. And all he did was to get out a little book, thumb about in it—and kindly told us the time of the next Innsbruck train.

"Thank's very much—and *Auf Wiedersehn!*"

So far, so lucky; but we hadn't got across the frontier yet.

The Brenner was brilliantly lit up; in order to avoid getting into the zone of lights, we had to climb a good way up the slope. We crossed ravines and steep slopes, with Martin always following a little way behind. Nothing stirred, except when the leaves occasionally rustled. Was it the wind—or wild animals?

Suddenly something moved in the undergrowth above me. I stopped to listen, heard steps—moving delicately, but plainly audible—until they, too, halted. I decided to risk everything on one throw. I pushed off, something crackled underfoot—and there was I running as hard as I knew how, trying my utmost to get across the Frontier ahead of my pursuer.

I did—but he came after me. Of course he did, for it was Martin all the time.

We went down to the main road and strolled down it quite safely, like two tramps. I went on ahead; Martin kept just in sight of me, a little way behind. At Gossensass we left the road and had a well-earned sleep in the woods. Next morning we caught a train to Brixen, where we retrieved the heavy luggage I had sent in several relays to friends of mine; then we travelled on in over-crowded trains by way of Milan to Courmayeur. Everything was full to overflowing, packed to the brim with summer holiday-makers and mountaineers. It was the *Fiera d'Agosto*, the peak of the Italian travel season—a regular hullabaloo!

It was a glorious summer's evening. The proud heads of the great 13,000-foot peaks shone in dazzling glory; at every step up the valley the gateway to the marvellous world of the snows opened wider. The whole Southern Wall lay open to our gaze from the imposing black spike of the Aiguille Noire de Peuteret, past the massive Brenva Face of the Monarch of the Alps himself and the gigantic tooth of the Géant, to the six-headed bulk of the Jorasses. It was an awe-inspiring spectacle.

We put up our little tent in a meadow outside Entrèves. We found some Innsbruck friends already installed there, having returned from the Gran Paradiso Group. An old ruined mill served as communal kitchen. Martin, who enjoyed cooking, started at once to set up our culinary arrangements inside that dilapidated edifice. A short time after he disappeared into it, I heard a yell and much bad language.

Our big provision-box had suddenly vanished a storey below, the floor of the mill having collapsed. So our noodles, our "basis of existence", were lying in the dirt down in the cellar. With infinite care our treasure was brought up again into the light of day. Supper was a long time coming.

We were astir very early, having slept in the open because our tent was too small; so that the very first light had awakened us, in face of a feast of loveliness on which we could not gaze our fill.

Martin and I got ready for our assault on the buttress of the Jorasses. Heavily laden we went up through the narrow alleys of Entrèves and, in order to save precious time, betook ourselves by the cable railway to the Col du Géant, 7,000 feet above. From there we loped down the long, crevassed Glacier du Géant, turned to the right at its foot and made our way up to the Leschaux Hut. We awaited our first sight of the North Wall of the Jorasses with ill-concealed impatience. Would it give us the cold shoulder again, or would it this time greet us with friendly conditions, promising success? We drew nearer, tense with expectation. Then, gradually, behind the crazy teeth of the Périades, the six-topped granite colossus of the Grandes Jorasses began to loom up, dominated by the 14,806-foot Pointe Walker, from which there falls, in a line as fine as if it had been cut with a knife, an *arête* breaking away in holdless flights of slab for 4,000 feet into the head-ice of the Leschaux Glacier.

"There's your Buttress," I told my friend, who was struck speechless. Rock and ice have come to a compromise on the North Face generally; but on that fearsomely steep buttress, rock predominates. Venturesome Youth fought a bitter fight for the Wall before Peters and Maier of Munich found a way up the granite mass in 1934; but the Buttress itself was considered unclimbable for long after that. In the summer of 1938, however, when the news that the Eiger's North Wall had been climbed electrified the Alpine world, a pair of young Italian climbing Aces from Lecco had already decided to make this very Walker Buttress of the Jorasses their target.

Their rope of three, consisting of that phenomenal climber Riccardo Cassin and his friends Mario Esposito and Tissoni reached the Pointe Walker after three terrible days, during which bad weather caught them on the climb.

They had succeeded in climbing the Buttress absolutely direct, and their route-finding had been perfect. In this way the other great Alpine problem after the Eiger North Wall was finally solved; the spell of the great wall had been broken, but its difficulties remained; and the aura with which the Buttress is surrounded compels respect in every climber who casts an eye upon it.

Directly after the War, a young and daring generation of climbers grew up in France; subsidised by national resources, they were trained in the Chamonix School of Mountaineering and in time became tremendously powerful teams. After many vain attempts, one of their ropes repeated the Buttress climb in 1945. Then in 1947 no less than three French ropes made successful ascents.

Martin, seeing the mountain for the first time, was overpowered by its might and majesty, which far transcended his imaginings. To our discomfiture the weather was growing rapidly worse; at first there had been only rainbow-like scarves of mist which dissolved again, but now definite cirrus clouds were forming and building up more strongly about the tops.

We had meant still to have a look at the approach to the Wall in the evening, so as not to lose too much time searching in the dark; the nearer we got to its base, the more unapproachable it looked. I must confess that no wall I have ever seen in my life has wrung from me such a shudder of respect. I felt almost too feeble to dare to test my powers out against it.

Just as we thought we had the Leschaux Hut to ourselves, two French climbers arrived, very late, from the Leschaux Glacier. Their equipment showed clearly that they had some very special climb of the first magnitude in view; could it possibly be the same as ourselves?

It was light when I woke next morning. I jumped up in a great state; I had set the alarm for three o'clock, and it had apparently not gone off. I looked out of the window. The sky was heavily overcast, with low cloud; no day for starting on a big climb. Relieved, I lay down again to sleep.

By mid-day the weather had improved visibly. The two Frenchmen were getting ready to start. They were going to try the Buttress, they explained briefly; so were we, we informed them.

We joined forces and climbed up to the base of the rocks together. As always before very big ventures, I followed our old track with mixed feelings. We soon crossed the *bergschrund*, about which we had been worrying furiously, on a slender bridge, and reached a small saddle by way of a very steep diverging gully about a hundred and fifty feet high. I was beginning to feel much better, though my rucksack was uncomfortably heavy, and I began to wonder whether I could manage it for such a long spell, with severe climbing to be encountered. Could I tackle it with sixty pounds on my back? All we had along with us for the day were two 120-foot ropes, one 120-foot rappel-cord, 20 rock-pitons, a few ice-pitons, 20 carabiners, sufficient slings, climbing-hammers, an ice-axe, two sets of crampons, two Zdarsky sacks, a primus-stove and provisions for four days: as well as enough clothes for the bivouacs that lay before us—a kind of Alpine junk-shop!

We climbed 300 feet of not very difficult rock, followed by some smooth slabs out towards the left and an even smoother gully. After a number of rope's-lengths we reached a steep ice-slope, which forced us to put on our twelve-point crampons. I had forgotten the rucksack's weight by then; the whole of my attention was taken up by the Wall. At the upper rim of the ice, after a traverse of two ropes'-lengths, we reached the start of the notorious "Hundred-foot Gully", the first super-severe pitch on the buttress. Here things began to get tough. The Wall was tremendously foreshortened from where we were, with a 600-foot belt of slabs cutting off the view upwards. Our target for the day, Cassin's first bivouac-place, must be just above that ring of precipices. I was just going to start on the gully when the Frenchmen—they were Marcel Schatz and Jean Couzy—later to win fame on Annapurna—called to us that they had lost their ice-axe and would have to go down again. We offered them our spare, but they still decided not to go on, pointing out that the weather (which we had not noticed) was rapidly deteriorating and that it was getting late. We now saw with great misgivings that heavy cloud had settled on the peaks and there was every indication of a serious break in the weather. Knowing what a forced retreat would mean on that Wall, we, too, decided not to tempt Providence, even though we knew we were giving up our last chance for this trip; but sound judgment was called for here, rather than blind enthusiasm.

Soon we were sitting in the Hut again, listening to the familiar buzzing of the petrol cooker. During the night a terrible storm broke over us, whistling and howling, clawing at the wooden walls of the refuge, banging the shutters back and forth. We were very grateful that we had turned back when we did and put a good roof over our heads.

The morning broke icily cold. While there was not a great deal of snow on the faces, the rock was clad in a thin, dangerous ice-armouring. We hadn't enough food left to try even the Peters route. Disappointed and depressed, we started on the way back to the Rifugio Torino on the Col du Géant. In order to reap some kind of a summit from this first expedition, we climbed the Grand Flambeau, whose 11,675 foot top is an insignificant feature in this royal round of mighty peaks.

Far below us lay the flat grey roofs of the pretty village of Entrèves, from which we had set out, and late in the afternoon we were back in our camp down there.

DREAMS COME TRUE

THUNDER ON THE AIGUILLE NOIRE

THE wind had gone round to the east and the clouds had cleared away. Our plans soared high; but our joyous mood was dissipated as if a bomb had burst on us, by the shattering news of the death of Karl Zinner, one of our comrades. He had been carried down by a stone-fall in the gully below the bivouac-box at the Brèche Nord on the Dames Anglaises; the recovery-party had already gone out to bring him back. There was nothing we could do but wait till they found him. I couldn't grasp that my friend, with whom I had shared so many lovely hours, had gone from among us. It was another reminder of the implacability of the Great Peaks; they are beautiful, but they are fraught with peril, even for the most competent. A police car took Zinner back on his last journey home.

We decided not to let the tragedy interfere with our plans. The all-compelling command of the mountains lay upon us: *Excelsior!*

Martin and I climbed up to the Noire Hut through the quivering heat of mid-morning; our aim this time was to have a go at the Monarch himself, by the Peuteret Ridge, the longest and most famous of his ridges. But it was not to be the usual abbreviated route from the bivouac-box; we intended to do the whole ridge with the Aiguille Noire thrown in. And just for full measure we were going to do the Noire by the South Ridge—a combination which had not yet been achieved.

A steep belt of cliffs, with a waterfall pouring down them, rises from the Val Veni, cutting off the approach to the Fauteuil des Allemands.

"A nice path up to a Hut," I remarked sarcastically to Martin. "At home in the Eastern Alps they'd bracket it in 'The Easy Climbs'."

Very soon the only sign of a route was the markings, as we scrambled from one red blob to another over the steep slabs for about 1,200 feet, till the view opened out again and we could see into a high ravine. There, clinging to the extreme right-hand wall of the rocks, we made out the small shape of the Noire Hut.

The night brought no relief from the heat. I kept tossing from one side to the other on my mattress, hot and stifled; it was midnight before I could get to sleep. Two hours later the alarm whirred me awake. A mild breeze was stirring in that high ravine—a bad sign—as we stumbled across to the South Ridge. It was still twilight when we laid hand on its rock and made rapid progress to the col behind the first tower, the Pic Gamba, just as the sun's red globe rose over the Val d'Aosta. There was a light covering of cloud and it was clear that the settled weather of the last few days was coming to an end. The ridge now banked steeply up in five huge *gendarmes* to the subsidiary summit, which is separated from the main summit (12,380 feet) by a col. There is nothing in the Northern Limestone Alps to match this ridge, with a height differential of 3,600 feet, and a length of a mile and a third. The second *gendarme* begins with a steep pitch. Our rapid assault came to a halt just underneath the two great rock-teeth, which combine to form the top of the tower; we were forced by a 60-foot step in the ridge to get the rope out of the rucksack and move on under its protection. It wasn't till we reached the third tower, called the Pointe Welzenbach, that we dared to move simultaneously again. It was only nine o'clock, so we could allow ourselves a short rest and a second breakfast.

I was still in an optimistic mood. "If we keep this pace up, we shall easily reach the Bivouac *Gîte* at the Brèche Nord this evening," I told Martin.

On the occasions when the sun broke through the cloud layer, it burned mercilessly down on us, and it was uncannily stuffy. We roped down two pitches to a saddle and then the ridge shot up much more steeply again. The climbing grew more severe and we had to use every application of rope-technique with great care. But the granite was marvellously firm; every hold was reliable, and the ascent was a veritable joy. As if on some mighty staircase, we climbed up over huge blocks piled high on one another. Occasionally we met a piton, but they seemed to us quite unnecessary luxuries here. The only nuisance was the weight of our rucksacks, which contained our whole equipment, none of which we had yet needed to use; but we should be wanting it later on.

The fifth tower, the Pointe Bich, on which we should be meeting our chief difficulties, started right away by setting us the problem of a completely smooth gully, which stood before us like a book someone had opened. . . . "Well begun's half done," thought I, and I got to grips with it without more ado. The first hundred and fifty feet were vertical and pretty holdless—comparable, in fact, with difficult pitches in our own home mountains. Further up, it was closed by projecting roofs; but about halfway up there was a prominent ramp leading out to its right-hand edge. I had been told about a traverse, and this was probably it; so I pushed my way across to the edge and only when I reached it did I notice a piton much higher up the gully. So I was doing "variants" again! But having got so far, and a return being a very difficult exercise indeed, I decided to try the *arête* above me, the first several feet of which overhung sharply. It was quite impossible to climb it unprotected, so I had to employ a piton to provide the necessary hold, and then it went all right. The depths below us were beginning to be beyond compute; to our right we looked down 3,000 feet of unbroken slabs on to the Noire Hut, while to the left of the ridge, sheer below our feet, the savagely crevassed Fresnay Glacier plunged towards the valley. All the time we could hear the thunder of ice avalanches, and collapsing *séracs* booming up to us from the depths.

About mid-day heavy thunder-clouds began to gather. Veils of mist crept up from the gulfs below and soon enveloped the ridge in a shroud of uniform grey. Away on the Jorasses, the storm was already rumbling. We held a council whether to wait, or climb on.

I was for pushing on to the summit as quickly as possible and Martin agreed. Soon heavy rain-drops, mingled with hailstones, were pattering down, though it didn't last long and the mist presently lifted; but the sky above was blacker and more threatening than ever. It seemed as if the weather was bound to make fools of us, though we still hoped to reach the summit before the thunderstorm broke.

A vain hope for, even before we reached the subsidiary summit, the full force of it was unleashed on us. The sluices of heaven were opened; hail and rain poured down upon us, with snowflakes intermingled. A fierce gale, breathtaking in its ferocity, blew up. We crossed the sub-sidiary summit, roped down to a saddle, and raced up the ridge towards the summit; by now we were in the middle of a lovely snowstorm. The gale was driving solid walls of snow- and ice-crystals horizontally across the ridge, lashing them into our faces. The organ notes of the storm boomed among the crags, howling around the faces: so thick was the pother that we could hardly see ten yards ahead. Suddenly the profile of a ridge loomed up—the East Ridge. We must have been quite near the Summit of the Noire then! The last bit to the top, though, where East and South Ridges meet, shoots up like a tower.

What on earth was happening——? My friend looked at me in aston-ishment. A high-pitched murmur filled the air, a most uncanny sound—but one I recognised at once. It was a static charge of electricity in the air, presaging the discharge of lightning. Everything around us was in a high state of tension. This was no time for hanging about; it was a signal for us to get off the ridge and down as far as possible in the shortest possible time, renouncing all ideas of our climb.

While we were still deliberating, a bright flash enveloped us and we were struck by a force which almost lifted us off our feet; a hot blast of air flapped at us. There we stood, half-blinded, concussed and deaf from the ensuing thunderclap. The next followed with hardly an interval, and then another and another; an ear-splitting, all-enveloping noise filled the Witches' Cauldron about us. Added to the thunder crashes was the howling of the wind, the lashing of the hail and the water roaring down like a tidal wave. We were caught in the hell of a high thunderstorm; flash upon flash, roar upon roar, as we raced like hunted animals down the upper part of the ridge, seeking at least to escape from the immediate danger zone. The blizzard hurled whole waves of sharp ice-crystals in our faces—which became so painful that we could hardly keep our eyes open. In a trice the rock was covered in a perilous glaze of ice. Steep cliffs kept on forcing us back on to the crest of the ridge from the slight shelter we had found on the South Face. Up there that ghastly murmur was always about us and with us.

The thunder gradually passed over, but the gale did not abate. Whenever the mist lifted we could catch a glimpse of what lay ahead of us. It was an endless way down and Time raced wildly. Dusk began to fall and we found ourselves engaged in a race with Night. Soaked as we were, we couldn't possibly bivouac. Every time we thought we had reached easier ground, the short respite was followed by another steep downward dip; such disappointments are a feature of the Western Alps.

We could hear from the rushing of the waterfall that there was still a steep pitch between us and the ravine at the bottom. We were going separately now, each picking his own line, until gullies down which we could not see brought us to a halt. We certainly couldn't rope down into that kind of unexplored pit—all experience, bitterly won, enforced that lesson. We tried gully after gully for a way out, but in vain. Were we going to have to bivouac after all? The thought chilled us to the very marrow.

We went feeling our way round in the dark. By a miracle I stumbled on an *abseil* sling, a clear pointer to the right way down. We roped down several pitches, most of them turned to waterfalls. Not that we cared; we were soaked through to the skin already. At last we reached the bottom. Just seventeen hours after leaving the Noire Hut, we found blessed shelter under its roof again. We had it all to ourselves; and while the storm raged outside, we were soon in a deep sleep. We had earned it.

*   *   *

I peeled off the heap of blankets, opened my eyes, and saw it was broad daylight.

"Look, Martin, I believe the sun's shining!" I cried.

Grumpily, we confirmed that it was in fact perfect weather again. As so often happens after heavy storms, Nature had chosen the next morning to show her most attractive mien. The sun was shining gently, if a little sardonically, out of a sky of deepest blue. What could we do about it?

Our clothes were wringing wet, our equipment soaked through. The best thing to do was to go down to our tents in the valley. We met some climbers at Entrèves, old acquaintances of ours; and washed away our bad temper together, with a glass of good wine.

A STORM ON THE MONARCH

REST day—it sounds like a time for leisure and for sleep: on the contrary, there is plenty to do all day long. Equipment has to be overhauled; wet clothes have to be dried; boots require the most exhaustive attention. Mine were past rescue, even in the most expert hands—their soles were full of gaping mouths. It was more worth while to look after oneself, by bathing in a quiet pool, and shaving for the first time in days. Then the route-books and climbing-manuals had to be studied; all part of a rest day. But the most important occupation of all is the forging of new plans and, of course, cooking, eating and drinking. And if there is any time over, a little nap isn't a bad idea.

Refreshed in every respect, we went on our mountain-way again, following this time a little track leading up the slope towards the recesses of the Brenva Glacier. The afternoon was sultry, and once again there was every sign of bad weather on the way. Black cloud-dolphins swam across the ocean of the sky.

The track soon petered out in moraine rubble and only little stone cairns indicated the direction. We had to cross one or two torrents; and as there were no bridges, we just had to wade barefoot through the icy glacier water.

Partly on moraine, partly on the glacier itself and, finally, along an endless rock rib, we made our way for hours to the bivouac *Gîte* at the Brenva Glacier, where we proposed to spend the night. The corrugated iron shed is so like in colour to the rubble around it that we nearly walked past without seeing it.

While my culinary friend prepared our supper—a spiced *risotto*—I reconnoitred the possibilities of crossing the wildly-crevassed Brenva Glacier. I obtained a fine overall view of the ice stream from a rock-cliff; what I saw was not encouraging—savage chaos and wild confusion. It was a wilderness of shattered ice-masses, which looked as if they had been bombed. Nowhere was there an obvious route through that labyrinth of crevasses. I returned to the bivouac shelter somewhat ill-at-ease.

Our night's rest, short enough in all conscience, was continually disturbed by one or other of us looking at his watch, so concerned were we not to oversleep. At about one o'clock I looked out of the window, to find everything enveloped in fog; but it was not quite hopeless for, here and there, a star could be seen through a rift in the mists, so that the sky must be clear. And the fog might only be a mountain mist which might dissolve at a moment's notice.

An hour later we left our cover and went down to the glacier and, seeing that there was in any case no particular route across it, we dived into the crazy network of crevasses as best we could. There were huge ice-chasms and enormous rickety ice-towers; the *séracs* stood around like a band of drunkards, oblivious of the laws of gravity, ready to overturn at any moment. Blocks of ice-débris the size of a room barred the way; a short while before, they had probably been proud shapes the height of a house. Everything was cracking alarmingly around us and there were rumblings and creakings in the depths of the glacier; water dripped ceaselessly from the *séracs*. There was nothing dead about the glacier; we could feel the dangerous life moving in it.

Soon we were in the bottom of ice-ravines from which it was almost impossible to see the sky any more. Then we moved on over narrow, vertiginous ribs of ice, with black abysses yawning on either side, balancing our way like tightrope walkers across their brittle edifices. We had to feel our way across, yard by yard.

Martin said: "There's no point in this, we'll never get across."

I didn't feel any too happy about it myself, but adopted an attitude of experienced superiority, to encourage my young partner.

With mixed feelings we continued to traverse under grotesque ice-shapes, inching across delicate bridges over horrid chasms. The ice glimmered blue and green and the many avalanche traces and ice-débris lying on it carried an unmistakable message. After wandering about in search of a passage for nearly four hours in all, we reached the other bank of the Brenva Glacier.

While we were so engaged, it had become broad daylight and now we could see overhead the wall of ice, the hanging glacier, by which we hoped to reach the summit of the Aiguille Blanche. Our day's programme was a grandiose one. We wanted to reach the Peutéret Ridge by way of the North Face of the Aiguille Blanche, only climbed once before, and then on to the Summit of Mont Blanc, following the rest of the Ridge.

We had the choice of two routes up the North Face. We could either go up the face to the left—by-passing the ice-bulge which cuts the wall halfway up—or pass directly under the bulge, and up by a hanging glacier. The second alternative had the advantage that we would be well protected from falling ice and stones, whereas on the open, even slope we should have no cover from those obvious dangers. Moreover the ascent by the hanging-glacier looked like being more varied and less exacting. So we decided for it.

Martin had not yet found his full confidence on ice, but he followed pluckily. We went up steeply, sometimes on snow, sometimes on smooth ice, with the great balcony of ice hanging poised overhead like a sword of Damocles; but it presently withdrew itself from our view, wrapping itself in mist. To our right, at a safe distance, rock avalanches went pouring down from the Col de Peuteret in an unending succession, to come to rest on the ice of the Brenva Glacier some 2,500 feet below. A dark secondary gully marked their deadly course.

After about a thousand feet we came to rock; it was a spur falling from the ice-bulge. Keeping to the left, we climbed the exceedingly steep, partly vertical upper lip of a *bergschrund*, which called for extreme care, because of fresh, moist snow lying on the sheer ice. Every rope's length called for a piton, and the snow kept on clotting under our crampons.

An ice ridge, narrowing rapidly as it led up towards the bulge, projected from this part of the face. That marvellous projection of solid ice, when seen from close to, proved to be about 300 feet high at its right-hand end and entirely overhanging. There was no question of trying in that direction; the left-hand side looked a little less uninviting; but promised to be quite a problem, for a slight re-entrant, protected by a sixty-foot perpendicular wall, offered the only means of progress.

I traversed towards it across the steep slope, and found a narrow crack leading upwards. "Just what I'd been waiting for!" I grinned at Martin, as I disappeared into it, like a mouse into its hole.

It was uncomfortable in there, with the water running down right over me, but it offered ideal protection, and Martin took up his stance in it as I tried my luck on the vertical ice-wall above.

The ice was very soft. Our rather short ice-pitons slipped into it as into butter, but equally easily out again, so I had to try something different. With the spike of my ice-axe in one hand and a piton in the other, I balanced from foothold to foothold with infinite care. That went very well for a little while; then, suddenly, both my hand-grips gave way, my body parted from the wall and I finished on the rope, some feet below my partner.

Who said "Pack it in"? We mustn't let a little scare like that put us off!

I tried again, even more carefully than before, pushing my way up an inch at a time. Owing to the continual pull of gravity on my body, I hardly dared to breathe. I had to keep my hand-holds to below chest-level, so as not to throw too much weight on them, while I followed mincingly on my crampon-points. I was really worried lest the next step, even the next movement, should upset my balance again. Fear kept on surging up and I had to master the paralysing emotion.

After sixty feet the angle eased a little, and I could trust my weight to my legs again with some confidence; the consistency of the ice, too, improved and I was delighted to see the pitons biting into it. Then a 150-foot ice-slope, again very steep and covered in wet snow, led to less tilted ground. As I looked back it suddenly occurred to me that the whole slope might have slid away in an avalanche, with most unpleasant consequences. The thought of where that would have landed us sent a cold shiver down my spine.

From above, the ice-bulge looked like a giant's ski-jump above a bottomless abyss: it was impossible to see down over it onto the slope by which we had fought our way up.

The way to the summit was now clear. We were separated from the ridge by an ice-slope of about fifty-five to sixty degrees; but it was good ice and we made good progress on our crampons without having to cut steps. We drew rapidly nearer to the summit till Martin hazarded a guess that it was only three to four ropes' lengths away; I knew the difficulty of judging those things and multiplied his estimate by four, for luck, and my calculation proved correct. At exactly twelve-thirty we stood on the Summit of the Aiguille Blanche. It was our first "Four Thousander", and we had come up a 3,500-foot ice-wall of great difficulty, to get there; but we could not yet give way to rejoicings, for we still had a long way to go.

The view was superb.

Far below lay the dark profile of the Aiguille Noire, and when the mists—which lodged so obstinately down below—parted, we could see a magnificent realm of ice. Opposite us, too, was the wonderful expanse of the broad wall, almost 3,000 feet high, of Mont Blanc de Courmayeur; we could hear the frequent clatter of stone-falls sweeping it—particularly the bottom thousand feet, which are heavily enfiladed during the afternoon hours, as the dark discolouration of the snow at its feet clearly testified. It was just the worst time.

After a short rest we crossed the other two summits of the Aiguille Blanche and climbed about 600 feet over very friable rock down to the Col de Peuteret below. We crossed the Col and cantered up the steep snow-slope to the start of the rocks, where we gathered ourselves under the shelter of a steep cliff. Then, managing to circumvent the danger-zone where the stones were falling, we climbed over the steep rock, to the "Corner Buttress" (13,920 feet) from which the fine-drawn line of the *arête* leaps up—at first in a series of steep pitches, later to lose itself in an even steeper slope of frozen snow, for another 1,700 feet, to the summit of Mont Blanc de Courmayeur (15,647 feet.)

The clouds came seething up from the valleys and presently blanketed everything from view. We managed to keep up our rate of progress, in spite of the rarity of the air, which had become noticeable, and we were delighted to find we were in such good trim, which was essential to our plans. The ensuing ice-ridge seemed endless, crest upon crest looming out of the fog. We moved on mechanically, along the narrow edge which appeared out of a grey monotony ahead, and vanished into it behind us. It is probably a glorious ascent in fine weather, a veritable Jacob's Ladder; in this mirk we could only surmise what gulfs fell away on either hand. Every now and then I glanced at my altimeter, only to pocket it again in disappointment, for it always registered less than I hoped.

The ridge eventually gave out into an enclosed slope which steepened abruptly. It was ground over which we could safely move unroped, and that made for greater speed. Hard snow gave way to smooth ice; our calves ached from continual climbing on the front points of our crampons, which we had worn since we got on to the Brenva Glacier, and we had to call frequent halts. We estimated the slope at fifty degrees, about the same as the Pallavicini Couloir on the Grossglockner. It grew darker and darker, and visibility was cut to about 50 feet by the mist. For a moment we thought we had misjudged the passage of time and it was already nightfall; but a glance at the watch showed it was only four in the afternoon. Perhaps the watch was suffering from the altitude—or was something frightful brewing behind that fog? It wasn't long before we found out!

The storm broke without the slightest warning, in a deluge of hail. Everything around us was suddenly alive; the very floor under our feet seemed to be running away, as a roaring mass flowed downwards all about us, in little avalanches of snow and hail, disappearing into the fog below. It was a good thing that we were as far up as we were, for the moving masses had not yet gathered sufficient strength to tear us from our feet. We pressed on unrelentingly through the uproar.

I encouraged Martin by reminding him that we couldn't be far from the Summit Ridge. When I looked at the altimeter again it showed 15,420 feet, and I began to wonder whether that useful instrument, on which we had always been able to rely, had let us down at last. If the altitude it recorded was correct, we ought to be quite near the ridge, but there wasn't the slightest sign of it. So we just had to plod on.

Then, suddenly, a shadow loomed up through the fog—a ghostly, distorted thing, magnified to great proportions by the mist. We hardly dared to believe it was the Summit Cornice as it drew rapidly nearer.

It was a huge wave of snow bulking above us—the mountain's last rampart. We found a weak spot in its defences and up we went. The wind screamed overhead; and, as I raised my head over the rim of the cornice, the full force of the icy blast smote me in the face. In a moment my wet clothes were frozen into a stiff armour plating. It was a good job that I had found out everything beforehand about the way to the Summit of Mont Blanc; otherwise we could never have found it in such a fog. We went down over a short ridge of rock into a hollow, and then on over a flattish snow-slope, groping our way forward step-by-step, with the utmost care in the all-enveloping grey of the flying mist and the sounding rage of the hurricane. We knew that gigantic cornice was on our right, overhanging the Brenva Face, but we also knew we mustn't keep too far to the left, or we might miss the summit altogether; in which case we couldn't hope to pick up our direction again correctly, for the summit is a great flattish dome. The storm was now coming from all sides at once; we looked like snowmen, ice in our hair and eyebrows, all of us sugared over with a frosty rime.

We could no longer tell whether we were going up or down; all sense of balance had deserted us, and we could hardly see the floor beneath us.

Abruptly we found ourselves standing before something thin, long and unidentifiable, apparently about twenty yards from us; at the first stride we took we nearly bumped into it. It was a rod, the Summit Signal. We were on the highest point in the Alps.

We shook hands; but there was no time to give vent to our feelings; somehow we had to get on—and under shelter. We quickly consulted the map and compass and checked our height with the altimeter— 15,781 feet. The wind nearly tore the map out of our hands; but we managed to plot our direction, and soon we were on our way down towards the Vallot Hut. We ran down the easy ridge as quickly as eyesight allowed us to, and that at last brought some warmth into our numbed limbs. Suddenly we stopped in sheer amazement. A wonderful picture opened up as a rift in the mists revealed, abysmally far below, a pleasant landscape of foothills. Far away, through a thin veil of mist, lay the trench of the Aosta Valley, with the cloud tatters of a retreating thunderstorm drifting high above it in a marvellous riot of colour— Nature in her most wonderful artistry. It only lasted a few minutes; then we were back behind the curtain again, with only the storm and the mist shutting us in.

We couldn't very well miss the Refuge, which stands plumb on the crest of the Bossons Ridge. It was half-past seven, and we fled from the storm into the shelter of that aluminium asylum just as we were, with the rope and our crampons still on us. It was already packed full; we had been looking forward to warmth—and relaxation, but here there was no question of comfort.

There was no firewood; everything was draughty; the floor was so wet and cold that we couldn't even take our boots off. We started the cooker up to melt snow, and tried to thaw out our frozen clothes. We spent the whole of the evening till "bedtime" attending to our feet, which had been numb for hours; massaging and rubbing the life back into them, jammed elbow-to-elbow with our suffering hut-mates. Nor did bedtime offer any improvement in the general discomfort; the iron frames of the "beds" gnawed into our bones and the only covering we had was the thin *batiste* of our Zdarsky-sack. We might just as well have been bivouacking in the open, and we lay there longing for the morning to come.

It did—eventually. The temperature in the hut had fallen to below freezing-point and the water in our cooking-utensils had frozen. Gingerly, and by a great effort of will-power, we got back into our wet, cold clothes again. My boots, however, were frozen stiff and objected; I had to soften them up for quite a time with the climbing-hammer.

It was a marvellous morning. Like the waves of a stormy sea, the carpet of clouds lapped the flanks of the White Mountain. It was bitterly cold outside—twenty below! The wind was chasing whole clouds of fine snow-powder over the smooth expanses of the summit. This morning we could recompense ourselves to the full for what yesterday's weather had stolen from us. We gazed and gaped, and marvelled at what we saw.

The route over Mont Maudit and Mont Blanc du Tacul, the so-called "Longitudinal Traverse" is, moreover, far more varied and more beautiful than the normal way down over the Dôme Glacier. I felt in splendid trim, though Martin was feeling the altitude—not that he complained about it. I felt like shouting aloud because the world was so lovely and life so good to live. In order to give vent to my joy, I rushed up the 1,400 feet to the Summit of Mont Blanc in threequarters of an hour, on the wings of an indescribable exaltation.

There are no words in which to describe the unforgettable impressions of that moment. An ocean of peaks, snowfields, dark walls lay spread beneath us. They were our kingdom; yet we were, at one and the same time, their mighty lords and their humble servants. Almost 13,000 feet below lay the Vale of Chamonix; the hideous, dull hotel buildings were from up here nothing but toys.

Unfortunately, it was too bitingly cold for us to stay long. We went down to the Col de la Brenva over snowfields of varying inclination, seamed by cunningly-hidden crevasses. The ensuing climb of 500 feet to Mont Maudit (14,650 feet) warmed us up again, and new vistas opened up at every stride. Our eyes were held by the glorious ice-adorned bastion of the Brenva Face, at whose left-hand edge we could clearly see the track of our yesterday's ascent; it was the first time we had seen the full immensity of that mountain wall. To the right a long, corniced ridge hemmed the precipice with great hundred-foot vertical snow-walls, overhanging the gulf. There was nothing pretty about it; everything was huge, sheer and overpowering in this world of great heights, which evokes so keen a love.

We crossed Mont Maudit and descended a steep slope beyond it. Then the fun began; we sat down and hurtled down on the seats of our pants, flying clean over the two *schrunds* that cut across the face. Very soon we were on the Col du Tacul, where Martin waited for me while I hurried up a broad snow-track to the summit of Mont Blanc du Tacul, in order to enlarge my collection of "Four Thousanders" at the earliest possible opportunity.

We could see the track to our objective, the Rifugio Torino, 3,000 feet lower down. A well-trodden path spared us the trouble of route-finding down the steep slopes falling from the Tacul. In a very short time, crossing rickety snow-bridges, past greenish-glimmering gulfs in which you could have sunk a whole block of flats, between ice-pinnacles the size of church towers, we reached the track on which we had been looking down so short a time before; but the sun-softened surface of the Upper Géant Glacier allowed us to break through into several hidden crevasses before we reached the Col du Géant.

I was rather tempted to make a diversion to the Dent du Géant or the Rochefort Ridge, but one can't do everything at once. Besides, my partner's condition was beginning to worry me—he looked in pretty poor shape. So we went down to Entrèves.

My boots were by now in such a pitiable state that they could not have stood another ice-climb, so we could only plan a rock-expedition. There was no lack of magnificent rock-faces hereabouts, so what about the West Face of the Noire? It was a name that had always had a special attraction for me; the very description spoke for itself. The upper half of this 2,000-foot wall consists almost entirely of penthouses and over-hangs; for instance, the climbing guide reads: "Two overhangs lead to a roof; you climb it to a second roof, where a hundred-and-twenty-foot overhang begins"—and pages more like that. The first two to climb it were the Italians, Ratti and Vitale. The guide-book mentions the time it took them: three days, with bivouacs on the Face.

Even if the climb is one of the severest ever made on granite, its lesser height and greater approachability forbid a comparison with the Jorasses Buttress. All the same, ten years went by before another rope, of French climbers, made the second successful attempt in July, 1949.

Martin was fit again; at least, he believed so, or wanted to believe it.

We agreed that the West Wall of the Noire would provide a fitting finish. So off we went again one afternoon, sweating our way up to the Gamba Hut, along a trail very much like that to the Noire Hut, only longer. On the right we had another opportunity of admiring the fearsomely dentated South Ridge of the Aiguille Noire. The nearer we drew to the Hut, the steeper looked the West Wall, towering overhead to the sky at an uncanny angle, terribly steep and smooth, above a chaos of shattered ice-masses. Tatters of cloud moved across the summit and formed into a cloud-banner drifting away to the west—an omen of bad weather. All the same, the face made a friendlier impression than the Buttress of the Jorasses; it wouldn't be altogether out of place in the Dolomites, I thought.

Martin had been too plucky; he was not at all well yet. His condition had deteriorated visibly on the way up, so he stayed at the Hut, while I went to explore the way to the climb, in the hope that he would have recovered by the morning.

At the Col de l'Innominata (10,171 feet) I had the whole Wall right opposite me. I soon memorised the way up and secretly hoped to be able to complete the climb in a single day. Below me lay the Fresnay Glacier, the steepest in the Mont Blanc Range, which falls 7,000 feet in a mile and a half, hurtling valleywards like a raging torrent frozen into rigidity. Emil Rey, the guide who knew Mont Blanc better than anyone, once said: "You can't get to know it, it changes from week to week."

I gave the glacier below me a long searching appraisal till I thought I had found the best way through, and was just about to climb down to it, when an ice-tower the height of a four-storey house collapsed with a terrific din—to go avalanching down the steep surface. After some consideration I realised that my passage was barred by a number of similar highwaymen and that to-morrow would be quite early enough for venturing on to their beats. So I left the ice-axe at the Col and took the opportunity of climbing the wonderful North Ridge of the Aiguille Joseph Croux (10,568 feet). I felt marvellously fit and hoped Martin would surely have recovered from his indisposition; then there would be nothing to prevent our crowning our programme with success.

Fortune had decreed otherwise. Martin was lying on his mattress, shivering heavily, though we neither of us knew the cause—unless he had eaten too much snow. Whatever it was, it was essential to get him to where he could rest and receive attention, even if it was sad to have to abandon our plans when we were so near to our objective. But Martin's well-being was the first consideration and down we had to go, leaving our equipment up there, in case it still proved possible to use it.

On the way down I remembered that our friends from Innsbruck were still down at Entrèves; one of them might still like to do the climb with me. Two hours later we were back in our tent.

We received a sarcastic welcome.

"How d'you do, Messrs. Ratti and Vitale?" they enquired.

But they soon stopped ragging us when they heard of Martin's misfortune. They had already packed their things so as to leave for Innsbruck next day; they at once offered to take the invalid home with them.

Sad at heart, I strolled up alone to the Gamba Hut and up to the Col de l'Innominata to fetch the ice-axe. On the way down I came upon a group of Italians who were watching the wall and continually pointing to it.

I asked them what was going on.

"*Amici,*" they answered. "*Sula pariete*—friends on the wall."

What a pity. . . .

But as I turned to say good-bye to the Peaks of the Mont Blanc Group, I promised myself that I would come back.

And I did.

THE SOUTH-WEST WALL OF THE
MARMOLATA, IN WINTER

I COULD not put the sky-raking Buttress of the Grandes Jorasses out of my mind; it had made an indelible impression on my heart and brain. I thought of it, dreamed of it, lived in a fever of imagination about it. But I am not the sort who is satisfied just to yearn for something I desire so hotly: achievement is the only final answer. And between desire and achievement lies preparation.

I have always taken preparation seriously. Perhaps it is because I am lucky enough to be able to visualise difficulties and dangers in advance, and have the gift of assessing mountains and the routes up them with accuracy. I have never wanted to belong to that class of climbers who underestimate their mountain and then give up at the crucial point. Such withdrawals are only the result of insufficient preparation. The first thing is to know ourselves; to establish—or at least assess—our own limitations. Then we have to see to it that our level of performance matches the difficulty and danger of the proposed climb. It is essential to take every mountain seriously.

I certainly took my plan to climb the North Buttress of the Grandes Jorasses to the Pointe Walker very seriously indeed. The months before I could make my attempt would have to be devoted to training and to preparation.

It was the beginning of 1950, and winter still reigned. I had found the ideal partner in Kuno Rainer. That cheerful, silent man possessed all the virtues of a first-class mountaineer—courage, absolute dependability and extreme virtuosity on both rock and face. He was not of the breed who recoil in horror if you suggest a plan which mediocre men would stigmatise as sheer lunacy, and he was just as ready as I to attempt the most difficult faces in our own mountains under winter conditions, so as to be completely adequate for the greatest climbs in the Western Alps in summer. We consequently climbed the South-East Gully of the Fleischbank in the Wilde Kaiser together in early February, a climb which ranks as one of the hardest in the Northern Limestone Alps and the severest among the faces dominating the Steinerne Rinne; this was one of the few repetitions of that formidable gully ever made, and certainly the first in winter. We took little longer than a good "rope" requires under summer conditions; so we were obviously in pretty good form.

But we wanted to improve on it, and therefore set ourselves new and even more difficult targets. Hadn't Fritz Kasparek first climbed the North Wall of the Grosse Zinne in winter because he had in mind the Eiger North Wall for the following summer? And wasn't there a Dolomite Wall—the South-West Face of the Marmolata steeper, harder and more dangerous than all others, waiting for us? The Italian team led by Solda were the first to climb it, years ago, after days of bitter struggle with the merciless rock, with grim nightly bivouacs on tiny ledges in the overhanging wall. We would have liked to have been the second party to do it, for this terrible wall is rather like a staircase whose top overhangs its base; but French climbers beat us to it. Their account of the climb was anything but comforting. And now I wanted to risk this most fearful of all Dolomite climbs in winter conditions.

I suggested it to Kuno, that responsible and experienced climber, whose harum-scarum days lay far behind him—not that he had ever been harebrained—and he did not shake his head. After a short period of consideration, he agreed; the battle was already half won.

The weather, however, was not yet agreeable, and all the reports from the Dolomites showed that there would be no point in making an attempt; so we lost the whole of February. There were now only three weeks of winter left; and on March the 4th the weather looked more promising. The peaks lay in a deep covering of fresh snow, but a steel-blue sky stretched over them. Four of us in a club-mate's car went spinning up the wide curves of the Brenner Road; our companions were Theo Plattner and Rudl Seiwald. The Frontier-guards who checked our passage were openly amazed at our equipment, particularly the immense amount of climbing-aids and material.

Down we went into the green, sunny Eisack Valley, straight into the forerunners of spring-time. At Bozen, where we slept, we made cautious enquiries about the state of the Marmolata; our friend advised us firmly to give it a miss—the snow was still much too "avalanchy" and it was far too early in the season—"yes, wait till April or May; then the Marmolata would be in perfect condition." Now our friend was thinking of the ski-tour; if he had known that we were contemplating an attack on the Queen of the Dolomites by her most difficult side, he would doubtless have consigned us to a madhouse. It was a good thing, really, that nobody knew. . . .

The next morning was taken up by a lovely drive to Auer and through the Fleimstal to Predazzo, but now we were back in mid-winter again. On either side of the road lay banks of snow, twelve to fifteen feet high, shutting off the view completely. The driver had his work cut out and, just to upset the time-table a bit, we had a puncture. It didn't take long to mend, and at about four in the afternoon we reached Canazei, where one leaves the road and goes up to the Contrinhaus. We asked the whereabouts of the caretakers of that hut, and were directed to Herr Deculian, who welcomed us in right friendly fashion; he has a most sympathetic understanding of climbers and their needs, and at once handed us the keys of his hut. A Canazei guide, who looks after the Contrinhaus in winter, came with us as we left the Valley and its hospitality. Our packs weighed heavily on our shoulders and our ski sank deep in the virgin snow; it was dark by the time we reached the Hut, so that we could not even take an overnight look at our Wall.

During the night I was shaken from my sleep by a fierce storm. I looked out of the window, but the Marmolata was veiled in mists. Towards dawn, however, the storm abated and gave way to the break of another marvellous day, by whose light we had our first sight of the South-West Wall of the Marmolata, deep in her winter robes. The whole wall was powdered with snow and the general impression was repellent; but we decided none the less to try our luck. We packed our climbing-rucksacks, taking only the bare essentials; in spite of which each of us still had 50 lb. to hump all the three-hours' way up to the foot of our climb. There a strong wind was blowing loose drift-snow over from the north side of the ridge; it came rustling down the wall like silver snakes, and the cold was bitter. Our spirits were pretty low as we got ready to climb. We had each a double rope about our torso; each carried a hundred-foot *rappel*-cord and each of us had an iron-monger's shop hanging from him; add to which a climbing rucksack apiece, say twenty pounds on our backs. Good show!

Kuno took the first lead. Every movement spoke of an outstanding master of his craft; everything looked so easy. But I knew the Marmo-lata rock and, sure enough, the first piton was soon in demand; and soon afterwards Kuno was safeguarding me up to him. I led the next rope, ploughing up to my hips in snow. My fingers were soon numb; there was ice all over the rock, and a fine powdering of blown snow lay on every hold. I went up into a 120-foot chimney, bending away to the left, which was partly filled with snow; higher up it became narrow, smooth and exhausting. I clawed on to the rock with my fingers, but I could only see that they were gripping, not feel it, so cold had they grown. What would it be like later on, I wondered!

With great caution I climbed the chimney, which broadened outward like a gaping gullet, threatening to spew me out. By the time Kuno joined me, my fingers were a little warmer.

And this was only the start. . . .

Most of the way up we were moving through snow. Pitches rated at only "IV" or "V"—that is "difficult" and "very difficult"—were on this occasion demanding the extremest "VI" of us.

We came to a series of snowed-up slabs, where every safeguard was but an illusion. The only thing protecting us here was our complete confidence in one another. I found a stance after about a hundred feet, and on we went. My hands went scratching round in the snow, searching in vain for a hold; my feet were on ice-coated slabs and sometimes I dared not risk the next step, for fear that the snow would not hold on the smooth, ice-bound stone. But at the last I managed even that fearsome pitch safely.

Kuno led again. He disappeared to the left in a crack, which petered out under smooth, beetling slabs. While we were suspended under their black roofs, the dusk began to draw in on us; it was already five o'clock. What should we do? We had only come up 600 feet—that is a quarter of the face—and it had taken us six hours; whereas in summer it takes one and a half to two. We might possibly reach the second terrace before darkness fell; but what about the overhanging crack above it; or the later traverses—among the most difficult anywhere, which would mean crossing three ropes'-lengths of holdless, snow/ slabs in darkness; to say nothing of the final gully to the summit!

There was nothing left but to beat a prudent retreat.

We left most of the ironmongery up there. We couldn't dream of an *abseil*, the rock overhung far too much and we should have been hanging too far out in thin air ever to get back on to the rock at the end of the rope-down. So we had to climb down the whole way, and the last 150 feet of it in the dark. We were very late back at the Contrinhaus.

We decided to wait a few days for the snow to melt on the Wall, and then have another go. So next day we did a ski-tour to the Cima Cadini by way of a change. It was very warm but, owing to its crossing the 10,000-foot altitude line, we could see no sign of any drying-out of our Wall. We came back to the Hut about mid-day and found visitors there—a guide from the Val di Fassa and the Hut-keeper—with whom we spent a very cheery evening.

Next day we ski'd to the Ombretta Pass and climbed the Cima Ombretta. From there we had our Wall under close observation directly opposite us, and could recognise every detail through binoculars. There seemed no sense in our starting out again; there was still far too much snow on the face. So we decided that I should go straight back to Innsbruck to fetch fresh supplies, while Kuno held the fort at the Contrinhaus.

No sooner said than done. In the evening, to the utter astonishment of some of my friends, I was back in Innsbruck. They would have had something to grin at, had they really known!

* * *

On Thursday, 9th March I was back at the Contrinhaus, arriving late in the evening. While Kuno was stowing the provisions I had brought, I lay down on my bed, dead-beat, and was soon in dreamless sleep. My friend shook me awake far too soon; it was half-past four when we shut the door of the hut behind us. There were light clouds in the sky, but they soon dissolved, till the vault of the sky shone clear and clean.

Conditions were decidedly better this time, and we reached our former point of return in a relatively short time. We divided up the iron-mongery—which we retrieved here—between us, and then I took over for the first super-severe pitch on the climb. I climbed over a roof to an overhanging crack which took me, after about 60 feet, on to a pulpit. The rock hereabouts was wonderfully firm. Then an absolutely smooth slab presented itself, with a vertical crack splitting it, to offer the only means of progress. The wall was defending itself, and a number of overhanging pitches held us up for quite a time. The rock was icily-cold, for the sun was still cut off by the enormous buttress to our right.

Suddenly I could see no way ahead, and in order to solve the riddle I consulted the route description. I had come up too far, and would have to go back a few yards and then across a smooth face to the left, where I ought to find a hidden crack leading on upwards. How easy it is to read a route when described on paper; how hard it is when you actually get on to it!

I worked out across the rocks to the left on a light rein. There I met the first piton, but it looked so untrustworthy that I didn't use it. Sure enough, a narrow "split" led upwards, to lose itself very soon in smooth protruding bulges; its rock was outward-sloping. Could I get up it? I was certainly on the right route, for I could see the next piton—20 feet higher up.

I worked up towards it with my hands in the crack and my feet splayed wide apart. Meanwhile, the sun's warmth had at last reached me, and I enjoyed its arrival to the full; poor Kuno was, however, still in icy shadow down below.

More and more overhangs presented themselves, and the crack was by now only a mere surface scratch, with a great lack of holds. In spite of the cold, sweat poured down me, and I gasped for breath. "No more rope!" I heard from below. I could only just manage to keep my balance, yet I had no choice but to let him come up to me. First, however, the rucksack had to be brought up on the rope. The wall overhung so much that I only caught sight of it a few feet below me and as I was hauling the sack up the last bit, it stuck among the rocks; so I had to try to free it by brute-force, precariously perched as I was. I managed it, but the back of the rucksack tore from top to bottom; by sheer luck, I had the bivouac-sack packed at the back, and it kept everything safely together. Then I had to do the whole thing up like a parcel and tie it on my back. When that was all done, I let Kuno come up.

Two easier ropes'-lengths brought us to the edge of the second terrace—we were halfway up.

It was two o'clock. We stood on astonishingly roomy snowbands in the midst of unbroken overhanging walls of rock. Menacingly heavy clouds were coming up the Etschtal from the west—to our discomfiture. We dared not rest long; soon we were on our way again.

We reached the huge yellow gully at the left-hand end of the terrace by a traverse over snow-laden ledges, in a savage setting such as is only found in the Dolomites. The right side of the gully was one mighty block, which might have been cast in a foundry, while on the left we were overhung by huge projecting masses of rock. Some 600 feet further up and protruding a good 60 feet above us, we could see the entry into the Summit Rift. Somewhere in between must lie the notorious traverse, and there was a black streak, probably ice, coming down the rock. We were committed inescapably to some very tough work ahead.

The gully pushed me remorsely outwards. I felt like a spider, as I hung with my hands and feet on the same level, maintained there by nothing but friction, in a series of acrobatic exercises, 1,200 feet above the floor. I reached a small belaying spike and wanted Kuno to come up to me, but he insisted on a withdrawal, pointing to the imminent break in the weather; and he was right. It was essential to get down as quickly as possible. I put a rope-ring round the spike and let myself down on the rope, while Kuno kept on bringing me back into the rock by pulling on the second rope; for anywhere on this Wall, roping-down means a journey through space, far divorced from the rock.

Meantime, it had begun to snow over the Rosengarten, and a hefty thunderstorm was brewing, over the Pala; a massive cloud came rushing at us, driven by a howling gale, in shape and colour appropriate to the end of the world. By the time we were ready to go on down, the mists were already creeping over the Ombretta Pass; it was half-past six and growing late.

We joined the 220-foot ropes, safeguarded ourselves with the belaying-rope and down we went into the depths—sheer acrobatics in space under the Big Top of the sky and with no safety-net below. Once again I went hurtling down on a spring-clip. I couldn't see the end of the ropes, as the pitches went by me—pitches which had cost us so much sweat on the way up, wrung us with alternating hopes and fears, and won us such a measure of hard-won success. I came to the end of the rope, but was still hanging a long way clear; so I tried to reach a lodging on the wall by setting up a lateral motion. There was I, swinging backwards and forwards like a pendulum, till at last I got a touch on rock, managed to claw on to it, and finally got something firm under my feet again.

While Kuno was freeing the *abseil* ropes and I was banging in a last piton, a furious storm was upon us. That put paid to any more roping down; we would now have to climb diagonally down the base of the wall, using the rope that way. The gale whipped the ropes out from the rock in a great loop, and it began to snow. We were thankful to the core that we had decided to turn back in time. At half-past eight, in pitch darkness, we were back at our skis at the morning's starting point.

We made our laborious way down to the Hut over friable crust; and even as we went down it was obvious that the bad weather was departing. When we reached the Hut the stars were twinkling again in a clear sky, but we were far too weary to be either pleased or cross about it; we lay down at once, to sleep.

The next morning was as lovely as the preceding ones; the weather had fooled us properly. All our equipment was, however, wet, and our bones were still feeling the previous day's exertions, so we did not even consider a return to the attack.

This meant saying good-bye to the wall for good. Kuno's leave was up and he had to get back. We turned our backs on the wall with heavy hearts. Was it good-bye for this winter only? Or was it for ever?

*   *   *

We were back at the foot of the wall the very next week-end, with Hugo Vigl and Karl Gombotz as our companions to the Contrinhaus.

At 3 a.m. on March the 19th the alarm rattled us awake, and we saw through the window that everything was overcast; but off we went, just the same. This time we had reduced our equipment to a minimum, so as to speed-up our progress. We just took one climbing-rucksack, far less ironmongery, one bivouac-sack only, no spare clothes and provisions sufficient for only two days—in fact the barest essentials. We

simply had to do the climb in two days, in the absence of emergency
provisions, or turn back once again in safe time.

We were at the foot by six o'clock. The sky was dark and lowering,
and there was a cloud-sea lying on the valley below, while the Civetta
and the Pala were completely veiled. The sun rose like a blood-red ball;
these were real Föhn conditions and we felt duly depressed. An icy
west wind chilled us; it was the coldest day yet, and we put on every
piece of clothing we could muster—two shirts, two pullovers and our
Anoraks. Though we could hardly move because of their thickness,
the cold still rattled our teeth. And then we had to take our gloves off
and get to grips with the icy rock into the bargain. Still, it had to be done.

It was only seven o'clock, but we had to start early if we were to reach
the beginning of the great rift, which offered the only suitable spot for a
bivouac above the second terrace, in one day. In spite of the cold, we
made swifter progress than the week before, because we did not have
to bring the rucksacks up on the rope every time. Changing the lead
frequently, we reached the terrace by noon. The weather had not
improved, but we were determined not to retreat this time and flouted
its implications.

Once again I was at work in the gully and soon mastered the first
rope; once again the world contracted to a few bare feet, composed of
holds for feet and hands; nothing else interested us, as we concentrated
whole-heartedly on the actual climbing. We were on exiguous stances,
as we peered upwards at the huge yellow roofs shutting out the universe.
If the wall had been stood on its head, I believe one could have walked
up it, as on a gigantic staircase, without even using one's hands.

A narrow, polished overhanging crack took me up the next 60 feet
to end under a wildly jutting roof; I got pushed further and further
outwards, till forced to straddle my way up the extreme outer edge of
the chimney. There I found a piton and promptly added another, to
make assurance doubly sure.

"Haul in!" With infinite care I pushed myself out under the overhanging mass, juggling with balance. Stretching and tatting over its
surface, with my body lying almost horizontal beneath it, back downwards, I found a hold, and soon my other hand followed the first. It was
superb climbing: no complaints here, only matchless joy and thrills.
I was in such excellent form that I got over those pitches, described
as insurmountable without artificial aids, by straight climbing, without
the help of a hook or a sling. The wall below me had by now disappeared
from sight; anyone who chose to fall off here would never once hit the
rock but would go straight down, yards clear of the face, several hundred
feet, into the ravine at the bottom. If there is anything which truly

merits the description of overhanging and exposed, it is beyond any question the South-West Wall of the Marmolata.

Meanwhile it had begun to snow, though we were so sheltered by the huge roofs above us that the scurry of flakes did not reach us. The mists drew up from the Ombretta Pass and enveloped us in a monotonous grey veil.

The succeeding pitches were pretty similar—overhanging, polished, wonderful—and so we came to the start of the traverse. The slab on our right was sloping and utterly unbroken. We could see the entrance to the Summit Gully. Climbing diagonally upwards, mostly by pure friction of my rubber soles, which acquitted themselves wonderfully here, I reached a small platform, from which a narrow crack shot upwards, with just enough room for an arm in it. I had to climb the next fifty feet under a projecting bulge, without protection from pitons.

We were worried about the weather, which kept on getting worse. In two days' time, for valley-dwellers, it would be spring; but here, for us in the middle of a face rated as the hardest in the Dolomites even in fine summer weather, it was winter in all his grim sovereignty. We must hurry; but hurrying in such a place is an impossibility.

The snow was by now lying on the rock, hiding all the holds. A short horizontal traverse took me to an *abseil* piton, which took me to climbable ground about fifty feet lower down, where a ramp led upwards again to the left. One more smooth gully was the last defence separating us from the bivouac-place. Time was pressing: I climbed the difficult pitch as quickly as I could and found myself on quite a roomy perch, only to find that the bivouac-niche proper, under the shelter of the rock, was still a couple of ropes' lengths further to the right.

At six p.m. we were directly under the Summit Rift, with little trickles of fresh snow continually pouring out and over our heads from it. The weather conditions were now serious; if we didn't want to get trapped on the face we should still have to prepare the pitch up to the lower entrance of the rift, which is the worst on the whole climb. The rock was ice-bound and there was snow everywhere; my fingers were so cold that it was only by the aid of several pitons and the use of all my reserves of energy that I made any upward progress. I had climbed the fifty feet when darkness drove me down, with only half the pitch prepared, leaving the ropes hanging in position. I was soon back with Kuno and we proceeded to look for a suitable night-stop by the light of an electric torch. Unfortunately the usual bivouac-spot was unusable, being full of snow and ice, but we found a ledge a little below it. It was about as broad as my hand, but it did offer the possibility of sitting down, which was better than standing up all night.

We knocked in some pitons, and hung seat-slings and irons from them; then we pulled the bivouac-sack over our heads. It wasn't exactly comfortable, as we dozed off, hanging rather than sitting. The sack only reached down to our knees, and powder-snow from the rift overhead poured into our climbing shoes. In such a situation we couldn't cook, so we had to content ourselves with cold stuff; but we were able to warm our hands a little over a candle, while the snow whirled down incessantly. Our position was somewhat forlorn; if this went on there would be eighteen inches of new snow by the morning. Would it then be possible to complete the climb? If not, our retreat was already cut off for an absolute certainty. Our feet had long ago lost all sensation, our legs had gone to sleep; time practically stood still. At last the monotonous trickle on our shelter ceased and, when we looked out of our spyhole at about midnight, the sky was clear! Even if the cold had immediately grown more bitter, we preferred that to the snow. Our confidence was completely restored.

At five a.m. we gave the agreed torch-signal to Karl and Hugo, waiting down below. It was understood, and our friends immediately started off for the summit with the necessary equipment. An hour later we crawled out of the sack, to be greeted by searing cold. We brewed a hot cocoa, and slowly thawed out, conscious of the beneficial effects of the warming drink as it percolated to our very toes. We could now see for the first time how fearfully exposed a place we had chosen for our bivouac; the wall broke away sheer from under it and went down without a break. All we could see were the slopes beyond the Ombretta Pass.

We started off again at seven. We were thankful that we had prepared the next pitch the night before; in such cold it would have been utterly impossible to attack an unprepared stage of such difficulty.

About six inches of snow had fallen during the night. I worked my way up on the rope with gloved hands, getting warmed-up in the process, so that I could then tackle some genuine climbing. Climbing indeed! —what I was doing the next moment was a desperate scraping forward inch by inch, for the snow denied me any kind of a hold at all. Still, the inches added up to feet, the feet to ropes' lengths and at last I was at the entrance to the rift, which was a good deal less steep, but fearfully smooth. A hundred feet up it there was an iced-up overhanging step, which pushed me out to the left-hand rim, where the rock was highly polished and outward sloping—even in summer a hundred-per-cent friction problem, but now thinly glazed with ice all over and powdered lightly with snow into the bargain. Where was I to find the extra bit of friction?—that pitch demanded absolutely everything we had to give.

I kept on thinking I had a footing, then slipped off to be held by the next piton. To try to move any distance here without those safeguarding hooks would be sheer suicide—and murder of one's partner as well. But the actual hammering of the pitons, whose iron shafts stuck in one's hands, was harder even than the climbing.

The weather was belying its early-morning promise, and a wild flurry of snowflakes was soon coming down the rift; but we were fighting for dear life now and struggled on upwards. There was one more difficult rope, then the angle eased off a little, at long last; we had reached a point from which we could see the Summit Ridge, and at three o'clock we stepped out on to the Punta Penia (10,965 feet), hardly able to grasp that the frightful wall had released us from its clutches. We shook hands in token of the mutual support which had fused the two of us into one during the struggle.

Our friends Hugo and Karl were over there on the top of the Punta di Rocca, where the famous ski-run begins, but it wasn't easy to reach them, for we had to climb down a ridge, from which we were forced out on to the North Face, which was in a very unpleasant state. There was sheer ice hidden under the fresh snow and we had to cut steps with the climbing-hammer, unprotected as we were and in rubber-soled slippers! After a long time we reached the deepest notch in the gap and from there reached the Rocca Summit in no time, using a fixed cable.

The clouds had come down, the wind was rising and it was snowing. The first thing we found was two rucksacks with our climbing-boots in them; while we were putting our boots on, our friends joined us, mightily glad that we were still alive. There is a tiny Refuge below the summit, where we were glad to find shelter and rest; in it we celebrated our success and there we spent the second night on the mountain. And how much more comfortable it was than the one spent out on the wall, exposed to the elements!

Another six inches of snow fell during the night and next morning the storm was still raging. Kuno and I went down on foot through the mists to the Fedaja Pass, while Hugo and Karl ran down on their skis; but the bad snow conditions didn't allow them to move much more quickly than we could on foot, and they reached the Hut on the Fedaja Pass only a little way ahead of us.

Before they could make out what was happening, they were mobbed by some Italians at the Hut, and fervently toasted as *Vincatori*. The true warmth of Italian enthusiasm and emotion made it impossible for Karl and Hugo to explain that the actual "victors" hadn't arrived yet; so they just had to let it go at that.

Meanwhile, Kuno and I, thinking our friends were far ahead of us, had decided to by-pass the Hut and go straight on down to Canazei.

There we once again enjoyed the hospitality of Herr Deculian, whose joy over our success and our safe return was unbounded.

Nor could anything damp our own joy at having made the first winter ascent of the most difficult wall in the Dolomites. Not even a final bivouac in Bozen's public park!

DOWN A CREVASSE AND AN
ALPINE WAGER

In the spring I enjoyed some wonderful ski-runs in the Stubai and Oetztal Alps, over miles of even glacier, with glorious straight running, down over perfect snow.

I was the complete ski addict again, devoting my heart and soul to it, and I didn't put away my "boards" till the valleys of Northern Tirol were lovely with blossom.

Now it was time for climbing again, climbing on warm, sunny rock.

At that moment I was invited to do some film work in the Oetztal Alps. Out came the stowed-away winter equipment again—wax, skins, repair outfit and all; but my ice-axe and crampons went along too. Our base was the Taschach Haus at the far head of the Pinztal, and a very restful time we all had up there. I don't believe anybody to do with films ever over-exerted himself. When the weather was good we went out on the neighbouring Taschach Glacier; everything lay at our very door. When we didn't have to stooge about on skis among the wild ice-falls, or the Director didn't want me to accompany him on searches for scenes, there was nothing to do but play table-tennis—a game I had despised till then, but which I now took up passionately and not merely as a change of exercise. But if the weather was anything like good, we spent the whole day out on the glacier, though even that was punctuated by long pauses for rest; consequently we never forgot to take cards along for the times when one just sat about and waited.

One day the clouds parted suddenly and a little oasis of sun appeared, far too precious to be wasted.

The Director thought it would be a good idea if I roped down quickly "into that crevasse over there". He waved his hand towards it.

The camera was firmly lodged on a safe snow-bridge over the crevasse, ready to take the "hero" as, daring all and risking his life without a care, he lowered himself down into the depths.

"Hurry, hurry!" I quickly seized both ends of the beautiful new perlon rope lying ready on the floor, tied on to it and shouted to the others—who were still playing a hand of cards—to secure me; then I dashed off to the selected crevasse. There was plenty of snow on the glacier and there were ten people to take care of me—so what could go wrong?

There was a shallow moulding which clearly revealed the hollow chasm lying beneath it. I took a wide stride across it, but before I had time to do anything, the ground gave way under my feet and I found myself swallowed in a crevasse. It got darker and darker. As I fell, I thought: "You can't go far, they'll hold you!" Indeed, I found it rather amusing, and a nice change from the monotony of the ordinary "manu-factured" film stuff.

But my trip didn't come to an end: I kept on falling. The rope was loose and neglected to jerk tight. My crampons scratched against ice, as I struck against the walls of the crevasse—now on this side, now on that.

It was black as night. I thought I must be nearing the bottom—the Hut-Keeper had told me that the glacier was about 600 feet thick. I wondered what would happen when I hit the bottom. It is astonishing what a lot of time there is for thinking. And still the rope refused to tighten.

Suddenly it occurred to me that I wasn't secured at all, and that the types at the top had just left the rope lying on the floor. Just the sort of thing that could only happen in Filmland, I thought. My next thought was the unpleasant one that I'd had it. Only two things could happen now: either I would go on falling till I stuck, helplessly jammed in a narrow spot, or else I should be smashed to pieces at the bottom. Oh, of course, I could also be drowned in the icy glacier stream, gurgling down below there. Any moment now!

Actually what happened was the one thing I could no longer have hoped for. The rope went taut. I took a fearful jerk and my fall was arrested. I was still alive! Funny, too . . . I could still see.

At least, I knew I could still see, if there was any light to see by— which there wasn't down there in a dark chasm; and in time I did even make out a faint glimmer, coming down from about a hundred and fifty feet above, as I judged, though it might be more. I was able, too, to make out the shape of the crevasse. I was jammed in a narrow passage, and was in fact suspended there; the black abyss went on down below me, I had no idea how far.

Damp, cold walls pressed on my chest and shoulders unbearably, and I could get very little air. My right shoulder was wedged in front of my chest and I had a difficult struggle to improve my position.

The rope now ran loosely up. What help could that beautiful new perlon rope give me now? It ran over a jammed ice-block and hung down into the abyss, about fifteen feet away from me; its other end must be dangling somewhere over there . . . if I could only reach the rope!

I could see that the ice was red. Blood? Yes, I had a gash just above my eye. Everything had gone down into limbo—hat, goggles, ice-axe. My right shoulder hurt.

There was no point in shouting; they wouldn't even hear me and I must save my little remaining strength. The types up above would surely notice that I was missing . . . or were they still busily engaged on Pontoon; was a "twist" more interesting than I was?

I found out afterwards that it wasn't lack of interest, but simply inexperience of the tricks a glacier can keep up its sleeve. Nobody was thinking about danger or death. It was nice and warm and sunny. There was a rope, lying on the ground. Someone had tied himself on to one end of it and had gone off across the snow surface. Coil by coil the rope ran out; a most amusing sight and certainly nothing to worry about. Suddenly there was no rope, any more. What had gone wrong? The man at its other end had disappeared and only a hole showed where he had gone to.

Panic! A concealed crevasse had swallowed him up. They tore after the rope, trying to catch the end of it; too late—the last little bit of it had disappeared into the hole, too.

Ashen-faced, they stood there, still holding the cards, and peered down into the hole; there was a man down there, no doubt about that.

Could he still be alive? Very carefully, one of them lay down on his stomach and shouted down into the chasm: "Hallo! Hallo!—Hermann! Hermann!" After a while a faint reply came up from below, as if from a different world. They lowered a rope. I could see it snaking down towards me: a few feet from me it stopped.

I shouted up: "Too short! Too short!"

I was beginning to feel pretty bad—my head spun and everything went black before my eyes. Knowing that a moment's weakness might mean the end for me, I pulled myself together; I knew I could only last out a few minutes longer. The rope disappeared up above; presently it came down again. This time it was long enough, but nobody had thought of putting a loop in it; with the utmost difficulty I managed to manufacture one. In order to gain support for some part of my body, I started by putting my foot into the sling I had contrived. With the help of the pull from above, I then succeeded in working my way far enough out of the vice in which I was held to have enough room in which to tie myself properly on to the rope.

At long last everything was in order.

"Heave ho!" was the signal for me to be hauled up as if I were an ox. Fragments of ice came clattering down and hit me. My tormentors dragged me through a contraction in the crevasse by brute force, mercilessly, as if subjecting me to some mediaeval torture.

The rope cut into me; they had me wedged under a projection. I shouted: "Ease off, ease off!"

They didn't hear me, but simply went on heaving. "Heave ho!" It was evidently a case of "Heave ho! Up with him—alive or dead!"

Everyone now lent a hand; it was as though they were determined to make good their previous neglect. "Heave ho!"

After an eternity I came up to the light of day, and stood there dazed and dazzled.

For all the smiling sunshine, I was absolutely all in. I had been down in that cold, wet slit for a whole hour; anything from a hundred-and-fifty to two hundred feet down. But I was still alive to tell the tale!

From then on everybody was meticulous about ropes, including those who had always laughed when we took our "string" along. In fact, they were the very ones to be so scared by the incident that they hardly dared to venture on to the glacier any more; practised skiers though they were, they now pottered about like novices, testing every hollow with their ski-sticks.

To cheer me up, they gave me two little white tablets called Pervitin. They wanted to carry me down the glacier, but I felt fit enough to go on my own feet. The only thing that hurt was my right shoulder. Had I broken my collar-bone? Or damaged a shoulder-blade?

The tablets acted marvellously and I soon felt as fit as if nothing had happened; I even ski'd away from the others. I raced up the slope to the Hut as if it were a real competition, but then I had to go straight to bed. They poured a quart of brandy, and then another, into me and then I went to sleep. Was it the Pervitin that gave me my strength back and revitalised my body so quickly? That was the first time I heard of the miraculous drug and felt its marvellous effects.

I had to stop my film-work soon after that. They made me stay in bed for a while and I had to wear a shoulder-bandage for a long time. The weeks went by in idleness enforced, and I began to worry whether the summer ahead would pass over me without my being able to do anything in the mountains.

Rest-days are always dangerous days for a mountaineer. During those weeks I made the acquaintance of a charming girl who was later to have a vital influence on my life; but at the time I had no idea of that, and merely found it very pleasant, as a confirmed bachelor, to be going about with one of the opposite sex for a while.

A climb on the Wetterstein marked the return of my old confidence. It was the Riffelkopf South-East Face, and Sepp Jöchler did it with me, but I had to put aside my climbing plans once again, for I received a fresh invitation from the Film Company, this time to work in the

Bernina Group, new ground for me. Also, I needed Swiss francs for the summer to come. The work was the usual pottering around on the icefalls, which were much more open, now that the year was advancing; they were also on a vastly larger scale than those in the Oetztal Alps.

We played about with artificial snow and took shots in ridiculously harmless places, while the Producer explained over and over again how a rope should properly be knotted. He ought to know, after all! We experts just smiled tolerantly on these occasions.

We moved over to the Boval Hut and the work became more strenuous. The scene was set by Nature herself and we chose the most impressive spots on the Pers and Morteratsch Glaciers. We soon came to know almost every individual crevasse and sometimes undertook quite daring ice-climbs. In the burning heat of day and at night by the light of torches we had to deal with quite a few unpleasant situations. On one occasion I had to be lowered ten times running into a crevasse, with a clutch of magnesium torches in my hands. The smoke from the torches blazing into my eyes upset my stomach, and my sight and appetite were affected. Sometimes we worked the whole night through. We blasted avalanches into motion, high up on the faces, and blew up enormous ice-towers into thin air.

On those occasions we had to stand by the camera, ready for instant action, so as to rescue the precious instrument if there was any danger threatening it. We carted the heavy apparatus the length and breadth of the Morteratsch Glacier's famous ice-labyrinth, along the edge of terrific crevasses and across their gaping depths. It was then I began to alter my mind about the idleness of film-folk; there are times when they can go to it as if possessed.

The night work was over; it was four a.m. and we had free time till ten o'clock.

"Just long enough for the Biancograt," I suggested to Rudl.

"The Biancograt?—You're crazy!" he replied.

"I said the Biancograt," I maintained obstinately.

"But it's impossible—in six hours!" he explained, and promptly backed his opinion with a bet of fifty Swiss francs.

Some of the Swiss guides who had overheard the conversation joined me; and within ten minutes the amount of the wager had grown to 200 francs. I could tell from their self-satisfied smiles that they had already credited that exact sum to their accounts.

I suppose orthodox mountaineers will wrinkle up their noses at me, full of righteous scorn to see me debasing honest endeavour to the level of money-wagers, and for trampling a holy ideal underfoot.

But, my dear respectable critics, just think for a moment how long and how high can one pursue an ideal with 200 Swiss francs.

Such a sum could assure the whole of my next visit to the Western Alps—and there was the Buttress of the Jorasses, calling me irresistibly. It wasn't really idealism I was short of—it was just money. . . .

So much for the moment. There wasn't enough time to do it that very morning and we had to use the settled weather period for the film work. But I hadn't forgotten. . . .

At last we got a day off, and the weather was lovely. At two in the morning four of us left the Boval Hut, ascended the Pers Glacier and made for the North Face of Piz Palü, that wonderful triple-fronted ice-rampart supported on mighty pillars and armoured with huge hanging-glaciers.

We chose the central hanging-glacier for our line of ascent, which lay over alternating ice-walls of great steepness and less abrupt slopes. We avoided the middle of the glacier because of falling ice, and a vertical wall gave us some trouble at a point where a grotesque *sérac* hung threateningly into thin air, creaking menacingly in its internal regions. Everything about it was soft, and we were very happy when we had got well clear of it.

Far below us now lay the realm which had confined us for weeks past. At last we were in a position to look out over it, instead of having to look up from it at the lovely heights about us, in home-sick longing.

We went straight up towards the central summit over a steep ice-slope; as the angle decreased we found wet snow lodged on smooth ice, a very uncomfortable feeling and not a very safe situation. Presently, however, we were at the top and the 3,000 foot face had been mastered; it was only nine o'clock, much too early to call it a day, especially such a day as we had been forced to wait for so long. So we followed the Summit Ridge westwards, down into a deep depression and up over rock beyond it to the Bellavista Summits.

Two of us had had enough for a day at this point, so they went down. Only Sepp Fürrutter fell in with my idea of continuing along the ridge.

From Piz Züpo, 13,000 feet high, we looked out over a vast prospect, newly revealed, to the south, across the Bergell, where Piz Badile's tremendous North-East Face was clearly recognisable. It was one of the climbs I had longed passionately to do, and we wondered if there might still be time when our film-contract expired.

Very soon we had traversed Piz Argient, then down by steep ice-slopes below Crast' Agüzza, for which we had no time to spare, and in soft snow across to the Fuorcla Confin, which we reached late in the afternoon, in a pretty tired condition.

We were racked with thirst, for the sun had been scorching and our drinks had run out; but we could not bear to forego a visit to Piz Bernina, for all that. We stamped our way up the slopes to Piz Spalla, where a beautifully airy ridge, whose far side fell steeply to the Rosegg Plain, helped us to forget parched throats and weary limbs; this picturesque cauldron is shut off by Piz Scerscen and Piz Rosegg. As the sun went down, we stood on the summit of Piz Bernina, our second 13,000-foot peak that day.

We looked back along the whole ridge to Palü, picking out our tracks, which lay deeply etched along the extended crests. It was quite a nice collection of summits for our climbing diaries and an unforgettable day for the tablets of our memory.

Down below, the Boval Hut was already deep in shadow; it was time to hurry away. A rock-ridge with a deep cleft in it took us across to the white head of Piz Bianco, and then we loped at speed, on our crampons, down the wonderfully-moulded crest of the Biancograt. We roped down into the depths over an ice-bulge, then sailed down a snow-couloir sitting on the snow, and stumbled over the débris at the bottom to the hut in the darkness. It was ten o'clock, and when we came in through the door we had anything but a friendly reception. They told us we were supposed to use our energy on our job, not go milling about on crazy ridge-climbs on our day off. Well, you never know. . . .

The next day we had to get up early again, resume our loads and hump them up hill and down dale, for hours on end, without a break, the whole livelong day. Our knees were fairly buckled on the way down to the Hut in the evening, after such pleasure-trips.

From time to time we made use of short intervals between filming to climb one or another of the more accessible peaks, like Piz Prievlus and Morteratsch. But it seemed all up with my 200 franc bet to do the Bernina in six hours—there and back. I wondered. . . .

Once again they were shooting at night and we climbed up towards Piz Morteratsch by torchlight, but presently the weather deteriorated and it finally began to rain. Washout!

It was about four a.m. when we got back to the Hut. I would have liked to get out on to something again, but everyone else turned in, so there seemed nothing for me to do but lie down on my mattress, too. Suddenly Rudl whispered:

"Hermann, what about doing a climb?"

"Oh, I've gone to bed," I answered, turning the suggestion down.

But the urge had been stimulated, and I could find no rest. Finally I got up, only to find that Rudl had by now gone to sleep and growled back at me that now he didn't want to do anything. And as I stood wondering what to do, I suddenly knew what the answer was—the Biancograt and my wager!

I dressed quickly, had a bite, stuffed a smoke-bomb in my pocket and at exactly five o'clock I quitted the Hut, which stands at 8,050 feet. I should have to get back by eleven, or lose the whole earnings of my film-service, for I should then have to pay up 200 francs. So I had to look to it.

I went up the moraine at a trot and very soon I was at the foot of the steep rock-rib which runs up to the Biancograt. Rock suits me, so I got on much more quickly than on normal walking-ground. I moved across to the left under a steep nose of ice and made straight and steep for the start of the Biancograt, moving on crampons, without having to cut a step, towards the finest of all ice-ridges, where the enormous precipices fall away on either hand. There was a narrow streak across the ridge, a hidden crevasse.

I crossed the snow cautiously; after that there was nothing to retard my progress. At eight I was on Piz Bianco, but in spite of my acquaintance with the ridge up to Bernina, I found winter conditions here and everything was different.

Here, with six inches of fresh snow on all the rocks, I could only move slowly. There could be no thought of bets and record-breaking in such a place; the only thing that counted was the law of prudent climbing.

I kept on looking at my watch and weighing-up the chances. The two alternatives were a glorious tour in the Western Alps or outstretched hands demanding a 200-franc note. I was very much in favour of the former, so I dealt firmly with the treacherous ground and, at eight-thirty, I was standing on Piz Bernina's 13,295-foot summit.

I let off the smoke-bomb and a thick plume rose to the sky—a signal they could not fail to observe at the Hut. I stopped only a moment to greet, in the course of a brief survey, the great peaks on whose account I had to win this crazy bet; then I was on the way down again.

I got back to the Piz Bianco sooner than I had expected and, from it, I ran down the ice-ridge as if I had stolen something.

A quarter of an hour later I was on the saddle 1,600 feet lower down, where I met a guided party, coming up. They thought they had met a ghost. The guide wanted a chat with the ghost but, alas, there was no time.

I excused myself and hurried on, to disappear over the ice-bulge which breaks away down to the Morteratsch Glacier. One has to take great care here, especially on the descent, because directly beneath it there is an abrupt cliff, hundreds of feet high.

This time I avoided the rock-rib and slid down various gullies to its left on steep snow, long-jumping several crevasses as I went. Then I ran out on to the open glacier, intending to climb down the slabs at its bottom. Fine débris-dust covered the rock, already polished to a high degree, and progress was very difficult. The second-hand was racing round. Time—whole minutes of it—was slipping away.

I had to go back, traversing to the rock-rib, further and further away.

Instead of idling back quietly to the Boval Hut, I had to race down the narrow track on the crest of the moraine, jumping over boulders and hollows, racing up the last hair-pins, and arrived at exactly eleven o'clock—neither a minute too soon nor a minute too late.

I had won my holiday in the Western Alps.

THE BUTTRESS OF THE
GRANDES JORASSES

A HOT summer's day brooded over the Vale of Chamonix. It was high
noon as we went up the Mer de Glace towards the Leschaux Hut. A
pleasant breeze blew off the ice to cool our sweating bodies. The giants
of the Mont Blanc group shone dazzling white about us; only at the
very back, closing off the Leschaux Glacier, a dark, gloomy wall stabbed
into the azure of the sky, its lower part hidden by the outliers of the
Aiguille du Tacul.

Two days earlier we had sat on the summit of the Dru, marvelling
at that wall in all its majesty. Its aspect had depressed us considerably,
for we had it in mind to suborn it to our will. The North Face of the
Grandes Jorasses, with its sky-raking Buttress, is a rampart of rock
and ice probably without rival in the Alps. We were luckier this time
than in the two previous years. Not only was Kuno Rainer with me again
but we had succeeded at our very first attempt in making the fourth-
ever ascent of the North Wall of the Dru by way of that severest of
severes, the Allain crack. We were obviously in splendid form.

We were late in reaching the Hut. Before we went to sleep we had a
look at the weather, and were satisfied. Then we studied the route-
book for the hundredth time for the description of to-morrow's climb,
though we knew every foot- and hand-hold by heart.

At two a.m. on July 28th we closed the door of the Leschaux Hut
behind us. Bemused with sleep, we stumbled over the débris to the
moraine and, carefully picking our way over the big boulders, were soon
standing on the main stream of the glacier, which is quite flat hereabouts.
In a deathly silence, broken only by the crunching of the soles of our
climbing-boots, we bore to the right, jumping a few torrents, and started
up the Mallet Glacier. We reached the end of the *névé* and had to
exercise great care among the many crevasses we met beyond it; a
labyrinth of criss-cross cracks held us up for some time. Our only means
of crossing a huge, apparently bottomless pit—a collapsed snow-bridge—
nearly proved the finish of us. Kuno stood absolutely unbelayed on the
nearer snow-slope, letting the rope run out carefully round his shoulders
to protect me.

Armed with our only ice-axe I proceeded warily over the dark abyss.
I let myself fall on my hands at the other side so that I was lying almost
horizontal above the icy gulf. I rammed my axe into the soft snow on

the other side, cautiously followed it with one foot and then the other; at which moment the axe—my only support—gave way. I just managed to heave myself up, throw my body across the rim of the crevasse and drag my feet up after it. Otherwise it would have been a nice start to our operations!

The glacier steepened, but became correspondingly less broken. A grey light was at last pervading the eastern sky.

We made our preparations for the severe climb ahead of us; this time our equipment was first-class, above all much lighter than before. "Once bitten, twice shy"! We crossed the *bergschrund*, high as a house, at the foot of the great couloir separating the Buttress from the Peters Route, and started up. This time the edge-crevasse was easily mastered, and after a steep ice-slope we were on the rocky spur below the Buttress. Now we were really off!

We soon reached the place where we had turned back last year. We zig-zagged up over steep, excessively smooth slabs to the foot of the "Hundred-Foot Gully", the first of the super-severe pitches on the climb.

I climbed into the left-hand of the two ascending cracks—the Rébuffat crack. The very first few feet left no doubt that this was extremely severe stuff. A Grade VI Pitch on the Jorasses Buttress is, of course, just as difficult as one in the Kaiser or the Dolomites, but much more exhausting. The narrow groove soon petered out into polished slabs, and I had to use a short traverse on an outward-sloping rounded ledge on the brink of nothingness to reach the parallel "Allain" crack, whose very entry was sharply overhanging, and a severe tax on my strength—but we couldn't let that defeat us.

We turned an *arête* and found rather less steep ground ahead of us; to compensate for that it was heavily plastered with water-ice and snow. The sun peeped half-heartedly over the Hirondelles Ridge and lent us a little warmth.

The mountain was in no mood to let itself be trifled with, but its presents were not very acceptable—small stones and ice-splinters. We climbed several ropes'-lengths, over mixed rock and ice up to the right, till we reached the edge of the Buttress; the water-ice was lovely to look at, especially when it caught the light, but it continually forced us to change our route.

All the same, it was still early morning when we reached Cassin's bivouac-place at the foot of the next notorious pitch—the 300-foot Gully.

The granite bulked up above us afresh. A slightly overhanging, apparently endless rift, of uncommon size, with smooth containing walls, shot up above us, to lose itself under a crown of protuberances, against the deep blue of the sky.

We were now in the full grip of the climbing-fever; I could hardly wait till Kuno joined me. A treacherous almost invisible glaze of ice lay on the knobby rock; a narrow fissure in the bed of the gully provided a way up. I worked my way slowly forward in the approved fashion, with my hands wedged in the crack and my feet straddling wide, gaining one inch after another from this 3,000-foot wall. My rucksack with the ice-axe in it constricted my freedom of movement embarrassingly.

This granite, bereft of all hand- and foot-holds, invited no elegant climbing of the kind limestone permits. At many places the only method possible was a hefty lay-back—a thing which I, whom Nature has endowed with modest biceps, do not find very easy. I kept on, panting for breath, while the rubber soles of my light climbing-boots went scratting over the lichen-covered rock, and my fingers tatted every slight unevenness in it. The climbing often bordered on the extreme of which a human-being is capable. . . . If only I were well over that roof above me!

Once above it, there were new surprises in store, and every yard had to be fought for. Our predecessors had left us few pitons indeed to witness their passage; each shaft had a history of its own. At last the gully eased back a little, which immediately meant more ice; so now the ice-axe came into play and proved itself a true and trustworthy ally.

Then back on to rock, with a chimney running up till a roof barred the way. Everywhere we looked we saw holdless wastes of slabs, and the way ahead was a perpetual query, daunting in its apparent impossibility, whose solution lay entirely with ourselves. I traversed to the right, where a steep ramp cut through between the overhangs, till an enormous, protuberance called a halt. Here two *abseil* pitons warned us to go down a bit, and we fastened the *rappel*-cord to them. Fifty feet down under a projection we found a narrow ledge, but the rock pushed my body so far out that I couldn't get a lodging on it; so I had to resort to the old acrobatic trapeze-act.

By swinging like a pendulum on the rope I managed to get on to a minute stance, and under a dark, ice-clad overhang I stretched the *rappel*-cord like a hand-rail between Kuno and me. Then he slid horizontally across the rock-face to me.

Looking up, we could see no end to such difficulties; the only thing that comforted us was that the weather seemed to be holding. Beneath us the rock broke away almost vertically to the ice of the Great *Couloir*. When we yanked the cord off we had cut our last bridge with the world below; retreat was now an impossibility.

Climbing slightly to the left, we reached the second fierce up-thrust of the Buttress, the so-called Black Slabs—the hardest part of the climb. There is no recognised route here. Pitons scattered about the rock showed that each individual party had chosen its own line, though they were all pretty close to each other. On those overhanging pitches my rucksack exerted a horrid outward drag; but we hardly noticed such things any more. We had forgotten the world and all its troubles and were absorbed heart and soul by the climbing itself, as we went on over outward-leaning cracks, vertiginous ledges, and tiny stances, for hundreds of feet. This merciless face gave us not a moment's relaxation. How we thanked our tough, unsparing training-days in such circumstances.

The disposal of one overhanging pitch simply led to the problem of mastering another, over and over again, in countless succession.

At last I was only a few feet from a resting-place I had already seen from below. At that critical moment the rope wouldn't come when I pulled it, and I had to go back along a hardly-won stretch, jerk the thing out of a crack in which it had jammed, and then climb up again, only to find it stuck a second time. It was no good losing one's temper; I simply had to do it all over again. I was very near the end of my strength when I finally reached the much-needed resting-place—the first for about five hundred feet.

I had to take a breather and restore my used-up energy before I could even bring Kuno up to join me. As I looked down over my partner as he waited flattened against the wall and obviously losing patience, my glance travelled straight down into the open crevasses of the Mallet Glacier which, at such a depth, appeared almost flat. So exposed was the situation that I couldn't help asking myself whether I was really in the Western Alps or in the Dolomites.

Kuno was soon moving up with his own inimitable certainty of movement; he could only enjoy our spacious rest-room for a few moments, for we had to get on.

We climbed an ice-rib, and reached a roomy, snow-covered terrace, a kind of balcony-like projection in the otherwise smooth wall; this was the second bivouac-place used by the first party to climb the Buttress. It was past mid-day, but the Black Slabs lay behind us and we had the comforting knowledge that what now faced us was all within the bounds of human possibility. We reckoned that we could now reach the top before dusk.

From time to time heavy stone-falls went clattering down the Great Couloir to the right of us, as we stopped for a short rest; but we were soon restlessly on our way towards the summit again, which had, till then, had all the characteristics of a wall, but now changed over to a knife-edged *arête*; we were able to look over on to the North-East Face, falling away in huge ice-slopes till, far below, it became rock again and disappeared from sight. The higher we mounted, the better became the holds. It was absolutely perfect climbing.

We were brutally shocked out of our mood of victorious upward movement. An enormous block had detached itself from the summit rocks of the Pointe Whymper and went tearing down the 3,000-foot face to the glacier at the bottom with an appalling uproar. . . . In spite of our great distance from the danger-zone, we instinctively took cover.

It was a long time before the last rattling ripples died away and silence was restored.

When there was time, we could now look out over the top of the Aiguille du Tacul to the wonderful array of the Chamonix Needles, but the beauty of the view was presently marred by the sight of a thunder-storm boiling up over them. Coal-black clouds heaved their menacing shapes across the peaks.

There was no time to think about the implications; we simply had to push on.

Rope after rope passed through our hands. Level with us, across the couloir, rose the second ice-slope on the Peters Route, a sharp icy edge lifting from the opposite wall. By it we were able to measure not only our progress, but the Lilliputian stature of men in such surroundings. We looked up overhead; the leaden-hued sky and the rolling of thunder counselled haste. The clouds were settling down on the summits. A moment or two later we found ourselves at the core of the thunder-storm, which broke without warning over our heads.

Flash followed flash; the walls hurled back the echoing thunder-claps a hundredfold.

There was never a break in the crashing din. The sky opened its sluices and drenched us with a deluge of rain and hail. The narrow world we lived in was in motion, swimming with the flood that poured down into the deeps. It was an experience we had met several times before, this racing river creaming down the wall, with the familiar melody of the avalanches thundering down as an *obbligato*. Every runnel in the rock was a gushing torrent. We could no longer hear one another speak; but we didn't need to hear. All we knew was that we must get off the wall, out of this inferno, somehow!

There was a brief break in the tumult of the elements, then they renewed their discord with greater violence—one thunder-clap hard on the heels of another.

A furious westerly gale smote the wall, whipping at the ropes. We searched feverishly for shelter; through the smother we caught sight of a tiny notch, the only possible place in which to take cover from the storm.

Surely this couldn't last long. . . .

We pulled the bivouac-sack over our heads and somehow felt a little protected. It was three o'clock and we were only 800 feet from the top—my altimeter showed just under 13,000 feet. Only 800 feet to go!

We waited and waited; but there was no break in the raging of the storm. We ate a bite. Weariness was now making itself felt; our feet particularly felt heavy as lead from the long, difficult hours of climbing.

The next time Kuno looked at his watch we realised, to our horror, that it was half-past seven. It meant a bivouac on the spot. We put on every available article of clothing—all too few. This was the occasion for trying out my new eiderdown jacket.

It was necessary to bang in a few pitons to give us the requisite protection; then we constructed a back-rest of rope, while our feet dangled over the 3,000-foot abyss. Finally we pulled the sack over us, taking tremendous care to give the wind no chance to get hold of it, and awaited the coming of night under our flapping shroud.

We dozed and dozed, listening almost in apathy to the organ-notes of the tempest, till I was at last overcome by sleep, and sheer weariness snatched me away for hours from this imprisoning world.

The cold jerked me awake again: I was brought back to reality, willy-nilly.

"Heavens, is it daylight already?" I asked Kuno, in astonishment.

I was not yet fully conscious. I peered out of the little window in the sack upon a world like a laundry. All the rocks near us were glazed white in ice and hoar-frost; the storm was raging as it had done yesterday, only hail-laden rain had given way to snow.

We didn't know what to think of the weather, but decided to wait a while. Kuno had spent a very bad night, for shivering-fits had allowed him no rest. Thank goodness for my own down jacket, which had triumphantly survived its baptism by ice!

About nine o'clock, when there had been no change at all in the weather, we decided to press on. We had no desire to let the wall make us its prisoners.

It needed a great effort of will-power to leave our warm sack and renew our fight with the mountain, in the gale and the bitter cold outside. Our bodies were completely stiffened, our muscles cramped, but the will to live is a strong incentive, and we were not going to give in so easily.

We strapped our steel rims on to our boots, got the perlon rope—

which was encased in a fur of hoar-frost—into decent order, knocked
out the pitons, by now totally hidden in ice—for we should certainly
need them.

I traversed back into the steep ice-gully from which we had retreated
yesterday in face of the hail. I hacked my way up its angle of very nearly
sixty degrees, still very unsteady on my feet.

A white patch loomed through the murk—a snowfield up which we
stamped our way—but very soon there were black, forbidding bulges,
thrusting out over our heads again. In spite of the cold, we had to dispense with our gloves—because the small holds could only be dealt
with by bare hands.

After a terribly severe traverse to the right, I came to the foot of a
steep fissure. It was just as though the wall were mustering its whole
might against its two insignificant attackers. The rock was disgustingly
outward-sloping, and brittle into the bargain; every hold had to be
cleared of ice before we could use it. Our rims did yeoman service here.

The fissure gave way to very steep ice. It was on this ice that Kuno
showed his superlative prowess, as he took over the lead. With the
skill of a mason he carved step upon step out of the brittle mass, which
covered the rock in a thin, treacherous layer. Ice splinters tinkled down
and struck me in their flight, but there was no time for self pity.

The only question was how to get out of this fearsome gully.

I couldn't see the slightest hope of getting up any further. There was
nothing but enormous black overhangs, fringed with great cascades of
ice, overhead. To our left the rock went down in one sweep to the North
East Face; to the right more overhangs cut off all view upwards. That
dumb witness, the rope, going up and down in jerks, told of Kuno's
fearful struggle with the difficulties. They were grim minutes of waiting. . . .

Then I heard a cry; something came banging down, took off into
thin air, as I put all my weight on the rope, ready for every eventuality.
God be praised, it was only the ice-axe, sucked down into the void.

But what should we do now—how were we to get on without it?
The loss of our axe might have the most dire consequences!

However, as always happens when things are really dire, we discovered—with the kindly aid of Providence—a small backdoor out of
our dangerous situation; a traverse to the right across smooth slabs,
leading under enormous bulges to some more rock. When the mist
lifted—as it occasionally did—we could see the Summit Ridge of the
Jorasses quite close at hand. There was one more overhang, after which
steep, ice-bound rock-gullies led upwards, though it was possible to
by-pass the ice with care; then the climbing grew markedly easier,

though the rock became rottener, a sure sign that we were near the top.

We wanted to quicken our pace, but found it impossible, either because we were feeling the altitude or just as the result of our long overexertion. The grey rock still piled up in front of us and we were just wondering whether there really was an end to this wall when something light appeared through the depressing gloom, and soon took shape as the summit cornice of the Pointe Walker (13,806 feet), the highest summit of the Jorasses.

At half-past four in the afternoon we took our final step on that colossal face, to escape at last from the horrific, magnificent abyss.

A dream of many years' standing had been translated into reality; we had reached the objective we had so long and so fiercely desired.

But, though we had climbed the Buttress, this was not by a long way the end of the tour. We had no mind to go down, like our predecessors, by the shortest way to Courmayeur; our aim was to traverse all the summits of the Jorasses Massif and finish by going straight down from the Col des Jorasses to Chamonix, thus avoiding the long détour by the Col du Géant.

And so, although it was late afternoon and the traverse of the Jorasses is normally a whole day's undertaking, we set off on our way to the Col des Jorasses. Our hope was that we might still reach the bivouac-shelter, a thing of corrugated iron, at the Col before nightfall. Luckily the weather was improving all the time, though we were still in a thick fog.

We climbed down southwards to a saddle short of the Pointe Whymper, the next summit, which we then climbed by a series of highly-exposed cornices. We were able to look down through rifts in the snow into the appalling depths, from which thick wreaths of cloud were swirling upwards. We made comparatively good progress to the Pointe Croz, but then the ridge narrowed to a knife-edge, so much so that Kuno, doubting whether we were on the right way, climbed down onto the South Face, where the slabs which break away from the ridge pushed us further and further down.

I didn't like our excursion at all, and was sure we were getting much too far off the ridge. We held a council of war and decided to climb up to it again.

It was on the way up that we really began to feel the effects of our two days' exertions, as we gasped our way up, step by step, along an exposed ridge which led to the Punta Margherita, over unusually rough rock. Our fingers were painfully sore from climbing and the cuts on them left bloodstains on the rock.

The ridge now became very dentated and we had to rope-down several times. Night enveloped us before we had crossed the Punta

Elena. We went sliding down the polished rock on the rope, in pitch-darkness. A north-westerly gale had got up again, tearing our ropes far out from the rock, with a sound like whiplashes.

I heard Kuno grumbling through the gloom: "I've had enough of this!"—I tried to encourage him by telling him we must be quite near to the bivouac-site, where we could have a proper sleep; but after traversing the Pointe Young, the last of the six summits of the Jorasses, we got hopelessly stuck in the darkness. For better or for worse, we simply had to resign ourselves to another bivouac in the open.

We judged we were still 300 feet above the Col des Jorasses. We found a roomy spot, out of the wind, of which there were fortunately several to choose from hereabouts.

Kuno hoped to get a better night, but the increasing cold kept us awake for a very long time. Waiting for morning to come was a bitter ordeal.

We were on our feet again by the first light of day. We found we couldn't climb down to the Col, because there was a steep icefield in between, which we could not negotiate without ice axes or crampons. The only way was by an endless rock-ridge, cutting down the North Face as a rib; we used the last rocks and some boulders frozen fast into the ice to rope down from it, and so made our somewhat precarious way in safety to the upper reaches of the Mallet Glacier. We jumped across the *bergschrund* and breathed again, for at last we once more had firm ground under our feet.

The sun, too, felt more kindly disposed towards us and shed its warming light on us once again.

As we went down the heavily crevassed Mallet Glacier, we kept on looking up to those unearthly heights where the gigantic rock-pillars of the Walker Buttress went sweeping to the very sky. And as I gazed, the realisation that it was no longer an aim unsatisfied, a rainbow-lure before me, gave me a pang akin to real regret.

Would there ever be anything more satisfying, more worthy of whole-hearted dedication?

FIFTEEN PEAKS AT ONE BITE

ALL our plans seemed to be materialising at once and at last. It is always the same with these Lords among Mountains; you have to pay court to them for ages before they graciously allow you to enter their domains.

Our climbs, this time, were very long ones, so that our rest days were short and scarce. We were in great fettle, and each climb added to our technique, stamina and determination.

We traversed the Rochefort Ridge in heavy new snow, from the Col des Jorasses to the Col du Géant and sat one evening, richer by a few Three- and Four-Thousanders, outside the Rifugio di Torino, watching the play of the last sunset glow on the teeth of the Peutéret Ridge.

Early next morning we waded through beastly crust to the Col de la Fourche (12,074 feet). We had been there a short time before, when a blizzard raged incessantly, imprisoning us for three days and three nights in the bivouac-shelter in the saddle of the ridge. Nor was it an improvement in the weather, but sheer dearth of food that drove us to risk the descent in spite of dire avalanche-peril and the fearful snow-storm.

There had been no option. Death by starvation has no great advantages over perishing in the snow; there was nothing more to lose, but there was life to be fought for—and won. We won it. . . .

But this time we had a glorious day before us. We raced our way up the Arête du Diable opposite, and finally that whole long difficult ridge lay below us. Then up and over magnificently-corniced ridges and deeply-indented rock. Conditions were wintry, but we didn't mind, for it was all training for bigger and bigger adventure. Perhaps we would catch someone's eye for one of the future Himalayan expeditions. Then the hard school in which we were learning would have repaid us for our efforts.

At mid-day we were sitting in a niche on the South-East Ridge of Mont Maudit (14,650 feet) in a mounting fog, which cut off every prospect. After a successful visit to the summit we felt our way down through the unbroken gloom over a steep ice-slope, found a route from one rock-rib to another and eventually hit the old trail to the Col du Midi. Then we hurried along the endless "path" to Montenvers. At the last moment we got caught by a thunderstorm and a cloudburst which left us looking like drowned rats.

A compatriot of mine, on holiday in Chamonix, particularly wanted me to take him up Mont Blanc by the ordinary route; and so I paid a second visit to the highest point in Europe. Once again I looked out over the vast distances below me, losing themselves on one side in the haze over France, on the other over Italy. I looked down over countless summits and spires and glittering glaciers. It was fairyland—Paradise itself. . . .

Our stay was drawing to an end. We had thought of something really big for our finale. We had often followed with our eyes the magnificent line of teeth, stretching from the Grands Charmoz to the Aiguille du Midi; and as we gazed a secret longing grew for those fantastic rock-shapes between the Mer de Glace and Géant Glacier on one side and the Chamonix Valley on the other. Those formidable needles of rock are a special magnet to draw true mountaineers, particularly those enthusiasts for whom the utmost severity has no terrors. The average height of these wild rock-pinnacles is between 10,000 and 13,000 feet; on their northern side they fall nearly 10,000 feet to the valley, on the south their shabby faces fall 3,000 feet sheer to the Géant Glacier. The views down either side of the Comb are magnificent; the granite of which they are composed is as hard as steel—there is none finer imaginable. They are a veritable El Dorado for climbers.

I had fallen in love with these sharp peaks two years before, when I first paid homage to them. In them the keen-edged sharpness of the Dolomites and the colossal size of the Western Alps unites to form an ideal combination, to be found nowhere else in the Alps. The needles have frequently been traversed singly; the difficulties of route-finding marks each of them as a magnificent expedition. The complete traverse, taking every one of them in a long-linked chain had, however, never been accomplished. Was it possible? It was a problem which invited a solution.

I deprecate talk of a "last" problem in this context; the phrase has been overworked.

Every generation of climbers has its "last" problems. What now attracted me was a desire for adventure, the longing for new and glorious delights. Besides which, I have a special affection for big traverses.

Kuno, that perfect partner, agreed immediately, but the weather was apparently against the idea; the mountain slopes were once again draped in grey cloud. All the same, we went up to Montenvers, for we had to make use of every available day.

Rain began to fall gently.

We met a Course from the French Mountaineering School on their way down to Chamonix: they advised us to go back. We thanked them politely—and went on.

"*C'est Buhl!*" the Instructor explained to his pupils, smiling at us with great understanding. The way he mentioned my name could only mean one of two things: it was either a complimentary tribute or he was writing me off as crazy. I didn't much mind which, so long as I got my way.

And these young Frenchmen, representatives of a magnificent *élite* of climbers were letting me have that.

We followed the hair-pins of the path up the steep slopes, which were covered by a lovely carpet of flowers. The gay flowers gave way gradually to the uniform grey-green of lichen-covered rocks. We were separated from the rocks of the East Face of the Grands Charmoz by a small hanging-glacier, and had to cross a gaping crevasse to reach the foot of the rock; from there on the "track" was difficult to detect as it led on over terraces and slabs of rock.

"How d'you like this for a Hut-approach?" I asked Kuno.

We were almost tempted to get the rope out; for a vertical, smooth crack forms the chief difficulty in this "stroll up to a hut". Kuno, who had never been this way before, was very much impressed. Meanwhile, the rain had stopped, but the weather didn't look at all settled. Kuno was equally surprised when he suddenly caught sight of a prehistoric wooden shelter on the steep face, consisting of three boarded walls, a corrugated iron roof and a plank floor.

This is the Tour Rouge Hut, which takes its name from the red *gendarme* a little above it, and bravely it fronts the world, built as it is on an edge of rock in most magnificent surroundings. It is a matter for wonder that this simple structure withstands the force of every storm that blows. The only sign of civilisation it boasts is the alarm-clock inside it.

While Kuno busied himself with the cooker, I went in search of water. I had to climb a long way up the face, to a snowfield from which a runnel was gushing; there I filled the water-tub and went back down the pitches with my wet and precious load on my back. In spite of all my care I could not prevent water flowing over the rim of the tub and, by the time I rejoined Kuno, I had given myself an unintended bath.

It soon began to rain again, and after a very short time whole torrents were rushing down the mountainside, close to our home. If only I had known it was going to happen!

As soon as we had fed, we threw ourselves on our beds of straw, and the steady drumming of the rain on the leaden roof of our shelter soon sang us to sleep.

We looked out at four next morning, to find heavy clouds down in everything, curtaining our Face from view. The rock was still sopping from the rain. However, we decided to start; we could always turn back, if the weather got worse.

We traversed to the right across broad ledges till a long series of steep cracks and gullies offered an upward way; yet another traverse to the right brought us on to the North-East Ridge of the Grands Charmoz, a little below the "Cornes de Chamois", two sharp towers, set on the ridge like the horns of a chamois.

We turned them on the Mer de Glace side and started up the face of the Aiguille de la République, where the climbing became more difficult and we were sometimes compelled to use the rope.

The rock was most deceptive; things that looked quite easy often proved extremely difficult, and *vice-versa*.

We went up the steep face for eight or nine hundred feet till we could see a col up above us to the right and, having reached it up a very broken gully, enjoyed a well-earned rest.

We reconnoitred the rest of the route to the République, which has not often been done before.

Leaving our rucksacks on the col, but taking the rope with us, we attacked a 500-foot crag simultaneously; we turned the overhanging face, which fronts the col, to the right. This brought us on to the Eastern *Arête* of this sharp needle, up which we proceeded, sometimes using the rope; the climbing was by no means easy and very airy. On a broad shoulder a hundred feet below the summit, which is a kind of monolithic block, we took stock.

Nobody had yet succeeded in climbing the top pitch of the needle without aids. The French had always used a kind of harpoon, with which they projected the rope over on to the north side; all the same, I do not see how they reached it on the overhanging, almost inaccessible North Face. It is a method the French consider fair and they have used it in other places; indeed, the unique formation of many of the summits in this slabby type of granite allows of no other solution.

We first of all tried to sling the rope over the summit by lassoing it, cowboy fashion. After this had proved impracticable, we found a rolled spool of string, with a small lump of lead on its end, hidden in a cranny of the rock.

"Aha!" we thought, "this is the answer to the riddle!"

It seemed, however, that we were too stupid to use it properly, for all our attempts failed. So we were thrown back on aidless climbing.

The wall on the right—an utterly smooth slab tilted at from seventy to eighty degrees—no longer gave any purchase for rubber soles, so I tried to scale the left-hand edge, which plunges down into the North Face. Though it overhung fearsomely, it offered some narrow wrinkles at varying distances. I managed, too, to throw the rope over a small projection in the edge, and to arrange it as a handrail; then I slid across the intervening impossible slab on the fixed rope, but once across it I had to unloop the rope from the spike in order to tie myself on again. That, of course, cut off my line of retreat.

The wrinkles were a sad disappointment. They turned out to be mostly too far apart to allow of a stride from one to the other, however much I "did the splits". So I had to climb the intervening bit, overhanging though it was to some extent and absolutely bare of holds. The impossible had to become the possible. I managed thirty feet of it, but then the rock pushed me fearfully outwards, so that I had to resort to a balancing-trick as delicate as it was perilous; but it was not long before I found it too much for me—and only forty-five feet from the top!

I wanted desperately to fix a piton, and only then recalled that I had none with me. Kuno, too, had relied on me, with the result that all our ironmongery was reposing safely in the rucksacks in the saddle below. But I simply had to have a piton!

So Kuno had to knock out the only one he had, which was safeguarding his stance, but which was now our only means of protection, for good or ill. Very carefully he passed it and the hammer across to me on the rope.

All in vain; the steel shaft was too thick and wouldn't go into any of the slender cracks in my neighbourhood. It was quite hopeless and the only thing to do was to try to climb down those hard-won feet unprotected.

What had been just possible in the upward direction now proved absolutely impossible downwards. The rock pushed my body out too far, and my feet were beginning to shake from having stood so long on most exiguous footholds. The "Sewing Machine" motion all climbers dread set in, threatening to hurl me off the rock. I had to force myself by might and main to quiet my reacting muscles. I felt all over the rock again. . . . At last I found a slightly wider crack and sent the shaft singing into the stone. I could have shouted for joy, and I expect Kuno down below me felt the same. I followed the invariable practice of testing the piton again for reliability, by giving it a sharp tug. It promptly came out and hit me in the face. I felt warm blood running down my cheek and neck; my nose had reacted to that trifling rap with a flow of gore worthy of better things.

I noticed that my strength was giving way little by little, and shouted to Kuno: "Look out! I shall be off in a moment'!'

My friend nodded with the utmost unconcern, in spite of the fact that he hadn't even his belay-piton any more. I knew he would do his best, but even that was probably no use; if I came off I should land plumb on the opposite wall and then go flying down about sixty feet on to a terrace.

I decided I mustn't put that responsibility on Kuno's shoulders.

I tried again to fix the piton and, with the last strength born of desperation, persuaded it this time to hold.

Quick! In with a carabiner—but of course I hadn't got one. So in that horrible position, I had to untie again, pass the rope through the ring and tie it around my chest again. Then, swinging through thin air, I reached the platform and, with Kuno's help, got back on to the Shoulder, where I sank down utterly exhausted. But the knowledge that I had escaped from so fearsome a trap soon restored my strength.

The effort had used up much precious time—something like three hours.

We gladly turned our backs on that little spike and climbed down again to the col. Even if one enjoys "Fool's Licence", it is better not to prejudice one's licence on such unimportant but highly dangerous objects.

We now climbed an almost vertical wall which, however, provided more holds than had seemed probable at first sight; and although it was difficult stuff, we climbed simultaneously, to make up for lost time. We were soon able to look down upon the slender tooth of the République. It was a very long ridge-climb and presently, as we neared the summit, the *arête* narrowed to a blade, though decreasing in steepness.

Over on the left yet another needle, the Aiguille Roch, raised its terrifically thin spire above a host of other rocky teeth. We were standing in the col where I had emerged two years before from the direct climb of the Charmoz North Face. I shuddered when I looked down it and recalled that experience. I could hardly believe that a human being could have come up such a place. I had my friends Hias and Luis to thank for being a human who had. . . .

Things became familiar, and we were soon across the summit of the Grands Charmoz (11,302 feet). A very narrow chimney was the obvious way down. On that popular peak all you had to do was to follow the litter of paper and the tins to keep on the right course.

Once again I stood on the Grépon; this time coming from the opposite direction—north to south. As I wriggled my way up the Mummery Crack like a worm, I thought with great respect of that incomparable Briton, who had climbed it for the first time seventy years before. It has not become any easier in the interval.

A huge, wobbly block, projecting half its length over the abyss, lies on the flat top of the Summit-Tower, precisely as if it had been laid there of set intent—truly one of Nature's miracles. We used it for an *abseil*, in spite of its somewhat untrustworthy appearance; though a host of old rope-rings bear witness to its actual reliability.

Once again I walked comfortably along "La Route des Bicyclettes", a horizontal terrace in this sheer wall, fully a yard wide, so that you really could ride a bicycle along it—except that the fearsome depths into which you look from it demand an absolutely steady head.

And once again, just as two years ago, we ran into cloud, and the inevitable noonday storm put in its appearance. Thunder began to grumble, but we couldn't afford to hang about if we were to accomplish our object.

An ice-cold wind struck us as we turned over to the west side. This time, however, it was no shock to find myself standing before a life-size statue of the Madonna on the Grépon's main summit. We roped down again, made a short traverse and hurried over blocks and crags to the next col, between the Grépon and the Blaitière. At moments when the mists parted we were able to cast a glance back at the colossal structure of the Grépon, whose towers shot up into the sky like gigantic massive columns.

We crossed some short snow patches and a few small cols, with grim rifts falling below us to the Mer de Glace. A knife-sharp ridge was the hardest part of the climb to the Blaitière summit. A good deal of up-and-down and back-and-forth brought us to the steep ice-couloir which falls from the col between the triple-headed Blaitière's summits to the Glacier des Nantillons. We crossed its somewhat brittle ice, which forced us to strap our steel-rims to our boots; for it was impossible to provide a belay in the absence of ice-pitons. We were enveloped in dense fog and felt our way tentatively forward; even the sketch-map of the route was a dubious guide in the thick cloud-wrack through which we were moving.

Almost as an answer to a prayer, the curtain parted for a moment, giving us time to memorise what we saw before us, and very soon we were standing on the first, easy North Summit. The other two crests were much more difficult, for it is hard enough to find a way on this primaeval rock in normal circumstances; in the kind of visibility then reigning, extraordinary care was essential.

Owing to the unique, square-headed structure of the rock, it was often a highly complicated business. Into the bargain, we frequently suffered from optical delusions: every crack and pitch looked quite small from a distance, then assumed gigantic proportions when we reached it.

The day was running out on us and we had to find a suitable place for a bivouac. Happily there were plenty of them and we made ourselves snug on a rocky ledge on the west side of the Blaitière. The weather had meanwhile improved, and the late sun came out to comfort us, as our feet dangled high over the valley; we brewed a hot drink on the cooker—our sustenance for the night.

Darkness came climbing up towards us. We sat on our lonely, lofty perch awaiting the night's coming, in a silence broken only by the thunder of the avalanches.

We gazed down on the myriad twinkling lights down there in the Chamonix Valley. Such quiet contemplative reveries are blessed things. Finally, the cold drove us under our sack; and at intervals through the long, long night we peered out to see whether the stars were not yet paling.

With chattering teeth we prepared our breakfast, and only waited for the sun to touch our rock-tooth before starting on our way again.

Crossing a steep, frozen snowfield we found ourselves at the foot of the next needle, the Aiguille du Fou, just another tooth in this innumerable chaos of teeth.

Kuno wanted to attempt a first direct climb of it, but I wanted to bag an intervening spike on the ridge, the Aiguille des Ciseaux, whose double-headed needle is shaped like the open blades of a pair of scissors. I left my rucksack at its foot and felt sure I could manage without a rope, too.

A smooth chimney goes up between the two "blades", of which I had selected the westerly one as my objective. I reached the edge of the arête by a steep face-climb. The slabs fell away hundreds of feet below that incredibly exposed and knife-edged sliver of rock whose summit is, in truth, a needle point—I could get hold of it in my two hands.

I was up; but I had quite forgotten about coming down. I had the painful feeling that I had fallen into a trap, though one can sometimes escape even from traps.

With quite extraordinary care, I climbed down the first sixty feet, every one of them critical, simply trusting to the friction of my rubber-soles. Some minutes later—minutes of acute anxiety—I was back at the col.

I rejoined Kuno at the foot of the Fou. The last block of the Summit —a grotesque structure—gave us a little trouble, but we were soon on top of the slender needle and looking down the steep South West Ridge, to the next dent in the ridge. We climbed down the upper part and came to an abrupt cliff, where rope-rings invited us to use the traditional method of descent.

It took six more roping-down operations before we stood on the roomy platform between the Fou and the Pointe de Lépiney. Although it was still early, the little niche tempted us to stay awhile.

Everywhere the eye could see, there were rock-teeth and more rock-teeth, lifting their grotesque shapes from the white levels of the Géant and Tacul Glaciers.

Tatters of clouds, sure harbingers of a thunderstorm, licked their greedy way up the walls and stirred us to activity. We had to climb some way down the North Face, where the frost of the night was still in evidence. Hard frozen snow and hailstones, relics of bygone bad weather, lay on the slabs.

A long and steep ice-slope, running up between the flights of rock, brought us below the needles of the Pointe de Lépiney and the Pointe Chevalier to the col at the foot of the Dent du Caïman. Once again we left our packs in the col and, as if borne on wings, climbing light, surmounted the steep cracks and spiral chimneys of the nearer peak, the Pointe Chevalier. Its summit was so small that we could not both stand on it at the same time, and thought it a good thing that this "Knight" wasn't allowing his head to be belaboured by several assailants at once. We roped down on the other side.

Kuno climbed back to the col, but I was attracted by the Lépiney which, in contrast to the Chevalier, owned a broad flat top, a great slab broken off at the edges. A most impressive and characteristic feature of this needle is a six-foot vertical absolutely smooth "step", only to be mastered by a positively acrobatic "lay-back"; and although I am far from being a gymnast, I have got used to dealing with places of the kind.

And now for the Caïman! After the Knight, the Crocodile. Our rock-dragon, the Dent du Caïman, starts with a perpendicular pitch, barred by a 250-foot high ring of polished rock-armour. The only possibility of climbing the summit, a thousand feet above our heads, was to turn the whole tower to the south. We had to rope down nearly 300 feet on its east side, and then traverse to reach the East Ridge, by which we hoped to complete the ascent of the 11,660-foot summit.

We held a long consultation as to the right way to reach it; finally I roped down, somewhat doubtfully and unconvinced, into a gully by way of some hazardous steps in the face; beyond it the way led over easy ledges and cracks to a tiny platform set in the midst of the great wall. I was seriously worried as to the rightness of the route. The difficulties, severe as those on the buttress of the Jorasses, were far worse than anything mentioned in the Climbers' Route-Book. Moreover, it looked very much like virgin ground, without any trace of a track broken before. Still, I was determined to get up to the ridge; the way led up terribly severe pitches and cracks which used up all my strength.

Even so, there was no hope of further progress, for I found myself separated from the shoulder up in the ridge by an absolutely smooth wall, a hundred feet high, without a wrinkle or a rift in it. We were just one "step" too far down, and we had to go down the whole wall once again in order to try our luck in what must be the correct set of chimneys; moreover, we had to climb down those bitterly-disputed pitches—some of the hardest I have done in this age-old granite—unprotected. There was not a place where we could fix a piton. I could manage to give Kuno some protection; if he slipped he could just hang on to the rope; but what could I hold on to as I came down on my own?

In the end, it went safely; but we had used up much time and energy.

We found another series of cracks further to the right—this must be it! Once again we had to climb up, meeting a very broken, ice-filled chimney on the way. Then the wall joined the ridge, which rose very steeply in a series of "steps" above us. Presently the moment arrived when it ceased to go up any further, and we were on the top of our Dragon's Tooth!

We had again been eleven hours on the way since morning, and still the end of our linked traverse was not in sight. Unseen rows of spikes separated us down below from the Aiguille du Plan. Huge flights of slab shot hundreds of feet down on either side of the ridge to small, savagely-cleft hanging-glaciers at the feet of the needles.

Our movements had by now become slow and weary; the eternal up-and-down had begun to bemuse us. Our surroundings were magnificent, but our receptivity had become blunted. We were heartily glad just to cross another summit off our syllabus.

Unexpectedly, mists closed down again and made it even more difficult to find the way on ground which was already tricky; and then on the way down from the Caïman we were battered by hail-showers before we had time to look for cover.

In any case, it was time to get on. We made a dead set at the last Tooth but one—the Dent du Crocodile. The French are truly experts in refinements when naming their peaks: Caïman—Crocodile. Respectively the teeth of an American and an African crocodile, both beasts being dragons!

Two smooth, recalcitrant *gendarmes* lay between us and the main summits, compelling us to make a tiresome détour by several exposed traverses on to its northern side. Icy rifts and ledges hindered progress, till a polished crack led us up to the ridge again, bringing us out on the extremely exposed Eastern Face. Just when we thought we had out-witted the first "Policeman" guarding the ridge, we found an un-climbable wall facing us; so back we had to go.

That was not the only time we went astray and had to look for another route.

To describe every pitch in detail would make an endless story. It seemed endless to us at the time.

At last we were at the foot of the Crocodile's summit structure. A perpendicular—nay, overhanging—face barred our way. We just looked at each other dumbly, for words failed us.

All around us the rock was holdless; there was no way but to try to climb the overhanging wall. Granite can be very deceptive. The rock proved to be uncommonly rough, but every hold hurt my fingers as though needles were sticking into them, for I had worn them raw with climbing.

Not surprising, after two whole days on rough rock, with bare hands! There was a profusion of holds, which revived my flagging spirits. We traversed into a chimney, climbed up under enormous piled-up blocks, found a way through them and were soon on the top.

The Crocodile had really defended itself with crocodile's teeth.

The thunderstorm had passed by and only a few isolated rags of mist were blowing about on the wind.

We looped the doubled rope for the last time—or so we hoped—about a spike and slid down a hundred-and-twenty feet through thin air, to fetch up on ice. It was the hanging-glacier which breaks away to the north from the col behind the Plan.

At the upper edge of the ice, where it abuts on the rock, a crevasse had formed owing to radiation. This enabled us to get across, and an easy climb took us up to a platform about 300 feet below the summit of the Plan.

It was seven p.m. We were on the last of the fifteen summits which form the Chain of the Chamonix Aiguilles, and had thus accomplished the first complete traverse; but we were almost too weary to get any joy out of the performance as yet—and it was a long way down to the valley.

I suggested climbing down to the Réquin Hut 3,000 feet further down; there was just a chance that we might reach it before night fell. But Kuno had lost all interest.

"Not one step further do I move," he growled.

I knew how he hated feeling around in the dark, so I controlled my irritation as best I could.

I would so much have liked to sleep in the Hut; and now we were going to have to bivouac in the open again!

We bestowed ourselves for the night on a roomy place on that airy ridge.

The sunset was gorgeous. All the highest spires in the Alps glowed rosy and gold. I followed the great red fireball in my thoughts as down it went.

The blue of the night climbed up the ice of the almost vertical hanging-glacier below us, and soon an icy wind chased us into our bivouac. My limbs were like lead; my weary body cried out for rest, but my mind went on working. I sat there brooding for hours before I joined Kuno in the Land of Sleep.

When we woke up, there were still black shadows in the valley and the lights were still on; but the Monarch of the Alps was dazzling-bright in the early sunlight. Our limbs were racked with cold and only a quick get-away could restore us.

With the Jorasses fronting us and the North Buttress outstanding against the sky, to remind us of what we had lived through on it, we climbed down to the Réquin Hut.

At the first spring at the glacier's edge we lay down to rest. The Earth's most precious gift tasted better than the most costly vintage of bubbling white wine.

We idled comfortably down the Mer de Glace, along the feet of those Chamonix Needles which had held us in thrall for the last three days.

Forgotten was all the toil, the danger, the hardship as we looked up to where the mists were at their daily play under the morning sun.

It had been glorious up there; but now we were looking forward to the delights of the valley.

I think we had earned them.

THE MATTERHORN AND A
FLAGON OF WINE

CHAMONIX—Vallorcine—Martigny—Sion—Visp were the stations on the direct journey to Zermatt, our next port of call. We wanted to pay a visit to the Matterhorn. It was overcast again; the mountains hid their heads in the clouds and even concealed their snowed-up slopes in them, as if ashamed of themselves. They might well be so; fancy wearing winter clothes in summertime!

"I think we've had it again!"

"Too late for the North Face, certainly."

We exchanged depressing remarks. Our thoughts were centred on our unattainable wish to climb the North Face of the Matterhorn. The guides sat about the main street of Zermatt, as we made our way out of the village, clad in their grey woollen suits, with huge badges on their coats, waiting for something to do; but the weather was no good to them either. This latest snowfall had ruined their business.

Outside Zermatt we found a rickyard, known as "Hotel Winkelmatten". We were surprised to find that a whole colony of Austrians and Bavarians whom the bad weather had condemned to inactivity were already in occupation. Kuno's leave was almost up and, as the weather showed no signs of improving, he decided to go home. It was a pity, for one could not ask for a better climbing partner. True, he doesn't say much, but that only led to a better understanding between us; the only words we ever used while climbing were the words governing manipulation of the ropes, and on the last few climbs we had almost dispensed with these, too. I was sorry to see Kuno go.

Someone told me that Luis and Ernst, those two old "extremists" were somewhere about the place; I might be able to rout them out. I toured the whole district, asking at every tent, till I found the right address. They were off together on a climb on the Matterhorn, but were supposed to be coming down that very day. I had to laugh when I saw the long and the short of it coming towards me; Ernst, the smaller, running vigorously ahead in his cheerful way, Luis stumping along behind on his huge elephantine legs. The former had a regulation ancient cow-string on his rucksack, the latter a ridiculously long ice-axe in his hand; they looked just like an exhibit from the last century in an Alpine Museum.

"Have you got parts in a historical climbing film?" I asked, after our noisy greetings were over. Then they explained that their equipment had failed to arrive, and that the guides had kindly helped them out, so it was not very surprising if they hadn't got the very latest kit. We had a wonderful talk, and before going to bed we agreed to do something together if the weather was kind.

The very next day actually proved fine, so we went straight up to the Rothorn Hut, where a couple of charming girls were in charge. Ernst and I, the bachelors, enjoyed ourselves, after sending Luis, the newly-wed, to an early bed.

In the grey light of dawn we approached the foot of the Zinal Rothorn's East Face, a rock-wall rising more than 2,300 feet and sharply defined from the neighbouring peaks and faces by its extreme steepness. This face, ranking among the most difficult climbs in the Alps, had only been climbed three times before. It was certainly a tough proposition. As soon as we started up, it welcomed us with salvoes of stones, so that we had to dodge for shelter under the upper lip of the *bergschrund*. Then we hurried upwards over less steep ground until overhangs afforded us protection from the bombardment.

A marvellous crack and a splendid traverse brought us out onto an *arête* to the right. One look round the corner established that stark winter was in possession here; there was nothing to be seen but snow and ice. This was August, yet the steepest pitches were decked in treacherous ice, whole curtains of it. It was, of course, a north wall and the sun had done precious little work on it since the last snow-fall. I crossed an iced-up gully and climbed a steep rib, using my axe freely. I had to search for holds under a thick covering of snow, as I worked my way slowly up, never quite sure of what I had under my feet—a feeling to which my winter training had fortunately inured me. We spent hours on this part of the climb, and things got more and more uncomfortable. Right under the summit we struck an overhanging belt of rock, while we stood on a steep snowfield below which the face plunged vertically down. We traversed an icy rock, with an angle of from sixty to seventy degrees. There followed a cold funnel, a chimney in deep shadow, and in the afternoon we reached the summit of the Zinal Rothorn (13,855 feet).

A magnificent view was our reward for that dangerous passage. It was the first time I had seen the Valais Giants from a high summit. They were clad in their loveliest robes, all silver. There were the glittering ice-slopes of the Obergabelhorn, the grim, dark wedge of the Dent Blanche, the hanging-glacier terraces of the white Dent d'Hérens; and best of all, every climber's dream-peak, the Matterhorn. We were looking at its most appalling aspect, the sombre North Face. Nothing was more certain than that we would not get a chance, this trip, of making its acquaintance. High above the Visptal, Monte Rosa's six summits flashed to the sun, with its neighbours, the Lyskamm, Castor and Pollux and at the end of the range, the Breithorn; and to their left the other two 14,000-foot Valais giants, the Dom and Täschhorn.

That evening we were back in Zermatt and spent the rest of the day pleasantly in a comfortable Valaisian wine-bar. A dance-band was playing, and our dashing Luis trod the parquet with his accomplished feet. At midnight we withdrew, for our time was up, and the three of us left Zermatt together. Luis had left his motor-cycle in a rickyard somewhere outside the village, for the regulations forbid power-driven machines in the Visptal. So those two had to shake off its dust in the mists of night, to avoid being fined.

Unfortunately the machine refused to start. We shoved and ran, but it wouldn't fire. At the end of an hour we had got as far as Täsch, nearly five miles down the road. There the precious two-stroke took it into its head to start. Ernst, notorious for his driving habits, offered to take me back to Zermatt; but our motor-trip nearly came to an end at the very first curve with a crash into the bed of the river. I dispensed with the rest of the proffered lift and made my way back on Shanks's Pony. After all, I wanted to climb the Matterhorn during the day, not fetch up in hospital.

I made myself some breakfast at Winkelmatten. Then I left the valley to its peaceful slumbers, at about three o'clock, pursuing my lightless way through the benighted woods; not till I had reached the open slopes near the Schwarzsee did the day begin to dawn. I could see a tiny light moving over on the Grenzgletscher, a guided party on the way up. The valley fell deeper and deeper below. After endless hairpins the path took me to the Hörnli Hut at the base of the Matterhorn. I didn't stop there long, for I was already pretty late. The last guided party had been away up for some time.

The Matterhorn's pyramid soared huge and steep above me, all its elegant dignity lost from that aspect. Everything was covered in débris and still more débris; everywhere rose steep, boulder-covered slopes on which, higher up, lay snow and ice. As I went on up, I glanced across at the North Face; what I saw left me quite happy and comfortable to be only on the normal Swiss *arête*.

Just below the shoulder I met the first guided parties coming down. From there on there was a thick coating of ice on the rock, which grew steeper and fell away sheer to the North Face. Cemented steel shafts and fixed thick ropes were a great help on the Shoulder and obviated the necessity for putting on crampons. It was nearly eleven when I crossed the sharp snow crest to the Italian summit, 14,705 feet up. A thick fog enveloped everything, but my short rest on the summit gave me great inner satisfaction, in spite of my seeing only a grey pall. It was very thrilling to be alone on that mighty peak, only eight hours after leaving Zermatt.

I climbed down south-westwards towards the Italian side, in the direction of the Dent d'Hérens. When the curtains of the mist parted momentarily, I could see, far down below, beyond the terrible precipices, the gleam of a glacier-stream. Ravines shot down into the depths from the crest of my ridge, the ice at the bottom black with fallen stones. On a sunny day this might all make a less forbidding impression; but in this drifting cloud-wrack and flurrying snow it all looked most grim and repellent. The mountain continued to veil its profiles in shame.

There were more fixed ropes to ease the descent. A short rise took me to the Col du Lion, then I continued down the ridge, turning the *gendarmes* now on one side now on the other. A tiny shelter bade me rest a short time, while I swallowed a mouthful of hot tea, then down I went again. . . .

The ridge went down and down and down. At last I came out below the cloud-ceiling and could see far down into the valley to Breuil, whence Italian climbers start out to climb their side of the Matterhorn. It was still a very long way off, over rock-steps, scree-shoots, rubble and débris, and still more débris. All the same I reached the shelter, the Rifugio Duca d'Abruzzi, at about two o'clock, only just in time; for a heavy thunderstorm, high on the peak, unleashed its fury as soon as I got there. I had a fierce thirst. Should I quench it with glacier-water? No; I ordered red wine, a whole flagon of it. After all, I was in Italy, and in Italy at this altitude wine is the cheapest drink; at least that is how I lulled my climber's conscience. After the second glass I began to feel extremely happy; after the third I felt at peace with all the world; by the time I had finished the flagon I thought life was terrific!

The rain had stopped, and I left the refuge laughing and singing, to cross innumerable gullies on my way to the Furggenjoch, right across the foot of the Matterhorn's South Face. Presently my exalted mood abated: I had sweated the alcohol out of my system—and about time, too. I had to put my crampons on again, as I had to traverse along, on steep smooth ice, right below the *bergschrund*, bulking high as a house, at the foot of the East Face of the mountain. The broad smooth expanse of that face is notorious for its fire of falling stones; so I quickened my pace and cast many a wary glance upwards as I went.

Suddenly I saw an enormous boulder, several yards high, deep and wide, detach itself from the face and come straight for me with a deafening clatter. I ran and ran and ran . . . clearing great boulders even with my crampons on my feet. It was the fear of death which lent me wings. Then I went flying, I felt a fierce pain in my ankle, sank to my knees, tore myself up again and drove myself on—with the inferno of stone-fall thundering close behind me. Somehow I found shelter under a projecting ledge, making my way madly through a chaos of boulders to get there. Then I fell down, exhausted. My right ankle, always a source of trouble to me, was obviously sprained and was swelling with uncommon speed. The din at my heels had died away. In the silence that followed, I could hear the blood hammering in my veins. I got up with difficulty, and went limping painfully over to the Hörnli Hut, which I reached at about five o'clock. Ordinarily the descent to Zermatt would be a trifle, but in my present condition I dared not risk it. However, the Hut was crammed with people, as it turned out, and they couldn't offer me a bed for the night.

I turned away disappointed and somehow limped my way down to Zermatt; every step of the way was agonising and laborious, but I gritted my teeth and dragged myself down from one rest to another. I reached my Winkelmatten home at about midnight and fell into a death-like sleep in its hay.

I couldn't put a boot on next day; my ankle was so swollen that I was scared, so I decided to find a doctor. He diagnosed severely torn ligaments and prescribed complete rest in bed, with cold compresses. For three days I observed the regimen prescribed, in my "Rickyard Hotel". Seeing that my ankle was in no way better, I resolved to say good-bye to the Western Alps for this occasion. There wasn't the faintest possibility of my being able to climb again in the foreseeable future.

Meanwhile an elderly, amiable gentleman had moved in as my fellow guest. He gazed incessantly at the Matterhorn. From early morning till late at night he sat in the open doorway, never turning his eyes from the Peak of Peaks, like a devout worshipper at the Almighty's own feet. That man's only desire was to stand, once only, on the summit of that glorious wedge of rock. He had tried a few days earlier, but had been compelled to turn back, because his heart was bothering him. So I expect his life's dream will always remain unfulfilled. In my sympathy for him, I forgot my own troubles.

I began to put my things together, for there really was no use in staying. The old man was still propped against the door-jamb of our "hotel" when I limped off on my homeward way.

I think anyone who loves the mountains as much as that can claim to be called a mountaineer, too.

GYMNASTICS ON ROCK—NORTH WALL
OF THE WESTERN ZINNE

OCTOBER of that lovely, successful climbing season of 1950 found me in the South Tirol once again. Kuno and I had joined a company of our club-mates. We meant the year, which had opened with a fanfare for our success on the South West Wall of the Marmolata, to close with chords in honour of another almost as difficult Dolomite climb—the North Face of the Western Zinne. This had been considered the hardest of all the climbs in the Dolomites till Solda and his friends made the first ascent of the Marmolata South West Wall. On such climbs, which touch the extreme limit of human capabilities, there is no saying whether one be more difficult than another. So much depends on the individual's condition at the actual time and on the subjective approach to the task in hand. In spite of our having already climbed what is admittedly the most difficult wall in the Dolomites, and that under winter conditions, we were prepared for a relentless encounter with the rock of the Zinne, and how right we were!

It was late in the evening when we reached the Umberto Hut, for a short night's rest. We were off again by four a.m. and crossed the Patern-sattel to the northern side of the Drei Zinnen, to follow the narrow track along the foot of their precipices. We kept on bending our heads back on to our shoulders, so incredible did it seem that human strength could be matched against what lay up there; and yet we had done similar things before. We stopped under the Western Zinne's North Wall. Imagination finally boggled at the idea of going up such a thing; yet we knew that, over the years, as many as fourteen parties had climbed it. But where? Colossal roofs and projections hid the top part of the face from our view, and the route must go on above them. But how did one get there? It looked an impossibly daring venture, and we thought with great respect of all the men who had done the difficult pioneering work until finally two plucky Italian youngsters, Ratti and Cassin, completed the task their forerunners had begun. Even then they were prisoners on that face for three whole days; they emerged so exhausted by their efforts and the nervous strain that they were on the borders of madness.

We roped up in silence. The rope had joined us in many a bitter struggle and taken us safely to the top; it had become the symbol of our unity in partnership. It was still bitterly cold, being already mid-

October, and we had to keep on putting our numbed fingers into our trouser-pockets to get them warm. The rock was very broken and I reached a chimney from which I thought I ought to traverse out to the left. Narrow ledges petered out into the smooth face. I tried my luck everywhere, but was always forced back again. The route description was very vague. Overhead a huge protuberance barred the view upwards, with only an exit to the right. I climbed up to it, to where a tiny crack led horizontally on to a platform in an overhang, a most airy stance, after which the way forward was a little more reasonable. We climbed a rock-band and found ourselves at the base of a tower.

"Now we must surely get over to the left," I surmised, knowing that we had to get out on to the face itself somewhere; but I couldn't see a piton anywhere—nothing but yellow, forbidding rock and brittle, too. That couldn't be right, so I started off up again where I found a ledge which led in comparative comfort out to the left on to the yellow, beetling wall. At its further end a vertical crack shot up, with a rusty hook sticking in it, and I was soon dangling from it. I had difficulty in pulling the rope through the carabiner; a sling was the only way to get a hold, and I brought Kuno up to me as I hung on it. The pitons were not exactly designed to give one confidence. It was a case of hanging from them in a sling a thousand feet above the floor at the bottom while one's feet, likewise in slings, splayed high up on the smooth, holdless face.

I managed to struggle up a few feet on the minutest of holds, content to make do with ridiculous unevennesses in the surface; I could not afford to be particular. The way ahead did not look very cheering. The only objects to catch the eye were a few pitons, sticking into the rock by their very points and heavily bent downwards. I remained hanging in thin air like that at one and the same spot for close on two hours. The rope bit into me, and all retreat was cut off, since Kuno had already taken up the stance below me. There was one hold, enough to take the rim of my fingernails, which I considered insufficient. In the end I contrived to knock a piton in between, but it only went a fraction of an inch into a cranny above me. I hung a sling on to it and put some weight on it with the utmost care. But suppose the piton came out—could Kuno possibly hold me?

There I hung on my hook, doubled up. I made a few cautious attempts to straighten out, gripping the rope-sling as I did so; but I went back to my original position each time, for it seemed much safer. On the other hand, I hadn't any choice; this way I couldn't make any progress. So I very carefully put my weight on the piton again, stepped into the sling and straightened out; the object being to knock in another piton higher up with the utmost possible speed. It didn't go in any further than its predecessor, but what could I do about it?

I called down, "Haul in gently." Or rather, I whispered it, as if to avoid scaring the hook. My feet tatted on the bare rock, as I measured each movement with absolute precision, for a violent jerk would certainly pull the piton out; and so I gambled my giddy way forward. After a long time I got up to an old piton which looked more trustworthy, and snapped a clip into it. After a short breather I moved again, not daring to leave my weight on the piton too long. The pull of the rope took me up again, and I used my hammer again; it was by protracted labour that I got a piton fixed and a clip into it. At that moment the last piton, with its carabiner, went sliding down the rope. And so the exhausting game went on till I finally reached a narrow ledge, where the first thing I did was to rest and massage my fingers. Then it was Kuno's turn and he was only too pleased to leave his uncomfortable stance; though the climbing was twice as difficult for him; because each time he retrieved a carabiner he swung away from the rock on the rope. Only his toughness and the assistance of the second rope enabled him to get up.

We stood on exiguous wrinkles, unravelling the "knitting" into which such manoeuvres inevitably entangle the rope. Above our heads the overhangs jutted from the right; the wrinkles led out into the yellow wall to our left, but soon got lost in yet another roof-pitch. The first few feet were all right, but very soon the fierce thrust of the rock was pushing the upper part of my body far out from the face. After about thirty feet the roof projected to such an extent that I could hardly find the holds on top of it any more. I was hanging in a horizontal posture under it, back downwards. At the same time I realised that I would have to go down some three feet—not as simple as it sounds. My arms were too short to reach the holds under the roof, so I had to fall back on a very queer idea. My feet were pressing against the rock fairly high up. I pushed my head under the overhang, still clinging with my hands to the holds above. Then I pushed against the roof for a moment with my head, and found myself able to hold the weight of my body for a split second nicely balanced between the tips of my toes and my shock of hair. I then withdrew my hands, brought them down in a lightning movement and got a swift, firm grip on the holds below. It was a real gymnastic performance, on sensationally difficult rock. By climbing down a few feet I was then able to reach easier ground.

If we thought that our difficulties were now behind us, we were badly mistaken. The worst was yet to come.

We were by now a little to the right of the lower exit of the great *couloir*, a steep water-washed gash in the rock, whose black streak cuts through the whole upper part of the face. Ice splinters whirred past us. It was a magnificent sight; a myriad glittering shapes sparkling against the background blue of the sky. But we had no time for Nature's loveliness, on this pitiless path of ours. Pitches, hanging-traverses, exposed traverses, all of extreme severity, followed one another, till the weariness in our fingers grew almost unbearable. Over and over again, when I thought I could manage to climb a pitch quite easily, I found I had to come back to the stance from which I had started. Down at the very bottom, plumb under us, some Italians were sitting, watching our efforts with the keenest interest; we could sometimes even hear them speaking.

We were on the great ledge in the middle of the face, with a last overhang bulging overhead. We had still to get up it, but we knew that above it the angle would at last ease off. Sixty feet to our left we found a weakness in this projecting armour. True, the rock jutted out further than ever, but there was precious little on the face that didn't overhang; our eyes had become accustomed to it and our nerves had become dulled to exposure and danger. I climbed a little rock-face to a narrow ledge and followed it to the left; fifteen feet further on there was a chimney, whose rock pushed me further out at every step I took. I was literally hanging only by my fingertips. Then, suddenly, I sensed that they were gradually going on strike. A terrible lassitude swept over me, as I hung there well clear of the ledge below, with the face plunging undercut into the depths beneath. It needed only one glance to bring the nature of my plight home to me. I hadn't the strength to go back to where Kuno was standing sixty feet sideways from me on the ledge, with the rope between us forming a wide bend. He wasn't even belayed to a piton. Yet I knew I couldn't hold on any longer. . . .

"Kuno, I'm coming off!" I yelled, as my fingers went back on me. They let go of the rock as if it were smeared with butter. At that moment I managed, with my last ounce of energy, to fling my body crossways into the chimney; and so I didn't come off after all. I managed to sprawl there for a few seconds, keeping my body moving and braking my fall at the very edge of the final plunge, though the undercut rock was pushing me furiously outwards. I have somehow always managed, when on the verge of a fatal slip, to find some way of maintaining contact by the friction of one part of my body or another against the rock. The desperate struggle lasted some minutes; sweat ran out at every pore. But finally I got completely into the chimney, and rammed a piton in. I glanced down at Kuno, who had been following my nerve-racking antics with marvellous control of his emotions. The rope between me and him ran over a single tiny knob; there could have been no question whatever that had I fallen, my partner would have had to come along—out, down, a thousand feet or more. . . . What a wealth of inner strength lies in the perfect trust between friends! I am eternally grateful that the kindly Fates provided me with such a companion in peril.

There was nothing more to bar our way to the top, though there were cascades of ice hanging in the couloir, whose right-hand retaining wall was plastered with the stuff. The difficulties now decreased measurably —nor had we any objection to offer; the occasional trickles of watery-ice we met didn't give us much bother.

About six p.m., eleven hours after we began the climb, we shook hands on the summit of the Western Zinne. We started down at once, for darkness was falling. Kuno knew the way, but night had soon enveloped us: we kept on down. Everything was uncannily quiet, as we came to a col, slid down a chimney and stood in a rubbish-chute. I wanted to continue down it, but Kuno warned me that it broke off into cliffs lower down and we must keep left across the rocks.

We went down from ledge to ledge, hardly able to see anything in the gloom, and feeling our way, as the rock grew steeper and steeper. At last we decided to bivouac; it was only eight o'clock, but the dangers of a descent through the night were too great. We could hear noise and the note of motors, from the Umberto Hut. We also heard people calling us by name. Down below someone was waving a torch to show us the way; one of our party. We shouted down that we were forced to bivouac.

The night was long and the morning cold. As soon as it was light, we peeled off our shell. We looked out in astonishment, which gave way first to fury, then to laughter. . . . There, not sixty feet to our right, was a débris-shoot, giving easy access to the bottom. It took us half an hour to reach the Umberto Hut.

Later, from Landro we looked up again at the yellow walls of the Drei Zinnen. It was good-bye to the Dolomites, for winter stood knocking at the door.

A CLIMBER WENT A-WOOING

I was a ski-instructor in Hintertal at the foot of the Hochkönig. That is a very healthy occupation. I was in the fresh air all day long trying to instil some of the principles of the white flight into my pupils. Mostly they didn't get much further than a gentle glide downhill. Even if I succeeded by the exercise of much patience in teaching the beginners how to change direction on skis, which made them feel like kings, my own personal skill as a ski-runner was degenerating rapidly. Something had to be done about it. So I found a training method—*Langlauf*. And a dangerous *Langlauf*, too. Time and again it took me over the frontier into Germany. I was ever making for the Ramsau in Bavaria, that romantic corner near Berchtesgaden. There, on the far side of a bridge, stood a pleasant country abode, a *Pension*. It was not as a guest that I made my frequent visits; indeed I came unannounced, when I called there. Nor had I always permission to come; but the daughter of the house and I did not ask permission.

As the crow flies Hintertal isn't really very far from the Ramsau, but between them stands a high mountain range, difficult and dangerous of passage in the winter months. It also happens to mark the Austro-German frontier. So, in order to reach my heart's desire, I always had to make the vast détour through Saalfelden, Weissbach and the Hirschbichl. Thirty miles is quite a step; when there was no transport available, I had to do the whole of it on foot. Then they used to see me hurrying away on my "boards" of an evening, at a *Langlauf* pace, uphill, downhill, always following the high road.

I mostly covered the return journey by night, so as to prolong the time spent with the Beloved to the utmost. On Monday morning I was always there, on the dot, in Hintertal, with my ski-pupils. Men mostly run for their freedom. I, on the contrary, seemed to be in a great hurry to surrender my bachelor freedom, at the gallop. Presently my colleagues at Hintertal began to notice my Sunday absences. So Hermann wants to wed; what's bitten him, I wonder?

It was a glorious spring day. I don't say that just because you *have* to say it about a spring day, if you are describing it in a book; it really was glorious. I didn't feel altogether at my best in a dark suit. But my bride in her white wedding dress was an enchanting, dazzling vision. And in that instant I forgot all my worries and cares and—I humbly beg their forgiveness—the Mountains, too.

At the ensuing celebration, quite a detachment of my club, the "Karwendler", turned up from Innsbruck. With tears in their eyes they congratulated me on my new estate as a married man. This was obviously a last good-bye—just as though I were lost for ever to my beloved hills and my friends.

I could forget the mountains for a short time; taking leave of absence in my thoughts to some extent; but in truth they remained my masters, whose law was my inexorable rule.

Life went on; the only difference was that it brought me more joy, though at the same time more worries. Meanwhile our honeymoon took us to the Sellrain. Our double ski-tracks scored unbroken slopes, sending the white dust of their powder-snow flying. We were happy and content. We climbed the Lüsener Fernerkogel in a frightful snow-storm and then went shooting down into the warm springtime. We travelled through a sea of blossom to Innsbruck, where the four walls of a little room, which were to spell "home" for the time being, took us to their heart.

In order to show my wife the loveliness of our Tirolean landscape, I took her to the Dolomites, where we climbed the Marmolata together. At Whitsun we went to Switzerland where, in the Bernina Group, she climbed her first "Four Thousander", Piz Bernina itself, and, on the very next day, Piz Palü as well. That made her as happy as a child, and I warmed myself proudly in my wife's reflected glory.

I took out one guided party after another that spring. I had now a family to plan for. I guided the sedatest of gentlemen on the rope among the mountains of the Oetztaler Alps; it was always on the same, very easy climb. As I did so, my glance used to wander in homesick longing across to the dark teeth of the Dolomites. Were the wise ones who had said, "That's the end of Hermann," right after all? A whole year passed like that, and the great climbs had to remain wishful dreams.

That was 1951.

We spent Christmas with my parents-in-law in the Ramsau. I was itching to do a serious climb again; it was more than a year since my last big effort in the mountains. Erhart Sommer of Berchtesgaden offered to come with me. Soon after Midnight Mass on Christmas Eve we left the Ramsau and drove up to the Hirschbichl in a Land Rover.

By eight o'clock we were at the start of the direct South *Arête* of the Grosse Mühlsturzhorn. I knew the old way up the usual *arête* well enough; the "direct" was new to me, and had only been done a few times. It is reckoned the hardest climb in the Berchtesgaden Alps, and according to reports has always meant a bivouac: yet the actual height is only a thousand feet or so, which speaks for itself. Now we were trying to make the first winter ascent.

I had begun to wonder seriously how I should get on. Rock and I had become well-nigh strangers: but hardly was my hand on it again, we were the old trusty friends once more. One can't forget how to climb, especially if it has become part of one's flesh and blood. It was an icy morning, even after we had begun to move in the sun; but presently it began to warm up till it was just comfortable. We gained height rapidly. Erhart mastered all the tough places extraordinarily well, considering he had lost several ribs in the war.

It was the old familiar picture. The rope rings did not lie on the rock, they hung from the wall. So did the rope itself, and the only way you could identify your partner's position down under the overhang was by the way the rope fell away to him. By mid-day we were at the succession of cracks which slants up to the right through a zone of completely smooth rock. It was a magnificent climb.

"Is this the so-called 'Crack of the Wooden Wedges'?" I asked Erhart.

I could see a few bits of decayed wood stuck in the rock here and there. I was almost sorry not to have brought any new wedges along; but I had wanted to prove that even here one could get on without them, for I love unassisted climbing best of all. Even here the holds were not too bad in the cracks; I could do without "hooks".

As the sun went down, the last difficulties lay behind us. We spared ourselves the walk to the true summit, and traversed instead across several snow-filled, icy ribs and runnels over to the left, to the South Face. It was already dark when we began to rope down it. We banged in our pitons and found our way down the face by the light of a pocket-torch. It led down steep chimneys smooth with ice. Suddenly I dropped my torch; the abyss swallowed it. It was pitch dark all around us. We just managed to get down to the bottom of a chimney and there to clear out a little snow platform for our housing plans. We comforted ourselves by telling each other that we had not brought the bivouac materials along for nothing. It was eight p.m. There we sat most uncomfortably under our smooth, cold shell of *Batiste*. It would be much nicer to be at home, we thought; a dangerous thought for a mountaineer to think. The sky had clouded over a little and soon there was not a star to be seen. We divided up what was left of our provisions and then each of us, more or less frozen, tried to bridge the gulf of time after his own fashion. I did it by going over the whole climb again in my mind. It had been glorious and we had been in such glorious form. I had everything to make me happy—I had found my way on again and that meant the stimulus to new things. And I had climbed the great ridge at which I had so often stared up during my repeated *Langlaufs* in love's service.

The weather began to worry us; a keen wind had got up, the clouds were descending on us. We kept on looking at the time. Obviously the weather was going to break up, but perhaps St. Peter would take pity on us climbers and on me as a newly-married man and put it off till after dawn? At any rate, till we were off the rock? Not a bit of it. In fact St. Peter doesn't appear to me to be at all on good terms with climbers. As keeper of the Heavenly Gate, he likes things done decently. And is it decent for a crazy loon to spend Christmas night out on a snow-covered crag, instead of with his young wife?

It began to snow before dawn; and helplessly we had to watch while it got heavier and heavier. How can anybody do anything in such conditions? The snow stuck to the face, swiftly hiding hand- and foot-holds, protuberances and ledges. Soon it was all one smooth, white, vertical surface. Buried under it lay that ultimate essential for the climber, rock with hand- and foot-holds in it.

It was already nine a.m. and probably broad daylight, but we were wrapped in a half-light, while the snow went dribbling down over our tent-sack. We could wait no longer; we must risk climbing down, come what may. The rigid ropes disappeared down below in the murk. We went sliding down them, yard by yard, with the utmost caution, an exhausting process. The ropes were so stiff and smooth with snow and cold that we could hardly manage them any more. We rootled around under the snow for holds, wrinkles, irregularities, more precious at the moment than the costliest treasure. Gingerly we went down from step to step of the white, perpendicular wall, till at last we were clear of it.

Then we went ploughing through the deep, fresh snow towards our well-earned Christmas dinner.

WE HAD TO BIVOUAC AFTER ALL—
ON THE TOFANA BUTTRESS

IT was the following spring. Our marriage held everything our love had promised. Our joy was unclouded, and the Hills smiled down upon it. We were happy indeed when after running down over the last brownish relics of snow, we unbuckled our skis and strolled homewards through a sea of crocuses in bloom. Delightedly we encountered the first primroses and stuck catkin branches into our rucksacks. Everywhere in the open new life was beginning to awaken; everything was budding and blossoming. Slowly the great walls darkened. The avalanches came thundering down from the peaks.

It was time to put our skis away. The rocks were calling now—yes, even to a newly-married man. During this year of 1952, after a whole year of neglect, they were to come into their own again. The first attempts were in the mountains close to home. Then I was off again into the Dolomites.

We were bound for Cortina. Monte Cristallo was still deep in snow, the Tofana still very wintry: for it was still very early in the year. A kind friend had taken us along in his car and brought us up along a disused military road almost to the very start of our climb. "Us"—Sepp Jöchler and me: "our climb"—the South Buttress of the Tofana. This was the third of three climbs reckoned by many as the hardest in the Dolomites. We had already done the Marmolata Walls and the Western Zinne. The two members of Cortina's younger generation of climbers, Constantini and Apollonio, who were the first to climb the buttress in 1944, reckoned it harder than the North Wall of the Western Zinne. And *Berti*, the Italian Dolomite handbook, says: ". . . *sesto grado superiore, arampicata effectiva—ore* 21!"

Twenty-one hours! We didn't intend to take so long as that. We expected to do it in ten to twelve hours. We left our bivouac-sack behind, so as not to embarrass our kindly "chauffeur" and his friends, who were due to climb the Tofana by the normal way. But we secretly took some rope-slings along and even some "step-boards", though I normally hate such ultra-modern gear.

It would be wearisome to describe in detail every successive pitch on such a "Giant's Causeway in Reverse". So let's start at the third roof which bars passage above the middle belt of the wall.

A crack goes diagonally up into the remotest corner of the huge jutting mass of rock. Climbing ends there. Eight or ten feet further out the wall starts vertically upwards again. There was not a sign of our predecessors' pitons, but plentiful holes gave evidence of furious "carpentry" hereabouts. What followed was horizontal climbing with one's back downwards. There was a fine crack in the roof's underside; I banged a piton into it, and hung a sling into it. Shakily I stepped into it and immediately swung outwards. I hung there under the roof like a fly on the ceiling, my feet dangling in thin air above a gulf 1,000 feet deep. The overhanging walls below me looked almost flat from my perch. I felt over the outer rim of the roof with my hand; managed to knock a second piton into it. A second foot-sling was soon hanging down from the corner of the rock.

I was at the uttermost edge of the overhang with my feet still hanging out over nothing; but now I could no longer find even a cranny into which another piton would fit. So I tried to climb the projection un-aided, which meant first getting my feet on to something firm. The friction of the rope was terrific and threatened to pull me off; my fingers were being tried to the last ounce of their strength. After a second overhang, also climbed without aids, I at last found a rickety stance of a kind. Now the same desperate game began all over again for Sepp. It was no easier for him than for me; when he retrieved the carabiners he swung right out over emptiness and spun like a top, on his own axis. I saw his mop of hair appear several times and disappear again as quickly as it had come. In the end he fetched up next to me, gasping frantically.

The reddish-white mottled rock continued in another overhang. Slender, partly-interrupted cracks offered the only means of getting up under the next roof. The rope ran through a carabiner every thirty feet. I saw a ledge above me and promised myself a stance on it. I would get there, somehow; but the last few feet were utterly smooth wall, which I managed to surmount without holds, using simply the pull of the rope and friction technique. But . . . there was no ledge, no stance, after all. The rock was pushing me out so far that I could hardly endure it. Only the use of a chair-sling made it possible for me to protect Sepp as he came up. Changing stance was a chancy, risky manoeuvre. There was only room for one to stand on this *Piazzetl*, as we had christened these exiguous stances. A jutting groove brought me up under the next great roof. It hadn't the same pitch as the previous ones, but made up for that by falling to the extreme edge of the containing wall. There was a broad crack in it, which refused to take a piton; as soon as I stuck one in, out it fell again, immediately. It was at the furthest corner of the roof that I managed to make one hold at last. I let myself be lowered out under the roof, lying horizontally under the overhang once again. My fingers searched the outer rim for a serviceable crack. My fingers felt one; but would it do? It would need another long iron spike to save the situation. I stuck it into the crack, turned it till it wedged itself and then gave it a couple of quick hammer blows, before my arm fell back nerveless. I had to go back and rest a bit. Then my body was leaning far out again. A couple more well-aimed raps with the hammer, in with a carabiner, and then a rope-sling into that. With the rope to steady me, my feet pressed down onto the sling, my body stretched upwards—I swung out to the utmost edge of the roof. Two more agonising yards and my feet had something firm under them once more. A hand-pull was enough to fetch out the piton which had given me support; I should have good use for it further up, I expected. After sixty feet more of exhausting struggle I found myself standing on a broad band of débris in the middle of the yellow, beetling crags.

We heard voices below. Somebody called my name, but it wasn't one of our party. We learned afterwards that it was some experts from Cortina, come to watch us. Sepp had a good breather next to me up there and felt better. We didn't want to talk—only to get in touch with our own friends below, at the start of the climb. Rudl shouted up that we had the worst of the difficulties behind us, which encouraged us to take a prolonged rest. It was half-past four.

"The rest is easy," I told Sepp. Who said twenty-one hours? That was a joke; but one should never start laughing too soon. . . .

A steeply overhanging chimney went up overhead. It didn't look exactly inviting, but not absolutely frightening. I climbed up on stalactite formations at its very back. Thirty feet up it closed in. So I had to come out into the light of day again, at the extreme edge of this steep, overhanging rift. There I found an old, rusty ring-hook to tell its tale of man's courage and human shortcomings. I hooked myself on and had a good look at the situation. The rock pressed heavily downwards; above me a smooth overhang prevented any further progress up the chimney. There wasn't even the shadow of a fracture into which to drive a piton. I straddled out towards the extreme edge of the bulge on "tension". From there I could sweep the whole lower part of the wall in one glance. The chimney thrust far outside the broad ledge at its foot. I managed a piton or two, but they didn't mean a thing. I tied them all together with a rope-sling in the hope that they would hold after such treatment; then I hung a foot-loop on to them, and so gained a couple of feet. But that was the extreme limit of my skill. I tried a rope-traverse to the right; but everything there was brittle and thrusting sharply outwards. Something didn't add up here! Perhaps the old piton was the legacy of a "boob"? And yet the description in the handbook clearly indicated this spot.

It looked a little better out to the left. I let myself down again to the ledge, where Sepp hauled me in. After climbing a little way, I tried to traverse on to somewhat easier-looking ground. I was almost there, when the traverse piton, my last support, came out—and seconds later I was back alongside my partner.

I tried the chimney again. Again I hung, exactly as before, up there and couldn't move an inch further. I began to have grave doubts. Such a thing had never happened to me before. What had become of my cast-iron theory: "Where one human being has got by, another must be able to get by too"? Our predecessors surely needed holds, too, to hold on to? They were surely not fitted with suction caps, any more than ourselves?

"Just miss this bit out, and get on with it above," Sepp called up to me. It's an old joke, though a good one, but at the moment I couldn't raise a laugh. I had to come back to the ledge again, for a rest.

Screeching and croaking, the daws fluttered round us, as if sensing a victim. If only I could sail in the air like them! We could only go on up; our retreat was cut off. But how, over those great vaulting roofs? I looked despairingly for a way out; on every hand the ledge petered out into unscalable slabs.

It was already six o'clock. Time had simply flown. We still hoped to get away without a bivouac. We had laughed about that . . . now we weren't laughing any more. But we would have to hurry, now. I had a go at another part of the wall, haphazard fashion. Thirty feet to the left the rock suddenly offered a variety of holds and I was able to climb a hundred feet without any assistance at all. To save time, we abandoned pitons, carabiners and slings in the overhanging part of the chimney. The rock was very solid, and consequently unfavourable to the use of pitons. My fingers had pretty nearly used up all their strength. I had reached the limit of what can be climbed without aids. I gave myself and every new pitch a searching test, to avoid a recurrence of what happened on the North Wall of the Western Zinne. An exposed traverse on small holds brought me back into the chimney above the overhanging barrier of roof. There was an abandoned rope-ring hanging from the rock just there.

We climbed the easier continuation-cracks almost at a run. But the wall still loomed huge and high above us, yellowy-red and vast; nor could we see any end to it. Suddenly, in a chimney the dusk was upon us. Sepp was 150 feet below me at a comfortable place. I was glad to climb down from my cold, narrow crevice to join my friend on the grassy platform where he was already making preparations for a one-night stand. How glad we were now to have our thick pullovers, which had been such a burden in the stark sunshine during the day. So we were going to finish the job in ten to twelve hours, were we? Without a bivouac, of course? One should never allow oneself such feelings of superiority; the mountains know how to curb one's self-confidence.

Slowly the night came creeping up out of the valleys. Down in Cortina the first lights were going on. We were only sorry to have brought discomfort on our friends on account of our bivouac. They ought really to have driven off home; we could have followed them back perfectly well by train next day. But they put comradeship first and would not dream of letting us down. That is the essence of the spirit of the Hills. We signalled to them with a candle; they answered by turning their headlights on and off. When we got hungry we burrowed into the rucksack and stuffed a handful of almonds and raisins into our mouths. We yodelled and sang at the tops of our voices, so that our friends shouldn't worry about us. Noise is the best evidence that things are all right: besides, the time passes more quickly. We had an inexhaustible repertoire, from operatic aria to pub-chorus, from cradle-song to army ballad. Our "Tofana Duet" was not silenced till after midnight. There were distant flashes—summer lightning. Sepp, always the optimist, said it was a good sign; I thought the opposite. Dark clouds were piling up above the Pala; lightning flashes split the dark night sky. We were blinded for seconds on end, then it was dark all around us again. Distant thunder rumbled heavily—a wonderful display by Nature. We hoped that was all it was. It was not all. . . .

The heavy mass of clouds drew steadily closer to us. From time to time our friends signalled to us with their lights. They had lit a camp fire; probably it had grown too cold for them. We were beginning to feel the cold too, but we couldn't light a fire; so we huddled close together through the endless hours. It was only two o'clock, and the weather was growing more and more doubtful. The last windows in the sky were closed now; not a star was to be seen any more; the cloud-pack was settling downwards menacingly. The summits of the Pelmo and the Antelao had already put on a hood; solitary shreds of mist came chasing over the Falzarego Pass. Fog was rising from the valleys, too, forming a wall which for a time cut off the view down below. Nearer and nearer drew the cloud-banks. Now fog was drooping down on us from our own summit.

The curtain closed in on us. Now we could feel the first raindrops on our faces. Rain? No, snowflakes; falling thicker and thicker. It lay on ledges and wrinkles, piling up and covering every projection in the rock.

It melted on our warm bodies and drenched our clothes. We waited there, freezing.

Slowly the grey dawn of a new day spread over the world, while the thunder still rolled in the distance. A cold wind arose and scattered the clouds; ghostly scarves of mist chased about the Nuvolao and the Cinque Torri; the floor of the ravine at the bottom was powdered with white. The wind blew banners of snow away over the ridge above us; the white crystals poured like a fine drizzle across the wall—and over us. It was an impressive place in which to have spent the night. Everywhere the yellow walls went plunging vertically away. It was like being on an island—in the middle of a rolling, raging sea. We got into touch again with our friends down by the car. A "Yo-ho!" from Sepp's throat was intended to assure them that we had had a tolerable night.

I wasn't keen on waiting; the weather was far from promising an improvement. It was time to get off the wall! The rock was cold and slippery; snow was lying on every hand- and foot-hold. The chimney was now considerably harder than yesterday. Our limbs were still stiff and ached at every movement. When I had to flex my ankles they just turned over; but after the first few rope's lengths, things began to improve noticeably. Our bodies were warm again and our joints had recovered their old elasticity.

The whirl of flakes began anew, but the climbing became definitely easier. We reached the left retaining edge of the face, to be met by a picture of fantastic beauty. The curtain of mist was torn asunder and there, out of the billowing grey, rose pillar upon pillar of rock, standing unbelievably sheer above their supporting slabs; between them the mists were still lodging. The whole scene was veiled in a gentle mist which lent a ghostly quality to the whole spectacle. Then the mirage was suddenly gone—we were wrapped once again in our uniform shroud of grey. The wind grew fiercer, the snow grew more dense, as we approached the ridge. Two more rope's lengths and we were standing on the crest of the ridge leading up to the summit of Tofana.

Everything on the northern side lay deep in snow. An icy nor'wester stiffened our clothes to the consistency of armour. We crossed the slopes between the Punta Marietta's rock outcrops in a slightly upward direction. We took frequent turns in breaking a trail through the deep snow, so as not to get too tired. It was a good thing that I knew the way down: for the lie of the land prompts one to go straight down the pleasantly-falling slopes which, however, soon break away into impassable cliffs. We kept on sinking more deeply into the rotten snow. The mists parted again for a moment, giving us an opportunity for checking our position.

We reached the saddle behind the Punta Marietta without any further détours.

When we got back to our friends, they met us with broad smiles, handshakes and congratulations; but not a word of reproach did they utter. The hardest thing said was Walter's: "You're a couple of mad dogs and no mistake!" We found such genuine team spirit very touching.

BADILE—NORTH-EAST WALL

It was the beginning of July. My wife had just gone off to Ramsau to visit her parents—I had to use the precious time somehow. For, though we climbers have a personality of our own, we do set the greatest store on harmonious family relations. So, where climbing absence is concerned, we have to make good in quality what we give up in quantity.

I had long had the North Wall of Badile in mind. My desire to quench the longing for that great experience was burning ever hotter and hotter; but the mountain always remained for me at an unapproachable distance. Something always interfered just when I was on the point of making the attempt to get near it. "Now or never!" must be my motto. My bicycle would dispose of the financial stringency.

I caught the evening express to Landeck on Friday, July 4th, 1952. There I mounted my bike. After miles of hard saddle-work I reached the Swiss frontier about midnight. I lay down for a couple of hours' rest by the side of the road, for I hadn't had a wink of sleep the night before, during which I had been on a search-party in Innsbruck's Northern Range.

At four o'clock I pushed off on the old "moke" again, pedalling away uphill in the vague direction of the Maloja Pass, at the other end of the Engadine. If you know the road up that long valley, you will realise on what kind of a "slog" I was engaged. I made slow progress; my legs and my seat shared the general suffering.

I had a drink at an inviting spring. My breakfast of bread, butter and gorgonzola went down there, too. A delivery van came by and took me in tow for a short distance. We pottered from village to village, and I helped the driver to unload his jam-pots. It was about mid-day when we reached Samaden. Then the van turned back and I was left to my own muscular resources again. On, past the pleasant Lakes of Silvaplana and Sils, tantalising me with their invitation to bathe in their clear, cool waters—for which the long road ahead left me no time—on to the Maloja Pass in stifling heat. There, to the south, the savage Bergell ridges greeted my eyes; far, far down below lay the Val Bregaglia, in a blue haze. Steep hairpins swung the road down to the valley with its southern, sub-alpine aspect; at each turn I grudged the loss of height, which I would have to make good later in the day. My body ran with sweat in spite of the wind of my progress. I rattled at a fair pace through the stone-paved streets of villages with old, weathered houses. Children

playing at the road's edge urged me on with shouts of "Koblet! Koblet!"
The comparison with the famous cycling champion naturally spurred
me on to greater efforts, and I pedalled harder than ever.

More than 3,000 feet down from Maloja lies Promontogno, the
place where you leave the road for the Sciora Hut. Its old, grey houses
cluster close at the feet of steep slopes. While I was passing—now
afoot—along its cobbly alleys I cast a glance upwards through the leaves
and branches of the rioting southern foliage. I stood there as if trans-
fixed. That, up there, was Badile, then!

Its faces and ridges swing upwards in clean-cut lines to a comb,
crowned by the glittering white rim of the summit-cornice. Dark and
forbidding, its flanks plunge valleywards. What a terrific wall! Was it
not perhaps a sheer act of presumption to dream of attempting the
North East Face, alone?

I bought a few things with the solitary five-franc note which now
remained to cover the rest of my travelling expenses, shouldered my
rucksack and moved on up the savagely-romantic Bondasca Valley,
at whose head towered the triple peaks of the Sciora Group, closing in
all the background. Three faces, hemmed in by ice gullies which act
as signposts to their summits. It was heaven to let the gentle rain of a
noisy waterfall spray my body, running with sweat. Dark storm-clouds
were gathering. Cloud-wreaths settled on the summits of Piz Badile and
Cengalo. Presently the blessed comfort of a cooling shower set in, this
time from the sky, as I went on up the valley. I reached the Sciora Hut
at seven p.m.

There were only two people there, the keeper and a guest from Milan.
Very sensibly, I kept my plans to myself and simply answered their
eager questions by saying I meant to do the Badile Ridge. Even that
seemed bad enough to them. "*La prima solo!*" was their comment—the
first solo climb! If only they knew what I was really aiming at!

In the meantime I kept on taking careful stock of this terrific granite
slab 2,500 feet high which is Piz Badile's North East Wall. I had seen
it a few months before from the Ago di Sciora, but then it had been
just a white surface and not nearly so impressive. Since then I had done
a thorough course of study at home on the literature, descriptions and
reports of various parties, which had convinced me that this, unlike the
other climbs on primaeval rock with which I was familiar from the Mont
Blanc area, was a technically straight climbing job. It was just that
which awoke my urge to do it. For I like technically tricky bits when
pure unmechanical climbing is concerned and am thoroughly used to
them. But now, face to face with the wall itself, a tiny doubt made itself
heard.

The first direct climb of this face was done more than fifteen years ago. Among the first to tackle it, all Italians, were Riccardo Cassin, often quoted by me, and his friends Esposito and Ratti. Two other Italians joined them in the siege. After 34 hours of actual climbing time, involving three bivouacs and a surprise storm into the bargain, the five of them reached the 10,853 foot summit of Piz Badile. The last two, unfit for the exacting demands of such an undertaking, died of exhaustion on the summit. This tragedy threw a deep shadow across the face, which was not cleared till Gaston Rébuffat and Bernard Pierre repeated the climb in 1948. They too had had to wrestle with difficulties for three whole days, so that the wall had yielded none of its early reputation and was still reckoned at the very top of the severest climbs in the Western Alps. But after that repetitions began to be more frequent and by the end of 1950 they numbered a round nine; almost all of them had forced their perpetrators to bivouac. The summer of 1951, a notoriously bad-weather season, and a huge rock-fall on the Badile Ridge, which swept across the North East Face and altered it extensively, seemed to have cast another spell upon this frowning wall. Could I, climbing by myself, exorcise it—to-morrow?

I had set my alarm for two a.m. When I woke up I noticed to my horror that there was daylight. A glance at the clock showed that I had slept through the alarm; it was four o'clock. I got ready very quickly, breakfasting as I went across the slopes, moving over boulders and slabs. Descending a little towards the end, I moved out on to the glacier which lies at the foot of the Cengalo and Badile. Not knowing the way, I got a little too high up. I wanted to traverse under Cengalo's rocks, but a huge edge-crevasse barred my way and forced me to take a time-wasting détour. The sun, rising behind the eastern Bergell ranges, threw its first rays on to Badile's North-East Face.

Then I was able once again to follow the approach-route, which was now easy enough to discern, etched in light and shade. As I looked at the wall it set me a few problems, which I could only solve when I actually got to them. Along the edge of dark, yawning gulfs I made my way to the head of a rocky spur. I thought things over for a moment, glanced up at the sky—the weather seemed to be settled—then got ready for my effort. I decided to leave behind the bivouac sack and every single thing I could do without. The only things to go into my climbing-pack were the 100-foot perlon line, a few rope-slings, spring-clips and pitons, the hammer, some food and the camera. Then I moved straight off over hard, steep, frozen snow, wearing rubbers, to the start of the climb. The sight of that uprush of gigantic, holdless slabs, in which the eye can hardly detect a break, gave me food for thought. But my attention

*11. I stood there spellbound at the first sight of the Piz Badile. Surely,
to tackle its North-East Face solo was presumptuous to a degree.*

12. *The North Wall of the Eiger . . . I had dreamed about it since I was a boy.
In the summer of 1952 my craving to test my powers against it was at last fulfilled.*

13. *The third ice-field on the Eiger North Wall is exceptionally steep, and raked by
an unusually fierce fire of falling stones. Safe under an overhang, I watched Rèbuffat
as, between volleys, he rapidly traversed the ice, which slopes at fully 55 degrees.*

14. *I had to do something to test my efficiency for the coming expedition. The highest wall in the Eastern Alps, the East Face of the Watzmann above Berchtesgaden, plastered with winter snow, seemed the obvious choice.*

15. *The veiw across the Bazhin Gap to Nanga Parbat's summit: I found it extremely painful to contemplate so great a loss of height but the final prize glittered before me and some secret urge drove me on.*

16. Nanga Parbat (top left) the Rakhiot route in profile taking a line along the upper edge of the Rupal Face. The Silbersattel is behind the prominent step of North Peak.

17. I was standing on the summit of Nanga Parbat (left). I got the Tyrolese pennants out of my anorak and tied them to the shaft of my ice axe.

18. Forty-one hours separated my departure from the tent and my return to it. Hans Ertl met me and took a snapshot (above). I was so dehydrated that I could not utter a sound, but Hans didn't mind. All he cared about was that I was back.

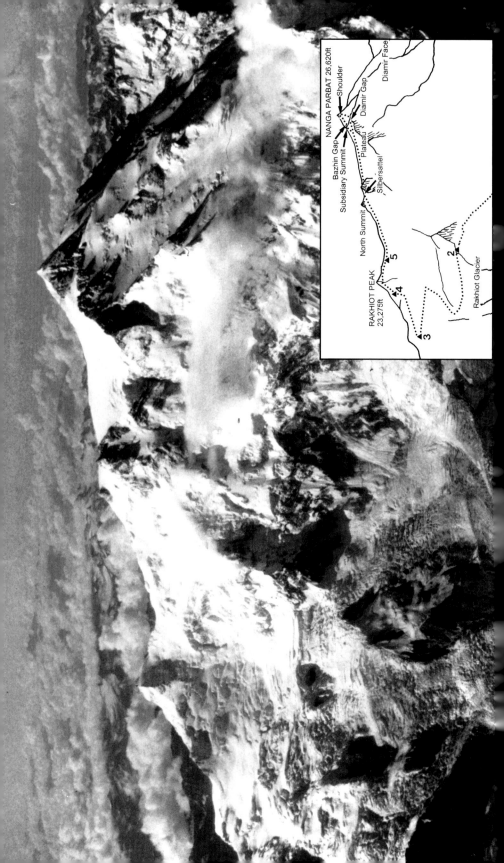

NANGA PARBAT 26,620ft

Bazhin Gap
Subsidiary Summit
Shoulder
Diamir Gap
Diamir Face

North Summit
Plateau
Silbersattel

RAKHIOT PEAK
23,275ft

5
4
3
2

Rakhiot Glacier

was immediately distracted by voices coming from the North Ridge, where there was a threesome already at work.

It was exactly six o'clock as I laid my hands on rock. The crossing from snow to rock had been easy. I made good headway to the right over good rocks with plenty of grips and footholds. A steep pitch was surmounted by way of a chimney—still easy work. That took me up the first 650 feet of the wall. How pleasant if it went on like this; but I must be coming to things soon!

Soon I was standing at the start of a hundred-foot rift, which I had almost overlooked. I had climbed quite a few feet on before I realised that things had suddenly got tough, and that it would be quite useful to have a "carabiner" handy. So I climbed down again to the first good stance I could find. There I took everything essential out of my pack. I slung the rope about me, hung the slings, ironmongery and camera about my person, and then—up I went!

I remembered at once the pictures in *Alpinisme*, that magnificent French climbing periodical, which illustrated this particular crack. But where on earth had all the pitons got to? On the right there was a smooth slab with only tiny corrugations for the feet; on the left one was pushed inwards by the overhanging wall. A narrow crack ran up the bottom of the rift. I clawed it with my fingertips, my feet tried to find friction holds to the right. Already at this point last year's rock-fall was making itself uncomfortably noticeable. The slabs were covered with a fine dust inches thick, which filled every wrinkle and almost nullified the friction of one's rubbers. All the same, I managed to reach the final overhang quite quickly, and found an ancient worthy of a piton sticking out. I tried it and it held. With some relief I snapped the split-ring into the rusty eye of the piton, panted a little, used the piton as a hold for a short while and then moved on up. There were plenty of holds on the overhang and I was soon over it. Then came more slabs, scored by cracks, opening a way up to the left. The climbing would have been easier if the cracks hadn't been full of silt, and so demanded extreme caution. Very slowly I pushed my way up.

I came to the edge of a small ice-shield lying on the slabs hereabouts and barring the ascent—just a small relic of the winter snows. It gave me a bit of a headache to come up—a two-foot layer of hollow ice lying on a smooth base, covering the route for a width of 70 feet. At its upper rim I had to traverse. With great care I hacked away the sharp upper edge of the ice, which groaned ominously at every stroke. It was with relief that I got off such a treacherous footing and climbed on up to the continuation of the line of cracks on good, safe rock. The climbing grew more and more enjoyable, and I managed at last to get out of the line of fire of the falling stones. After a short *arête*, the wall went leaping steeply up again. I was at the start of the second gully, one of the supreme difficulties of the climb, indisputably classed as in the super-severe category "VI". This was for me a critical spot.

If I find it easy, I thought, I can go on above it with a light mind, for there won't be anything harder to come: if not I can still go back from here, and would be well advised to do so.

An overhang slanting upwards to the left next occupied my attention and offered me the safety of some excellent handholds. Where they gave out, a short gallery of pitons began, the shafts making a most reliable impression on me. Probably they were a legacy from the first ascent ever—to judge by the patina of age on them. After them, a fairly vertical gully went shooting a hundred feet to heaven. Its rock was, however, quite unusually rough, so that I was able to "friction" up the whole of its length. I gave silent praise to the "profile" soles of my climbing rubbers, whose advantages in a place like that are absolutely invaluable.

I wriggled, heaved and straddled myself up the face, foot by foot, with the free end of my rope following me like a faithful companion. There can scarcely be a more wonderful feeling than balancing upwards like that, unburdened and light of foot, free of all adventitious aids—like a Paul Preuss or a Hans Dülfer in earlier days, entirely self-reliant, wary of eye and sensitive to the tips of their fingers and toes. The only thing required here is a good natural climbing style and pure technical skill. I could have shouted aloud for sheer delight, but I did not want to disturb the solemn hush. Not a sound disturbed the silence. Down below, the valley was still wrapped in the soft veils of a fresh and dewy dawn.

On with the dance! There was another glorious pitch ahead of me. The gully was cut into by great overhanging roofs, with an exit under them to the left on to a smooth slabby wall. Here there were plenty of small but firm holds, till I reached a place where I was not quite sure about the continuation of the route, for the description isn't any too clear. All around me the rock fell away like tiles on a roof, with tiny cracks everywhere in evidence. I explored them all for old pitons, and finally spotted an ancient, weathered shaft some way off. I reached it after some wriggling over places which all looked worse than they proved to be when you got there. Then there was a series of marvellous pitches. At about eight o'clock I reached the snow-patch half-way up the face; there to sit down on a warm boulder to pant a bit and summon up new strength for the difficulties to come.

To the left of the snowfield was the beginning of the Great Gully. Climbing-fever and inquisitiveness soon had me on the way again. I had been worrying a good deal about the gully. It looked damnably smooth. But plenty of straddling and a good friction technique enabled me to climb it unassisted. I only used the piton or two stuck in the rock here as momentary hand-holds.

Then I ran into the expected difficulties. About 130 feet up the gully a sharp overhang barred my way. There I found a piton and a carabiner, both of French provenance, trade-mark "Allain". I tried to take the overhang direct, as it was, but soon found myself hanging like a fly on the wall, which was in a highly resistant mood. I was actually almost up, but couldn't find the necessary holds on top. So I went back and had a second go after a short rest. With a considerable effort, I managed to knock a piton in above the lip of the overhang. I used it for a foot-sling, the only one I employed on the whole climb. I was still 30 feet from the sundering roof. Unable to spare a valuable piton, I knocked another in higher up and let myself down again on the rope to the overhang. A couple of hard knocks with the hammer and the ring-hook was mine again. With the help of the rope I then climbed to the overhang again. There I discovered the initials L.T. on the French split-ring; they could only stand for Lionel Terray. I climbed on, delighted with my find. But I could find no vestige of a traversing piton under the roof; yet it was obvious that one had to get across to the right here and down into the parallel gully. Then it dawned on me. Sixty feet lower down there was a rib joining the two gullies. I had been doing a "variation" route, a real "work of supererogation". And now too I knew what the meaning of the French carabiner must be; Terray had also come too far up and had roped down again. But I didn't want to lose height again and so attempted a descending traverse into the parallel gully.

I rammed another spike into the rock, and explored around the corner with great care. A smooth slab shot up to the right. Six feet lower down a narrow ledge, thirty feet long and about a finger's breadth, offered the only possibility of effecting the crossing. With the utmost caution I pushed myself inch by inch to the right in a "Dülfer-seat" on the rope—not a hand-hold anywhere. The slab fell away so steeply that I was only just able to maintain balance by the aid of the rope. After some ticklish minutes there were at last some holds for my fingers. I was in the gully; and the rope came away without any difficulty. . . .

The next part of the route was much easier, but "honeyed ease" didn't last very long. A few more small overhangs cropped up, but all of them furnished with the necessary holds. Vertical ribs and wrinkles, behind which were hidden splendid hand-holds, proved welcome allies. On the debit side, one's feet were rather worse off again, for no support had been laid on for them. A jutting roof forced me out on to a pretty exposed traverse along a horizontal crack to the left, leading to the edge of the Great Gully. The first 30 feet were nerve-racking, but if the holds were minute, there were at least plenty of them. "Poor things, but mine own," thought I.

So there I was at last in the gully. Occasional stones whizzed past me, without disturbing me unduly. In the bottom of the gully a positive streamlet was bubbling its way cheerfully into the abyss, offering me precious comfort—for I was pretty dried-up by the last hours of scorching sunshine.

Leaving Cassin's second bivouac-spot on my right, I followed a long succession of cracks, which eventually broadened into a chimney. In that kind of chimney, where there is absolutely no danger, because you can jam yourself into it like a wedge, "technique" ceases to have any meaning; the thing becomes nothing but a straightforward scramble. I wriggled my way up like a snake. Presently the chimneys broadened out and formed a kind of miniature gorge, too wide for me to straddle any more; so I made use of two delicate cracks in the bottom of the gorge. First the right-hand crack, then the left afforded excellent upward progress, with one or two small overhangs for variety's sake.

I could feel a cool breeze blowing down on me, so I couldn't be far from the summit now. I traversed out above an overhang on to the left-hand containing wall—and soon I could see the summit. There was still plenty of snow in the couloir running up to the ridge, so I traversed a rope's length further to the left on an exposed wall with small holds. Then I looked up again—and saw quite a collection of people on the summit. I could only see their heads sticking up over the cornice. I had been observed, and they were following my every movement with tremendous interest. One doesn't often get a chance of watching a "rope" actually at work on this particular wall, of course. *My* rope was snaking its way gently up behind me. I had to rope down twice before getting into the bottom of the Great Couloir. Then, still carefully avoiding the snow and ice, I balanced my way up a kind of *arête* with rather loose stones. The last few feet of the wall kept my climbing soles occupied for quite a time. Then I was on top at last!

I greeted the company of young Italians with a *"Bergheil!"* They answered with *"Saluti"* and *"Bravo!"* It was just half-past ten. The whole of the day remained at my disposal. I lay down contentedly on one of the summit's stone blocks and enjoyed my well-earned rest. I could read the excitement and astonishment on the faces of the Italians. One by one they came over and introduced themselves: Mauri, Ratti. . . . I began to take notice. The names were very familiar and added up to the cream of the Italian mountaineering world. I had to

summon my whole miserable vocabulary to answer their flood of questions. My Italian friends continually expressed their recognition with
truly southern warmth of feeling. They kept on repeating the words
"*Grande Impresa*". Our conversation was friendly, nay cordial; which
goes to show that there are no national frontiers for mountaineers. All
that counts in the mountains is the man and his performance.

Our forgathering and our pleasant talk lasted an hour and hardly
left me time to enjoy the glorious prospect which Badile commands.
Chain upon mountain-chain, sharply outlined, ranges along the
southern horizon. To the west glitters the blue eye of Como's Lake.
The Italian foothills lie dreaming in the horizon mists. To the east
gleam the great Bernina snow-summits, the ice-edge of the Biancograt
shining clear and clean. Every corner of it all is full of memories for me.
I can just see the friendly green of the Maloja Pass, the watershed
between the Black Sea and the Adriatic. Behind the outlying spurs of
the Forno Basin the Lakes of Sils and Silvaplana peep out shyly. Deep
down at our feet, in the shadow, the Valley of the Bergell wound past
the pretty villages—Promontogno, Soglio, Casaccia. From one of them
the sound of the mid-day bell carried all the way up to us.

My newly-won mountain-friends wanted to take me straight down
to Lecco, but I explained that I must go down to Promontogno because
my bicycle was there; besides I had to be in Innsbruck next morning
without fail. We shook hands cordially and my friends from Lecco
started off to the south, while my way down led down the Badile Ridge
to the northern foot of the peak. I gave one more glance to the steep
slabs of the North-East Face, plunging to lose themselves in the abyss.
From here they seemed more terrible than while I was finding my
lonely way up among them.

Not knowing the way, I kept as near as I could to the crest of the
ridge. Fine, exposed climbing took me down into the depths without
having to use the rope. My eye roved over the steep faces of the peak,
heavily-armoured with granite, now to the right, now to the left. In
places the rock was heavily lichen-covered; it was noticeable how much
more exposed to the weather the ridge was than the North East Face.
I was making swift progress down my 2,500 feet of descent; the walls
about me gaining rapidly in height and grimness. The Cengalo Couloir
went straight up above me now. The Cengalo itself lifts its broad mass
above savagely piled boulders; its flanks were smooth and sheer. Giant
forces had been at work here; every wrinkle and step was decorated
with a kind of dazzling white filigree-work. Shields of unmelted snow
three feet thick hung poised on its steep slabs, ready to crash down.

I crossed a snow-slope to reach the Sass Fura Comb, a promontory of the ridge, which I followed until I found a good place for descending to the floor of the glacier. The silver diadem on Badile's summit now glittered high above me once again; the North-East Face stood there, huge and defiant as ever. But I looked at it quite differently, now that I knew all its secrets. I had still a short snowfield to traverse, then I was back at my belongings.

The first thing was to quench my raging thirst, then I let the kindly sun warm my hide. There were ages of time; it was only three o'clock. A cool breeze got up, so I began to get ready for my journey. Thrilled by the success of my climb, I slid gaily down the snow-slopes, stumbled over débris . . . loitered with tremendous relish across the carpet-like green lushness of soft meadows.

It cost me my last centimes to retrieve my bicycle. A last silent parting glance up at Badile; then into the saddle again, with a nice grind facing me—a height differential of 3,700 feet to the Maloja Pass is a matter of twelve miles. It took me two hours; at eight p.m. I was on the top of the Pass. From there I had ninety miles of high road to deal with. I hoped nothing would go wrong with my bike, or I should have to take to Shanks's Mare. Once again the Lakes of the Upper Engadine bordered my road with their shores, their surface smooth as a mirror's. St. Moritz—with its busy life of a great city, set among the eternal Hills. I squeezed my way through between the rows of parked cars. Slowly the violet hues of evening faded into the monotonous grey of the twilight; night spread her veils over heights and depths alike. I followed the slightly lighter ribbon of the road, which lost itself in the darkness ahead, laying back the milestones behind me. And so the rhythm of my muscles bore me down the valley for hour upon hour; about two a.m. I crossed the Swiss-Austrian frontier near Martinsbruck.

As in a dream I pedalled monotonously on. Time and again my weariness overwhelmed me and only by a supreme effort could I keep awake. Once or twice I found myself terrifyingly near the stones or trees at the road's edge, but I managed to control my mount and avoided the obstacles at the last moment.

Gradually the light broadened in the east, bringing a clear, cool morning with it. Ten miles more to Landeck! Straight as a die, slightly down hill, the road rolls away down to the Bridge of Pontlatz. Swiftly and silently my wheels go flitting over the asphalt. Then with a sudden violent crash, my onrush is stopped dead. In a trice I am catapulted like a hawk through thin air, to land head first on something hard, where I turn a somersault into something wet and cold. Still drunk with sleep, I open my eyes, to find a broad expanse of water before them. Can I have fallen into a lake?

But I very soon felt the chill of the water, noticed the current, caught sight of the other bank. Then I knew all right where I had landed—in the Inn; I was standing up to my neck in its main stream. The painful chill of my somewhat odd resting-place soon brisked me up. There was my trusty steed, too, and my pack; both about to move off, but I grabbed hold of them somehow. It was quite a job getting myself and my battered companions back on to the road, but I did it in the end. There I stood, wringing wet; chilled to the bone. Everything stuck to me and dripped. Very soon there was a little lake about my feet, and a streamlet was running merrily out of my rucksack. It was half-past four in the morning; not the right time for a dip in a swift and icy mountain river.

Now look at my poor bicycle! The frame is heavily buckled, the forks bent backwards. That can't be repaired on the spot. No more riding from here on. Not a soul, not a house in sight. . . .

My head was hurting and a great bruise was swelling up on it. There was nothing for it but to shoulder the bike and start walking. The Bridge of Pontlatz, where in A.D. 1703 my ancestors fell heavily upon a column of transient Bavarians, will now remain more firmly engraved on my memory than ever it did at school. It was some miles before I came to the first house, the old "Toll House" Inn. After long hours of waiting, during which my clothes at last began to dry out, I caught a bus to Landeck. The civilised world, the world of the valleys, had taken me back to its bosom.

But what do labours and sacrifices, an unintentional bath, a buckled bicycle and the beginnings of a head-cold amount to? Very small beer in relation to the tremendous experience which was the prize of my long journey. The bodily suffering and the little discomforts are soon forgotten. But the joy can never be expunged from memory's tablets.

*　　*　　*

My friend Roland Braunegger took pity on my bikeless state and invited me to join him on a motor-cycle trip to the Dolomites. True, he had only a feeble 125 c.c. machine, but it none the less made sensibly faster progress than pedalling on a push-bike. We were aiming at the Brenta. We reached the Rifugio Agostini, a Hut situated in a marvellous rock-cirque, one evening. As the next morning was Sunday, we took part in morning service held in the little mountain chapel next to the Hut. Praise the Lord for the joys he gives us—the joys of mountaineering. . . .

Above the Hut stood an exciting, largely overhanging wall, fully

1,000 feet high, the South Wall of the Cima d'Ambiez. With my personal and particular eye for overhangs, it appealed to me immediately. The guide-book said it was comparable with the North Wall of the Grosse Zinne, that is to say, Grade VI in severity, and that the first party to climb it took ten hours. It had only been done three times; all the same I decided to try it. Unfortunately, my companion wasn't keen on difficulties of that calibre; in any case, he didn't feel like climbing that day. So off I went, alone once again.

After a short foundation-structure the face overhung at once. A smooth strip of wall went shooting up, above the top of a crag. There was an old piton in it already. For caution's sake I pulled the thin *rappel*-cord through it and fastened it back to my chest-loop. The rock was uncommonly bare of decent holds. Just as I was over the main difficulty the line decided to jam, down there behind the crag. So much for safety measures! There was nothing for it but to climb down and then up again over what afterwards proved to be the most difficult part of the whole wall. The climb continued over marvellous rock, with one's body mostly hanging out backwards beyond the vertical and the arms taking the bulk of the weight. Once I sensed just in time that a huge block was being loosened by my load on it, but by then I was well on my way above and the unstable rock fell back into its old place.

An hour and a half after I started, I was standing on the summit of the Cima d'Ambiez. On my way down I met my friend coming up a snow gully; he hadn't been able to stay down below after all. Together we climbed the Cima Tosa, the chief summit of the Brenta Group. He enjoyed himself hugely and the hour we spent on top left an unforgettable impression on my mind, too. All around us the dark rock and light snow-streaks of the Brenta stood tumbled, their vast, vertical walls seamed with clefts and gullies, and beyond them in the distance lay the foothill country. A lovely group, the Brenta Dolomites.

There was a pleasant human sequel to my climb of the Cima d'Ambiez wall. A little later, Cesare Maestri, the young master-climber from Trient, climbed it, also solo. He knew nothing of my climb, and so his compatriots congratulated him delightedly on the first "solitary". When he learned that it was actually only the second, he wrote to me, apologising for his mistaken claim. That was thoughtful and fair of him, and I should like to take this opportunity of wishing my Italian "rival" much success in his future Alpine career, already so full of the highest promise.

PREPARATION FOR A
GREAT OBJECTIVE

THE MOUNTAIN CRUCIBLE—
EIGER NORTH WALL

The North Wall of the Eiger. . . .

Ever since I was a boy it had drawn me to it. Knowing little about mountaineering then, I heard about the assault on that gigantic face, of the bitter struggles of brave men upon it, of ghastly tragedies and the death of keen young climbers. They went to it again and again, full of confidence and hope, but they didn't all come back; a slight obituary, a few kind words, were all the reward they won. Sedlmayer, Mehringer, Hinterstoisser, Angerer, Rainer and Kurz paid for their daring with their lives; but their spirit lives on after them.

The first pair to come back alive from that terrible wall were Hias Rebitsch and Ludwig Vörg.

The chief hazard of the Eiger's North Wall is its exposure to sudden disturbances of the weather. This mountain of almost 13,000 feet is the most northerly ice-giant of the Bernese Oberland, in Switzerland. Owing to this geographically exposed position, it gets the first onslaught of the weather. The enormous North Wall, itself close on 6,000 feet high, catches all the bad weather and traps the storms among its crags. And when the avalanches of fresh snow go sweeping over its precipices, when stone-falls pour ceaselessly down and rushing torrents are unleashed over the rock-terraces, the whole huge face becomes a veritable hell. That was what the young dare-devils learned about the North Wall of the Eiger, when they attempted it.

Rebitsch and Vörg were no less daring than their predecessors—but they were not just blindly set on success at all costs. Their valuation of the wall was accurate: "An ice-wall complete with all the difficulties of a super-severe rock-climb." They chose their equipment and laid their plans in accordance with that judgment.

Those who went before them had perished because their retreat had been cut off. Rebitsch and Vörg had no mind to find the face a prison from which there was no escape. So they safeguarded their retreat by leaving a rope hanging at the critical spot. Like the others they got two-thirds of the way up the wall; like the others they were overwhelmed there by fearsome weather. But thanks to their precautions they managed to retreat safely over the downward route which had brought death to the others. So they were the first to come out of that inferno alive; they reported in detail on it and so laid the basis for a successful climb later.

Success came in 1938. Unfortunately Rebitsch could not share in it —he was at the time with Paul Bauer's party on Nanga Parbat, in the Himalaya. But two ropes, Heckmair and Vörg and Kasparek and Harrer climbed the wall after days of struggle and lifted its shroud of horror. Their names are for ever engraved in the history of Alpine endeavour.

It was in the summer of 1952 that my old wish to pit my own strength against the wall was at last gratified. We intended to enjoy a daring major climb, based on careful preparations; it turned out to be a desperate fight for life. But we had no prescience of that when we arrived at Grindelwald on July 26th; Hans Jöchler, who had juggled his Opel of ancient vintage—we had rather disrespectfully christened it "Kalafatti"—along the endless hairpins of the roads of Switzerland; Eugénie, my young wife, Sepp Jöchler, who was to be my rope-mate; and finally myself. We were all glad to get out of the car and stretch our legs properly again. The drive from Innsbruck to the foot of the Eiger Wall had been venturesome and exciting—but that is another story.

The Jungfrau Railway took us up to Kleine Scheidegg. The nearer we got to the wall, the higher it loomed above us; but it seemed to be in good condition and impressed us as a good clean rock wall. We felt confident of success. We hadn't yet discovered that the very dryness of rock had increased the difficulties to the limit of human capacity, just because stones which the ice had once held fast were now hurtling down the very way human beings had to go up. And that there was ice there just the same, a thin, glassy covering invalidating every hold and yet denying the fundamentally safe ice technique of cutting steps and fixing pitons. . . .

We made our preparations.

All our equipment lay piled up in a jumble. Rope, ironmongery, extract of malt, jam, socks, spare clothes, ice-axes, chocolate, bags of provisions, bivouac equipment, cookers, shoes and all sorts of small things, all mixed higgledy-piggledy—a regular still-life picture. The time had come for it all to disappear into our climbing rucksacks, but they were too heavy when we had finished and we had to start taking one thing after another out again. At last they were just the right weight for managing on difficult pitches. We left our heavy underwear behind, for this time we intended to return the same day, so as to get our rucksacks as high up as possible before coming down again and only starting the climb seriously at night. So we left our two companions sleeping their enviable sleep; there was no point in waking them, they knew we were coming back in the evening.

It was quite a job avoiding all the Nosey Parkers and sensation seekers. A woman came up to me and asked me if I were going to climb the Jungfrau. Did I know that three climbers had been killed there the day before? She advised me to stay down below; it was much too dangerous. She would only let me go when I assured her that I was only going to the Eiger Glacier. Then at last we were alone and able to go on our own sweet way.

We followed no track as we crossed the great grassy alps which stretch at the foot of the wall, now up, now down, endlessly it seemed. We kept on underestimating the distance hopelessly; only gradually did we begin in this way to recognise the enormous size of the rock-face above us. It is quite exceptional to be able to approach the foot of one of the most fearsome faces in the Western Alps over meadows and scree-slopes—almost like in the Dolomites. But here everything was on a titanic scale. There were enormous avalanche-cones at the foot of the huge precipice. Its lower steps were partly vaulted over with snow. At last we were really standing at the foot of the greatest rock-cataclysm in the Alps. So much has been written about the Eigerwand that I can take a good deal of knowledge for granted and spare readers details such as the names given to different parts of the wall.

We went on across bone-hard snowfields to the foot of the "Massive Buttress". "Look—look, Sepp!" I pointed to a dark shadow flitting through the ravine—a hare.

We couldn't help laughing aloud. What on earth did he want there? Sepp suggested he was going to climb the wall, too, and was waiting for his partner. Our amusement was a little overdone, I think. Neither of us probably wanted to admit to the other what an impression the wall was making on us. . . .

We crossed a deep *bergschrund* in our stride; then our hands were on rock at last, but not on our old familiar friend, whom we could trust. This was downward-stratified, holdless stone, wet, slithery, with fine débris lying on every projection. We each took our own line over it, but both of us were frequently stuck on steep pitches. So we zig-zagged up the lower, easier part of the wall which constitutes its proper plinth, keeping on towards the "Vertical Pillar".

To our surprise two figures appeared above us. They were coming down and we could not avoid meeting them. They were two brothers from Allgäu, both very young. They continued on their way down into the hollow at the bottom.

The rock now became steeper and more broken. Half an hour later we reached the bivouac cave below the "Hinterstoisser Traverse". The two boys had just reached safety at the bottom of the wall; but we were by no means safe, where we were. Stones began to rain down, by way of the Rote Fluh. After falling hundreds of feet they struck quite close to us, scattering over the whole lower part of the wall, leaving little white clouds behind them. We decided to wait a while, for we had no desire to expose ourselves to the peril of a bombardment by stones. . . .

It was half past five. The missiles kept on whistling and whining through the air, past us. The mountain kept up a steady, defensive fire. Some of the stones came unpleasantly near us, and we were not so sure that our dugout was safe. We found a better place a little further up. Mist was now settling down on the Rote Fluh and its cold breath sometimes struck further down the face. We could hear hailstones pattering on the rock, but the sun was still out where we stood. It was probably a short storm on the upper part of the wall. After waiting an hour, during which the stones kept rattling down with unabated force, we decided to stay where we were. Our two down there, my poor wife and Sepp's friend, would have to wait miserably—and we hadn't even taken our leave of them. 2,000 feet below we could see two tiny dots, moving up towards the foot of the climb. It was Eugénie and Hans, trying to get within shouting distance. . . .

Sepp lighted the spirit-stove while I went in search of water. That wasn't quite such a simple matter, but my war experiences stood me in good stead. I moved quickly from ledge to ledge. When I heard a whistle, I hugged the rock—just as when under fire. Every yard of the face bore signs of bitter struggles for life. Old ropes and rusty *abseil*-pitons bore witness to a day when this was unknown territory. My search for water was a risky business; but at last I put Sepp on the way to preparing a hot drink.

Long shadows were moving across the valleys. The faint sound of a woman's voice came up to us, a little forlornly: "Hermann. . . ."

We answered and said our good-byes. The two down below turned back slowly towards the valley. We could see they were not happy about it. They kept on stopping and shouting up: "Sepp—Hermann!"

A crackle of stones interrupted their affectionate voices.

A cold wind blew down on us. Slowly the mists descended, but they did not reach our level. We wrapped our Anoraks around us. The stars came out, one by one, in the broad tent of the sky. Far away there was a glint of silver on the Lake of Thun, illuminated by the light of the moon. Presently the slender scimitar of the moon itself emerged from behind the West Ridge, hung for a short time from the vertical wall like a climber, then parted from it but, unlike a climber, did not fall. We sat there for ages, motionless, looking down from our cave on to the myriad points of light down in Scheidegg and Grindelwald. Our thoughts gravitated between our friends down below and the gigantic wall which lost itself in one shadowy sweep in the star-studded sky above our heads.

To-morrow and to-morrow and to-morrow. . . . Would we be at the top by the end of it? That would be grand! How glad we would have been at that moment of our warm underwear, though it wouldn't be too bad, if we only had to bivouac once. At about midnight we crawled into the shelter of our tent-sack and tried to sleep. At about three we saw two tiny lights moving up towards the wall—obviously yesterday's pair, the two brothers from Allgaü, coming up. We waited for the first light to break.

Our morning toilet was short and by the time I had got things ready for the day's move, they were close below us. I was still moving rather clumsily, but a difficult crack soon provided the necessary livening-up process. I gave myself a proper warm-up while the leader of the pursuing party went up past me by acrobatic movements on a faded rope— a relic of the rescue attempts all those years ago. The second soon overtook me, too.

"In a bit of a hurry," said Sepp. "Are they trying to make a race of it?"

"They're taking risks," I replied. I for one certainly preferred good solid rock to that ancient, weathered bit of rope.

We caught them up at the Hinterstoisser Traverse, where the others had abandoned their rucksacks.

"Look out! Stones!"

The wall was sending down its morning greeting. My old climbing-hat, which I was now handling in most cavalier fashion, would have to look out again to-day. Under it, for further upholstery, went my cap. Sepp remarked that I looked more like an outsize mushroom than a mountaineer. A little leg-pulling, however, never killed anyone; stones have. On a débris-cone at the start of the traverse we made our final preparations for serious climbing. The first few feet were made easier by some old but solid lengths of rope fixed in the very smooth rock. I pushed myself over to the left in a sling-seat.

This 120-foot interruption had already brought many to grief. When, after bad weather and the resulting failure to climb the face, a quick retreat was the only way off the wall, it was this traverse that denied exhausted and dispirited men suffering from frostbite a way of escape. In 1936, by removing their traversing rope after them on the way up, Hinterstoisser and his companions sealed their own tragic fate.

I found a stance behind a corner and protected Sepp's approach, which was helped by a rope balustrade. We left it in position for the use of the party following us. After another 150 feet we reached a niche.

All the way there were traces of the Battle of the Wall; here too there were bits of rope and jam-tins. The "First Icefield" must be round the next corner. But the mountain had altered its countenance; there was not a trace of an icefield. Instead we found holdless rock, planed smooth, with a layer of water-ice only an inch thick all over it. With the utmost caution I worked over to the left in a kind of a groove. Every now and then stones went whistling past, with increasing frequency as the warmth of the day set in.

The approach to the "Second Icefield" was barred by an insurmountable barrier of watery ice, which pushed us over to the left, while the rock piled ever more steeply overhead, and always of the same dreadful consistency—sloping outwards, smoothed to glass by avalanches and stonefalls; there were neither hand-holds nor foot-holds, not even a wrinkle to take a piton. On every ledge and excrescence lay a fine dusting of débris. We tip-toed upwards, as if walking on eggs, hardly daring to breathe. It was a horrible feeling. Suppose the friction of our rubber soles failed us? It didn't bear thinking about.

Sepp led the next rope's length. I didn't grudge it him, for now it began to overhang into the bargain. He clung desperately to the rock. I couldn't imagine what he was hanging on to; every moment he looked like coming off. I looked away comprehendingly, so that he need not be ashamed of using his knees to the full. The rope moved out slowly through my hands. Splinters of ice came tinkling down; I could hear steel clinking on ice. Sepp was obviously knocking a piton in. Then it was at last possible for me to follow him up. When I got there, I said: "Well done, Sepp—a masterpiece!"

The boys from Allgäu were close on our heels. Sixty feet above us was the lower rim of the "Second Icefield", and Sepp continued to lead up to it. He could hardly find a stance, and I was no better off below him. We strapped on our twelve-point crampons in the most difficult conditions. I was to lead the icefield. It was only a layer of thin, black ice. At the first axe-stroke the whole surface gave a hollow groan; it would not stand any step-cutting. Well, we would have to do without steps, then. I tiptoed cautiously to the right. Looking down between my feet, I could see our two followers on a horrid spot, and a little lower down—I could hardly believe my eyes—five more figures. I couldn't contemplate a slip here; if I came off, I should certainly sweep the whole long line of followers from the face!

After about 30 feet I risked knocking a piton into the glassy surface. It only went in half-way, then impinged on rock. Gradually the consistency improved and finally turned from brittle ice to hard-frozen snow. Our five pursuers revealed themselves as two separate ropes and very soon I recognised old friends of mine from Chamonix. In the lead was Rébuffat—we shouted our greetings to each other. Among the rest was Magnone, whom I had met two years before on the North Wall of the Dru. Just recently he had brought off a *tour de force* by climbing the Dru West Wall, one of the last unclimbed faces in the Mont Blanc Group. I yelled my congratulations down to him. That was something to shout about, I thought. I felt very small and unqualified in this company of international stars.

So the nine of us tackled the "Second Icefield". We soon got used to the whistling stones; they seemed to provide an essential background music. Fatalistically, we persuaded ourselves that not every stone finds a billet.

We crossed the top lip of the icefield towards the left. That sounds simple enough; but I counted ten rope's lengths. What a stupendous wall this was, if this little passage of ice alone took ten lengths of rope! We could only surmise how much rock still towered above us. We were using precious time without gaining an inch of height. That is a feature of this wall—one-third of the whole climb consists of traverses.

I found an overhanging crack and moved up into it. It ended in ice, water-ice and still more water-ice; in between it brittle, precipitous rock. I began to wonder when this ghastly, perilous stuff would give way to better things. There must be good firm rock with holds in it *somewhere* in the wall. The conditions were, of course, the result of excessive drying out. This had been all ice; now there were only fragments of it left, black, rubble-filthed relics, clinging in the flutings, revolting to look at.

We had to get on. . . .

A broken rock-rib let us gain some height; water was plashing down it. We had reached the point where Sedlmayer and Mehringer had died in their bivouac. My altimeter read 10,600 feet; we had come up 3,000 feet of the wall, but that was only half the grim business, and the easier half at that.

It was mid-day and our stomachs demanded attention. The landscape lay like a relief-map below us—Grindelwald's tiny houses, the buildings on the Little Scheidegg, the sinuous curves of the Jungfrau Railway. There was an overhang just above us; some 20 feet up we could see an old piton. The icefield probably extended up as far as that at one time. It might even be the piton to which Sedlmayer and Mehringer were attached during their last night?

Uncannily steep was the "Third Icefield's" plunge into the depths. It shot down without any lessening of angle to the even steeper rocks below it, which bent swiftly out of our sight. Dark secondary grooves testified to the exceptional weight of stone bombardments. Sepp had to wait for a lull in the fire before leaving the protection of the overhang; but the stones began rattling down again close beside us. The missiles hurtled down in unusually swift succession, while my partner stood completely exposed to them on ice whose angle was fully 55 degrees. His choice of language was a clear indication of how he felt about it. His luck had been out all day to quite a remarkable extent. The Gremlins seemed to have been concentrating on him; for he had already been ungently handled—mercifully only by splinters—on three occasions.

"Your nerves have to be sound," he remarked, laconically.

When we had mastered that ugly bit in its turn, climbing became a little easier as we crossed diagonally to the foot of a ramp which carved crossways into an overhanging belt of rock. We thought we were fully protected by the rocks above us, but soon found out that there is not a foot of dead ground on the whole of the face. As we climbed on, the "Egons" started coming down the ramp. The rock, however, was much better and we moved on at quite a good pace. If this went on, we should certainly reach the top to-day, was our joyous reaction. Our joy was premature. . . .

We had to halt at the bottom of a chimney jammed with ice. Icicles hung from the walls and the smooth rock was sheeted in glassy ice. I tried again and again; my hands invariably slid off the mirror-like surface. Rather than be beaten, I tried my luck on the severely undercut walls to the right of the chimney. Two hours later I had put a hundred feet behind me, and there were still six feet or more between me and the stance above the chimney.

The crack petered out. Meanwhile the others had all come up and stood bunched at the bottom of the chimney. The sun actually shed one of its rare greetings on us here; it was in fact the first time its rays had penetrated into the wall. Life began to awaken, very slowly, in the chimney. Icicles broke in two with a clink like glass.

I couldn't get any further, and was forced to rope down through thin air till Sepp hauled me back on to the face again. The ice was now changed to water and veritable waterfalls were pouring down the chimney. The two Allgäu boys took a turn and were soon busy fighting the torrent, till they couldn't breathe any more.

Then it was my turn again. By the time I was at the top of the chimney I hadn't a stitch of dry clothing on me. It was small consolation to know that the others were no better off. We continued in the lead, continually drenched by further hateful douches. The pitch ended in another overhang, cased in ice, with water trickling down as well, and above it stratified rock like tiles. It was just like trying to climb out on to the shingles of a steep roof.

More stones came whistling down. I tucked my head in, and after a short salvo all was quiet again. A steep icefield, the originator of the bombardment, soared overhead. The rock became very wet again. We made this dangerous passage easier for those behind by linking ropes. And there, up on the right, was the traverse to the "Spider"; but to reach it we had to cover a fearfully bad bit of stones resting loosely on one another, which had been exposed by the rapid retreat of the ice. It only took us a couple of steps to see that it would be useless to proceed, because of the danger to which those following would be exposed from the stones we must inevitably dislodge. We stood there waiting, waiting, wasting valuable time. . . .

It was five p.m. before they were all up with us. We could not be certain of finding a bivouac-place later on, so we decided to make one here and now. The Frenchmen found a platform on a rocky spur a little lower down, while we looked about for something that would do for us. Essential number one was cover from stone-fire.

"Here we are," Sepp called as he disappeared round a projection. Almost in the same breath, I heard a groan.

"What on earth's the matter?" I asked, as I hurried round to join him. He was leaning against the rock, completely dazed. A stone the size of a nut had just selected his head as a target. Luckily his skull can stand a good deal!

We pushed everything loose over the edge till we had a tiny place to sit on at a pinch. The young brothers ensconced themselves a little to our left. Hot tea was the right thing to warm us up in our chilled, damp state. We got "Esbit" and vestas out, but everything was wet; I emptied the box of sulphur matches in vain, trying to get a light. I sent it over the edge with an appropriate quotation from the classics. The only thing was to get straight into our bivouac-sack. We were racked with thirst, and food stuck in our mouths; even chocolate tasted like sawdust.

It was dark again. Someone down near the Little Scheidegg was blinking a torch signal up at us. "That's for us, I think," I told Sepp; but alas we could not answer.

"What about a song?" At that very moment I remembered a most suitable parody: "Don't go up the Eiger, Daddy; don't go up there!" So I serenaded my companions with it.

"Don't go up the Eiger. . . ."

The night was endless; every minute seemed an hour long, and the weather was beginning to worry us. The sky was overcast and the lurid light of the moon grew paler and paler till she finally hid in the clouds for good. The clouds darkened, and hung black and menacing over the gulfs. Suppose the weather broke, could we ever hope to reach the top? The most dangerous bit, the "Spider", was still ahead of us; and if avalanches were to sweep it, what then? Yet we could not for a moment contemplate a retreat. The icefield traverses would almost certainly spell disaster, for avalanches of fresh snow were at work there with increasing fury. And we were two-thirds of the way up, now.

The endless hours of inactivity were becoming a martyrdom. Every minute our hopes of an improvement in the weather were dwindling. We kept on peering out of the spy-hole in our bivouac-sack with increasing frequency. Scarves of mist were draping themselves about the wall in ghostly fashion. Slowly the darkness of the night gave way to a milky grey. The atmosphere weighed heavily on our spirits.

At last it grew light, and we were soon on our feet, for the break in the weather was obviously only a question of time and every foot we could gain while reasonable conditions lasted would be a precious asset. The Allgaü brothers had spent an uncomfortable night; having no bivouac-sack they had been mercilessly exposed to the bitter cold. By contrast, the bright blue of the French eider-down bags was a cheerful note in those grim surroundings.

Brittle ledges brought us to the next steep pitch. The rock shot up perpendicular to the sky, with a few snowflakes floating round it. Hereabouts there were plenty of holds.

Suddenly a heavy snow-flurry engulfed us as if we had been ambushed. Hand-holds and ledges were soon covered in snow, which melted at once under the warmth of our fingers and formed a thin, treacherous layer of ice. Conditions grew more critical every moment; yet to be engaged in the struggle, the very activity, was far more bearable than the dreary waiting for what we knew lay ahead.

By common consent we now joined up as a single rope. Before us lay the so-called "Traverse of the Gods". It may be divine in fair weather, for directly beneath one's feet the rock breaks away sheer to the "Third Icefield". 4,000 feet below lie the meadows of Alpiglen. But under present conditions its only association with the Gods seemed to be the idea of making a rather abrupt acquaintance with them. We had to free every foot- and hand-hold from snow with the greatest of care. There was very little that could be used for safeguarding measures. The storm howled round the face, and the snowfall grew much heavier; the sky poured flakes down on us as if the clouds had broken apart. The snow started pouring down the walls with a rushing sound. Each one of us had to fend for himself in this Witches' Cauldron. Only the rope told each of us that he was not alone; that there were comrades sharing the ordeal, ready to help. . . .

A vague shape loomed out of the mist. When it got to within 15 feet of me I recognised Sepp by the outlines: he was clothed in ermine. "You've got your furs on," I called to him, trying to make a grim kind of joke; but it was no time for laughing.

Five more rope's lengths brought us to the "Spider". We strapped our crampons on in a most exposed place. We had an opportunity of observing the play of the avalanches and tried to get the hang of their rhythm, their "time-table". Every five to ten minutes a white stream went hissing down the left side of the icefield. At much longer intervals of about half an hour came a main cataract, assuming huge proportions and sweeping across the whole expanse of the ice. I waited for one of these to pass, and traversed immediately after its passage into the middle of the ice-slope leading up to the final exit-cracks. It is called "The Spider" because it reaches out its icy tentacles in every direction over the rock like a spider's legs.

At moments the fog parted and gave us glimpses of soft green meadows shining up from sheer below, like some glimpse into a different world. I made progress up a narrow rib about a yard wide, which the avalanches mostly spared. I hacked my way step by step up the tough ice, for I had to have firm foot-holds in case an avalanche flooded over it in spite of everything. After every rope's length a piton went ringing into the ice. It was exhausting work, carried on to the accompaniment of the roaring of the avalanches.

The mists lifted a little, revealing the final cracks sweeping steeply upwards. At the same moment another white wave filled the gully above, came pouring down the cracks and divided in two at a rocky spur. A good part of it took the right-hand route and came straight for me. I dug my ice-axe in, braced my body and waited in agony for the snow to crush me.

The white stream tore down into the depths with incredible speed. Everything around me seemed to be moving; or was it I who was flying upwards? What on earth was the matter with me? Was I still upright on my feet or was I already hurtling down to the depths? My sense of balance was playing strange pranks.

After an eternity the pressure eased. A wedge of snow running sharply up into the wall had formed over my head. I owed it entirely to that that the downrush of snow had not swept me away into the abyss. Slowly the hissing died away and silence was restored. The fringes of the avalanche were still pouring over my companions below me, the loose snow sweeping over their bodies and tugging at the ropes; but soon they too were out of danger.

In the next half-hour another six inches or so of snow piled up. Up there just under the summit it would be worse, and the gathering weight of snow would be likely to bring down the whole summit cornice in an avalanche, probably by the convenient route of the upper cracks, which form a kind of a gully. We had been seven hours on the ice-slope. I marvelled at the patience of my companions, who had to wait an hour in a bunch after every 100 feet of progress, while I was pouring with sweat at work ahead. Our cavalcade was so extended that I could only catch an occasional glimpse of the French climbers. We felt it to be a particularly sporting gesture that those two far-famed climbers made no attempt to push past us; though it must be admitted that it would be almost impossible to vary the order just at this point.

Meanwhile the snow had become very sloppy, and so had our clothes. The ice-slope shot steeply up to the rocks, now covered with a treacherous layer of new snow. The next piece of climbing—probably not very difficult in normal circumstances—was probably the riskiest I had yet met. It wasn't really climbing any longer, but a continual fight upwards against a tendency to slide off the mountain; any means of progress was allowable provided it paid dividends; there was no question of correct method or style. Elbows and knees afforded the best technique. Whenever I managed to get a piton fixed I felt better, knowing I had wrung another snippet from the wall; every couple of feet forward amounted to a victory, as I crept forward at a snail's pace. Time raced on by minutes, hours; we took no toll of its passing, but one thing was by now certain—we couldn't reach the top any more to-day. That meant a third bivouac on a wall like this, in such conditions! There was no escaping it. It was no longer a question of achieving a successful climb; it had become a fight for very life itself. . . .

We were on the spur, which parted the avalanches like a snow plough. The traverse across the main gully was comparatively easy. I could hear a piton being hammered below. Could the tail-enders have found the pace too slow and broken away into an independent party again, so as to come up past us? The rock below me fell away undercut to the "Spider".

Then—another white wave creaming down the gully.

"Look out—avalanche!"

It was a matter of seconds before the sharp jolt, all over again, and another inferno of snow-smother, like some devil's merry-go-round. . . .

It lasted some minutes. By some miracle I was still alive when it ended. A deathly silence reigned down below. The Frenchmen had been struck by the main weight of the cataract. Had they been swept away into the gulf?

Mechanically, like a dreamer, I started up again. Quite remarkably, in that moment of terrific tension, I felt hungry. No use trying to swallow anything; I couldn't, for my thirst was greater than my hunger. I had hardly eaten a thing for two days, but it didn't matter. The main thing was, where were the Frenchmen? Then out of the fog below, at first muffled, then clearly, I heard a voice: " 'Ermann—'Ermann—Bühl— *corde* . . . !" Silence again; then a repeat of the call.

It was Rébuffat who had been trying to get up separately to the main gully, but the avalanche had put paid to his effort. But the Frenchmen were alive!

Sepp quickly lowered his *rappel*-cord. It wasn't long enough; the Allgaüers' reserve rope had to be joined to it—barely enough and a tricky manoeuvre, but it worked. After a longish while they all stood together again, panting; the little experiment had proved a heavy drain on their slender reserves of strength.

In the meantime I had managed to reach a miserable stance, 100 feet higher up in a perpendicular face. Sepp joined me while the others stayed on the rib, for there was only room for two on my precarious perch. It was already evening, though it was hardly noticeable, for the fog had long been turning daylight into a dusky mirk.

During the whole day we had only gained 800 feet. . . .

Overhead loomed the wall, mist-girt, storm-lashed, menacing. Our immediate prospect was an endless, grim night's vigil. Would we all survive it—for we were all one party now?

Our resistance had ebbed considerably since yesterday. Luckily, this time the French could offer some shelter to the Allgaü boys. We were all one party now. . . .

Our precious dripping bivouac-sack had to be brought into action once again. It had often protected me from the elements. The only food our parched gums could in any way deal with was Biomalt in viscous form. Our feet were soaked and without sensation. We would have given a lot for our heavy underwear, reposing safely in our rucksack at Little Scheidegg. My old climbing trousers were pretty well finished with, too. As a matter of tradition, they had been a "must" for this particular climb, before final relegation; anyhow, their ventilation arrangements were perfect. I had stabbing pains in my lungs and kidneys, and breathing had become difficult. Sepp complained of similar symptoms.

Night fell with startling suddenness.

"Don't go up the Eiger. . . ." The stupid song-hit came up again in my mind. What was it that had lured us to this place; what had moved us to embark on such exertions as a matter of course? We knew the perils of this wall well enough; we knew, too, that climbing purely for its own sake can give no ultimate satisfaction—and we had come in spite of that. Well that is just the fundamental mystery of all mountaineering. But to-night was neither the time nor the place for unravelling that riddle. Only our faith and our will-power could keep us alive now—faith and our will to live. . . .

The walls dripped on to our sack; fresh snow rustled down over it. We were wet through and it was in water that we sat. The cold penetrated to our very bones and shook us till our heads bumped. We were racked with cramp, especially Sepp, who could not stay in one position for any length of time. With a submissiveness dictated by sheer will-power we resigned ourselves to waiting for morning. No more singing now: our rattling teeth were the only music.

I don't know how often I had bothered Sepp to look at the time, but I did it again. "Eleven o'clock," he pronounced.

After what seemed several hours, I asked again.

"Half-past eleven," came the terse reply.

My neck ached from being so long in a crouching position. The bivouac-sack weighed down on my head, for my feet wanted to be in its shelter, too. At times my thoughts strayed out into that distant, safe world below. How my wife and Sepp's friend down there at Scheidegg would be worrying about us—those others in that other world! A burning thirst in my throat brought my thoughts winging back to the relentless present; I reached outside the "tent", scraped some snow together and stilled the pain. There was grit in the snow which jarred my teeth, but it helped for a short time. I felt around till I located the mug of Biomalt. I dug the last gluey remnants out with sticky fingers. That kept my stomach quiet for a while.

I was soon thinking again about the wall above us—another 1,000 feet of it between us and the summit. Had we two been alone on its mighty face we should indeed have felt small and helpless. But there were nine of us now, all responsible to each other; that thought provided a wonderful moral support. Could we do it, even so, or would the avalanches defeat us?

We *must* win! If one of us failed, there was another to take his place. A team of nine doesn't go under so easily, I kept on persuading myself. How trivial seemed the daily bothers, which occupy one so busily down in the valley, at such a time. The cold had become almost unbearable. The condensed water which had run down inside our tent-sack at the onset had now turned into a sheet of ice; our clothes were frozen solid.

Slowly the grey dawn crept into the sky.

I peeled myself gingerly out of our shell, to be met with cold that seared—at least 10 degrees below zero, at a guess. Overhead lay a storm-washed clarity; below lay a billowy cloud-sea, lapping the wintry wall. My heart sank as I looked at our repellent surroundings, at the icy rocks about us, from which a chilling breath blew down upon us.

A horrible feeling came over me. I turned to Sepp and said: "I believe my sense of balance is disturbed. I can't stand up without support."

The cold soon drove me back into the tent-sack. The very idea of climbing in such a temperature was sheer lunacy.

An hour later we decided to give it a try. We mustn't waste a moment, so as to make absolutely sure of getting to the top to-day. We looked at the continuation of the route and then we looked questioningly at one another. I was shocked when I saw my friend's pale-greenish face— and yet it was a determined face, full of courage.

The way up was by another overhanging crack, with icicles hanging in it. The rock was covered with snow and rime. The rest of the party was still cowering on the rib of rock like a handful of lost men. The perlon rope was like a wire, my rucksack like a tin canister, and the hood of my Anorak was frozen so firmly to my head-covering that I could not push it back. My trouser-legs were like a battered drainpipe and bumped against my bare legs like tin. Our gloves were frozen stiff, too. But I tried to shake off my misery and despair.

I fastened my crampons with jointless fingers, and stamped away up a wedge of snow. My hands sought a hold, but everything was glazed and they slid off. I tested the rock with my hammer and got a piton in. Then a carabiner went in, my feet splayed far apart, my crampons clawed on the rock.

"Haul in a little!" Sepp was on a good stance and gave the necessary pull. I got a second piton out from my belt and placed it, but I could hardly hold the hammer any longer. After every second or third stroke my arm fell back tired out. It was difficult to handle the carabiners with thick gloves. Then my feet slipped again and I was hanging on the rope like a sack; it needed a tremendous output of strength to get back onto the rock. It was a fearfully exhausting game.

I had used up all the ironware, pitons and split-rings and we had to send down for replenishments. My armpits ached from the continual strain of the rope on them. There was a horrid jutting overhang ahead. I think I would have thrown my hand in, had circumstances been different. But here, how could I? We simply had to get up. I used my last remnants of strength banging in piton after piton: every stroke of the hammer seemed an enormous effort. It was the last upsurge of the thing called will-power—the very will to live. . . .

Four hours later I had managed all of 60 feet, and was standing on a minute stance.

"Sepp, I've had it," I called down. "That crack has finished me off."

Sepp was soon up with me, and without a word he took over the lead. I now had the double responsibility of looking after the third man and protecting Sepp up above me. But my hands had given in and I couldn't grip any more. It took all I had to keep the rope taut between me and the next man below. Meanwhile Sepp had already traversed out to the left, and reached the continuation of the series of cracks by climbing down a little way.

Now the rope could move forward again simultaneously, for the difficulties were gradually relaxing. Loose powdery snow kept on rustling down through the cracks overhead. The wind was having fun and games with the snow, but we were pitilessly exposed to its venom.

The wall was apparently endless; up and up it banked above us. The view down into the abyss below was appalling—enough to put one off climbing for good.

The crest of a long ridge ran up to the summit icefield. We kept on stopping to rest. Our hearts and lungs were refusing to do their work any more. At long last we reached the final rocks, and there for the first time in two days felt the warm comfort of the sun's blessed rays. Through gaps in the mist we looked down on the Lilliputian roofs of Grindelwald, 10,000 feet below, while we waited for the others at a point some 300 feet below the summit ridge. Little by little we revived; life began to re-awaken in us with the sight of the top so near at hand. The French party unroped now, wishing to follow a little later. There was smooth ice here, in spite of the fresh fall of snow. One last effort from ankles and stiff muscles driven unwillingly to a final output of energy; then we were standing on the sharp crest of the Eiger's Mittelegi Ridge.

A few last steps up on to the Summit, where two compatriots were waiting for us. With the true mountain spirit of comradeship they had hurried up there to see in what kind of shape we arrived and whether we needed any help. We shook hands dumbly. We felt none of the joyous feelings one might expect from such a triumph. The ordeal of the last three days still weighed far too heavily on our spirits; it is impossible to adjust oneself so quickly. We were almost incapable of grasping that the fight was over, that we had in fact been able to achieve what had come to seem to us the almost impossible. We had only too recently fought our way back to life.

It was five o'clock. We decided on the easy way down to Eigergletscher Station by the west flank of the mountain. But first we slaked our craving for water, greedily licking the wet summit rocks. Around us stood the peaks in their splendour—Jungfrau, Mönch, the Fiescherhörner and the Finsteraarhorn's slender spire. The sun was only with us a short time before we plunged down into the sea of mist below us. Only now was any kind of sensation returning to our frozen feet. From the deadness of our toes we knew that we had been slightly frost-bitten.

Down near the bottom Sepp heralded our coming with a yodel—perhaps my little Eugénie and Hans were waiting for us somewhere round here, or coming up to meet us. Then two shadows detached themselves from the uniformity of grey . . . we fell into each other's arms. All the worry, all the torture of the last few days was gone; we were together again. My wife's misery was magically transformed to indescribable joy—life had taken on a meaning again. We had had to fight hard for that life.

They were waiting for us down in Grindelwald. The rescue section of the Innsbruck Club had heard of our ordeal and had come hurrying across, ready to help if wanted. But they saw our final arrival on the summit in time to disperse a rescue operation which had been organised. The greatest of all walls was shining again now in conciliatory mood; we looked up through wreaths of mist to its gigantic summit structure. It glittered in its robe of new snow, in the lave of the bright mid-day sun. All's well that end's well! The hardest fight of my climbing career had come to a successful close.

If anybody asks why we did it, we must respectfully beg the question. Cynics will say, "Notoriety Hunters!"; but one doesn't risk one's life for the sake of notoriety. Years ago, when Mallory was asked, on his return from an unsuccessful attempt on Everest, why had he set out to climb the mountain, he replied, "Because it's there!" Even after reaching the summit in 1953, Hillary himself could find no other answer. Every mountain we climb—we climb because it is there. . . .

Sepp and I bedded down comfortably on a mountain of rucksacks in a jeep-trailer and were soon fast asleep. I heard somebody say, "We've run out of juice." It seemed only a few minutes before someone woke us up again. We were in Innsbruck and it was past midnight.

THE DAILY ROUND INTERVENES

LIFE sees to it that the everyday round of things does not spare one's mood of mountain-born elation. There was a nice surprise awaiting me at home: a compulsory order to vacate. The shortage of houses was growing more dire every day; we as sub-lessees would have to clear out of our rooms because the lessee had been discharged from hospital after a long spell there. They offered us accommodation in the shelter for homeless people. Personally, I would sooner lead a nomad existence in a tent, but in a modern, civilised place like Innsbruck they don't allow that kind of thing; besides which I had to consider my wife and our small daughter, then only a few months old. At the very last moment I managed to secure a stay of execution for six months, and was able to breathe again. The results of the Eiger climb were only beginning to make themselves felt now. Sepp and I had both contracted frost-bitten feet. His case was much more serious, for his toes had broken open, whereas mine only showed by the dark discoloration and the daily loss of a toenail. It was quite enough for my taste. I lay awake many a night, tossing from one side to the other. As soon as the blood began to circulate my toes felt as if they were crawling with ants. Bathing them was the only thing that did any good. My feet had never met so much water in all their lives.

Kuno Rainer had received an invitation to join a Himalayan Expedition. He and Peters, a Munich climber, were both to go out to Makalu, one of the "eight thousanders" in the Everest group, which nobody had yet approached or reconnoitred closely; they were to look for the best route on to and up the mountain, but the main objective was to be a neighbouring peak of only about 23,000 feet. I welcomed Kuno's trip with all my heart; but secretly I couldn't help envying him too. I asked myself why no one asked me to join that kind of an expedition; if I wasn't qualified, then by heaven one must produce fantastic credentials to be worth one's salt in the Himalaya. But the leader of an expedition must, of course, have the final say about what he demands of the men of his choice.

I was asked to give a lecture in Bavaria about my Eiger experiences, and when, in the normal course, talk among an intimate circle turned to the subject of expeditions, I could not avoid mentioning to my friends my disappointment at being left behind again. Was the whole of my training to go begging, I asked. One of my friends answered: "Oh, you're *too* good for them!"

"Too good?" What could that mean; one can't be too good for the Himalaya? No, that couldn't be the real reason. Didn't I fit in with the others, just because I always demanded the extreme limit of endurance from myself as well as from my comrades? But what was the use of aiming at the very highest, if we didn't know the depth of our own resources and their utmost limitations?

The Peters Expedition eventually fizzled out because they couldn't raise enough money for it. To offset that, however, another enterprise suddenly came to the fore. I was sitting talking to Heini Harrer, who was busy writing his book *Seven Years in Tibet*, at Kitzbühel; we were talking about the future and its problems. Presently he showed me a picture periodical and pointed to the name of Karl Herligkoffer, a medical man, who was planning to lead an expedition to Nanga Parbat in the following summer. I had never heard the name, nor had Harrer; but he seemed to have very definite plans and to be a master at propaganda, if the periodicals were publishing articles about him. For not a single mountaineer had ever heard of Dr. Herligkoffer.

Time passed, and there was more and more in the news about the Herligkoffer Expedition. Was it all idle chatter, or had the man really the organising ability to set such an enterprise on a sound footing? He was said to be Willy Merkl's stepbrother—Willy Merkl, who had twice gone out to Nanga Parbat but had not come back the second time. They said that Peter Aschenbrenner, another veteran of Nanga Parbat, was signed up for the new party; likewise Kuno Rainer. But a number of names were mentioned which I had never come across in my mountaineering experience.

Meanwhile the day of my compulsory eviction was drawing very near. Winter, too, was at the door. I gladly accepted a promising job as a salesman in a Munich shop, "Sporthaus Schuster", and started work on December 1st, 1952. My wife and the baby moved to her parents' home in the Ramsau, while I found an emergency lodging in the house of some Munich relatives. Sick at heart, I left my old home and at the same time Innsbruck, my birthplace. I had lived there for 28 years, all the days of my youth!

A surprise telegram arrived. What I had thought could no longer happen had in fact happened; they were asking me to join the expedition. Excitedly I said yes, and plunged wholeheartedly from the first day into the preparatory work. Almost every evening found me in the expedition's office, where everyone was busy packing, making arrangements, writing letters. I had stopped asking who Dr. Herligkoffer might be, or what his qualities were. For me, now, he was simply the man who had given me my chance of going to the Himalaya and the chance perhaps of proving myself there. Besides, he had promised to hand over leadership of the expedition at Base Camp. On the mountain itself Peter Aschenbrenner would be in charge; so everything would be in the best possible hands.

Dr. Herligkoffer shaped his plans on the basis of his step-brother's notes, which now stood him in good stead. At times it looked like becoming a mammoth organisation and we tried to put the brake on; but Herligkoffer would listen to no advice and continued to work out his plan in adamantine fashion. Next, we had to sign a contract which had so many legalistic clauses that we viewed it with some suspicion, but our leader allayed our fears by explaining that it was all a mere formality. The basis of the whole thing was, after all, team spirit, and the only consideration was the fulfilment of a solemn mission. A company for the Furtherance of German Exploration Abroad was founded; each of us was bound by his signature to become a member. The company—that was what they called it—was intended to deal with the winding-up of the expedition, when each of us would receive a share of any profits there might be, in proportion to his contribution to the performance achieved. In any case, the tax regulations made it imperative to form a company.

We were taken aback by the sudden withdrawal of the well-known Guide, Anderl Heckmair, the first man to climb the Eiger North Wall, from the team. Could it be the contract and all those conditions which one had to sign that had scared him away? It also seemed a little remarkable that Rebitsch, Harrer and Erwin Schneider, the collector of seven-thousand-metre peaks, had refused Herligkoffer's invitation. But I did not begin to see the red light till one day when one of the other members of the team, Dr. Walter Frauenberger, the magistrate of St. Johann in Pongau, remarked: "If Kuno and you weren't in the party, I would withdraw."

Our names kept on appearing in the Press and I did not like it at all. As a mountaineer I found it, to say the least, unusual to start beating the big drum and gathering laurel wreaths in advance; there was no avoiding the outcome of that. All manner of sharp things were said and we had to listen to a great deal of doubt being expressed.

"You won't do it, you know. What a colossal waste of money!"

"You won't get any further than the others did."

"Why, you haven't got the experience—you've never even been in the Himalaya!"

"And what an outfit! Full of people nobody's ever heard of."

That was the kind of thing, and plenty of it, we had to put up with. The most discussed person in the expedition was its leader. The reason, of course, was that he had yet to fill in the opening page of his mountaineering story; so the top-ranking clubs in German Alpine circles would have nothing to do with him. Only the Munich Section of the Alpine Club remained loyal to the enterprise, which was understandable, since two of its members were taking part. And the Austrian Alpine Club, too, supported Dr. Herligkoffer's plans, obviously out of consideration for us, the Austrian members.

Something had to be done to put an end to the continual bickering and to prove the fitness of the expedition to tackle its job. I myself had not done a big climb for six whole months. I simply had to regain complete confidence in myself, by putting every fibre of my body and spirit to the test before the time came for us to sail.

ALONE ON A WINTER'S NIGHT—
EAST WALL OF THE WATZMANN

It was just noon on a February day in 1953. Laden with rucksack, skis and ice-axe, I wriggled my way like a slalom runner through the throng of people on the way to Munich's main station. The express whistled me up into the Hills. "Berchtesgaden—all change!"

It was still deep winter up there. I bought a few things, left my ski at the luggage counter and pushed on towards the Königssee.

The people there know their business. Not till I had bought an entry ticket was I allowed to launch out on the frozen surface of the lake. A good many people gave me the once-over. "Rucksack . . . ice-axe . . . alone . . . going towards Bartholomä . . .? Surely he's not meaning to . . .?"

To add to my misfortunes I met a neighbour from the Ramsau. Suppose he told my wife? The inquisitive brute wanted to know all about everything.

"Alone, eh?" he enquired.

"The others are following," I explained.

An hour later I reached Bartholomä.

I took a furtive look up at the highest wall in the Eastern Alps, the East Wall of the Watzmann. It was difficult to gauge the conditions from down below. The first thing I did was to satisfy my raging hunger to some degree. A jolly party sat at the same table, apparently a party of hunters. They ordered the menu for the evening—roast pork, plenty of beer, and then a flagon of red wine for good measure. I asked for a plate of hot soup. I could hardly avoid bringing to light some article of Alpine equipment if I started grubbing about in my pack for my provisions. I could already read the same questions on the faces of the strangers:

"Why the ice-axe? Why no partners?" I avoided the necessity of an answer by making myself scarce as soon as possible. I took another quick look at the climbers' guide. The "Salzburg Route" looked the most suitable; it was so steep that there would be less snow lying on it. It was just light enough to make a quick comparison, outside, with the real thing: and to impress the outstanding features of the route on my mind.

I left Bartolomä at about seven p.m. The comfortable log-road soon ended and with it every trace of human existence. I frequently went into the snow knee-deep. The moon rose behind the great bulk of the Göll;

it was a full moon and it bathed the whole district in a flood of silver light. The mighty wall I was going to attempt soared overhead like a phantom. How different it is here in summer, when a noisy crowd of over-enthusiastic people use Nature as its playground. Now only the lonely chamois breaks a trail in the deep snow; the only sound to mar the silence is the occasional roar of the avalanches plunging down.

I climbed steeply up to the back-most corner of the "Ice Chapel", over fresh avalanche-cones compressed into hard ice. The first steep pitch lay buried in deep snow; the masses of snow pouring down with the weight of whole goods trains had ground out ice-walls, hard as concrete, 10, 15 feet high, down below. I had been wise to choose the night for the lower part of my climb, for the frost was binding the snow firmly; but I had made one slight miscalculation—the resulting hard snow-surface would not support my body weight. The few hours of sunshine during the day were insufficient to transform the snow on the slopes of the wall into glacier-snow; all it had achieved was a friable crust, a loathsome, brittle crust. . . . At last, however, harder avalanche tracks allowed me to gain height more rapidly; but there the snow was so hard that I had to resort to crampons.

I stopped several times to listen to the terrifying thunder of avalanches coursing down over in the opposite face of the Hachelkopf, looming monstrous and menacing in deep shadow thrown by the moon. My over-strained nerves began to play tricks with me, conjuring up grisly visions before my eyes.

I kept on seeing the lifeless bodies of two dead climbers on the snow-slope. Only a few months before, when making my first acquaintance with the East Wall of the Watzmann, I had joined some colleagues from Berchtesgaden in a search for two missing mountaineers. The wall was already deep in its winter robes as we followed a track which lost itself in the course of a recently-fallen avalanche; our eyes searched the foot of the slope below it, straining anxiously.

And then, piecemeal, we saw a rounded shape, a rucksack, then a bivouac-sack, a provision tin. We climbed upwards into that chute of ruin. Again, a glove, snow-bindings—and something black lying in the snow. It was the first of the two men we were searching for. Not a nice sight for a climber full of high-flown plans; but it is part of the game. We picked up the track again a little higher and followed it. In a steep snow-gully we found traces of a slide and then—a dead body hanging on the rope and a lot of blood reddening the snow below it. . . . But away with such dismal memories; they were no fit companions for me on this risky enterprise of mine.

A simple traverse landed me in the Schöllhornkar. My normal peace of mind had returned by then. The deep avalanche scores helped me now to gain height swiftly. A dark wall of rock loomed above me. I knew how deceptive moonlight can be with its distorting shimmer.

I climbed a narrow ramp and a short, steep ice-slope, then the sheer bare rock began. Still standing on the ice, I unstrapped my crampons and stowed them away in my rucksack; I shouldn't be needing them for a long time to come.

It was nearly ten p.m. My altimeter read 4,600 feet, so I had already come up 1,600 feet of the wall. An exceptionally smooth slab almost forced me into a very long détour, but I climbed it in the end and so reached the foot of the "Salzburger", the most difficult of all the climbs on the East Wall.

Of course, there had to be a thin cake of ice-glaze on all the corrugations, which would otherwise have given safe support to my cut-out rubber soles. Water was trickling down every face. The night seemed unnaturally mild to me; or was it my own warmth, engendered by my exertions? The rock was repellently smooth. I climbed up to the left into a kind of trough, using an uncomfortable scoop for the first few feet. The presence of rusty ring-hooks confirmed that I was on the correct route. A steep ramp led upwards to the right. My body threw a dark shadow on the rock and at times I had to move aside to find hand- and foot-holds close to me.

Something was happening high up above me on the wall—snow coming down off it. Over yonder on the Schöllhornplatte I could hear ice chocketing down, but I was in no danger from it.

I reached a narrow stance—a very airy perch. Above it was a great overhang, with two pitons in it, which I tested carefully. The rock pushed me savagely outwards and my rucksack straps bit into my shoulders. I had to retire to the little platform. There I hung my heavy rucksack by a sling from the lower piton. Things went much better without its burden; a little lay-back and I was up over that key-point of an overhang. I hauled the rucksack up and studied the climber's guide by the light of a pocket torch till I was sure about the continuation of my route. At greater distances moonlight robs one of all ability to judge correctly, removing all the relief of the ground to be covered. I took note of every possibility of beating a retreat. My store of iron-mongery and the 120-foot rope would do, though there might be all sorts of surprises in the final chimney—ice cataracts, snow-balconies, and so on. And how would the traverse to the first terrace be looking?

I turned a few glazed slabs by going out to the left, where a narrow ledge led onwards to an *arête* of rock rising steeply overhead. The limestone, normally so warm and sunny, was cold and grim to-night; though the holds were firm enough, even in the depths of a winter midnight. I had one or two doubts about my route; once or twice I went astray on "works of supererogation" and had to come back, traversing briefly with the aid of a sling. Then I was at the exit chimney which led out of this precipitous pitch. I was agreeably surprised, for a way seemed to open out above; there was some ice in the bottom of the chimney, but it hardly interfered with my upward movement. A row of slabs led out to the left to the start of the first terrace. A sheer passage followed from rock on to hard snow which broke away below into ice-gullies. The Schöllhornplatte already lay far below me. A gleam from a lighted window struggled up from Bartolomä, where the hunters' feast had perhaps by then reached its climax.

The moon had strayed away far to the south; its light was climbing up the Schönfeld Ridge, a silent companion on my nocturnal climb. . . . A broad white surface now ran up to the left and after a short breach deposited me at the "Giant's Terrace". There were cracks here and there in the snow, affording me glimpses down into black chasms; the depth of the snow hereabouts was anything up to 30 feet. The terrace narrowed continually and I was soon looking down steep gullies falling away from my feet; the snow-slope above me was almost vertical. The wall was plastered with cascades of ice, but they were pretty stable on the whole. The front prongs of my crampons and my ice-axe were the only anchorage on this precipitous ground.

Shortly afterwards I reached the start of the traverse to the final gully. It was the spectral midnight hour, but not a spectral sign was there! An uncanny silence lapped the whole great face. I could count on my fingers the tally of those who had ever seen its slopes in winter. Even in summer it is a climb which occupies a whole long day; those who had done it before me in winter had been imprisoned on the wall by its masses of winter snow for from two to four days. They too must have found the silence and the loneliness uncanny; but at least they had not been alone in the wintry night, like me.

I freshened my dry gums with an orange. The moon disappeared behind the Watzmann's Ridge and the great dark shadow crept further and further across the wall. Eagerly I moved into the final gully, which began by looking almost inviting, for a steep snow-groove led up it almost unbroken. At first the snow was as hard as glass, but gradually it got worse, becoming steadily looser. I could measure my rapid gain of height by the way the neighbouring summits sank below my own level. I was level with the Hachelkopf now and the Watzmannkinder were only a little way above me. The dark streak over there must be the south *arête* of the third "Child", a climb I had had on my programme for a long time past.

I was moving less quickly by now, stopping for frequent short rests—forcing a way through the snow was terribly exhausting. Finally I reached a small projecting rib, with the wall falling steeply to the great terraces below. This must be the place where the Kederbach route comes up, the route by which the first climb of the wall was accomplished 55 years ago. Since then route after route had been worked out; but this Salzburger route remained the most difficult. I was surrounded by unreal snow structures—mushrooms, projections like balconies, great cartloads of compressed snow hanging from small wrinkles, ready to collapse. The whole face was buried under the white masses. Steep snow-slopes too went winging up to the ridge, covering every projecting step in the wall and lending it an aspect of extreme exposure. The whole face was one sheer unbroken sweep of white.

I traversed to the right, but after moving a few yards found myself swimming in bottomless snow; the conditions had undergone an instantaneous transformation. The wall faces slightly northwards hereabouts and does not catch the sun much. I moved on by delicate snow ridges, bridging the way from one projecting crest to another. I was almost sorry to disturb these lovely manifestations of Nature, but it was no time for aesthetic considerations. I had to get on. . . .

It was almost impossible to make progress close to the rocks. Deep hollows had formed between rock and snow, often necessitating laborious détours. In the south-east glittered the summit snows of the Hochkönig; to the right the dark pyramid of the Hundstod.

I ate my last orange under a sheltering rock, where a freak of the wind had constructed a big bulge, a kind of tray, which provided me with a comfortable resting place. This was where the bivouac-box must be, probably buried deep under the snow. I moved on up steep gullies and over sharp snow-ridges; there were short rock-pitches in between and, for variety's sake, some tiring traverses. The wall still bulked steep and high above me, deep in shadow which prevented me from recognising any detail. A chimney jammed with snow ran up a steep pitch; I wormed my way up it, past great snow structures which leaned far out from the face. The angle steepened perceptibly. Overhead, the profile of the summit ridge cut like a broad white band into the dark night sky, looking almost near enough to grasp. But the wall wasn't going "to give in" as easily as all that; it made me fight for every precious foot. There was a short step in the wall . . . then a steep *couloir* running up to the ridge. Was the way really open? I could hardly wait to find out. I hurried upwards, pounding, racing impatiently on.

Suddenly I was standing in the full light of the moon again. A cold wind met me. A few more strides and I was on the summit. . . .

No handshake this time, no friend anywhere near; nobody to whom I could express my feelings. And yet it was a marvellous moment; a moment of such importance for me that silence spoke volumes more than speech. Below me lay the dark abyss with the highest face in the Eastern Alps, 6,000 feet of snow and ice, plunging down into it; and far away out there a streak of light—Berchtesgaden. Where I stood peace reigned ineffable; no sound was heard in that blessed hour of deathly cold and deathly loneliness.

I sat under my damp tent-sack. My watch said four o'clock. The bitter cold went through me, but I had decided to wait for daylight. The way down, a sharply-crested ridge, would be difficult enough then. The first lights were beginning to show down in the valley—as the early risers got up. And down there in Bartolomä the party was apparently still going on. It was nine hours since I too had sat at the table in the warm guest-room.

Many a time have I sat on a summit after a difficult climb, ravenous, my nerves worn out, my strength exhausted, but blissfully happy. It is that feeling which drives us climbers ever and again up into high mountain tracts, remote from all life; which impels us to undertake the most fearful exertions, which drives us far beyond the narrow confines of the world. And while in spirit I was retracing the thread-like way which had led me up out of the abyss, my thoughts were already winging away to the greatest mountains in the world, to Asia's sky-raking summits, to Nanga Parbat itself. For the sake of Nanga Parbat I must strengthen and equip myself; only then would I be worthy to approach it. . . .

My anticipations of the coming expedition were so pleasant that night passed comparatively quickly and the first rays of the sun were soon welcoming me. The ridge to the Hocheck provided marvellous views back into that glorious wall and my glance kept on following the slopes across which my way had led me all last night. I took deep draughts of the warm comfort of the dawning day. I passed along a few more cornices and, crossing a fallen-in snow-crest, went hurrying down to the Watzmann House. How I longed for a hot drink of tea! Yet every step nearer to the house only increased my disappointment. The shutters were closed, the doors were barred; so much for my precious tea! I pushed on down towards the valley, a tedious scramble, down and down and down, until I reached the first well-trodden track in the snow.

I was once again snaking my way through Munich's streets, laden with my rucksack, axe and ski; but this time glowing with an inner peace and satisfaction, in the certain knowledge of a lovely experience and the performance of a successful effort which was still only the preparation for something even bigger.

* * *

The nearer the departure day arrived, the more feverish became the work. I spent the last three weeks before the start in the office without a break; I even ate and slept there for the most part. The only time my wife got sight of me was if she looked in at the office; but what usually happened if she did was that she got roped in too. I sat driving a typewriter till two or three in the morning; then I started my duties again at six o'clock after snatching a short nap. All the equipment had to be registered in English and the values worked out in dollars.

There were financial worries for our expedition, too. We had to cut down our strength. They started trying to boot Kempter out, but the Munich section of the Alpine Club, to which he belonged, vetoed the proposal with the utmost energy. Kempter was reprieved. To balance that, though, Eschner, who had done a lot of spadework out in Pakistan, had to withdraw. But Hermann Köllensperger, also a member of the Munich section, remained on the list of participants.

The final addition to the party was Hans Ertl, the famous Vagabond of the Hills. Dr. Herligkoffer had invited that great climber and photographer to come home all the way from Bolivia; we were thrilled when he agreed, and admired the way he had subordinated his own plans among the Andes to this new call. We knew Ertl as a first-class performer right in the world class, and at the same time as a climbing partner well worth his salt. A man, too, of incalculable value to any expedition. Our own was indebted to the trust reposed in him by a film company for an advance of the considerable sum of 80,000 Deutschmarks in respect of a Nanga Parbat film which he was yet to make. It was, in fact, this sum which finally assured that our expedition would actually come into being.

It was April 16th, 1953. The city of Munich had prepared a great send-off for us. Ertl gave a last lecture before a wildly enthusiastic audience. Munich's biggest hall was sold out to the last seat, and the profit went to swell our finances. But we ourselves didn't exactly look like needing a send-off, for we hadn't yet managed to obtain permission to enter Pakistan. In fact, our passports were still in Bonn, though our train was supposed to leave for Genoa at noon next day, for Genoa where the whole 12 tons or so of the expedition's equipment were already stowed in the hold of the *Victoria*.

We needed a miracle. . . . It happened. Our Pakistan visas arrived at the very last minute!

NANGA PARBAT

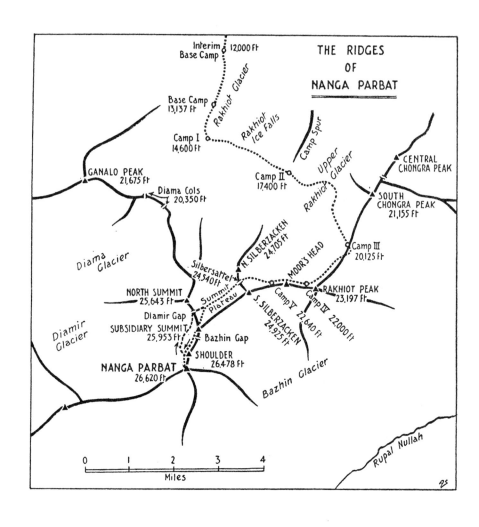

THE RIDGES
OF
NANGA PARBAT

Interim Base Camp 12,000 Ft

Rakhiot Glacier

Base Camp
13,137 Ft

Rakhiot Ice Falls

Camp I
14,600 Ft

Camp Spur

Upper Rakhiot Glacier

CENTRAL CHONGRA PEAK

GANALO PEAK
21,675 Ft

Camp II
17,400 Ft

Diama Cols
20,350 Ft

SOUTH CHONGRA PEAK
21,155 Ft

Diama Glacier

N SILBERZACKEN
24,705 Ft

MOOR'S HEAD

Camp III
20,125 Ft

Silbersattel
24,540 Ft

Summit Plateau

RAKHIOT PEAK
23,197 Ft

NORTH SUMMIT
25,643 Ft

Camp V 22,640 Ft Camp IV 22,000 Ft

Diamir Gap

S. SILBERZACKEN
24,925 Ft

Diamir Glacier

SUBSIDIARY SUMMIT
25,953 Ft

Bazhin Gap

NANGA PARBAT
26,620 Ft

SHOULDER
26,478 Ft

Bazhin Glacier

Rupal Nullah

0   1   2   3   4
Miles

BELOW 26,000 FEET . . .

NANGA PARBAT—a symbol to conjure with in the world of mountaineers and for millions elsewhere, too. That peak of many names—sometimes called the Fateful Peak, or the Mountain of Terror; that cloud-piercing giant which had already devoured thirty-one victims; that pitiless domain demanding its holocaust and giving nothing in return, luring men into its thrall, never to set them free again.

We all knew the history of the huge, lonely, north-western corner-stone of the Himalaya; the desperate efforts men had made to pluck its virginity, the devasting drama of the disasters unfolded on its slopes and ridges. We knew the story of what had been done up in its lofty realm in 1895, 1932, 1934, 1937, 1938, 1939 and 1950. And now it was to be our turn. . . .

Were we a strong enough party to face such odds? Or were we presumptuous to follow in the tracks of those who had gone out before us, had struggled, attacked, defended themselves and still, in the end, been struck down? Could we hope to succeed where they had failed? Grim queries those, but overlaid with a fierce joy—our joy at a great and weighty venture, at our chance to prove our mettle. We built up the mountain and what we were to live through on it in our imagination. Our imaginings fell far short of the reality.

I remember my first sight of the mountain from the Dakota that was lifting us from the lowland world of men into the flashing, glistening world of the Earth's highest peaks. There it suddenly was; and the sight was overwhelming. Nobody said a word for long minutes; the very thought of climbing afoot to its summit seemed madness. And when I recall that first shattering impression it seems also a fairytale or a dream —a glorious, wild, impossible dream—that it was granted to me to stand up there, all those weeks later.

My experiences on the mountain were so tremendous and so impressive that I find it difficult to marshal them into an orderly account. Indelible pictures keep on interposing themselves on the actual chronological sequence of events. They are pictures which obliterate mere human happenings, shining, alluring visions which sear one's heart and wipe out all memory of distress, worry and disappointment.

I can see the Base Camp now. It lay high, by Alpine standards, almost 13,000 feet above sea level; low in the Himalayan scales; set in a moraine trough at the rim of a gigantic river of ice. Home and the homeland hills were 6,000 miles away.

It was a huge hump of a moraine, which seemed to have been placed there by prescient Nature as a protection from the menace of the avalanches which thundered down from the North Face of the regal mountain. At Base Camp one could only hear a muted version of the bursting, roaring, cracking and droning of the ice. This was still a place fit for human habitation, over which the gods did not exert their sway.

But above the moraine, for nearly 13,000 unbroken feet, towered the sheer North Face of Nanga Parbat, its precipices ice-armoured, its rocks snow-powdered. High up in it hung a wedge-shaped hanging-glacier; to the right fell a delicately-chiselled snow-ridge, from whose cornice-crowned crest descended apparently vertical snow ribs and ice-runnels, marvellously formed, falling several thousand feet to the Ganalo Glacier. Each of these snow flutings was an individual masterpiece.

Opposite, to the north-east, stood the rounded heads of the Central and South Chongra Peaks. At the extreme left, the summit of the North Chongra Peak fell away in a steep ridge to the comparatively low Buldar Peak. In the distance, far beyond the foot of the valley, shimmered the distant ice-castles of the Karakorum, veiled in mist, yet compelling, alluring, exciting, beguiling heart and mind. A landscape so mighty, so magnificent that poor, pathetic words are too feeble to begin to describe it, and fade out into a reverent silence.

About 4,500 feet above Base Camp there was a levelling out of the chaotically-tangled ice-masses of the Rakhiot Glacier, whose ice is forced and churned under indescribable pressure through a narrow passage. In that small flat expanse there was a small projecting rock-rib —Camp Spur, 17,609 feet above sea level, cleaving the broken ice of that glacier torrent, hundreds of feet in depth, like the prow of an ice-breaker. Opposite it, projecting from the North Face, rose a huge spur, the size of the Matterhorn, but almost lost in these gigantic surroundings. The ice masses piled up into a steep ice-fall, like a heavy sea lashed into furious movement. Troughs and ridges of ice-rollers, ice-towers like gushing jets of water; and behind them, like sky-scrapers, great clusters of glass, more than 300 feet high, indescribably lovely in shape and slender grace, to which we loaned a beloved name from our own mountains at home—the "Vajolett Towers" . . .

Through this land of ice-magic ran a trail. It ended at a hollow in the middle of a flattening of the glacier. Overshadowed by ice-walls as high as houses stood a few tents. That was Camp II.

The establishment of the camp was an adventure in itself, spread out over long weeks, compact of danger and indescribable exertions. For the mountain used every weapon it had against us interlopers. It sent snow and gales, then unbearable heat alternating with crippling cold. And it sent avalanches. Now I thought I had had a fair experience of those phenomena; but all my past avalanche-adventures were meaningless when compared with the avalanches we met on the slopes of Nanga Parbat. Pictures rise to my mind again. . . .

Kuno Rainer and I were climbing up the ice-fall from Camp I to where Camp II was yet to be, through a labyrinth of clumps, towers and caverns of ice so dense as to make one lose one's bearings. It was like being in a maze of streets in a strange city whose house-walls met overhead. Deep snow covered the treacherous abysses underfoot. True, we were roped, but at 18,000 feet or so it is no fun falling into crevasses. This was ideal ground for photography, and I was looking forward to leading our cameraman to such perfect subjects—now a glimpse through an arch in a *sérac* to the North Face, whose profile was becoming more impressive at every foot of height we gained, now a pyramid of ice lifting against the dark haze of the Indus Valley, or a shot of the Kongra Group or the distant line of the Karakorum.

Then a steep slope made us forget all such loveliness again. We often took more than an hour over a short step of forty or fifty feet, moving forward like moles. In spite of everything I had ever done, I had never felt so tired. From ten o'clock on, the sun was so scorching that we sought shade at every halt; in the shade it was icily cold.

Suddenly there was a detonation high above us on the North Face. Judging by the size of the report it must be a pretty big avalanche on its way down. We felt quite safe and looked forward to enjoying the magnificent spectacle from our lofty view-point. Minutes had elapsed since the report. It seemed that the avalanche must shoot out down below there any moment.

And then—so suddenly that I could hardly believe my eyes—a great cloud formed overhead, mounting stupendously, growing and growing, moved over from the right, out over our heads, and began to settle on our perch. In a flash we knew that this was the avalanche.

Instantaneously I threw myself face down on the slope, buried my face in the snow and bit into my flannel shirt. I waited for terrifying seconds—minutes. Then everything went dark; a fearful flapping wind enveloped us. Snow drove into everything, into my shirt, into every stitch of clothing, and the hideous fear that there was more to come seemed to last an endless time; it was the heavy stuff, the ice fragments, I was waiting for, as I buried my head still deeper in the snow. But at last I saw something glinting and it was daylight again.

I lifted my head very carefully at first. I could see the blue sky again; the danger was past and I got up.

It was icy cold standing there in my shirt with rolled-up sleeves, full to the seams with snow, and I shivered from head to foot; but the sun soon warmed me. How came it that we could be exposed to avalanche danger here, more than a mile from the North Face? But here anything was apparently possible. We had survived our baptism of fire, and now we knew how to treat these monsters. The astonishing thing is that an avalanche of such proportions could pass and leave no trace behind it. Our hearts had been in our boots a few minutes before; now we were able to laugh at our experience.

That first taste of avalanches was followed by many others.

After one very sultry day the snow had shrunk enormously and set again; there was a heavy frost that night, and next morning the going on the hard-frozen surface was splendid—it was a real pleasure to be climbing. Kempter and Köllensperger were with us as reinforcements, but just as we were leaving Camp I another enormous avalanche came tearing down the North Face. No one who has not seen one of these displays staged by Nature can imagine its impressiveness. It is like the end of the world. Monstrous masses of broken-off ice plunge tens of thousands of feet into the depths with a terrifying thundercrash, to burst on the flat surface of the glacier beneath and dissolve into microscopic particles of ice-dust that form into a mounting tidal wave of snow which with incredible swiftness races out across the glacier levels. A human being is an object of naught; a house would be just a small toy and would be submerged unnoticed in such a cataract. These avalanches are often as much as a mile and a half wide and 600 or 700 feet high. There is naturally a terrific wind-blast accompanying them, and their suction is their most dangerous feature. We saw the white cloud sweeping down the face, growing and growing; as if someone was pouring water on to sherbet. A vertical wall moved towards us and in an instant we were enveloped in thick fog. The avalanche swept all the way up the opposite slope, nearly 700 feet, to the crest of the moraine, and the fine curtain of ice-dust took a long while to disperse. One of the most unpleasant features which invariably accompanies these phenomena is a sharp, momentary drop in the temperature. So we never went into the danger-zone without warm clothing from then on. We only saw the results of that particular avalanche two days later; where there had been bottomless powder-snow, every vestige had been swept away down to the floor level, exposing the sheer ice as though a hurricane had blown furiously upon it for days. Ice-fragments the size of our heads lay scattered all around. The snow formation bore eloquent witness to the force with which the blast had carried all before it.

At times we got the impression that mountaineering in the Himalaya consisted of nothing but breaking trails and superhuman exertions; but memory has cast over those heartbreaking days of toil a kindly veil of beauty, bringing to the surface of one's consciousness pictures of loveliness absorbed unbeknown at the time, when our breath was rasping and the racing of our pulses obscured everything else. One example: a glimpse, through an arched crevasse, tunnel-like, far away to the Karakorum, where gleamed a mighty pyramid—K², 28,250 feet high, the second highest mountain in the world. . . .

But the accompanying melody is no soft, sweet tune. The idyll is immediately interrupted by heroic chords, by the roar, the rattle and the rush of the avalanches. . . .

On one occasion I had to go down from Camp II to Camp I. I went slowly down the virgin slopes, for fresh snow had covered up our tracks. In the "Winterrasse" I met Albert Bitterling, coming up with porters. We were only a few yards apart when the slope suddenly cracked across its whole breadth, started to move and carried us away with it. I was lucky and got clear of the slide at once; so did Albert. But the porters were not so fortunate, being roped together; they dragged each other down in a flurry of feet and arms.

Providentially, the snow came to a halt before reaching a steep ice-cliff. The porters lay motionless on the slope, praying to Allah. We had great difficulty in getting them on their feet again; then we stowed their loads in a safe spot and all went down together. Although we often had cause to complain of these Hunzas, there were some first-class men among them; we had soon picked out the best of them, among whom Isar stood out for his fine performances.

I started up again for Camp II with six porters. Hermann Köllensperger escorted us. We were just crossing the level glacier below the North Face when a report made us cast a quick look upwards; one of those dull crashing roars which always chilled us to the marrow of our bones. An avalanche had broken loose up there. We ran for our lives, for we were straight in its line of fire. At the last moment we flung ourselves down in a crevasse, as the wall of snow overtook us. It grew icily cold and a hurricane got up. We gasped for breath, feeling as though we were suffocating—and everywhere fine snow-dust forced its way into everything. I bit hard on my pullover, to prevent the fine ice-particles from getting into my windpipe. After a long time the storm abated, we could breathe again; but the porters lay in the snow, praying to Allah and, in their terror, never even noticed that the whole thing was over.

We went on, but only five minutes later there was a new rumble, up on the left for a change. This time we didn't run, but just found a sheltered spot, pulled our balaclavas and pullovers over our ears and faces, stuck a bit of sacking in our mouths, filled our lungs with air, and waited. The minutes seemed like hours, but once again we came to no harm. We thought it enough for one day, though. As it happened, we had no more trouble on the rest of the way up. Ertl later expressed regret that he had not been able to capture it all on film from where he stood, and had waited hopefully for the events to repeat themselves. We, however, were quite glad that his hopes were disappointed.

But now it is high time for me to give my memories, which conjure up pictures haphazardly, only to fade away again, a proper sequence, and I will try to get them into proper order with the aid of my diary.

Early June: at Camp II. The weather had at last grown more settled, but Peter Aschenbrenner was taking his time; he only smiled tolerantly at our growing impatience up above, so we supposed he must know best. The next thing we heard was that the Sherpas we had hired had gone back to Darjeeling; although they had actually reached Pakistan nobody seems to have met them. That was a mistake pregnant with serious results, for our porters proved far too few. What use were fifteen porters to ten Sahibs, especially when three, and by no means the worst, were retained at Base Camp for orderly duties? The rest of them were perpetually on the sick list, and the chapatties, which are their staple diet, never came up. Ertl cursed and swore when nobody called up at the agreed times for communication on the radio. At that point he took the initiative and went down to make all the necessary arrangements; porters would have to be brought up from Gilgit and food for them, too. Hans was making himself more and more our champion. . . .

Hardly a decisive order ever came up from Base Camp. Walter was still busy with the thankless task of sorting out the equipment. In Camp I, night after night, he got up at two o'clock, to prepare breakfast for the climbing party; there were still about 80 loads for the high camps to be carried up. It wasn't difficult to work out how long it would take them to get there with that ridiculous shuttle-service of porters. I was beginning to think about a post-monsoon expedition. If we were to succeed in July either the equipment would have to be seriously lightened, which would result in very short periods on the mountain for each of us, or we would have to get hold of more porters.

No sooner had this become crystal clear than an order came up from Base Camp that the Sahibs themselves must carry loads. A grand idea, seeing that we had been doing so for weeks past!

The shortage of porters almost drove us to desperation. We had to get up at three o'clock to cook breakfast for them and for ourselves, because those bright lads couldn't learn to use a cooker. If we did leave the cookers to their tender mercies, we had to provide a new burner every day. When called, one or two of them got up at once, but others—one soon got to know them—turned over once or twice more and were then promptly sick. At three o'clock we reckoned on twelve men and arranged the loads accordingly . . . an hour later we had to begin striking them off the list. Then, at five o'clock we set off with five bodies. Those five were at least reliable and had already learned a good deal. They were very self-reliant and wanted to do everything without any help from us. It required a good deal of tact and hard work to get them to do what we wanted; if we had left them to their own sweet will they would have started a series of accidents. . . .

June 10th. After a poor night's sleep, Köllensperger and I started out at four a.m. to break a trail up to the plateau below Rakhiot Peak. We meant to establish Camps III and IV that day. Kuno Rainer, who had been up with us till then, went down to Base Camp with Otto Kempter for a well-earned recuperative spell.

It was bitterly cold. We got warm at last, thanks to the hard work spent on an ice-rib which went up through steep cliffs of ice. Hermann Köllensperger followed us up. The altimeter showed 19,030 feet and it seemed a very suitable place for Camp III, but it was still very early. So I played a little trick on the porters, who certainly didn't know that this was where Camp III was intended to be, and we went straight on up to Camp IV. It was a measure which would save valuable days later on; and where ignorance is bliss. . . . Well, they didn't know, and so our party moved slowly but cheerfully upwards while Walter Frauenberger followed a little way behind with his smaller group of porters.

By seven o'clock I was on a level plateau half a mile wide, with nothing between me and the slopes of Rakhiot Peak, the extreme excrescence of Nanga Parbat's East Ridge; it was all quite familiar to me from pictures, reports, descriptions. This was where Camp IV had stood in 1932 and 1934. In 1937, though, they had neglected that safe place and put up Camp IV about 300 feet lower down; an ice avalanche had obliterated all traces of human courage and endurance, burying under it the youth and keenness of a whole expedition—those splendid men, Carl Wien and his comrades.

I couldn't believe, as I stood there, that the mountain could be so brutal. There it stood opposite me, peaceful, transcendently beautiful, with the Silbersattel, the gateway to the summit, shining silver up there. The beauty and grandeur of the scene would permit of no sorrowful mood. One thinks on quite different lines at great altitudes; much more soberly, in a way more suited to the stature of the great scene about one. I remembered the heading of Hans Hartmann's diary

V

when they dug it out of the ice of the avalanche—"Target—Nanga Parbat". Yes, the great peak was the target; we ourselves must try to grow in stature to match it. We were certainly not approaching it in any spirit of idle frivolity, but in all seriousness of purpose, with high hearts, tough wills and passionate zeal. Those men, of similar spirit, whom the mountain had struck down, were still alive as we saw them in our memories. They accompanied us not as messengers from the dead but as guides for the living—guides to take up to the top.

I laid aside my rucksack at about 20,350 feet. It was too cold to wait there for the others, so I decided to use the opportunity to climb my first "six thousander". The plateau stretched endlessly towards the north and, in spite of the good pace at which I was moving, it was an hour before I reached the foot of the precipices running up to the South Chongra Peak. The snow got deeper and deeper and trail-breaking grew more and more laborious. I rested on a small saddle; to my right lay a gigantic cornice, beyond which the face fell steeply southwards. It was a fine example of those wonderful flutings typical of the Himalaya, almost vertical, knife-sharp snow-mouldings, true witnesses to the force of the winds and the tremendous extremes of temperature.

I traversed the Chongra's Western slopes, watching the snow texture with some apprehension; but it held firm. At one point I felt thin air under my foot and left a black hole behind me; then I moved on over firm snow to the summit at 21,162 feet. So well was I acclimatised that the climb took hardly anything out of me. My delight was such that I let loose a huge yodel, which was swallowed up by those vast spaces. I now had an opportunity of looking up at Nanga Parbat's summit structure, to which my devout hopes went winging. I got back to my rucksack after a terribly laborious descent through the softened snow on the plateau. The porters had already cleared a smaller platform and there were soon a couple of tents on it; everyone was glad to take shelter in them from the red-heat of noon. Köllensperger and the porters went down, while Walter and I made ourselves comfortable together—he, the Himalayan veteran, and I the enthusiastic novice. The weather was grand and we regretted bitterly that we had no porters at our disposal, for we could so easily have pushed the high camps upwards in such conditions. We just had to control our impatience; it seems that the porters were wanted down below.

The next day Walter followed my trail and also climbed the South Chongra Peak, thereby adding yet another "six thousander" to his collection from bygone days. He told me later that down in Base Camp people were not at all pleased with these side-shows, possibly because they thought we would be using up our reserves on them; but they were, after all, only proof of our fitness. And I couldn't help thinking of Peter Aschenbrenner's extravagant stories, told down there to make our mouths water, of his individual excursions during the 1934 Expedition.

That day Hermann came up again, accompanied by three of the Hunzas, to stock us with petrol and supplies. Very soon all I could see of him was his boots sticking out of the entrance to the tent; he was sleeping the sleep of the just after his labours. If a capacity for sound sleep is a sign of fitness, Hermann was a very fit man indeed. Meanwhile I worked away at the cookers, to brew some tea for the porters, without the least success, for two hours. The brutes of machines sometimes lit at the first touch; at other times they refused altogether. When at last a tiny blue flame flickered and I tried to put the pot full of snow on top of it, the burner suddenly began to splutter and in a moment a spurt of flame shot up. In a fury, I threw the thing out into the snow, whereupon my porter, with astonishing patience and oriental phlegm, went and fetched the sooted-up cooker back for the fifth time; then I started all over again. It was these small everyday irritations that used up our nerves most.

My pocket alarm woke me next day. It was still pitch-dark. I rummaged in the flap-pocket of the tent and soon had a candle alight. Clumsily peeling out of my sleeping-bag, I dressed and went over to the other tent to get breakfast ready. The cooker played the fool with me again. Before I knew where I was the whole provision-case was in flames and I was just in time to hurl the case and the infernal machine itself out of the tent before the whole place caught fire.

We left camp at five o'clock. We could see clear up to the Silbersattel and it was encouraging not to have the menace of *séracs* overhead any more. We had to surmount the steep slopes to the Rakhiot Peak in long diagonal sweeps; the very first slope didn't look very inviting to me, but the snow proved unexpectedly firm. It was another lesson that here, at these great altitudes, you can take much more on trust than lower down. At the top of the slope, I waited for my companion, but he wasn't coming up. Had anything happened, I wondered; had he met a wind-slab? Then I saw a dark spot right at the bottom on the level glacier. I went down to see why he was still down there, only to discover that he had lost his hat, which had gone rolling down; and you can't desert an old friend like that, can you?

It was the chilliest morning yet and I could even feel the cold through the soles of my boots. We waited for the sun on an ice-bastion. The Silbersattel, shining down on us in truly silver light, kept on catching our eye and I couldn't really imagine what there was to dispute one's way up there. Of course it might be an effect of the thin air and the deceptive light-conditions, but everything looked so orderly.

Steep slopes deep in powder snow met us, as we went on. We were feeling the altitude and were forced to breathe through our mouths. The difference between the number of breaths we had to take going ahead or following in the broken trail was most noticeable—the leader had to take four to every step, those behind, only one. A prolonged *bergschrund* compelled us to make a long traverse, till I found a place where I could cross the deep rift on to a vertical wall of snow. Every jerky movement or sudden exertion made itself severely felt; our bodies seemed crippled. By noon we were at the foot of the Rakhiot Peak's steep ice-wall, looking for a good place to pitch a camp—at 22,000 feet. But we had to turn back immediately, for a rapid change in the weather had enveloped us in thick cloud. However, we found our way back to our tents along the trail we had made.

Snow fell during the night. By morning there were three feet of it and it was still snowing. The cookery-tent was buried in snow and the tent-poles were cracking in spite of reinforcement. We provided emergency support with our ski-sticks and puttees and kept on clearing the camp of the encroaching masses of snow. No porters came up that day; but there were enough provisions for the two of us for a few days. There was a momentary clearing in the evening, and we had a wonderful view across the Buldar Peak, now well below us, and the colossal precipices of Ganalo Peak, with the mists moving up and down them.

The clouds closed in again and we were glad to get inside the tent, where conditions were just bearable. Exceptionally heavy snow poured on our roof all night and the walls of the tent pressed heavily on our sleeping-bags. Walter got up and cleared our shelter of the enormous weight, but very soon it was as bad as ever, and the layers of snow threatened to crush the tent altogether. Those heavy storms lasted several days; the space in our tent became too small, so I moved over into the kitchen-tent. We had to get up at all hours of the night to dig the tents out. What a contrast, between a warm sleeping-bag and the blizzard outside! But if we didn't do it, the wet roof of the tent was pressing on our noses, waking us with a start, so that at first we didn't know what was going on and had the horrors. We would try to sit up, then the tent pushed us down again and we would have liked to slit its walls open, if we had had a knife in our hands. If we closed the entrance at night, we had difficulty in breathing, or woke next morning with bad headaches; if we left it open, the snow piled up on our sleeping-bags. It was the same with the sleeping-bags. If we crawled right in, it was nice and warm, but we were soon looking desperately for the opening and suffered agonies if we could not find it at once; for the result was a real Alpine nightmare. We crawled out, gasping for air, only to find ourselves numb with cold. Eventually we found the right technique and tried to sleep with only the tip of our nose sticking out.

I had had a bad altitude-cough for some days, caused by the dryness of the air so high up. I invariably got persistent attacks when I lay down to sleep, and woke in the morning with a headache. My sleep wasn't any too good, either; but I didn't want to take tablets. Walter, by contrast, felt very well. Gradually time began to hang heavily on our hands, as we conversed for the umpteenth time about the things we cared for most.

"What a pity we haven't got the Sherpas; we miss them at every turn," I remarked to Walter, who agreed that we could easily have been much further up the mountain by now. I mentioned my fear that it might lead to our failure; he talked about his beloved Garwhal peaks, those mighty Central-Himalayan peaks, and reminisced about the Caucasus. In between, we took turns at shovelling snow, a most exhausting occupation, which I always took too quickly at first, and paid for with immediate headaches.

In the evening it cleared up as usual. Then it started snowing again and threatened to undo all our hard work. We hoped that our day's work hadn't been in vain, for this time we had gone to great pains, clearing a veritable sun-bathing terrace with all amenities laid on. Heavy snow gave way to an unusually fierce gale. The wind screamed across the high plateau and very soon our camp was level with the snow again, with only the tent-ridges sticking out a few inches. Shovelling and still more shovelling! We took turn and turn about and we were at it the whole night long.

The next day, June 16th, the storm raged unabated—its fifth day. Suddenly I heard voices, or was it an illusion? I could hardly believe that anyone could be coming up to rescue us in our cut-off position. But the voices sounded nearer—I could hear them shouting. Soon five figures appeared through the impenetrable gloom. It was Ertl, Rainer, Aschenbrenner, Kempter, Köllensperger and some porters. They had got tired of waiting and had decided to occupy Camp III. We hadn't had the wildest suspicion that they might turn up, seeing that Peter Aschenbrenner was supposed to be taking rest days and nobody had been able to spare a porter for us two up here. Perhaps we were really off in earnest this time?

The news they brought us was astonishing. Everest had been climbed! I was immensely impressed by the information, for I had never thought it possible that that giant peak would be conquered for another year or two. It was certainly a great spur to our own endeavours. Everyone was busy putting up the necessary tents, while I busied myself with the cooker. It was no longer possible to eat cold stuff and every bit of tinned food had to be cooked.

I had to smile at my early optimism. According to my time calculations we ought to have been at the Silbersattel long ago. They reckoned this way: "To-day we'll break the trail to Camp IV; to-morrow we'll establish it, and next day Camp V." Easily said, but instead we sat in the tents for days, snowed up and cut off from the world; and, when it finally cleared up and the upward trail had been broken, the porters went on strike or reported sick.

This is what I had written to my wife in my last letter: "The day after to-morrow we hope to establish Camp IV with three porters and tents. Then we go on to Camp V, the last one below the Silbersattel and the springboard for the assault on the summit. It will have three tents, to house four Sahibs and three porters; two climbers will then go on to the top, with the others in support. It will be full moon in a fortnight; that would be the right moment. We hope the weather will hold till then—cross your fingers for us! When I look up at it, it all looks so simple that I believe we must be going to pull it off. It all depends on how we adjust ourselves to the altitude. . . ."

Next morning my tent was all silted up again, to the very top, and Kuno had to make an exit for me before I could get out; but on the following day the weather had changed and it was beautifully warm. Aschenbrenner gave instructions to move the camp down 300 feet, explaining that we were in a wind-corridor; the order didn't cheer us up particularly, but we obeyed it dutifully.

The morning of June 18th dawned gloriously fine, though our thermometer showed 21 degrees below zero. All the slopes were dazzling white in their new snow, and our trail up above had, of course, vanished. Frauenberger, Rainer, Kempter and I broke the new track towards Rakhiot Peak, through much deeper snow than a week before. It was that kind of loose, floury, bottomless snow one so often meets above 20,000 feet, where it does not change in consistency. At the foot of the steep rock-wall leading to the peak we dug a burrow in a snow-slope. Presently we came upon a crevasse, but Kuno thought it did not matter, and as we had done so much we continued till we had made quite a roomy cave for two; the crevasse had the advantage that we were spared the work of removing the snow, for there was ample room in it for what we had dug out. Finally we plugged it with blocks and went down, relieved to have that hard work behind us. One day later Kempter, Köllensperger and I, with some porters, stood on top of the ridge below the Rakhiot ice-wall.

While the others went down and Otto worked at the "Primus", I dug out another hole in the slope and put up a tent in it.

Outside, the organ notes of a fresh storm sounded across the ridge; in next to no time our tracks were obliterated—normal Camp IV weather. But we felt safe in our shelter and no longer had to listen to the oppressive flapping of tents.

I awoke from a deep sleep to find it was already eight o'clock, though in our cave it was still dark. Our sleeping-bags glittered with rime, everything was frozen and an icy-cold draught blew from one corner; the crevasse had opened up again! The entrance to our den was silted up, so I had a nice morning's work; three feet of snow lay on the tent-flap we had stretched across the aperture. Outside I was met by an icy wind. A little later we started out, hauling 800 feet of belaying-line to the *bergschrund*, whence I climbed, with the rope crawling behind me, up the precipice; the weight of the hank almost dragged me out of my steps as I went up. I wouldn't have got anywhere without crampons.

The rope only reached half-way up. I anchored it to a rock-spike and climbed down, thankful that the drudgery was over. No porters came up to us that day; probably the weather was too depressing.

There was another frightful storm during the night, and our entrance was drifted up again; luckily we had a spade with us. The crevasse had opened again, which was probably a piece of luck or we would have had difficulty with our breathing; but its ventilation was now too much of a good thing. We estimated the temperature was at least 20 degrees below zero. We could do nothing, not even cook, without gloves. The tent next door was completely snowed-up; drift-snow, blown down the slope above, poured down incessantly into the crevasse, between the tent and the slope.

At half past eight we were off again, with another 300 feet of rope, to climb the Rakhiot Face again. The rope now reached almost to the shoulder above the slope; we used a few rock-teeth, a worn-out ice-axe and an old tent-pole left by an earlier expedition, to secure it.

Then we traversed to the "Moor's Head", over bare, blue ice.

I was very glad to have my crampons, which many had considered superfluous. I cut step after step into the brash surface, great "bath-tubs" of steps, so that the porters could come this way safely; it was no easy job. The weather was fine, though there was a strong wind blowing.

Now there was nothing between us and the summit massif: we could see the Subsidiary Summit, the Bazhin Gap and the rocky ridge to the Shoulder. I cannot describe the immensity of the South Face. I made a track through deep crust towards the summit of Rakhiot Peak, but leaving it to my left, steered a course towards the Rakhiot Needle, a sharp rock-tooth. The urge to climb swept over me; I decided to climb the Needle and so capture my first "Seven Thousander". The tooth was only 60 feet high, but by no means easy and I almost forgot the altitude in the excitement of the climb. Of course I had to take my gloves off and I waited for lulls in the gale to gain each three-foot rise up the vertical rock. It was wonderful to have the feel of rock under my fingers again! The summit was minute—just big enough for me to stand on it —and it is given on the map as 7,070 metres, 23,197 feet. I climbed down the other side, without a rope, of course; it had been left on the traverse. I had to use extreme care, for right under me hung a cornice, ready to break off and plunge down that monstrous South Face.

Otto had waited for me, and together we went down to the "Moor's Head", that dark rock tooth, where Willy Merkl lies buried in the ice. We left a shovel up there, but it was now too late to build a hole in the snow for a camp. Clouds were curling up the South Face, creeping across the ridge, enveloping everything in a grey pall. Then they parted again and let us look down into the Rupal Valley where, thousands of feet below, distant beyond all reality, a blue lakelet flashed up at us. Yet the summit pyramid, glowing in the last sunlight, still towered immensely high overhead.

On the way down I cut a solid staircase of steps down the steep slope, for we intended to bring the porters up here next day. Down on the levels near Camp IV I could see five little dots and I began to look forward tremendously to the morrow.

"Cheers!" I said. "To-morrow we're going to the 'Moor's Head' and then on beyond it."

We were, however, not to be spared the inevitable disappointment.

Next morning the porters were sick; these were our picked men and the hope of swift progress died away rapidly. Their tents looked like a home for incurables and we were continually met with the word "*pimar* —sick!" They would neither eat nor drink nor would they go down, and this time we were convinced that they really were ill. It started to snow; we were stuck in a white waste. I realised that we couldn't rely on porters any longer; but we couldn't beat a retreat with nothing accomplished. So we must help ourselves. I consequently suggested that each Sahib should hump a small load up to the "Moor's Head"; the suggestion earned me a pitying smile. So I took a sack of tinned stuff and a rubber mattress, and went off on my own. My load weighed at least 20 lb.; yesterday's trail had vanished and the work of renewing it had to be undertaken. Nowhere on that slope of about 45 degrees was there any possibility of putting the load down for a rest. I was therefore pretty exhausted when, some hours later, I reached the shoulder, where I dumped the load. I then hung a fixed rope on the traverse to the "Moor's Head" and came down the face on it.

The curtains of the storm opened from time to time and I could see the small dots near Camp IV again, those who had remained behind—or could it be the porters, risen as though from the dead? I was starving by the time I reached the snow-cave, for I had only had a taste of Milo before starting out in the morning; but I got nothing warm till the evening. The night was a bad one. Over and again I recalled Erwin Schneider's remark: "A bivouac in the open once a week would be more endurable than several weeks spent in the shelter of high camps."

My heavy cough, which I could not shake off, kept me awake a long time, and not even some warmed-up beer helped. When I had recovered from the attack—very much like whooping-cough—I was wide awake and lay there for hours thinking. I tried hard to side-track my thoughts, but only succeeded for a few minutes; then in my imagination I was up on the ridge again, studying and studying again what one could do to get things forward in spite of everything. I sometimes cursed the mountain, but much as I longed for warmth and greenery, I couldn't think of going down. I was prepared to try anything, to avoid reproaching myself later for not having given my all. I got to sleep at last after midnight, and that happened night after night.

Kuno, who came up with the porters yesterday, was in very poor shape. He is one of the best, and was obviously most unwell before he would admit it. He went down again to Camp III with Köllensperger and his porters. That left Otto Kempter and me alone together. Our petrol had run out and we had to cook with Esbit, a process so slow that it took hours before we got anything even lukewarm; moreover it smoked, so that we preferred to be out in the open in spite of the gale. Altogether, very uncomfortable! My thoughts strayed very often to the lowlands, but I could no longer imagine that furnace down there.

This kind of hunger-cure in the midst of plenty struck me as too stupid. In the morning I went down to Camp III to fetch petrol, while Otto stayed in his bag; by mid-day I was 2,000 feet lower down in wonderful, comforting warmth and sunshine, an astonishing contrast. There was no wind, one could stay out in the open, the cookers worked perfectly and my appetite recovered. It was remarkable what a couple of thousand feet could do. Instead of returning to Camp IV the same day, I enjoyed the amenities of that advanced base-camp overnight.

Next morning at four, I started up again with four porters, one of whom turned back immediately. I wallowed in deep snow; yesterday's track had almost disappeared. It was one of my bad days and I was glad indeed to be back in camp at the end of it. Otto had now had enough of life in a snow-hole and went down with one of the porters.

I was left alone with the remaining two Hunzas, my personal servant Hadji Beg and another Beg. Perhaps they would go on with me next day? My orderly had agreed to do so in Camp III, of course only in return for every kind of promise if he did come along. I had had enough of the draught-hole after five days in that cave of winds and I now preferred the tent. There was a raging gale, and a raging fight with the cooker; the vestas would only glow, perhaps every tenth one lit, smoking and stinking, with the result that my coughing attacks came on again. When, in desperation, I opened the tent, so much snow blew in that the entrance was full in a twinkling; and if, by any chance, the cooker happened to be burning it blew out immediately. And if it didn't do that, it spat and flared so violently that I had to get it out of the tent with all speed to prevent a conflagration.

It took me an hour to get tea ready. Then one of the porters came over and shouted "Cha!" So his lordship wanted tea, did he? Of course I gave him my tea; for if I didn't, he would obviously be "*pimar*", meaning sick, in the morning. I started melting snow all over again. Meanwhile dusk had fallen, I had a job to light the candle; the cooker went out, then the candle followed suit, the tent was plunged in darkness, I couldn't find the matches, the water got cold again, finally the cooker consented to light, only for the petrol to give out immediately—and the water only tepid. By that time it was nine o'clock. I tipped some fruit juice into the water and went to "bed" depressed and hungry.

The day's work in the Himalaya isn't all heroics. . . .

Next morning I was up at seven, getting the cooker going, to melt some water; I could hear the steps of my orderly outside as he shovelled snow. It almost deserved a hymn of praise. I handed him the can, half full of hot water—the result of about an hour's cookery—and asked him to add snow to it; whereupon he brought me back the empty can, having tipped the water out. At that my patience evaporated. I rushed out of the tent, knocking over the sausage-meat which was to be my breakfast in the process, so that everything went floating on the rubber mattress. I really didn't know how to deal with that bird of ill-omen. I explained to him that as a result of what he had done we shouldn't have any hot water all day, whereupon he departed without a word; of course, he may have misunderstood my tone of voice, besides which they had all learned certain good Tirolean and Bavarian expressions. It only remained for me to start all over again.

When at last tea was ready, neither of my neighbours was astir. I shouted across to them five times, without a word of reply. So I took the tea over to them, only to find they were both sick again. One of them pointed to his chest, so I advised him to go down at once: not a movement resulted. Beyond all patience I pulled his sleeping-bag off him, but he just pulled it on again, pointing to his bandaged foot. In the meantime a furious tempest had started to blow again; it was almost impossible to stand up outside.

Everything considered, I decided to go down. Of course, those two had left their tent open, knowing perfectly well that their Sahib would close it for them. Right again!

I needed a couple of days' rest before I could go on up, and Camp III very soon restored my mental balance. I went up to Camp IV again with energy renewed. Meanwhile Base Camp had come on the air:

"Either the summit is captured next week or——"

Or what?

Aschenbrenner and Ertl now tried to get the porters up the Rakhiot Face; it was hopeless from the start. They wouldn't go beyond Camp IV, and without a Camp V we couldn't hope to push further up the mountain. The valleys were full of heavy cloud-layers; could it be the monsoon? Our efforts seemed a forlorn hope in the face of so many obstacles. Frauenberger, Kempter, Köllensperger and I were now in Camp IV again. Heavy mists wreathed every slope, and the atmosphere was oppressive; we could hardly get enough air when resting, but when we were on the move we felt as if we were suffocating. The porters sat about listlessly in the snow, letting the gale blow over them. Our morale dropped below freezing-point; but while our weather expert down below, Hans Bitterling, saw no future in things, Ertl still maintained there was a chance.

That night it cleared up; the summit lay serene in the light of the full moon. My thoughts went winging up there again, and I would dearly have liked to start off on the spot; sleep finally put an end to the idea. Otto and Hermann had lost the will to go on, but I still did not want to give in.

I remembered the words of our experienced leader, Peter Aschenbrenner. He had said that whoever were fittest should form the summit party; personal considerations, in excess of normal service duties, were to be ruthlessly eliminated. Above 26,000 feet each of us would have quite enough to do to manage himself. I suggested to Walter that we should go up as a foursome, carrying only my personal belongings, and dig a cave by the "Moor's Head"; I would then try to go on, while they could come down again. Walter didn't like to refuse my request and the others agreed too. It was still fine in the morning. I broke the trail, while the others followed slowly carrying my stuff, but I could see that altitude was having its effects on all of them.

Small snow-slides kept on coming down the slopes, but not enough to be dangerous; they just gave us a cold shower. By four in the afternoon we were at the shoulder and traversing across below Rakhiot Peak, where I reinforced the rope anchorages, to make it easier for the others. I was in really fine form. While crossing a steep ice-slope Köllensperger put too much weight on the fixed rope, with the result that he pulled the old ice-axe out and himself went head over heels. Luckily the slope eased a little below, so that I was able to hold the lower end of the fixed rope and he came to rest just before a considerable cliff. A fall like that above 23,000 feet isn't any kind of a joke!

We were now in the thick mist again and the wind was gaining in strength. But we knew that in these weather conditions it would clear up again by nightfall. We were within about half an hour of the "Moor's Head"; true it was late in the evening, but we were nearly there and then the others could go down unladen. At that moment Kempter stopped suddenly and said: "I suggest we turn back—there's no point in this!"

That immediately awakened doubts, and very soon a defeatist mood had set in. Naturally I didn't want to influence anybody, but I was furious inside me. So down we went all the way again, carrying the heavy rucksacks; the whole effort had been a waste of time, and just as darkness fell we were back at the tents. It cleared up again during the night and there lay the beckoning summit, bathed in moonlight. But now I had had enough, too; no more for me!

Next day it was stormy, though it was noticeable that the layer of cloud only came up to 23,000 feet. Hermann's condition gave us cause for anxiety. So we decided to go down, probably for keeps. Heavily laden—for we didn't think we were coming up again—we moved off through the stormiest weather yet. The fog was so thick that we could hardly distinguish the snow a few yards ahead; we were swallowed up in a whitish-grey mass of even texture, with nothing to fix the eye in it, as I broke the trail. Suddenly I felt I was treading on air—a crevasse perhaps . . .?

Instead I sensed a yawning abyss. I had stepped out on to the cornice which overhangs the South Face.

We steered further to the left, on steeper ground. There was a rushing noise, which startled me; the snow was moving and avalanches were plunging away below my feet, starting as quite small snow-slides, then rapidly unfolding into the usual wedge shape. But I knew it was safe to climb down over the waste of scattered lumps in their wake, though I went in chest-deep in the loose snow-masses. It wasn't a question of walking any more, but of dragging oneself along. You pushed your body forward and your feet had to be pulled after it. I no longer noticed the weight of my pack; route-finding occupied the whole of my attention.

I climbed down another steep slope, which grew rapidly more precipitous, to my great discomfort; I therefore turned back and traversed to the left; just then the mist parted for a few seconds and I caught sight, back there, of a *bergschrund* and, a few yards below where I had been breaking the trail down the slope, an overhanging ice-cliff 150 feet high. Another proof that one often has a kind of sixth sense in dangerous situations.

The slopes steepened again, though we only realised it from the fact that the snow-lumps were now rolling downwards again. A dark shape loomed up, an ice-wall, whose outline I remembered clearly, and so I held on down and past it. There were from three to six feet of fresh snow on the faces, but at last we reached the broad plateau near Camp III and were out of the avalanche danger-zone. But where was the camp?

We were very lucky. I was apparently on our old track, for I could feel something hard under my boots and when I stepped to one side I went in further. That gave me my line, through the wildly deceptive mists. A shadow was moving behind me on that milk-white expanse; just as I was making out its contours we bumped noses—it was Walter.

At last we saw a touch of red—one of our pennants! We let out a yodel and in another 100 yards we were at the door of the kitchen-tent in Camp III, where the tireless Hans Ertl was getting a meal ready. He thought he was seeing ghosts when we loomed up at close quarters in the fog to confront him. He remarked approvingly that he hadn't expected to see us in such weather. Quite a tribute from Hans. . . .

He was alone in Camp III. The others had all gone down to Base Camp, worn out with mountain-lassitude, in search of rest and recuperation! Apparently no one was giving a hoot for the summit any more. Hans saw how depressed we were about our successive failures and tried to cheer us up by suggesting that there would be things one could do here even during the monsoon. He knew that from having been in the Karakorum years before with Professor Dyhrenfurth. We had plenty of provisions, so that there was no point in turning our backs on the mountain so soon. Then he told us that when, two days ago, he had come down from Camp IV with his three porters upon the empty tents, a porter came crawling out of one of them and explained in broken English that Aschenbrenner had taken all the Hunzas down with him except himself. As he didn't want to go down he had hidden himself and stayed up. He was our best man.

We were ravenous and Hans found it difficult to satisfy our hunger. We were particularly thrilled by the boiled goat's meat, which was really meant for the porters, but we let them share our rations in exchange. Then there were stewed plums into the bargain and in the evening Hans brewed us a soup from one of his countless recipes; they combine all three courses of a meal in one and taste wonderful. As usual, it cleared up in the evening.

We had a grand night's sleep and when the morning sun shone into our tents we all felt very differently about everything. The weather was glorious, with a rain-washed sky, and the Silbersattel, the gateway to the summit, shining wonderfully above us again. Down in the valleys, the last of the bad weather was moving away; the thick cloud agglomerations were continually dissolving. Had they given us the monsoon warning too early? For according to Radio Rawalpindi it ought even now to be breaking upon us with its storms.

A ring on the Teleport; a repeated call from Base Camp. Aschenbrenner, they said, was leaving for home to-morrow; we must come straight down to Base Camp. "We want to give Peter a proper send-off," was their one idea.

"Come down—what for?" we asked. "Why, when we still have a last chance of getting to the top?"

We couldn't comprehend it. The Teleport rang again: "Down you all come!" was the order, "you are all in need of rest and recuperation." And yet, only a few days ago, Aschenbrenner had been saying: "Now we must be tough and see the thing through." Something didn't seem to tally at all. . . .

They told us they had a new plan of campaign down in Base Camp.

"Couldn't we perhaps hear what it is?" asked Ertl.

"No," echoed the earphones. "Come down."

At that Hans could not control himself any longer and made it clear beyond all doubt to those down below that none of us except Köllensperger, who had raging toothache, had any intention of coming down. We were well acclimatised and saw no need for a descent to Base Camp in search of recovery. We intended to make the best use of the good weather. Camp III was as good a convalescent home as we could wish for.

"The weather is glorious up here," Hans explained to them, down there in the clouds. "It looks like holding; it's our last chance, and we're going to use it."

Quite unmoved, they repeated the order to withdraw, over the earphones. The barometer was going down and down, they told us, from 6,000 feet lower down in the valley.

Hans left it open to each of us to do what he thought right. Otto said he wouldn't go down, because he knew he would never come up again if he did; in any case it would lose too much time.

We spent those decisive hours sitting together in the kitchen-tent, in an atmosphere all our own. Why whistle us down like that, when there was really no sound reason? Hans made several requests down to Base Camp on our behalf; all were refused. So they were withdrawing all support from us. That meant a head-on clash, and the clash strengthened our unity. I wrote a quick letter home; it was dated June 30th and read:

"... we have been up here for weeks and can't bear to think it has been in vain. We are going up to Camp IV to-morrow and then to Camp V, close under the Silbersattel, from where we will set out on our summit bid. I hope it will come off this time; it will not be my fault if it doesn't! And I can tell you this—if we do get to the top, then it will have been entirely to our own credit...."

That evening in the kitchen-tent was a historic one!

... ABOVE 26,000 FEET

THE next morning was the first of July, and we were early on our way to Camp IV. The cloud-pack down in the lowlands had broken up and only a thin haze, the surest sign of good weather, slightly veiled the bottom of the valley. As far as the eye could see there was not the faintest suspicion of a cloud and it was undeniably cold—what more could we ask? Everything combined to heighten our drive to the topmost level. I was in terrific form; it looked like being my best day yet and, in spite of the wastes of snow, I hardly noticed the labour of breaking the trail. We all felt that it must come off this time.

In order to climb an "eight thousander" you have to have certain definite conditions, and it is extremely rare for them to coincide on a given day. One's own state of health and mind is subject to continual variations; one day you feel like uprooting trees, on another you are in a very poor state. One thing is certain: the right man has to be in the right place at the right time.

Otto Kempter wasn't feeling quite fit yet and wanted to stay one more day to recuperate at Camp III; he and his porters would follow next day. We took the other three Hunzas—the "Tigers", as we later christened them—along with us. They were very keen that day, but we couldn't risk loading them too heavily if they were to do their job next day. They only carried the bare essentials, a tent and some food, and of course the Teleport equipment; we carried our personal belongings.

There was a sudden ring on the radio, a call from Base Camp. Ertl took the receiver off.

It was another order to come down; they were bent on recalling us. Ertl began to doubt the sanity of the inmates of Base Camp, whose attitude seemed to us one of increasing self-righteousness and thick-headedness. Hans explained that they ought to be delighted that at last the wind stood fair up here and that we could go on without let or hindrance. At that point Aschenbrenner, who had not after all left Base Camp but had handed over the climbing leadership to Frauenberger the day before, came on the line. A fierce argument developed, punctuated by good strong Bavarian words. Aschenbrenner announced that he had taken over the climbing leadership again. . . .

On we went. An hour later we rang through to Base Camp and reported that we were making good progress on our way upward. Once again the order to retire came thundering over the air, this time in

Aumann's voice. We tried a third and last time to put things right.
"You'll be glad yet," we said. All to no purpose.

When this last attempt to convince them failed, Hans told them that
Faust wasn't the only poem he knew by Goethe, and finished the
conversation with a famous quotation. That was the last, pointless
talk that day.

We reached Camp IV by mid-day. It was almost invisible, except for
a few elevations in the otherwise level snow; those were obviously our
tents. The whole place had changed. The big hollow by the tents was
completely filled with snow, and we had to start a serious snow-clearing
operation, first establishing the exact position of our tents, some of
which were buried several feet deep in snow, with our ski-sticks. We
could hardly find the entrance to our snow-burrow, which still housed
valuable provisions; at last the ice-axe found a hole—the little opening
was jammed with ten feet of snow. It took hours to dig the whole camp
out.

Next, Hans and I each took a coil of rope in our packs and climbed
up the Rakhiot Face. We were much helped by the fixed ropes and soon
reached the traverse to the "Moor's Head", which we made safe with
this fresh supply of 600 feet of rope. Fixing pitons at such a height is
a laborious process. Then we cut a clean set of steps through the ice-
slope—a real spiral staircase. Necessary preparations these, if we
were to get the porters up there next day; and we were very much
heartened by having set up an unbroken rope-anchorage all the way
from Camp IV to the "Moor's Head". We reached our tents at seven
o'clock absolutely worn out after a strenuous but highly successful day.

Next morning, Ertl, always an early riser, was up betimes. The porters had headaches, which yielded to tablets, and they then seemed to
be fit and keen. Walter had done invaluable preparatory work the day
before by getting everything ready and even fitting the porters with their
crampons. We had been handling the men the last few days as if they
were on holiday. Walter, though a devout Catholic, had started praying
to Allah, to let them come along with us.

To our surprise there was a call from Base Camp. Perhaps they were
at last going to give us permission to go on?

It was however the usual order to come down at once. Walter argued
back and forth for half an hour before finally wringing the word of
absolution from them down there at the bottom. We breathed again
when we heard it: "All right, then. Go, in God's name; you have our
blessing!"

Otto had now joined us, feeling rather better. Our numbers were
complete, four Sahibs and three porters. I went ahead all the way,

W

improving the whole route, with Ertl following with his heavy film-camera to capture the climb, and behind him Walter, whom the porters called the "Kind Sahib". They came along behind him on the rope like trusting animals. Otto brought up the rear.

I couldn't suppress a shout of delight—the porters were coming along well; and when we saw them cross the *bergschrund* our faces positively beamed. They had shed all their fear of the heights and the Face didn't seem so full of terrors any more; a great achievement, for just to our left the ice fell away steeply into the far, green floor of the Rakhiot Nullah.

It took us a relatively short time to reach the traverse below Rakhiot Peak. I worked away at the rope, trying to anchor it better, but couldn't find a hold for the ice-axe anywhere. Meanwhile the porters were resting on the Rakhiot Shoulder, till presently I had succeeded in what I was doing and they were able to follow me, going very cautiously. Madi had to stay there, for we hadn't been able to find any crampons to match the size of his boots and he couldn't manage the steep rocks and icy slopes without. So he went back to Camp IV, while Walter shouldered his load. It was hard work making a track along the hard-pressed snow of the ridge which joins Rakhiot Peak to the Silbersattel. I stopped to take an almost involuntary look round.

Below us the steep face fell away to the level glacier-floor near Camp II. Further down lay the Camp Spur, a small rock-rib as seen from here, and on the slope alongside it some microscopic dots, the tents; still further down, the grey, débris-dirty tongue of the Rakhiot Glacier, crawling out like a snake towards the Fairy Meadow and Tato beyond it. Somewhere down there, in the greenery, near the further-most kink of the glacier must be Base Camp. We wondered if they were watching us. In the distance shone the icy Karakorum peaks, Gasher-brum, K²'s stupendous pyramid, Rakaposhi and innumerable unknown summits.

A sheer wall fell away to the south and it was only by taking a step or two forwards that we could see the upper half of that gigantic face, the South Face of Nanga Parbat, the highest mountain wall in the world, plunging 17,000 feet in one sheer sweep from the summit into the un-plumbed depths.

I went on ahead a little, more impatient than ever to get even a few feet nearer the summit; and as I forged across the "Moor's Head" over a gallery of magnificent cornices, new impressions broke upon me every few yards. We came to the snow-shovel we had left up at the rocky knob; from there on the ridge falls to a deep level indentation at about 22,700 feet. A sharp-crested snow-ridge leads up to the Silbersattel from it and I went on up it, anxious to site the camp, from which we were to tackle the summit, as high as possible. But soon I heard objections coming up from behind me, and saw the porters put their loads down, and I suggested that they be allowed to go down again, for we wanted to keep them in good humour, if they were to be ready to pull their weight during the next few days.

Hans and Walter would naturally have been only too pleased to stay up there, as they were going extremely well; but someone had to go down with the porters, and in any case there would only be room for two in Camp V, which was to consist only of a small hurricane tent. They sportingly stood down from the attack on the summit, being the older men, leaving the great chance to us youngsters; then, after a cordial leave-taking, they started down for Camp IV. It was most comforting to know that two comrades on whom we could rely to the last gasp would be protecting our rear. For there was, in truth, a horrid vacuum behind us—a gap of fully 10,000 feet; all our communications had been cut and the intervening camps were vacant. . . .

We stamped the snow flat in a little hollow and set up the tent on it for our night's shelter. The sun soon disappeared behind the Silberzacken on either side of the Saddle and the evening chill drove us under our protecting roof. We packed the rucksacks and made the next day's tea, which took up the last hours of July 2nd. It was soon dark and the two of us crouched huddled in our sleeping-bags over the hissing "Primus".

I said to Otto: "It's a waste of time our both hanging around. Do you mind if I have a bit of a lie down? I'll do breakfast in the morning to make up for it."

Otto agreed. I was very tired and tried to get to sleep before my cough could start racking me again, but I couldn't; it was eight o'clock. In spite of everything I could do, my thoughts, which are always terribly active at night, weighed heavily on me. An hour later Otto blew out the candle. My spirit was up there on the Summit again. Would we do it? I knew to-morrow must be the decisive day. We were still 4,000 feet below the top vertically, and nearly four miles from it as the crow flies. That was a tremendous distance; nothing like it had ever been done at such an altitude in the Himalaya, and it was wildly beyond reasonable practice. But what could we do? The porters wouldn't go any higher, and we had to make an effort without them. The two or three camps which there would have been, in normal circumstances, between us and the Summit simply didn't exist.

Then I went over the whole route again in my mind's eye. I knew the snow-ridge to the Silbersattel; it steepened further up, but I hoped not into polished ice, which would delay us. Aschenbrenner had once said that five hours was good time on it. Then the Summit Plateau, fearfully long, an unholy grind! We could only hope the snow up there wouldn't be too deep. But after that everything was guess-work, in unknown country. What would the descent to the Bazhin Gap, and the opposing ridge beyond it up to the Shoulder, be like? It had always been reckoned as relatively simple. And the last bit from the Shoulder on? Erwin Schneider had called it a "mown meadow, over which you could take anything from a push-cart to a light motor-car." So the whole thing might simply be a question of how we stood the altitude. The only thing that really worried me was the short rise to the Subsidiary Summit on the way back, an unavoidable matter of some 300 feet. The only way back to the camps lay over that Subsidiary Summit; that small ascent might be almost impossible if one was in an exhausted condition after one's labours. It would just *have* to be possible! To-morrow was the decisive day, one way or the other—certainly the most important day in my life. . . .

Otto lay motionless by my side, apparently sleeping peacefully. Suddenly a violent storm got up, rattling the sides of our tent, pressing on my side of the wall, pushing me more and more over to the middle. It blew across the ridge with hurricane force and went screaming down the South Face. Our tent was only 15 feet from the edge of the cornice; beyond lay the abyss, and our shelter was only anchored with quite ordinary, short rings. It was only meant to do one night's duty and we hadn't counted on that sort of storm at all. The idea of being hurled, tent and all, down the South Face terrified me. For a long time I lay wondering what we could do; something was bound to happen. If once the wind managed to get in under our flat roof, it would be the end of everything. I had to make a stupendous effort before I got out of my warm sleeping-bag into the open outside the tent. The sky was clear, but the gale threatened to blow me over. I used our ice-axes and ski-sticks to anchor the tent on the windward side, and went back to bed feeling mightily relieved. Now it could rage and rattle as much as it liked—and in any case it was only till to-morrow morning.

And so the hours went slowly by while I lay thinking and thinking, and still I couldn't get to sleep. The storm abated a little after midnight. I looked at my watch—it was half past twelve. It was still too early to get up; two o'clock was zero hour, so as to get as long a day as possible for the climb and avoid being benighted at the end of it.

It seemed ages before the luminous hand said one o'clock. I dressed in my sleeping-bag, boots and all, tying up my trouser legs particularly securely. Then my puttees over them; I had always found them a success. And, as a special measure for to-day, I even put on my blue Ninoflex overalls. I had on three layers of underwear. The cooker consented to burn after several attempts and I soon had a hot drink ready. It was half past one, time to rout Otto out.

I called to him, "Otto—time to get up!" No reply, no reaction of any kind. He must be sleeping uncommonly well. I took more energetic measures, shook him. "D'you hear?" I asked. "Almost two o'clock. Time to be going."

He mumbled something unintelligible. All I could get was: "Much too early. We said three o'clock yesterday."

"Even if we *did*," I explained, "we need the time. It's a long way and we have to be back by nightfall." It was past two o'clock and still Otto wouldn't budge. I simply couldn't understand it.

I tried to goad him into activity. "Otto, haven't you got any will-power?" I asked. "To-day of all days—when everything's set—and we're going for the Summit?"

I heard a mumble come from his sleeping-bag: "Not me—I ain't got none."

That settled it for me. I packed my little storm-rucksack with things for an attempt on my own. I put in bacon, Dextro, Ovosport and a few cuts of Neapolitan; I added warm clothing, my own Agfa Karat camera —the Expedition unfortunately didn't supply me with a Leica as sup- plementary equipment—then the little flask with Ertl's precious Coca- tee, which he had brought all the way from Bolivia, and my crampons. Finally, a packet of dried fruit and the Pakistan flag which Ertl had handed to me yesterday, and of course my Tirolese pennants, as Kuno and I had promised the members of our Climbing Club when they saw us off at Innsbruck Station. I had with me a few tablets of Paludin—a drug which stimulates the circulation and wards off frost-bite; a few pills of Pervitin in case of extreme necessity—we had carried them ever since Base Camp.

Just as I was on the point of leaving the tent at two-thirty I noticed that Otto was beginning to stir himself. I asked him if he meant to follow me and he said he did. So I gave him the bacon to put in his rucksack, so that I shouldn't have to carry everything.

As I left the tent I said: "You'll catch me up somewhere. I'll go ahead and break the trail for a while."

The wind had almost died away; the sky above my head was brilliant with stars, but it was dreadfully cold. The slender crescent of the waning moon threw its ghostly light on the sharp snow-crest tilting to the Silbersattel. The curved ice-edge between the dark heads of the Silber- zacken hung like a shining crescent of purest silver.

I stowed my ice-axe through my rucksack straps and used only my ski-sticks to support me, as I went on over the hindering crust, always hoping it would give way to firm snow; but as I went on up the ridge I continued to find the same trying conditions. Suddenly I was aware of an immense shadow, the shadow of a snow wall, the size of a block of buildings, in front of me; it was the "Whipped Cream Roll", that colossal cornice structure. There, in bygone years, fourteen first-class Sherpas had been in position, with another group of eleven up above, on the Silbersattel; and that expedition of outstanding mountaineers had nonetheless ended in a shattering tragedy. A sense of desolation swept over me. But you mustn't think of death or indulge in thoughts of horror when you are on your own. . . .

I went on up a steep funnel to the ridge, still on unusually deep snow, and, when eventually snow-conditions improved, the ridge steepened considerably. I could sense the great drop to the right as I looked into a vast dark pit. The ridge had been blown firm, thank goodness; it soon became so hard that I had to strap on my crampons. The only sound in the world was the crunch of my ten-pointers. Soon a keen wind, this time blowing up the South Face, struck me. I turned my face away and tried to work over to the north side again, on steep slopes, turning enormous broken-off cornices to the south. Here I met deep snow again, dislodged by the wind, till I came to a steep gully falling away between the dark guardian shapes of isolated rock-towers. I couldn't see very much, but I knew that the slightest slip here would land me at express speed many thousands of feet below. I no longer had the company of the moonlight, which was now cut off by the Silbersattel, but I managed to find my way pretty well. I traversed steep slopes on the northern side and was well satisfied with my progress. I was only taking two breaths to a stride, which is pretty good going.

The ridge steepened and I drew nearer to the rocks of the left-hand Silberzacken. A belt of light appeared to the north-east and slowly the sun's fiery globe rose over the ranges of the Karakorum, promising a glorious day. The sky was clear to its uttermost limits; down in the valleys, where no doubt they were still asleep, lay a transparent haze.

It was five o'clock. I sat down on the snow and ate a few crumbs while I watched the drama of day's rebirth. The magic world unfolded itself little by little. Things only dreamed of till now confronted my reeling eyes. That broad wedge of rock over yonder must be the Mustagh Tower, with a host of rock spires like Dolomites to the right of it. My eyes followed my own track downwards. Right at the bottom I saw a small dot, which was Otto; he must be fully an hour behind me!

Soon the sun had enough strength to bring me comfort. The finely-drawn curve of the Silbersattel now seemed quite near, with bare ice glittering on it; I ought to be there in half an hour. I moved on over more crust, with huge cornices above me, followed by wind-whorls; compact snow followed with something hard underneath it, till I reached that shining strip of bare ice. I cut step after step in it, moving with extreme care, for one careless movement, one small slip would certainly finish up 6,000 feet below in the neighbourhood of Camp II.

What about my half-hour now? I had been climbing for a full hour since then and the Silbersattel seemed just as far away as ever. The thin air robs one of every means of measurement, makes a mockery of all one's assessments. It was two hours before there opened before me a vast snow-plateau, seamed by wind-drifts many feet high, with blue, bare ice between them—the gateway to the Summit, the Silbersattel. I pressed on upwards, anxious to see how the way continued; but the slope hadn't flattened out yet. Somewhere at the back a slender snow-spire raised its tip—the Subsidiary Summit. Then I could see the whole of the plateau, a gigantic expanse of level snow. I was on the sill of the Silbersattel, at the rim of the summit snow-plateau, 24,443 feet up. I sat down again in the snow and took a modest swig from my flask. Otto was only at the beginning of the traverse down below. To the right and left of me stood two tall pillars, the Silberzacken; the western spike was quite sharp and the desire to climb it almost overwhelmed me. Beyond the furrow of the Indus, the Hindu Kush and Karakorum peaks ranged far and wide; indeed, I could see further still—those mountains in the distance must be the Pamirs, in Russia!

I couldn't stay long; I had still far to go and mustn't waste a precious moment. I thought for a while; ought I to wait for Otto? But surely he would catch me up, for the way ahead was laborious to a degree, an endless undulating way, a kind of obstacle race over steps many feet high. I know there have been plenty of climbers who found themselves fully capable of action at this altitude, even when, like myself, they had no oxygen. And I was fully acclimatised to the height. Yet I found it terribly difficult to make any progress; and I was breathing five times to each step I took. The sun was beginning to be unbearably hot, too. Could it be radiated heat? How extraordinary, I thought: the snow is dry, the air cold, yet the sun's heat is merciless, parching my body, drying out the mucous membrane, lying heavily on my whole being like a ton load! It grew more and more insupportable; I sat down again and tried to eat, but I couldn't swallow a morsel. If only I had the bacon with me, I thought; I could have got that to go down. But Otto had it in his rucksack. So on I went.

I forced my way on and up, but had to rest more and more frequently; and so I dragged myself over the rim of the Summit Plateau. I hoped for a fresh breeze off the South Face; but there wasn't a breath of air stirring. I wondered whether it was always like that just before the monsoon breaks; I knew the English climbers used that weather-phase on Everest. These are the only windless days in such altitudes; but it can be a very dangerous time, because storms often break without any warning. I thought of Aschenbrenner and Schneider, who had been up here, close under the Subsidiary Summit, nineteen years before. They had told how their cigarette-smoke had risen straight into the air —yet the very next day that inferno had started to rage. . . .

Now the slopes tilted more steeply to the Subsidiary Summit. It was ten o'clock. I lay in the snow face downwards on my rucksack, panting, panting, panting, This looked like the end. . . . Far away over there, on the Silbersattel, I could see a dot—Otto. How glad I should have been to have him here with me, not just because of the bacon, either. I was so tired. Was it hunger, or thirst, or was I just feeling the altitude? I could now see almost horizontally across to the Bazhin Gap, no great distance away; but between me and it lay a vertical wall, with rocks in it, the South Face. To try to cross it alone would be suicide. I racked my brains how to circumvent the rise to the Subsidiary Summit. Perhaps I could do it on the northern side, and so be back by the evening? Yes, but if I was going to try it, I should have to travel much lighter, for my rucksack was weighing terribly on my shoulders; true, it wasn't very heavy, but up here every extra ounce was an affliction. Food was useless, seeing that I couldn't force myself to eat, so that commodity could well be left behind. I looked over again at Otto: the dot was motionless. I could not wait for him.

I stowed the rucksack away in the hollow of a wind-furrow, tied my Anorak around my middle, slung my axe sword-fashion by my side, pushed my flask, spare clothes, summit flags, into various pockets, hung my camera round my shoulders, with a spare film in the case, and started off again. Then I remembered that my heavy pullover was still in the rucksack . . . but I hadn't the energy to go those few yards back to it. I tried to persuade myself that the thin one I had on would do, as I should certainly be back here by the evening. For a few minutes I felt relieved, but very soon all the old sensations had set in again. One of the most painful efforts was getting to my feet again after rests; all I wanted to do was to stay on the ground and sleep. The dark background of the Indus Gorge, which now appeared over the Silbersattel, gave some rest to my eyes; I should dearly have liked to remove those bothersome snow-goggles, but that was against the rules, even when taking photographs—

the light is too fierce and dazzling. There were occasional small crevasses, but they were quite easy to detect and avoid; then I reached a point about 25,600 feet up close under the Subsidiary Summit, whose northern flank I then traversed, ploughing my lonely furrow over endless undulations in the snow. Looking back, I caught a glimpse of Otto, the size of a pin's head, this time below the Silbersattel; he seemed to have given it up, and wasn't coming up any more, so I went on by myself. I could have bagged the Subsidiary Summit, quite a prize at 26,248 feet, but that would not have satisfied me. Crossing snow-rib after snow-rib I reached a small saddle 120 feet below the Subsidiary Summit, at the very top of the Plateau. I gave a miss to the short slope leading to that peak, for I had to husband my strength.

Below me lay the Diamir Gap, easy to cross, but involving an infuriating loss of height. It must be possible to get across the Bazhin Gap somehow from here, across uncharted ground, on which no man had ever set foot. A steep, rocky crag lay before me, with a steep snow-slope at its foot and a sharp rock-ridge opposite, a slabby face scored by countless gullies, and above it the Shoulder. I found it exceedingly painful to contemplate so great a loss of height, and longed to be over there, across the Gap. I climbed down a gully, crossed some boulders to the left, but soon found myself facing a vertical rock-face, to climb which seemed to me a sheer impossibility. I was finding great difficulty now in keeping myself upright. I kept on sitting down on the rocks, wanting to go to sleep, overcome by a terrible feeling of lassitude. But I had to push on; the final prize glittered before me and some secret urge drove me on, its daemonic energy planting one foot ahead of the other, endlessly.

I climbed back and tried higher up, where there seemed a better chance. Steep gullies full of ice led downwards; I went on, asking myself the grim question, "Can I get any further after the next corner of rock, if not, will I have the strength to come back this way?" I remembered the Pervitin, knowing its effects and also its reactionary after-effects, and fought a fearful battle with myself. My body wanted it desperately, but my mind wouldn't take it. I thought I could get as far as the Bazhin Gap without drugs.

I finally reached the Gap at two o'clock and stood in that deep notch between the subsidiary and main summits at 25,658 feet. Completely exhausted, I fell down on the snow. Hunger racked me, thirst tortured me, but I knew I had to save the last drop as long as possible. Perhaps Pervitin was the answer? It couldn't be many hours before I got back again and the effects would last that long. Doubtfully, I swallowed two tablets and waited for them to take effect; nothing seemed to happen and I felt no benefit. Or was it that they had already done their work

and that without them I would never have been able to get up again?
You never know with tablets!

Once on my feet again, I clambered along an enormous chain of
cornices and could soon see the rock-ridge rising to the Shoulder
straight ahead of me. I had often looked at it from Camp IV and the
"Moor's Head", but had never been able to make up my mind definitely
about it. I had remained sceptical about it; now my pessimistic views
seemed to be confirmed. It was a sharp rock-ridge that ran up in a
series of saw-toothed crags, dominated by rock-towers, and there was
snow and ice all over it. Up above was a knife-sharp crest crowned with
a rim of cornices; while to the right a slabby face fell hundreds of feet
to the Diamir Gap. I could not guess what happened below that; but
I knew that I had that terrific South Face on my left. Out of force of
habit I searched the face on the right for possibilities and eventually
detected some weak spots in it. If it wouldn't go by the ridge, that
would be the only solution; but the last snow-slope had a steep rock-
step above it.

I stood on the sharp-crested snow right at the foot of the rock-ridge
and looked out over my boots at the abysmal deeps of the Rupal Nullah
17,000 feet below. The awesome sight hardly affected me, so apathetic
had I become. Perhaps the climbing on the rock wouldn't be so bad
after all. . . . .

For a very short time on the first short pitch it wasn't; then exhaustion
set in again. Completely breathless, I had to sit down on the next step
and pant for a longish time. Then I went on to the knife-edge, where,
in order to avoid the slabby rock to the right, I had to tread on the
snow-cornice. Would it hold me? Through a crack I caught a glimpse
of that horrific southward plunge, whose upper half was an Eiger Wall
in itself. The delicate cornices arched from one rocky head to the next
like carefully built bridges.

A vertical step lay ahead—I only hoped I had the strength to climb
it. I got a few feet up it in a snow-filled crevice; with my last ounce I
pulled my body up over the rocky crest and lay prone for a long time on
a flat slab, fighting for breath; then I sat up. There was the Summit at
last, but still a long way off. I felt quite desperate; but I couldn't give
in now. I decided not to look and find each time that the Summit had
come no nearer. I would set myself my own target, fixing my eyes on
some point only a few yards away, and that would be my target for the
time being. I would look at the next step, the next ledge, the next spike
on the ridge, and not until I got there would I look any further ahead,
and then only for 10 or 20 yards. I was no longer interested in the
Summit. I had stopped thinking about it; I had in fact stopped thinking

altogether. I walked and walked, climbed and climbed, for hours and hours. My earlier climbs had taught me not to give in before I got to the top; and I had never given up or turned back on them, just out of bodily weakness. But this was quite different; now it was an incredible irresistible urge that drove my exhausted body onward.

After an age the Shoulder loomed into my field of vision. The ridge grew flatter and more broken. Just when I thought I was over the worst, a sheer tower unexpectedly barred my way—a real *gendarme*. It is a habit of *gendarmes* to bar the way, but this one seemed to me to have put a final halt to my activities. It shot up nearly 200 feet above a quite insignificant indentation in the ridge. Had I really got to admit defeat so close to the end? It almost looked like it. I knew it couldn't be climbed direct, without a rope or any other climbing apparatus; in any case it would be crazy, seeing that I was alone. At first I didn't even consider the south side and tried the only possibility—to the north. I traversed across the broken rock of a rock scoop, in which a small vertical ice strip, equally brittle, interposed. There were lumps of loose rock hanging from the solid mountainside. I turned a rock-edge and found myself after about a hundred feet face to face with a projecting cliff; 15 feet below me there was a partly snow-filled gully leading straight up to the crest of the ridge. But how was I to get into the gully? It was protected above and below by overhanging crags. I was now prepared to risk anything. With my crampons still on my boots, I climbed the rapidly steepening face of high, friable, rusty-brown gneiss by a crack which gave me my only hope.

Once again I pocketed my gloves, and jammed myself in the bottom of the crack, as I had so often done in my own native mountains; but now speed was the essence. It was only about 30 feet, but my crampons got wedged in the narrow crevice, my fingers threatened to give up altogether. It was climbing of the severest order, comparable with the Salzburg route on the East Wall of the Watzmann. I had that horrible feeling in my fingers again; yet, only a few feet above me, I knew the way lay clear to the Shoulder. It just had to be done and presently I was safely in the gully. They had been terrible minutes.

That put the tower behind me. A short, much less steep rock pitch and a steep firm snow-slope now lay before me; the tension relaxed. I was on Nanga Parbat again, and appallingly tired. I simply slumped to the ground and lay there fighting a desperate battle for that essential commodity—air. All the old altitude symptoms were there again; only worse—or was it just my raging thirst? I forced myself on again, struggling to gain every yard, and after a long time gained the crest of the Shoulder. I was over 26,000 feet up, and it was six o'clock in the evening. The realisation of that gave me a horrid fright; I had thought it would only take an hour from the Bazhin Gap. I was finished. For my eyes the Summit was almost near enough over there for me to touch it; for my condition it was an eternity away. I took a last gulp from the flask; surely that would help!

Apparently the Cocatee had its effect. I felt a little fresher and after laying everything I could dispense with on a boulder, I staggered to my feet again. I took nothing but my ice-axe, the flags and my camera. Indescribably wearily I dragged myself along a horizontal rock-ridge. I realised that I was only obeying the dictates of a subconscious which had only one idea—to get up higher; my body had long since given up. I moved forward in a kind of self-induced hypnosis.

To the south the steep snow and ice slopes plunged away; to my surprise great bouldery rocks appeared to the north, rising steeply. I was astonished, and tried to think why. Did the gales up here sweep all the snow from the rock, so that it couldn't settle? I crossed some gullies and short patches of snow and stumbled laboriously over boulders to the foot of the summit structure; the highest thing I could see was a projecting rock, behind which the Summit must be. But how far? And had I the strength to get there? That ghastly fear obsessed me. I could no longer stand upright; I was but the wreck of a human being. So I crawled slowly forward on all fours, drawing imperceptibly nearer to that rocky spur, towards which I was struggling with such grim doubts.

To my joy and relief, there was nothing but a little crest, a short snow-slope, only a few yards long, easier now, easier. . . .

I was on the highest point of that mountain, the Summit of Nanga Parbat, 26,620 feet above sea-level. . . .

Nothing went up any further, anywhere. There was a small snow-plateau, a couple of mounds, and everything fell away on all sides from it. It was seven o'clock. There I was on that spot, the target of my dreams, and I was the first human being since Creation's day to get there. But I felt no wave of overmastering joy, no wish to shout aloud, no sense of victorious exaltation; I had not the slightest realisation of the significance of that moment. I was absolutely all in. Utterly worn out, I fell on the snow and stuck my ice-axe upright in the hard-beaten snow, just as if it were something I had practised over and over again. I had been on the way for seventeen hours on end and every step had become a battle, an indescribable effort of will-power. I was only thankful not to have to go uphill any more, not to have to think about the route ahead, not to have to keep on looking upwards with the frightful question, "Would I get there?" always torturing my mind.

I took the Tirolese pennant out of my Anorak and tied it to the haft of my ice-axe. The sun was low on the horizon and I should have to hurry if I were to get any pictures. I knelt down, with the axe and the pennants in the foreground and, behind it, a glimpse of the Silbersattel, part of the Plateau and the drop to the South Face. The long shadows of evening were creeping across the scene and I could identify the wind-flutings on the Silbersattel clearly. There was a bit of the ridge down to Camp V in the picture too; and over the top of the axe, far and small and low, the peaks of the Hindu Kush and the Karakorum.

I finished the film and wound it off; then I opened the back of my "Karat 36" with great care, for I knew how important that picture was, and put in a new Agfa colour-film. In spite of my utter exhaustion, my mind attended to these operations with precision. Having complied with the wishes of my fellow club-mates in the Tirol, I removed the Tirolese pennant, pocketed it and then fastened the Pakistani flag to the axe, as agreed. I took a few more quick shots—the light was getting rather bad and I had to use my exposure-meter. I took one towards the Subsidiary Summit, one towards Rakhiot Peak and Camp V, and one straight down into the Rupal Nullah, so as to capture that terrific downward view as well. That was sufficient documentary evidence and I put the camera away.

Not till then could I take a quiet look round. On every side steep faces fell from that little platform of a summit towards the valleys appallingly far below. They fell away so steeply that the first objects the eye could fasten on anywhere were the débris-covered glacier-tongues crawling out into the nullahs thousands of feet down in the abyss. I felt as if I were floating high above everything, out of all relationship with the Earth, severed from the world and all humanity. It was like being on a tiny island in an enormous ocean. To the north, a hundred miles away, great ranges melted into the distance; to the east, a similar sea of peaks, innumerable, ice-clad, unclimbed, unapproached—the Himalaya, though it was but a small sector of that mighty mountain range my eyes beheld. Westwards, too, as far as the eye could scan, rose a wall of great peaks; only to the south did the land fall deeply away to a great, black, haze-enveloped plain, where lay Pakistan and India. Plumb below me rose a chain of 17,000-foot peaks, revealing their height by the snow which just lay on their topmost crests; and far out and away beyond them there fell upon the land the mighty shadow of the pyramid at whose extreme point I stood.

The sky was flawless; not a cloud stirred in the length and breadth of the firmament. The sun went down behind a mountain range and in the instant the cold was penetrating. I suppose I had been up there half-an-hour, and it was time to be going down. As a sure sign of my ascent—for nobody could possibly have observed my movements—and as a symbol, too, I left my ice-axe with the Pakistan emblem, the white half-moon and star, on a green background, up there. I also carried a few stones to add to the summit-rocks as a small cairn, but very soon found the effort too exhausting. It was sufficient, though; something built of man's hand now stood there.

I took a last look back, and turned to go. Then I remembered another promise I had given and went back those few yards to add a small stone for my wife, waiting at home so anxiously; then I started down for the Shoulder. I immediately felt a change come over my body; I was suddenly much fresher, probably because I knew I had accomplished what I had set out to do. I moved quite quickly over ground where I had crawled on the way up and was soon back at my belongings, where I had left them at the Shoulder. I knew well enough the difficulties of the rock-ridge running down from there; it would be almost impossible to descend it. I had only just managed that last *gendarme* on the way up and I had no rope with me. So I had no choice but to find another way down.

There was a steep ice-slope falling away below me, whose bottom part I could not see. There might be gullies running down from it, and it might do. I had taken a good look at the right-hand side on the way up and spotted a number of possible routes. If I could go down that way I could easily climb the snow-slopes to the Subsidiary Summit from the bottom of the rocks, 1,200 feet lower down. That must be the top of the rib by which Mummery, that great mountaineer, whose monument the glaciers and peaks of Nanga Parbat had become 58 years before, tried to scale the mountain. And I had been granted the luck to be the first to reach its Summit!

I couldn't yet grasp that fact. All I wanted was to get down to its foot again, back to people, back to life. . . .

So I went northwards down the ice-slope, losing height rapidly. The first part looked all right, but the rest was conjecture. I was very glad of my crampons, for ski-sticks are no substitute for an ice-axe; but I would far sooner do without the axe now than without the sticks later on. I still hoped to reach the Bazhin Gap before nightfall, so as to be able to cross the Plateau by moonlight and so get down to Camp V without having to camp for the night in the open at such a height. Suddenly I felt something dangerously loose and wobbly on my left foot; I was startled to see the strap-fastening of my crampon disappearing down below me. The crampon had come off and almost precipitated a disaster for me. I grabbed it quickly, but only just in time; I had, however, no spare strap with me, not even a piece of string.

And even if I had, how could I fasten the crampon again in so exposed a position?

I was standing on one leg, with my two ski-sticks as my only support. To my right and left, above and below, there was nothing but snow and ice pressed bone-hard by the winds. I tried to scrape a shallow dent with the points of my sticks; it wasn't so much a dent as a scrape, sufficient to give my smooth boot-sole a moment's hold while I moved the foot that still had a crampon a step further on, where the points could get a bite. . . . It was a most hazardous movement, but it was successful. In time I reached a snow-rib, but found I could not proceed downwards any further; so I tried to get off the slope by the shortest possible way, traversing towards the ridge, balancing from one snow-rib to another, until I felt rock under my rubber sole again. I moved like one walking in his sleep; there is no other way of explaining how I escaped from that slope. . . .

I got back into the gully behind the *gendarme*, and made swifter progress; the actual climbing occupied the whole of my attention to such an extent that I almost forgot how high up I was. The rock grew slabbier and I worked my way carefully down a smooth, fairly holdless rib. Then it suddenly began to get dark—could it be nightfall already? I had been so preoccupied that I had quite forgotten the time. I searched frantically for a better perch, for it was impossible even to stand where I was. In an astonishingly short time it was pitch dark; there is no noticeable twilight in these parts. Where could I find a place in which to spend the night?

At last I found something firm beneath my feet, and immediately felt safe again. It was a stance with room for both feet on it, though it was too small to sit down on; I should have to spend the night standing up. Over there, towards the ridge, I could see a big, dark shadow thrown by a huge block; I could sit, or even lie down, over there, but the rock in between was polished and glazed with ice and to attempt the passage in the dark seemed too great a risk. For better or for worse, I should have to make do with my perch. I put on everything I had with me, my woolly well over my ears, my balaclava well down over my head, two pairs of gloves, drew them all as tight as I could, and settled down to my long wait. I had a rock face, angled at from 50 to 60 degrees, as a back-rest. I could have done with my heavy pullover, but that was far away, in the rucksack which I had left behind, down there. . . . Otherwise I was splendidly equipped, thanks to everything the Schuster Sports' shop in Munich had done to carry out my personal wishes, particularly in respect of my splendid boots, which were such a comfort in my hour of need. Of course, I should have had a bivouac-sack to protect me from the cold, and a rope to stop me falling off the mountain, but somehow I viewed the prospect of the night which lay ahead of me without any great qualms. I was amazingly relaxed; everything seemed so normal. It had to be like this; all part and parcel of what I was doing. I almost faced that night at 26,000 feet with complete equanimity. I knew I should have been much better off higher up, where I could have lain down, but this is where I was, and that was all there was to it. Then I remembered the Padutin—a drug which stimulates the circulation and protects one against frostbite. I forced down five of the little pellets, which almost stuck in my throat. My left hand clutched the ski-sticks; I hoped they wouldn't escape my grip, for I should need them, how I should need them! My right hand clung to that solitary hold. I looked at my watch again—it was nine o'clock. I prayed the wonderful weather would hold. . . .

Utter weariness came over me. I could hardly stay upright, and my head kept falling forwards, my eyelids pressed on my eyes like lead, and I dozed off. . . .

I woke with a start, and straightened my head up. Where was I? I realised with a pang of fright that I was on a steep rock slope, high up on Nanga Parbat, exposed to the cold and the night, with a black abyss yawning below me. Yet I did not feel in the least as if I were 26,000 feet up and I had no difficulty with my breathing. I tried hard to keep awake, but sleep kept on defeating me. I kept on dozing off, and it was a miracle that I didn't lose my balance.

Oh God, where are my sticks? Keep calm! You've got hold of them. I clutched them in a grip of steel. Cold shivers ran down my spine, but I didn't care; I knew it would have to be a tough night. I wondered whether my mind was by now in such control of my body that I could no longer feel bodily discomfort. I longed for the moon to come; if it came out, as I hoped, at midnight, I could start on down, and the night would not seem so long. Next time I tore my eyelids apart, the plateau below was agleam with silver; everything down there, the Subsidiary Summit, the North Summit, shone in a ghostly light, edged by dark shadows. Where I stood, it was still dark; why didn't the moonlight come? It looked as though I should after all have to spend the whole, long night till the dawn came, on this minute spot. By now that seemed to be bordering on the impossible.

I kept on looking across at the dark shadow of the block over there, thinking how nice it would be to be sitting down. An occasional breath of wind moved gently over the slope, then everything was still again, in the wide hush of eternity. . . .

I discovered that my body had after all not achieved insensibility. The cold grew more and more unbearable; I felt it on my face and, in spite of my thick gloves, on my hands, which were nearly numb, and worst of all in my feet. It crept further and further up my body; my toes had long ago gone dead, though at first I had tried to keep them moving by trampling on my little stance, but I had to be careful, because it was loose. Never mind, I thought: I had often had cold, dead feet before without suffering serious frostbite as a result.

I was caught up again in the immensity of the night . . . in the glory of the starlit sky stretched overhead. I gazed up at it for a long time, seeking out the Great Bear and the Pole Star over there on the horizon. A light flared down in the Indus Valley—a car probably. Then it was dark again.

My body began to take charge again. Hunger and thirst asserted their needs, but I had nothing to give them. Time passed incredibly slowly, so slowly that I thought the night could never come to an end. Then, behind a toothy mountain range in the far distance, a streak of light broadened and rose gradually higher—the new-born day. For me, its light was the light of salvation.

There were still stars in the sky, and the morning never seemed to come. I looked longingly across to that strip of sky, till my eyes grew almost fixed; for that was where the sun must be coming up. Eventually the last stars grew dim—day was dawning at last.

I leaned against my rock, motionless, my right hand still clinging to the hold, my left still gripping the sticks like a vice. My feet were like blocks of wood, my boots frozen stiff, my rubber soles clogged with rime. The sun's first rays fell on me with their blessed comfort, resolving my stiffness and immobility. I began to move again and got back into the gully. But now I really had to watch my step; everything was twice as dangerous under the smooth glaze of ice. I went down in the gully for ages, still wearing a crampon on one boot, while the other reposed in my Anorak pocket.

During those hours of extreme tension I had an extraordinary feeling that I was not alone. I had a partner with me, looking after me, taking care of me, belaying me. I knew it was imagination; but the feeling persisted. . . .

There was a steep pitch interrupting the gully; its rocks were splintery and friable. I had to take my gloves off and pocket them, while I tried to regain the bed of the gully; but everything I touched came away. It seemed too great a risk, for one small slide or fall would be the finish of me, and I should certainly drag with me my companion and friend, non-existent though he be. . . . I had to exert extreme care every foot of the way down.

In the mountains at home I should just have jumped down into the
gully. Here I climbed back again and wanted to put my gloves on once
more. I couldn't find them. Horrified, I asked my mysterious companion:
"Have you seen my gloves?"

I heard the answer quite clearly: "You've lost them." I turned round
and there was nobody there. Had I gone crazy?

Was I being mocked by some phantom? I recognised a familiar voice,
but did not know to which of my friends it belonged. All I knew was
that I knew it. . . . I looked for my gloves, but couldn't find them anywhere. They must be lying about somewhere, or could they have fallen
down the slope? I hunted through all my pockets again, and as I did so
I remembered the terrifying tragedy of Herzog's hands on Annapurna
—till I discovered my reserve pair of gloves and felt better again.

I went on down, succeeded in getting into the snow gully and out of
it again on to the rocks beyond. There on my right, almost level with
me, was the Bazhin Gap; but I had to go still further down, to the bottom
of the rocks. The whole of this time my companion was with me, that
staunch companion whom I never saw, and whose presence was more
definite at danger spots. The feeling calmed me, lulled me into security:
I knew that if I slipped or fell, this "other man" would hold me on the
rope. But there was no rope; there was no other man. A moment or
two later I would know that I was quite alone and dared not risk one
moment's heedlessness. .

There was one more steep pitch, an almost vertical crack, which took
all the breath out of me; then at last I was on the snow. I had escaped
from the clutches of the Face, which now lay behind me. Steep snow
slopes, hard as iron, led down to the rocks which plunged from the
subsidiary summit. Here crampons were indispensable, and I tried
to fasten the second one to my foot; I used the cord of my overall-
trousers to tie it to my boot, but after a few steps it was at right-angles
to the sole. Patiently I fastened it on again, only to find the spikes
standing away from the sides of my boot very soon afterwards, so that
I had to repeat the dangerous game every ten or twenty yards. Bending
down was a fearful exertion, which got me completely bemused. I raged
at my partner behind me for giving me such a wretched crampon. (He
was still following close behind me!)

Then I sat down on the snow again, with my head in my hands,
resting and panting. My ankles ached from being flexed so much and
I found the going fearfully exhausting, but I eventually reached the
rocks below the Diamir Gap, where I dived under a huge snow-mush-
room for shade. The way the time went was fantastic; it was noon
already. I was racked by a terrible thirst, but had nothing left to drink.

The sun burnt viciously down, but there was no water anywhere, though the rocks were plastered with ice; not a drop trickled from them.

Now I had to face the rise to the Subsidiary Summit, which had worried me on my way up. I wanted to recover a bit before tackling it and sat down in the snow again. My reasoning processes were suddenly blotted out, though it was quite a pleasant feeling.

I opened my eyes and looked about me. I must have fallen asleep, for another hour had gone by. Where was I, anyway? I saw tracks and cairns everywhere. Was I on a ski-ing trip? Gradually consciousness returned: I was nearly 26,000 feet up on Nanga Parbat, and all alone. The ski-tracks were nothing but wind channels and the cairns over there—rock towers. Up among the rocks of the Subsidiary Summit I heard voices, or was it only the wind? Perhaps my friends were waiting for me up there. I staggered to my feet again with a great effort and circumvented a steep crag, from which a rubbish shoot went up. I worked my way up it from stone to stone, hanging on to my ski-sticks for support. After every step my weary body sank down on the débris, and this time I really thought my strength had given out for good. How often have I said it? But I had to go on, for I knew there was no other way of getting back to living people; so I had to get up that slope. It took me an hour to cover a hundred feet, and as I felt then, the long ascent I had made yesterday seemed more and more improbable. Some flat snow-patches followed, apparently without end; but I had reached the Diamir Gap at the lowest point between the Subsidiary and North Summits.

Before me there now lay once again that enormous wavy snow plateau, scored and furrowed—far away behind it, the Silbersattel. My eyes sought the horizon, working inwards over the sill of the Silbersattel, across and along the plateau's snow up towards where I stood. I hoped to see someone coming up to meet me, but could distinguish nobody. If only I had a drop of tea—one single drop—that might see me safely across the next few hours. I could think of nothing but drinkable liquid; my thirst had become a torture of hell, driving me literally mad. I had swallowed my last drop yesterday, and now there was this murderous heat, this positive dehydration. My gums were like straw, my blood must be thick and viscous. . . .

As I went slowly on I kept my eyes fixed on the Saddle. At last I saw some dots, or were my eyes deceiving me? No, those must be my friends. I wanted to shout and cheer, but could not produce a sound. Anyway, they were coming. Should I wait for them? No, it was too far for them to come, I would go on and meet them. I went on, step by step, mechanically, stumbling, weary. Next time I looked across the waves of the plateau the dots had vanished. The disappointment was shattering, till I caught sight of them again; then—no—the vast expanse of snow was empty! I was definitely alone in that endless, hopeless waste of ice.

Hunger became as unbearable as thirst. I knew there was a packet of Ovosport in my rucksack, somewhere over there. Somewhere . . . where? I crossed slopes without end, going a long way off the direct line, just to get a bite of something, in the hope of renewing my strength. All the time I had to take great care not to hurt my ankles, which were giving out on me, with my crampons. A slight sprain would be enough to put paid to me. I looked at the Saddle again; the dots were in a different place and I realised that they were rocks on some mountains thrusting up from behind it.

But this time I heard voices, most distinctly. I heard them calling me by name: "Hermann—Hermann!" I even heard people talking to each other; but there was nobody in sight. These must be hallucinations. Could this be the beginning of the end, or was it the end itself? Where was that rucksack of mine, which was so difficult to find?

Perhaps I could find my old track, by climbing down and across to the right. It went on interminably, back and forth, up and down. I knew I couldn't keep it up much longer. The only thing that kept me going was the thought of having some food inside me. I had almost decided to give up the search, when I saw the clear imprint of a boot—I was back on my trail. Which way, though, to my rucksack—up or down? I went on down, but was soon racked by maddening doubts. I ought to be able to see a rucksack. . . .

I found it at last. I fell down and rummaged in it as I lay there, but couldn't locate any Ovosport; instead I found a package of Dextroenergen. When I tried to swallow a tablet it stuck like flour in my mouth, so I did the only thing left and grabbed some snow. I wasn't keen about it, as I knew it might have disastrous results, but there was no other way out. I crushed the tablets, mixed them with the snow and ate the remaining mess. It tasted wonderful and revived me beyond expectation; I found I could swallow again, there was spittle in my mouth once more and I tried to move on again. Very soon, however, my thirst was more searing than ever, my tongue stuck to my gums, my throat was as raw as a rasp and I foamed at the mouth a good deal. So I took another dose of the same brew, but the relief was very short, and my thirst came back even more unendurably than before. The snow robbed me of my last vestige of strength and my progress across the plateau became a veritable torture.

I moved on at a snail's pace, finding it necessary to take twenty breaths to a single stride. Every yard or two I fell down on the snow. My ski-sticks were my last succour; Samaritan-fashion they supported me and saved my life.

I suppose I fell down again and slept. When I woke my eyelids were like lead, and when I tried to get up I collapsed again, utterly exhausted. This was it, I thought—journey's end. . . . But the will to live still flickered in me. I looked for my sticks; only one of them was there. Fear gripped me, but it acted like a whip-lash, revitalising my body. I saw now that the other stick had rolled down a little way, and crawled after it on all fours. Once I had them both firmly in my grip, I was able to get up again, to stand, to move on. . . .

I could see across to Rakhiot Peak now, and there was a dot—the tent. Over by the slope I saw what must be rocks or friends. I tried to shout, though the distance was far too great, but I had no voice. Perhaps they would see me if I waved the ski-sticks. . . .

Evening was drawing on; once again the sun was going down and long shadows moved slowly across the snow. I knew I could not survive a second night in the open and fought my way onward, using my last reserves. I stumbled on, pursued, hunted and confused by my own shadow. I was no longer myself; I was only a shadow—a shadow behind a shadow. I cursed the wind-whorls which made my way so fearfully difficult. At length I was at the plateau's lowest dip, with only a few hundred yards separating me from the broad sweep of the Silbersattel, opening like a gateway before me; how the tempests must have raged to produce the upheavals on these flat expanses! There were no means of avoiding the snow-structures, many feet high, however much I tried to skirt them. I was staggering like a drunkard, falling, crawling, standing, walking, falling again . . . then I remembered the Pervitin again. It was the only chance; its brief renewal of my strength might last long enough for me to get down to the tent. That is, if I hadn't already used the last reserve of strength left in me, for I felt absolutely finished. Blood and spittle were coming out of my mouth, which was completely gummed up; and I had to force the three tablets down as if they were wooden wedges. I began counting the yards, as the rim of snow drew nearer.

At half past five I was on the further rim of the Silbersattel, and at last I could see down to the Rakhiot Glacier and the Camps on it once again. The whole route of the climb lay spread before me, and I could see the tents clinging, half buried, to the slopes. It was an indescribably comforting sight; I felt just as if I were coming home. Yet I could see nobody moving about down there. Surely they could not have evacuated the camps? Peace unbroken reigned over everything, not a soul stirred, not a sound marred the silence. I looked across to Rakhiot Peak and again I noticed the dark spot, the little hurricane tent—and then, two smaller dots. Those were definitely people, on the Rakhiot Traverse, porters perhaps. This time there could be no mistake, they really were people!

Then at last I knew I was safe. The knowledge that I was near my team-mates gave me new-born confidence. My old tracks were still in good condition and I traversed slowly along them to the ridge. For the moment I felt fresher again, either because of the Pervitin or because of the blessed feeling of relief; breathing became easier, too, but I still had to use extreme care. The crampon came loose again and I took it off in a rage and threw it out over the South Face, without further ado. I made relatively rapid progress down the exposed ridge, moving forward through crust past the "Whipped Cream Roll", till at seven p.m.—forty-one hours after leaving the spot—I approached the tent.

Hans now came to meet me. He did not know how to hide his emotion and buried himself behind his camera. We embraced, speechless. I was so parched that I could not utter a sound, and Hans was satisfied to see me back safe and sound. We sat down outside the tent and he called Walter back from where he was standing near the "Moor's Head" on his way down to leave room for the two of us. Walter was happy enough to do no more than shake me by the hand, with tears in his eyes. There are times when it is no disgrace to weep. . . .

Neither of them knew what had become of me and both had feared the worst. They had agreed not to go down to Base Camp without me. If I did not turn up by the evening, they had arranged to start up over the Silbersattel and that limitless snow-plateau above it, in the direction of the Summit, not with any intention of climbing it, but to search for me. It was grand to have such good friends, and at that moment I felt happier than ever before in my life. I forgot that all the camps down the Rakhiot Glacier had been evacuated.

I could read joy and relief in the eyes of Walter and Hans, who set to to look after me with paternal care. Hans poured pints of tea and coffee into me, which eventually began to restore life to my dehydrated body. They never even asked whether I had got to the top; all that seemed to matter was that I was back safely. Our close communion at that moment was for me the most significant experience of the whole expedition; for we had established something more than the cameraderie of team mates—a true and deep friendship. Walter soon had my boots off and it was only then that I became aware that the mountain air had extracted its tribute. The first two toes of my right foot were discoloured and without any feeling in them; apparently I had failed to notice it on the way down. Walter worked away at my frost-bitten foot.

Once the three of us had crowded into the little shelter-tent, I began to tell my story and poured out words like a torrent or a fully-wound clock which refused to run down. I was incredibly restored, though it was probably only a wave of nervous tension. They both listened intently, as I described the difficulties of the climb; at about midnight I suddenly realised that they had fallen asleep, so I tried to go to sleep too. I lay there wide awake, feeling wonderful, warm and safe in a tent with my team mates; thankful beyond words, absolutely unable to grasp that I had really been on Nanga Parbat's summit. I had so often dreamed of it and it had been so different in reality, so utterly incredible. And to have survived a bivouac—looking back, that seemed the greatest of all the miracles the kindly Powers had granted!

On July 5th we were up and about quite early. It was still cloudless and calm, but we had to get on down. My frostbites needed urgent medical attention and we knew that the monsoon might break any day. We wanted, too, to get off the mountain, for we had an unpleasant feeling that it would still take its revenge on us; Fate so often takes a hand at the last moment. And, now that we had succeeded in climbing it, we wanted to get home without casualties. I took a last look up at the Summit—of course distance made it impossible to see the axe and its flag—and we took our regretful leave of the mountain which had come to mean so much to us. We sent the tent down the Rupal Face, a sacrifice to the mountain, and left the rest of the gear lying there. I was in remarkably good shape as I followed my friends down the trail, along past the "Moor's Head", where a memorial tablet to the dead of 1934 had meanwhile been put in place, and down the ice wall at the end of the Rakhiot traverse. Just thereabouts we met Otto and the porters on their way up to Camp V to salvage the gear. We stopped at the tents of Camp IV for another refresher—I could hardly eat because of the inflammation of my throat, which had naturally got worse—and then moved down through burning heat and mushy snow to Camp III.

Spent and weary, I lay down in a tent, at about five o'clock in the evening; I was soon in a deep sleep. It was glorious to sleep again after several days of wakefulness. Somebody shook me—I thought, to call me for supper; but instead I found it was the next morning, and I had slept like a dead man the whole night through. We had to make the most of the time during which the snow would remain hard. Each of us had to carry his own equipment, a heavy load. There was no escape for me, though I had fierce pains in my right foot and my weariness lay on me like a leaden weight. Halfway down, we met a group of porters, an evacuation squad, led by Aumann and Köllensperger, who had left Base Camp the day before. There were 15 Hunzas, more than had ever been seen on the mountain during the whole expedition. But then, this was the homeward trek and that in itself engendered fresh enthusiasm. The porters showed their delight at the good news, then we went off again in our different directions.

The glacier was in a dreadful state. Our old tracks were ruined, under a covering of avalanche débris, for nobody had come this way for a whole week. Fresh crevasses had opened, *séracs* had collapsed, the whole area was unrecognisable. Near Camp II the desolation was at its worst; everything was wide open and the snow-bridges had disappeared. Movements of the glacier and the sun's heat had brought about a fantastic change in the course of four weeks. We couldn't find a way through; so we sought refuge from the sun's scorching heat in the evacuated camp, while Hans and Otto went to search for a route, leaving me in Walter's care. Hours later they came back without any results, having found the ice soft and unreliable, in altogether too dangerous a state to warrant going on down; so we were forced to spend yet another night on the glacier. My frostbite injuries made it almost impossible for me to sleep. My feet had begun to swell, so that next morning I had to rip the felt linings out of my boots and abandon my second pair of socks; even then I could hardly get the boots on. I could still not eat anything dry or hard without feeling that I was swallowing tintacks. The snow had frozen again during the night, so we could go on again. The Buldar Ridge and the Chongra Peaks already rose high above us again; the Silbersattel was a remote, high edge against the sky and the Summit had long gone into retirement behind it. Our route down led dangerously near to the North Face. That didn't worry Hans, whose long legs gave him a means of escape. I followed, limping painfully and dragging myself along in his tracks. We were exposed to the danger for more than an hour. I kept on looking nervously up; the slightest noise startled me. Yet after awhile I became resigned and kept on telling myself that if I caught my packet at this stage, it was just sheer bad luck, and that was that.

Down at Camp I there was no more snow and everything was clear and dry. The tents stood there like mushrooms on narrow ice-hummocks and we even met water welling up from a spring. There were plenty of provisions, too—all the greatest delicacies. I began to feel better and ate whatever I could force down. I swallowed beer and apple purée, little sausages, marmalade, honey, meat and other things as well—just as if I had to make up for everything I had missed on the previous days. Of course, I did not escape the effects. I felt terribly slack and the heavy air, to which I was not yet attuned, didn't help.

At last we came to vegetation. Even though we had stared curiously at flies and butterflies in Camp II, there they had been visitors from another world, harbingers of summer. But now we could really wallow knee-deep in grass, with the colour and scent of flowers around us again. It was like being born anew, after all those weeks spent among snow and ice. We stretched ourselves out on the greensward and dreamed peacefully, forgetting our hardships and exertions, while a warm breeze caressed our rough bearded faces. There were white alpine roses to welcome us, and we took it all gratefully to our hearts.

It was evening when we drew near to Base Camp. What on earth could be going on? We hadn't seen so many people for a long while. At first we thought they were preparing a special reception for us, and were delighted at such a thoughtful recognition of our success, thrilled that all the agony we had put up with had not been in vain.

But when we had covered the last few steps to the tents we met, instead, the coolest of receptions! The only people who showed any joy at all at our triumph were the porters, who could now return to their wives with heads held high; they decorated us with garlands of flowers. When I went to meet the Leader of the Expedition, he greeted me with: "Well, how did it go?" and later, "How are you?"

I had first to give him the details of the climb to the summit; then he asked about my foot.

There was a coming and going of porters which bewildered us. The fact was that our baggage was already being sent on ahead of us to Gilgit; we were to follow to-morrow. Herligkoffer and Bitterling were bent on catching the very next ship, which sailed in the middle of July. We, who had only just come off the mountain—and, particularly, I myself, were not at all pleased about it, for we felt strongly that we needed a few days' rest and recuperation at Base Camp, to which we had been looking forward with nothing short of longing. Bitterling was engrossed in packing the provisions and equipment, which was to do for some expedition or other next year; most of it was already disposed of. Even the medical supplies, except a small store of tablets, had already gone on their way to Gilgit. There was a good deal of talk about K²—I don't know why, for an American expedition was still at work on the second highest peak in the world. A very peculiar atmosphere descended on Base Camp.

We all gathered in the kitchen tent for the evening, and there was a "gala dinner", consisting of—noodles!—all that was left of the provisions. And we would have been so thrilled to get something really worth eating down in Base Camp for a change!

Then, where was Aschenbrenner? As soon as he heard the news of our success, we were informed, he had left for home. At that point Bitterling rose to his feet and made a speech of thanks to our leader for the great success he had been instrumental in achieving. An oppressive silence followed this highly appropriate speech. Then an amazing message from Gilgit arrived telling us to stay a few more days after all; so I retired to my little tent once more.

Hans and Walter took me into their care and worked devotedly over me. I could not walk any more; my injuries had broken open and my frozen toes had gone black. I began to put down some impressions of my lonely journey to the summit on the typewriter, since the leader of the expedition was demanding them with such impatience. At times I looked out through the tent aperture, up over the gigantic North Face to the high plateau, lifting like a white hem against the blue sky. And as my eye rested on it my thoughts were always on those fateful hours I spent up there; but already, with only a few days fallen between, that struggle to the very Summit had begun to seem absolutely unreal—a dream whose true import I could not grasp, a dream at once incredible and yet a dream that had in fact materialised.

EPILOGUE

A YEAR LATER

THE storm has died away. It was a storm raised by men, to whirl up a hideous cloud of dust, which for a time obscured even the shining magic of the Mountain. During those unpleasant days breath was scarcer than at great heights, vision was obscured, the right relationship with men and things—even with oneself—was lost. It was like a concert in a hall into which penetrated all the noises from the street outside. The lovely melody could hardly be heard for their interference.

The street noises are stilled; the dust of the plains has been laid. The image of the Mountain stands clear again, the melody sounds pure as before. Joy, inexpressible in words, has triumphed over all the bickering —our joy in that marvellous mountain, in having climbed it and in our friendship, which brought us together again in July 1954—Hans Ertl, Walter Frauenberger and myself. We were celebrating an anniversary: it was just a year since we were together in the tiny tent that was Camp V, to which I came down again after it had been granted me to reach Nanga Parbat's summit. This time, however, we were on no mountain, but at my home in Munich. There was also a quite private birthday to be celebrated; my wife had presented me with a second daughter. So our glasses clinked not only in honour of the Mountain, but also to wish good fortune to a child of man which had just uttered its first wail. Hans Ertl, that old vagabond of the hills and many lands, was there to keep the festivities within bounds. He always liked to hide his feelings under a mask of good-natured frivolity and to draw remarkable parallels between Alpine performance and national policy.

So the early part of our reunion was gay with laughter, though it was far from likely to become a noisy, riotous occasion; my gratitude for the friendship of these men, which the wonderful mountain had forged, was too deep and strong for that. And together we went over it all in memory. . . .

We thought of the journey back from Base Camp. The pain in my frozen foot had become too severe for me to be able to walk at all; so our Hunza high-camp porters, those same splendid men who had been with us during the days of danger and decision, carried me down, absolutely refusing to let anyone else shoulder the burden. Hans and Walter were ever at my side, anticipating my every wish. Nonetheless we formed a miserable rearguard to the Expedition, which had gone on, leaving us far behind. I couldn't help thinking of Maurice Herzog's painful journey back from Annapurna. I know there was nothing enviable about the condition in which the brave leader of that French expedition found himself, but I almost found it in my heart to envy him. For he had only friends about him, and then, too, there had been a first-class medical man, Dr. Oudot. . . .

I had really nothing to complain of. On that journey back, I met doctors, who gave me their devoted attention; one Pakistani, one English and, finally, in Lahore, a German doctor. But there was no Dr. Oudot among my team-mates.

My memories are still too fresh to have been purged of recollection's tricky play; the humdrum is still the humdrum; the petty, petty; the ugly, ugly. But what was great and beautiful must transcend it all, containing everything else within its own narrow limitations. I shall never forget our leave-taking from the porters. Forgotten were the many occasions when we had to scold them; I still remember them as they were that day at Gilgit, when they ran after the jeep in which Walter Frauenberger—"the kind Sahib"—and I were seated, as they waved to us, wished us luck and said good-bye with tears in their eyes. None of us would ever forget them.

And the flight past Nanga Parbat . . . the same magnificent spectacle as on the way in, and yet completely changed for us. For then there

had been grim, feverish looking forward; now in their place were
fulfilment and gratitude, tinged with a faint regret, somehow as if
one had lost a valuable present. Just as in daily life, achievement may
always be a good-bye to the past.

We said farewell to Pakistan, that young country of fine, zealous
people, where we had made so many friends. How grateful we were for
all the manifestions of real goodwill shown to us by its countrymen and
its Europeans alike!

As we touched glasses to the memory, we were conscious of a deep
truth. Memory can erase all the discord which arose between human
beings over many an issue, masquerading under the banner of Nanga
Parbat, but totally irrelevant to the mountain and its ascent. Now
Walter Frauenberger, the bridge-builder between individual and individual, found the appropriate words to steer memory on to its proper
course—the way to the Summit.

It was as if we could see the men who had been on the great peak
long before us; those who had perished on it and live on in memory.
The men who had contributed to the building of the pyramid, whose
last stone it had been granted to me to add. This comparison is none of
my own; John Hunt, the leader of the successful British expedition on
Everest, used it before me, but it fits Nanga Parbat as exactly as it
does the highest mountain in the world. They all helped to build
it; every one of them strove with all his zeal towards the great
objective, though they were all repulsed or slain by the mountain.
Now, at our birthday anniversary, it seemed as though they were all
with us.

First, Mummery, that great English climber, one of the outstanding
climbers of his day. He failed to recognise the overwhelming size of the
mountain and attacked it by a face from which an experienced, Hima-
laya-wise party turned away appalled forty-four years later. It was in
1895 that Mummery laid the foundation-stone of the pyramid which
grew to be the history of Nanga Parbat. He is the first of the men to
whom I feel moved to report and to render my reckoning; I want him
to know that I climbed Nanga Parbat without the assistance of any
modern climbing aids, that is to say, in the way he would have wanted
it, under my own steam, by what he himself considered "fair
means".

The second is Willo Welzenbach, the most prominent German
mountaineer of the period after the first world war. It was he who
revived Mummery's plan which Walter Schmidkunz had so carefully
stored in his mind, and brought Nanga Parbat out of its obscurity into
the strong light of the aspirations of a new generation of young German

climbers. When, in 1932, he was unable to take part in the expedition he had brought into being, he entrusted the leadership to his friend and climbing-partner Willy Merkl; and in 1934 the great-heartedness of Welzenbach, who had been the first to climb the great faces of the Dent d'Hérens and of the Berner Oberland peaks, was demonstrated when, able this time to go out himself to Mummery's great mountain, he never for a moment disputed the leadership with his friend Willy Merkl.

It was on the morning of July 3rd, 1953, that I passed the spot where Willo Welzenbach had died nineteen years before. It would surely be out of place to let that fine man, who spent eight days without hot food or drink in the hell of the storm-imprisoned mountain before he died, hear a whisper of my complaint about my reception at Base Camp, which at the time hurt and disappointed me so deeply. I now know that my mind was then fixed not on what had been achieved but on the manner of its achievement; in the face of Welzenbach's sacrifice, the question of how things were handled is hushed into silence and my only thought remains my wish to report to him that the Summit was reached and his death and that of so many others finally justified. And I know, too, that Willy Merkl, in whose commemoration our own expedition went out to make its attempt, would, on my return from the Summit, have shaken me by the hand ungrudgingly, as is the way among climbers.

Next in my mind came Pert Fankhauser, the young Kitzbühel climber, whose countless daring first ascents in the Wilde Kaiser are his eternal monument. I never actually knew him, though we belonged to the same climbing club. He too died on Nanga Parbat, but not in vain. The pennant of our Karwendler Club has been unfurled on the Summit, and I brought it back, not least in his honour.

Is it proper for me to mention my two amputated toes, which earlier attention might have saved, in the presence of Hans Hartmann, whom in 1937 they dug, with Carlo Wien and the rest of his team-mates, out of their icy grave in Camp IV? For he had in his time lost the front part of both feet from frostbite, and yet not only contrived to carry on with his climbing, but often assumed the arduous labour of breaking the trail on Nanga Parbat's slopes. Hans Hartmann, whose study of high-altitude physiology remains the most important scientific contribution ever retrieved from an avalanche; and whose diary is one of the finest human documents in the history of Himalayan endeavours. I can only quote the lines he placed at its head:

> "Though frost be fierce and pain be dire,
> My oath shall be my burning fire."

I was fired by the same oath; and a kindly Providence allowed me to fulfil it. That is my message to all those who died on Nanga Parbat.

You cannot climb a great mountain, least of all a 26,000 foot peak like Nanga Parbat, without personal risk. The leaders of the 1953 Expedition would not face this truth or the responsibility underlying it. They were entitled to take the line they took—from their point of view, which was influenced by well-founded caution and erroneous weather reports. The summit party shouldered the risk involved. They were entitled to do so, for they were in a position to interpret the conditions and the weather correctly. There was nothing wild or rash about our decision; it was governed by deliberate judgment We, moreover, were moved by our oath to do justice to the Mountain and those who had given their lives on it.

I myself took the risk on my final ascent of the Summit; and I was entitled to do so and to say so.

It is probably not essential, in order to become a first-class Himalayan climber, successfully to have endured the greatest perils in the Alps, or there to have inflicted on one's body and spirit exertions which used up the last ounce of strength and endurance. All the same, I was glad I had become accustomed, by force of long training, to exact from myself the uttermost of which I am capable. I have that to thank for being alive to-day; and, believe me, I love life. . . .

That night the great mountain stood shining down on the three of us, reunited; a milestone of the past, a signpost to the future.

Thank you, friends of mine!

Our glasses touched.